CREOLIZING THE MODERN

D1264578

CREOLIZING THE MODERN

Transylvania across Empires

Anca Parvulescu and Manuela Boatcă

CORNELL UNIVERSITY PRESS   ITHACA AND LONDON

Copyright © 2022 by Cornell University

All rights reserved. Except for brief quotations in a review, this book, or parts thereof, must not be reproduced in any form without permission in writing from the publisher. For information, address Cornell University Press, Sage House, 512 East State Street, Ithaca, New York 14850. Visit our website at cornellpress.cornell.edu.

First published 2022 by Cornell University Press

Library of Congress Cataloging-in-Publication Data
Librarians: A CIP catalog record for this book is available from the Library of Congress.

ISBN 9781501765728 (hardcover)
ISBN 9781501766565 (paperback)
ISBN 9781501765735 (pdf)
ISBN 9781501765742 (epub)

Contents

Acknowledgments

We would like to thank our editor at Cornell University Press, Jim Lance, for his generosity and editorial support throughout the publication process.

This book benefited from numerous conversations with colleagues and friends. We would like to thank, in particular, participants in the Telciu Summer Schools in 2018 and 2019 and in the 2019 Annual Meeting of the Political Economy of the World-Systems Section in Freiburg, Germany—in particular Luis J. Beltrán-Álvarez and Agustín Lao-Montes—for their inspiring feedback and suggestions. Gratitude is due to Cornel Ban, Valer Simion Cosma, Laura Doyle, Abram van Engen, Tabea Linhard, Christian Moraru, Santiago Slabodsky, Marius Turda, Ovidiu Țichindeleanu, and Immanuel Wallerstein for taking the time to provide feedback and make suggestions on some or all of the arguments in this book at different stages in its emergence. We would like to extend special thanks to Bogdan Vătavu and Ágota Ábrán, who provided invaluable research assistance.

This project benefited from the financial support provided by an American Council of Learned Societies Collaborative Research Fellowship during 2018–2020, a Summer Research Seed Grant from the Center for the Humanities at Washington University in St. Louis, a Collaborative Research Seed Grant from the Center for the Humanities at Washington University in St. Louis, and a publication stipend from the Arts and Sciences Dean's Office at Washington University in St. Louis.

We would like to thank the following presses for permission to reprint parts of the following articles: Taylor & Francis for "The Inter-Imperial Dowry Plot," *Interventions: International Journal of Postcolonial Studies* 23, no. 4 (2021): 570–95; Wiley for "The *Longue Durée* of Enslavement: Extracting Labor from Romani Music in Liviu Rebreanu's *Ion*," *Literature Compass* 17, no. 1–2 (2020); Brill for "(Dis)Counting Languages: Between Hugó Meltzl and Liviu Rebreanu," *Journal of World Literature* 5, no. 1 (2020): 47–78; Illinois University Press for "Creolizing Transylvania: Notes on Coloniality and Inter-Imperiality," *History of the Present* 10, no. 1 (2020): 9–27.

INTRODUCTION

Transylvania: Inter-Imperial Creolization

The photograph frames a smiling old woman holding a book.[1] She is dressed in black, a sign of her widowhood, and wears the signature head scarf of elderly peasant women in Transylvania. An intricate tapestry and a golden mass-produced wall clock stand out in the background. The woman is not posing as a reader; the book is closed, and she handles it reverently, as if it were a sacred object (figure I.1). A reporter asks the woman about her mother and father, who served as models for the characters in a 1920 novel set in the village. Her parents are famous, having had their tumultuous youth fictionalized a hundred years ago in what is now a canonical Romanian novel. The old woman has not read the novel that immortalized her parents. She does not own a copy; the edition she holds belongs to the reporter. She knows from other villagers that the novel improvised some elements of her parents' lives and outright lied about others. She confirms, however, the veracity of one aspect of the fictional text: all her life, she worked the land she inherited from her parents, the land her father, in particular, was passionate about. Like him, she cherished the land. Her rough, cracked hands testify to the labor she has dedicated to it. "Nobody works the land anymore," she laments. "All youngsters have gone abroad, only us older folks are left." The statement comes across as tragic. This is the same land that generations of Transylvanians of all ethnic and racial backgrounds fought over, among themselves and against the background of multiple conflicting empires. This is the same land that Liviu Rebreanu's famous novel *Ion* took as its

1

FIGURE I.1.   Photograph of Xenia Pop, daughter of Ion Boldijer, the model for the main character in Liviu Rebreanu's novel *Ion*.

protagonist. The woman's lament is witness to the most recent shift in the land's history. While global investors rush to buy large tracts with the hope of cashing in at the opportune moment, local landowners have all but abandoned their small plots to join a new wave of international labor migration. This book examines this perceived tragedy against the history of land in Transylvania and the economic, political, religious, and cultural struggles that have marked it. Its aim is to include Transylvania in the ongoing, interrelated, critical conversations about world literature, world history, and world-systems analysis. In a complex dialogue with the novel held by the old woman in the photograph, we position these struggles within a global inter-imperial predicament whose entanglements have shaped our understanding of modernity, rurality, migration, and patterns of racialized and gendered inequality.

This book has two authors: a literary critic and a sociologist. We use the interdisciplinary perspectives afforded by this coauthorship to foreground Transylvania's unique historical position at the intersection of a number of empires (Habsburg, Ottoman, Austro-Hungarian, Russian). The central concept we develop, in dialogue with the work of Laura Doyle, is that of inter-imperiality.[2] We turn to Transylvania as an example of a multiethnic, multilingual, and multiconfessional region of the world, a condition that stems from its exemplary positioning across empires. Since its emergence as a geopolitical entity between the thirteenth and fifteenth centuries, and following a series of heterogeneous migrations, Transylvania has been claimed serially by a number of empires and neighboring states. We argue that, far from being an intra-European affair, Transylvania's situation is inflected by global arrangements of power, most centrally coloniality.[3] In the following chapters, we concentrate on Transylvania's role in conflicts between and among empire-states in a critical effort to historicize, question, and transcend the methodological limitations of country comparisons. We derive our unit of analysis from Transylvania's shifting inter-imperial and structurally semiperipheral condition. We demonstrate that this semiperipheral condition determines Transylvania's presence not only in economic and political affairs but also in global cultural production and in what Pascale Casanova has called the "world republic of letters"—including the novel held by the woman in the photograph.[4]

Our project is to place Transylvania's inter-imperiality in a comparative perspective that provides new insights on comparatism—starting with its unit of analysis. Our wager is that, in addition to being a fascinating object of study, Transylvania's exemplarity can crystallize a methodology. The inter-imperial, multilingual locale is a world-historical phenomenon; many regions can be described in relation to their inter-imperial predicaments and trans-imperial connections—from Taiwan to the Philippines and from South Sudan to the Caribbean. Locating these regions across empires, as we do with Transylvania, offers a critical analytical framework that effectively creolizes the predominantly "ethnic lens" of methodological nationalism.[5] In the following pages, we strive to both analyze Transylvania's inter-imperial condition and develop the Transylvanian perspective as a method.[6]

What does the world look like from the standpoint of a small village in Transylvania, a region in East-Central Europe?[7] Seeing the world from the perspective of rurality challenges the conventional view of capitalism as a linear process of urbanization, industrialization, and depeasantization, pivoting around cities as motors of modernity, trade, and increased communication. The critical task is to trace world integration from the constitutive entanglements of the rural and the urban—that is, within the dynamic of Raymond Williams's "the country and the city."[8] As the flip side of debates about the global city, this project participates in an effort to think about the global countryside.[9] Our focus on a Transylvanian village foregrounds the region's capitalist transformation from local production to production for a world-market, while integrating the village into networks of consumerism and desire, struggles for women's and minorities' rights, cycles of secularism and postsecularism, and literary innovation. This shift in attention has the potential to revise preconceived notions of power dynamics in small rural places and to reveal local agencies creatively deployed in multidirectional ways.

Significantly for the thrust of our argument, Transylvania's location on the European continent, yet in the rural periphery of several of Europe's imperial powers, renders it a comparatively eloquent candidate for the larger decolonial project of "creolizing Europe."[10] Originally coined to describe the processes of racial, cultural and linguistic mixing in the Caribbean, the term *creolization* has increasingly been defined as a mode of transformation premised on the unequal power relations that characterize modernity/coloniality—dispossession, colonization, and enslavement.[11] Importantly, unlike terms such as *hybridity* or *transculturation*, with which it is often compared, *creolization* does not refer to a mixing of equal elements.[12] In the following chapters, we draw on critical approaches that emphasize the mutually constitutive character of colonial and imperial entanglements to trace a process of inter-imperial creolization as seen through Transylvania's history. As in other parts of the world (places in the Indian Ocean and Africa), linguistic and religious creolizations are central to this process—as is the existence of a heterogeneous ethnic and racial field that yields complex forms of creativity and resistance.[13] When used to denote structural transformation, as it is here, *creolization* also names a relation to other "translated societies" around the world.[14]

The project of creolization involves the rethinking, reframing, and creative recomposition of the received categories structuring our respective disciplines—from Europe to Transylvania, and from the modern to the comparative method. This necessary reframing starts with an analysis of the power relations that have shaped these entities in the context of both coloniality and inter-imperiality.[15] As articulated by a growing critical literature, this deployment of the concept of creolization contests the prevailing notion of a geographically, culturally, religiously, and racially coherent entity: Europe. In the particular form employed here, the project involves the creolization of one of Europe's subaltern formations, Transylvania, by replacing any of the ethnic lenses that claim the region for a national project with the framework of a multiethnic and multilingual entity across empires. This exercise necessarily relies on the creolization of theory by retrieving subaltern histories and experiences in both colonial and imperial situations and reinscribing them into literary and social theory. Creolizing Transylvania therefore represents an instance of what Françoise Lionnet and Shumei Shih call "the becoming theory of the minor"—thinking through and with invisible, peripheral, or subaltern formations.[16] An important dimension of this process of creolization remains anchored in the politics of multilingualism, which we redefine in chapter 4 as *interglottism*.

Across Empires: Transylvania between Coloniality and Inter-Imperiality

The question of inter-imperiality sits awkwardly with critiques of coloniality. We therefore do not simply "apply" postcolonial theory to Transylvania's historical configurations. Rather, we employ the methodological lens of reading across empires, empirically anchored in Transylvania's history, to bridge three otherwise disconnected critical conversations: postcolonial theory, decolonial thought as it intersects world-systems analysis, and recent scholarship on inter-imperiality. Textbook knowledge of postcolonial theory typically posits that the emergence of postcolonialism as both a descriptive term and an academic field of study occurred in parallel with the creation of the Third World at the end of World War II. Chronologically as well as logically, the newly independent states that resulted from the administrative decolonization of European empires in Asia and Africa formed the object of what would later become postcolonial studies. This conceptualization neglected an array of places that—for very different reasons—did not correspond to either the category of the Third World or the conventional postcolonial timeline. Among them were regions that had achieved independence long before the end of World War II and had therefore been postcolonial *avant la lettre*, such as Latin America; territories that were occupied in the immediate aftermath of World War II but were not perceived as Western colonial outposts because of a long history of ideological legitimation of Western control, such as Palestine; countries that profited from and participated in the Western colonial enterprise, but only after being colonized themselves, such as Ireland; and areas that continue to function as colonies today, such as Puerto Rico, the British Virgin Islands, and the French Antilles. Also among the regions omitted from the standard postcolonial category were semiperipheral areas with an inter-imperial history, such as Transylvania.

Shortly before 1990, Edward Said's plea to include Ireland—alongside India, Africa, the Caribbean, Central and South America, China, Japan, the Pacific archipelago, Malaysia, and Australia—on the list of world regions sharing both colonial status and cultural dependency failed to mention any part of East Europe.[17] It was only after the demise of state socialist regimes in Europe in 1989–1990 that scholars started to signal the so-called Third Worldization of the former Second World in East Europe.[18] Almost immediately, debates about the adequacy of the postcolonial category for an analysis of semiperipheral East Europe emerged. Influentially, historian Maria Todorova—whose concept of Balkanism was intended to be an explicit departure from, rather than a variant of Said's concept of Orientalism—objected to the application of postcolonialism to the Balkans. In Todorova's words, "Postcolonial studies are a critique of postcoloniality, the condition in areas of the world that were colonies." She argued against considering the Ottoman, Habsburg, and Romanov empires colonial formations. Todorova asked, "What are the benefits of comparison" between postcolonial areas of the world and the Balkans?[19] The question has received various answers but remains largely unresolved.

Latin American theorists of decoloniality have offered both a systematic cri-tique of the overgeneralization inherent in the postcolonial category and a con-sideration of the historical heterogeneity of colonial experiences.[20] Rather than easing the way to cultural and epistemic decolonization, they argue, many self-designated postcolonial approaches risk a revamped version of Western post-structuralist thought projected onto a select group of colonial realities—for the most part, the former British colonies. This limited focus on British colonialism and Anglophone colonies results in a primarily English-speaking postcolonial theory, reproducing one of the most enduring tools of empire: language. This perspective systematically leaves Iberian, French, and Dutch colonial endeav-ors and their legacies in Latin America, the Caribbean, and Southeast Asia un-accounted for, as well as outside the scope of the definition of postcolonial.[21] In response to this critique, the Americas' centrality to an understanding of both the geopolitics and the geoculture of the modern colonial world-system started to come into focus.[22] A critical conceptual change in the notion of coloniality was the acknowledgment that colonialism as a formal administrative status had come to an end, yet the hierarchies established between Europeans and non-Europeans—the coloniality of power—continued to underwrite social, political, economic, and cultural realities in these regions of the world. Crucial dimensions of the process of decolonization were still pending. At the same time, the centrality conferred on the Americas in the creation of coloniality had a theoretical cost: by focusing on the impact of colonial power in the emergence of alternative modes of labor control, weak state structures, and subaltern epistemologies that subsequent waves of decolonization left in place, this perspective implied that the ongoing socio-economic and epistemic colonial relation between the core and the noncore in other parts of the world was a later step within a postulated temporal sequence. As a consequence, regions that had been subjected to imperial or colonial control both before and during West Europe's Atlantic expansion did not belong to this revised timeline. Histories of imperial domination and of anti-imperial struggle in East Europe were consequentially omitted.

Work on East Europe by world-systems authors in the 1970s, East European historians since the 1980s, literary and cultural theorists, as well as a growing body of recent studies on the political economy of modernity/coloniality, has re-vealed that economic, political, and ideological domination in various parts of East Europe since the sixteenth century followed a different path to coloniality than that described by both modern Atlantic history and postcolonial studies.[23] Analyses by scholars of East Europe foregrounded patterns that were typically linked to situations of imperial, not colonial, domination. Occurring over about two hundred years, the dissolution of the Habsburg, Ottoman, and Tsarist im-perial states often led not to the liberation of the previously occupied provinces but to a shift from imperial systems based on the exploitation of peasant labor to systems under the jurisdiction of Western capitalist powers. These powers were interested in increasing agrarian production and thus reinstated the enserfment and exploitation of rural labor. By the end of the nineteenth century, the terms of political discourse, national identity formation, and cultural change in these newly emerging states were transformed by the geopolitical reshuffling that made West Europe a renewed metropolitan center.

The inter-imperial approach espoused in this book provides an important corrective to, and a productive complication of, the narrative of linear progress toward industrialization as a necessary (and even sufficient) characteristic of capitalist economies. We argue that the political, cultural, and economic legacy of empire in East Europe left indelible marks on both the socioeconomic organization and the self-conceptualization of its subjects, which placed them in a different relationship to the West European core than the American colonies. While the racial, ethnic, and class hierarchies erected in the colonies marked the *colonial difference* from the core (the colonizer-colonized dichotomy), the less overtly racial but more pronounced ethnic and distinct class hierarchies accounted for the *imperial difference* between European empires and their former subjects (with language, religion, regional location, ethnic allegiance, and economic status complicating the divide).[24]

In turn, world-systems scholarship helps account for the role of semiperipheries in the world-system. Semiperipheries have been credited with ensuring the survival of the modern world-system since its inception; their intermediate position has placated the system's tendency toward polarization between an exploiting core and an exploited periphery. By preventing the unified opposition of the periphery against the core, semiperipheries not only fulfilled a significant economic function in the capitalist world-economy but also accomplished the major political task of providing stability to the system, one region at a time. As Immanuel Wallerstein put it in the wake of the 1970s economic crisis, "The essential difference between the semiperipheral country that is Brazil or South Africa today and the semiperipheral country that is North Korea or Czechoslovakia is probably less in the economic role each plays in the world-economy than in the political role each plays in conflicts among core countries."[25] Specifically, for regions in East Europe, being semiperipheral triggered two conditions: First, not being the core entailed political and economic domination akin to that in peripheral areas and the need to develop theoretical and practical solutions to such domination. Second, not being the periphery permitted a certain degree of visibility in the production of knowledge that intellectual projects in the silenced societies of the periphery did not have. Unlike the peripheral "Orient," which was constructed as an incomplete Other of Europe and as the locus of barbarism, irrationality, and mysticism, the semiperiphery in East Europe—which undeniably contains many of the attributes that went into the construction of the white, Christian, European Western self—is featured in the Western imagination as Europe's incomplete Self.[26] Geographically European (by twentieth-century standards) yet culturally alien by definition, the European East, like the Orient, has conveniently absorbed the political, ideological, and cultural tensions of neighboring regions. Its existence exempted the West from charges of racism, colonialism, Eurocentrism, and Christian intolerance while serving, in Todorova's words, "as a repository of negative characteristics against which a positive and self-congratulatory image of Europe and the 'West' has been constructed."[27]

These critical conversations have taken a consequential turn in recent years, as scholars such as Laura Doyle and Shu-mei Shih have called for complementary comparative work on non-European empires and, importantly, the spaces between various European and non-European imperial formations—Mughal, Ottoman, Russia, Japan, China. Increasingly, this call is heeded by a growing critical literature focusing on sites that are marginal to the conventional postcolonial gaze and that decenter, in the words of Miloš Jovanović and Giulia Carabelli, "two imagined geographies: that of postcolonial studies and the scholarship on so-called continental empires."[28] The corresponding shift in attention and historical scale renders various parts of East Europe, including Transylvania, recognizable as inter-imperial spaces. Anti-imperial themes and structures become legible in relation not to one empire but to multiple conflicting empires vying for control in the region. Likewise, the unequal agencies of various subjects come into sharp relief when viewed through the prism of a negotiation across empires. This shifting emphasis echoes critiques of world-systems analysis such as Abu-Lughod's *Before European Hegemony* (1989), A. G. Frank's *ReOrient* (1998), and John Darwin's *After Tamerlane* (2007), which called for a reconsideration of Asia in accounts of world-system expansion yet, in the process, glossed over East-Central Europe, which functioned as a structural link between regions of the world even before European colonial expansion.

One way out of this mosaic of omissions of East-Central Europe is to trace a historical and analytical relation between coloniality and inter-imperiality.[29] We do this through an analysis of Transylvania's cross- and trans-imperial entanglements. In doing so, we build on the Latin American literature on decoloniality, with its roots in world-systems analysis, and on Doyle's notion of inter-imperiality, developed within the realm of world literature and in dialogue with world history. Our aim is to offer a framework for the analysis of world regions that have been controlled by various colonial and imperial powers throughout their early modern and modern history. We show that a focus on such regions illuminates situations of coloniality and imperiality in ways that decenter our understanding of empire and transform our assumptions about comparison and its benefits. We turn to Transylvania's history to argue that its location at the crossroads of several empires is structurally comparable with that of other multilingual and inter-imperial locales and provides an entry point into the creolization of the dominant notion of Europe as a geographically, culturally, religiously, and racially coherent entity.

For Doyle, inter-imperial predicaments reveal anti-imperial themes and structures to be graspable in relation not to one empire but to multiple empires in the *longue durée*. Critiques of Eurocentrism have cautioned against extrapolating the term *empire* to non-Western imperial formations such as the Ottoman Empire.[30] Because we are writing from and about one of Europe's inter-imperial regions, we are more concerned with the perception of the peoples subjected to occupation by Ottoman armies and forced to pay tribute to them than with Ottoman self-perception. Romanian-speaking subjects referred to the Ottoman entity as *Imperiul Otoman*. In Ottoman Turkish, the word for the Ottoman imperial formation is *Osmanlı Devleti*, which refers to the state founded by the followers of Osman. Ottoman subjects most often referred to their state as *Bâbıâli*, after the name of the sultan's palace, which was translated into French and then into English as "the Sublime Porte" or simply "the Porte." Neither form of self-naming smoothly translates into *Ottoman Sultanate*, which has been proposed as an alternative to Ottoman Empire. In addition, starting with the Tanzimat period, the Turkish word for *empire* was very much at play in Ottoman discourse. Modern Turkish uses the term *Osmanlı İmparatorluğu*, the closest translation of which is "Ottoman Empire." Deeply aware of translation as a mediating factor, we decided to use the word *empire* when writing about this imperial entity, retaining the Latinate word that people in Ottoman-occupied areas used in the Romanian-speaking principalities and a word often used by the Ottomans themselves. In the case of Russian imperial entities, our analysis is rarely concerned with the period 1547–1721, for which we use the designation *Russian Tsardom*. It more often deals with the Russian Empire after 1721, which is why the term *empire* is more prevalent here too. Likewise, throughout the book we discuss and problematize the sense in which the Habsburg Empire functioned *as* an empire.

In proposing the concept of inter-imperiality, Doyle resists the assumption, implicit in most postcolonial or world-systems theorizing, that either a region is a postcolony of the West or it has not been colonized. Instead, she highlights the dialectical role of vying empires before and after European hegemony to account for both imperial and colonial differences. In what she terms "the inter-imperial method," where "inter" refers "both to multiple interacting empires and to the multiple subject positions lived within, between, and against empires," the link between macroscale politics emphasized in world-systems analysis and microlevel interactions and cultural production becomes graspable:

> An inter-imperial method incorporates the insights of both transnational and world-systems analysis while aiming to supplement their insights. Our understanding of the conditions of diasporic displacement, economic exploitation, or international resistance changes, for instance, when we look not only at western European cores and peripheries, but also at these as they interact with Ottoman core and periphery, or Chinese core and periphery, or Russian core and periphery, or all at once. Each state's core-periphery policies and instabilities shapes that of others. And together these relations structure the larger force field within which all populations must operate—creating specific kinds of inter-imperial positionality and burdens for each community and person.[31]

We turn to these specific modes of inter-imperial positioning to assess the core-periphery dynamics shaping one of Europe's most undertheorized regions, Transylvania, both before and after the imbrication of inter-imperiality and coloniality. In particular, we examine the constant tension between Habsburg, Ottoman, Austro-Hungarian, and Russian imperial formations as inter-imperial rivalries. We resist, however, the reification inherent in the assumption that empires interact with each other only *as* state formations by revealing connections, exchanges, and mobilizations *across* empires as well as *below* the state level. In distinguishing between *inter-imperial rivalries* and *trans-imperial processes*, we build on Kristin Hoganson and Jay Sexton's work on trans-imperial connections. We untangle the fact that the actors who were engaged in anti-imperial struggles in Transylvania "positioned themselves *inter-imperially* (meaning between empires), but they also navigated . . . layered empires so as to advance their own interests"—that is, they acted *trans-imperially*.[32]

As a telling sign of its inter-imperial nature, Transylvania's population has included (and continues to include) Romanians, Hungarians, Germans, Armenians, Jews, Greeks, and Roma—as well as myriad combinations of these identifiers. Historically, several languages have been spoken and written at any given time, leading to widespread creolization of Transylvanian languages as well as multilingual practices and translations, all of which were negotiated transimperially. Place names have historically been a matter of dispute, a symptom of the region's inter-imperial history. Transylvania itself is known by multiple toponyms: Erdély in Hungarian, Ardeal in Romanian, Siebenbürgen in German. We employ the three most widely used languages of Transylvania for each toponym, in no particular order (Siebenbürgen/Erdély/Ardeal), unless the historical context requires a different approach. Ideally, all Transylvanian languages, including so-called minor languages (Romani, Yiddish, Armenian) would be represented in toponymical practice.

Modernity as Inter-Imperiality in Liviu Rebreanu's *Ion*

A Transylvanian standpoint exposes a deep-seated methodological nationalism that still reigns in the humanities and social sciences. Although many scholars have criticized the prevailing theory that society is implicitly bounded by the nation-state, few have addressed the limitations of this perspective, and offering alternatives is the exception rather than the rule.[33] Taking Transylvania's inter-imperial position as the starting point of our analysis requires several alternative methodologies—some transnational or transregional, and others inter- or trans-imperial. We conduct our study from the vantage point of a small village in Transylvania in 1920, a year that marked a momentous shift in the imperial projects of European states. In an interdisciplinary methodological experiment, we undertake this project through a multilayered engagement with one document: Liviu Rebreanu's novel *Ion*, published in 1920—the book held by the old woman in the photograph.[34] Engaging this document as an extended case study allows us to place our theoretical arguments alongside the novel's narrative.[35] Narrative has an important pedagogical dimension; it placates the risk of abstraction by offering consequential details for both literary and sociological analysis. We read this novel as an extended archive of a range of "sedimented legacies," in Doyle's terms, understanding Transylvania's inter-imperial position as constituting "a condition of aesthetic production and an object of literary representation."[36] We analyze Rebreanu's novel both as a product of inter-imperiality and as its chronicle.

Throughout, we place the small scale of the textual detail in relation to the large scale of the world. In the spirit of bridging the humanities and the social sciences, we engage a constellation of texts. We bring transcripts of debates in the Vienna and Budapest parliaments, legislative and court records, economic data, maps, literary texts, memoirs, and oral testimonies into dialogue with Rebreanu's novel. The Năsăud/Nassod/Naszód region of Transylvania, where Rebreanu's village is situated, has a rich historical archive maintained and made available by a group of dedicated historians who have published census data, property records, court decisions, and family data. In concert with this material, we analyze the novel's canon-forming force and its impact on culture and history. We trace the text's negotiation of fictional and documentary impulses, both of which are equally forceful. We place these impulses in the novel's immediate milieu and in its travels around the world through translation. Ideally, our archive would comprise all editions of the novel and its translations in multiple languages and locations, as received by comparative audiences.[37] An inter- and trans-imperial approach connects the macrostructural perspective with the microhistories reflected in one of the most canonical literary documents of the region, allowing us to examine both large-scale political maneuvers, such as an imperial decree, and small-scale shifts, such as a change in the culture of sexuality.

We engage Rebreanu's novel as an exemplar of "the great unread" on the global stage.[38] *Ion* is considered the first modern novel in the Romanian language.[39] As such, it takes its place in an archive of such firsts around the world: Mohammed Hussein Haikal's *Zainab* in Egypt, Futabatei Shimei's *Ukigumo* in Japan, or Lu Xun's *The Real Story of Ah-Q* in China.[40] Like these texts, Rebreanu's novel encodes questions related to semiperipherality in the world-system, empire and inter-imperiality, nationalism and its myths, vernaculars and multilingualism, race and ethnicity, secularization and gender relations. The novel is well known to Romanian-speaking audiences, as it has been required high school reading for generations; however, it remains virtually nonexistent for global audiences, even after modernist studies have presumably gone global. The rationale behind our choice to write about one novel thus has another pedagogical ramification: we hope that readers unfamiliar with Transylvania and its literary traditions but interested in expanding the debate on world literature and comparative empires will consult this novel in translation, alongside our study. At the same time, we write without assuming such prior reading.

In the wake of recent debates about the intersection of world literature and coloniality, we believe it is paramount to revisit the canon of so-called "small literatures" developed in minor languages.[41] Small literature canons yield substantial power; they do so in a restricted space but with world-historical implications. The exercise of rereading the canonical texts of small literatures at this critical juncture between world literature and coloniality opens avenues of inquiry into equality, domination, and power as they relate to the world literary system. Stylistically a mix of realism, naturalism, and modernist experimentation, Rebreanu's *Ion* opens these theoretical debates anew. If we retrace Transylvanian history as world history, we read *Ion* as world literature. This book thus participates in a reframing project, in conversation with *Romanian Literature as World Literature*.[42]

Scholars occasionally confess to the embarrassment of not having read some foundational or otherwise canonical works—an exercise in modesty meant to reinforce their competence. There is the English literature scholar who never read *Hamlet* or the German literature scholar who never read *Faust*. And yet many highly erudite scholars who have not read a single text from entire regions of the world seldom feel any embarrassment because knowledge of such works is not a standard of professional competence. This lack of embarrassment signals what postcolonial theorists have called sanctioned and asymmetric ignorance.[43] In this case, the scales are reversed: one has not missed one important text; one has missed most or all texts. This stark asymmetry has prompted advocacy for what Boaventura de Sousa Santos calls a "sociology of absences," which charts the structurally unequal distribution of attention.[44]

Knowledge about East Europe falls within the purview of sanctioned ignorance. Not to have read the primary texts, not to know the history, and especially not to engage theory developed in languages from peripheral and semiperipheral areas of the world are legitimate options because of a colonially and imperially enforced division of academic labor. On the one hand, the theory-producing metropole, overwhelmingly associated with the Global North, is credited with having the science, the concepts, the methods, and the literary canon. On the other hand, the periphery is reduced to a source of data and a repository of myth, folklore, and indigenous art—from which it can derive neither concepts nor canonical literature. Academic convention too often adheres to a canon of theory in one or two languages—a function of the international distribution of knowledge production.[45] Our project takes up the question of knowledge production in relation to inter-imperiality. It does so methodologically, through the decision to focus on Rebreanu's novel, and it does so thematically. Finally, it does so by engaging historians and theorists who write in Transylvanian languages as well as other so-called "minor languages"—thereby creolizing the theoretical conversation alongside a range of units of analysis.

The project here is to creolize the modern in both modernism and the modern world-system by rereading a small canon otherwise hijacked by national literary history and by repositioning *Ion* as multilingual at the moment of its production. We examine Rebreanu's novel as an example of a minor text in an effort to rethink the meaning of the minor and to model the kind of sustained critical work that can be advanced alongside a minor text. The fact that the novel is highly canonical in Romanian literature yet remains minor globally is arguably a predicament it shares with a large majority of literary texts in the world. For the purposes of our project, this condition is an invitation to creolize both theory and comparative methodology. Although we agree with many tenets of Gilles Deleuze and Félix Guattari's theory of minor literature, the text we study here is not a minor novel within a major-language European tradition.[46] Instead, *Ion* is the equivalent of Franz Kafka resisting the monolingual paradigm of the German language and writing in Czech instead—a regional Czech that enlists five or six other languages in its composition. From a literary studies perspective, one of our aims is to theorize the question of the canon in minor or small literature and to situate the conversation on canonicity in relation to the debate on the canon in modernist studies. From a sociological perspective, we aim to question the understanding of rurality as a minor formation in an increasingly urbanized world, thus creolizing modernity as a normative canon.

Ion is considered the first modern novel in Romanian literature because of its perceived synchronization with European literature.[47] Upon its publication, literary critic Eugen Lovinescu, one of the main proponents of the Occidentalist theory of synchronism, praised the novel as "the strongest objective creation of Romanian literature."[48] For Lovinescu, the local and the national were associated with the barbarism, irrationalism, and antiprogressivism that civilization, modeled on the European West, would eventually abolish. He maintained that, for peripheral locations, "light comes from the West: ex occidente lux!" Lovinescu insisted that the urban character of Western civilization provided such luminosity: "light does not come from the village."[49] Given the sanctioned and asymmetric ignorance with which Rebreanu's novel was met in the West, clearly synchronization was a one-way street; despite a large number of translations, the "world republic of letters" did not register *Ion* as a literary event.

For the past one hundred years, Rebreanu's biography upheld Romanian Transylvanians' claim to political sovereignty through aesthetic authenticity, a symbiosis Rebecca Walkowitz captures in the dictum "original art and original nations grow up together."[50] Contrary to conventional readings of Rebreanu's biography and the novel's reception in the context of Romanian Transylvanians' claims to national sovereignty, we read *Ion* as an inter-imperial text emerging in multiple languages (Romanian, Hungarian, German, Romani, Yiddish, and French) and incorporating translation and future circulation into its production. After initial translations in Czech (1929), Italian (1930), Polish (1932), German (1941), Slovenian (1943), and Croatian (1943), *Ion* was translated into French, English, Russian, Turkish, Persian, and Japanese. Although translation is usually taken as evidence of a text's transnational destiny, the translation of minor literature often results in what we call minor translation—that is, translation that does not save a text from the sanctioned or asymmetric ignorance reproducing the core-periphery divides of knowledge production.[51]

An inter-imperial framework of analysis, coupled with insights from migration studies, helps us identify, retrospectively, a young man becoming a writer in a multilingual inter-imperial space and attempting to build a writing career in Budapest and then in Bucharest.[52] In both capitals, Rebreanu was considered an immigrant. As Walkowitz submits, "viewed from the perspective of migration, the concept of literary belonging may have outlived its usefulness."[53] This does not mean that Rebreanu does not belong in the canon of Romanian literature or, for that matter, in the canon of Central European literature (for the latter, Carl E. Schorske's *Fin-de-Siècle Vienna: Politics and Culture*, with its use of Vienna as the main reference point, remains central).[54] Rather, we show that Rebreanu and his work belong to multiple literary and sociological frameworks—local, regional and global.

In world literature, debates about the canon have been most consequential in the field of modernist studies. In *Geomodernisms*, a pioneer project in the exercise of globalizing modernist studies, Doyle and Laura Winkiel write: "so much depends on *which* modernism, written when and why and from what place—which city, which hillside, which seat on the train, which new nation or new colony, and before, after, or during which war."[55] A focus on what Doyle and Winkiel call "placedness" reveals a range of global modernisms formed in relation to one another—and sometimes through an antimodernist impulse held in strong relation to modernism. Doyle and Winkiel invoke as examples Latin American modernisms explicitly framed as "modernism at the margins" or "modernism of underdevelopment."[56] These modernisms require a revision of modernist periodization, genealogy, and formal innovation. Indeed, both naturalist and realist forms appear within the various modernisms of the modern world-system. Importantly, Doyle developed the notion of inter-imperiality, which she employs in a reconceptualization of global modernism, in dialogue with Sanja Bahun's concept of interpositioning; Bahun, in turn, proposed the latter through an engagement with the imperial histories of the Balkans as seen from a world-historical perspective.[57] With our analysis of Rebreanu's work as an exemplar of emplaced semiperipheral modernism, we aim to contribute an account of a region that, until now, has not been visible within the purview of modernist studies.[58]

On Collaboration

C. P. Snow's *The Two Cultures* (1959) started a complex conversation concerning the divide between hard and soft sciences in the realm of knowledge production.[59] In recent years, significant work has been done to overcome this divide. There has been much less discussion about the divide within the so-called soft sciences—that is, between the social sciences and the humanities. Snow understood that the tension (epistemic as well as affective) between the two cultures was related primarily to the abyss between those he called the "literary intellectuals" and the scientists. Despite a genealogy of modernist sociology that intersects literary modernism, sociology and literary studies largely resist each other.[60] This divide is particularly telling in the debate over the world in our respective subdisciplines.[61] One field, comparative literary studies, organizes its debate around the concept of world literature. The other field, at the intersection of macrosociology, world history, and political economy, works with the notion of a world-system. Social scientists tend to be skeptical of the idea that the world is a flow of information and culture. Humanists, in contrast, are skeptical of the oneness of the world-system, which they see as being tainted by Eurocentrism.[62] Attempts at dialogue—such as those undertaken by the Warwick Research Collective or by Doyle—or calls for overcoming the divide altogether are rare. Among other things, at stake is institutional power, itself an outgrowth of the intellectual division of labor that established the divide in the nineteenth century in the first place.[63] We propose our project as an experiment in collaboration. What does this debate look like if social scientists and humanities scholars work together and, in this case, write together?

Both this study and its authors are symptoms of the globalization of scholarship on small places and small literatures. We write in English, the language of this globalization. We bring to the project a number of other languages that diasporic scholars are often tasked to represent. We too have linguistic limits, which we have tried to overcome through additional collaboration. We foreground our own positions within the institutions that mediate knowledge production. The irony is that sometimes it is easier to find a nineteenth-century Transylvanian text through the interlibrary loan system in a US library than it is to access it in Cluj/Kolozsvár/Klausenburg. Sources of funding, such as the American Council of Learned Societies collaborative fellowship that facilitated the research and writing of this book, are more accessible to scholars based in the United States and Germany than those based in Romania or Hungary. By theorizing our institutional and disciplinary positions, as well as our use of English, we frame the ways in which disciplinary and geopolitical contexts have shaped comparison, academic legitimacy, and the notion of the modern.

We start with an introductory sketch of Transylvania's inter-imperiality, which provides historical background for the following chapters. Chapter 1 offers an analysis of the "land question" in Transylvania as a function of both individual and collective property. The crucial question of land distribution in an inter-imperial context sets the stage for an analysis of the structural position Transylvania occupied within the world-system at the turn into the twentieth century. We discuss this position in chapter 2, revealing the imbrication of capitalist integration with a very specific form of antisemitism. In a comparative arc, chapter 3 foregrounds relational racialization processes by weaving the neglected history of Romani enslavement and its aftermath into the analysis of inter-imperiality. Chapter 4 picks up the question of language and multilingualism to provide a fresh account of Transylvania's credentials as the birthplace of literary comparatism. Chapters 5 and 6 focus on the overlapping of gender with the other categories of analysis operative in an inter-imperial situation—specifically, through an analysis of women's labor and violence against women (chapter 5) and women's education (chapter 6). Chapter 7 brings many threads together to trace the intertwining of religion and inter-imperiality.

Transylvania's Inter-Imperiality: A Historical Sketch

Transylvania's history has been highly contested scholarly terrain for historians writing within national paradigms.[64] Our analytical framework refocuses this historiography on migrations and empires in the *longue durée*. This double attention to empires and migrations—which straddle, crisscross, and transcend past and present state borders—challenges methodological nationalism and allows us to assess the empires of the region *as* empires, in a global comparative framework.

The layering of multiple migratory and imperial formations shaped what would become Transylvania in the medieval period—Avars in the sixth and seventh centuries, Bulgars in the eighth and ninth centuries, Hungarians in the ninth century, and German-speaking migrants invited by Hungarian rulers to occupy border regions in the twelfth century. The Hungarian migration, known as the Hungarian Conquest in nationalist historiography, involved movement from an area between the Urals and the Volga to the Carpathian basin.[65] Famous for its fertility, land in the east of Europe was thought to be sparsely inhabited during the Middle Ages and was often described by chroniclers as empty—an early *terra nullius* argument inviting and seemingly legitimating settlement in territories where documented rural communities existed. Subsequently, the Crusades as a mass movement sparked the interest of many settlers who chose the land route to the Holy Land through Moravia, Silesia, and the Carpathian basin.[66] The Mongol invasion passed through Transylvania in the thirteenth century, including the region within the global purview of the Mongol Empire, which extended from China to the Caucasus.[67] The Romani migration, which started in India and passed through Persia, Armenia, and the Byzantine Empire, occurred between the ninth and fourteenth centuries, resulting in Romani communities settling in the region. Sephardic Jews expelled from Spain in the fifteenth century arrived in Transylvania through the Balkans from the Ottoman Empire, adding to Transylvania's Jewish population. They were followed by Ashkenazic migrants. Short-distance migrations of Romanian-speaking populations between Wallachia, Moldova, and Transylvania occurred throughout the early modern period as well.

These migratory waves put the region on the world map extending from China and India through Central Asia to West Europe and North Africa. Transylvania became an estate-based principality between the thirteenth and fifteenth centuries. There were three "nations" (in a premodern sense) in Transylvania within the estate system. One group consisted of the Hungarian nobility, a fluid, nonethnic category anchored in privilege and landownership. The second was made up of Szekler nobles, a Hungarian-speaking population in the eastern Carpathians and close to the Hungarian nobility. The third were the Transylvanian Saxons, a German-speaking and increasingly urban group.[68] These three nations participated asymmetrically in the exploitation of Romanian-, Hungarian-, and German-speaking serfs. The institution of serfdom provided the region's economic infrastructure for a few hundred years.[69] In pockets of Transylvania, the enslavement of Romani peoples was entangled with serfdom to create a structure of racialized labor.

Migrations continued throughout the history of Transylvania's early modern estate system. Armenians, who had arrived in neighboring Moldova in the fourteenth century, were violently persecuted and migrated west in the mid-sixteenth century.[70] Some found refuge in Transylvania, where they enjoyed commercial privileges and established Armenian colonies. Best known was the "free royal town" that came to be identified by a series of toponyms: Hayk'aghak' in Armenian, Armenopolis in Latin, Szamosújvár in Hungarian, Gherla in Romanian, and Armenierstadt in German. Armenians' presence put Transylvania on a major global travel route, as the Armenian diaspora and Armenian trade routes stretched from China and India to the Caucasus, North Africa, and England.[71]

As an estate-based principality, Transylvania was located at the intersection of a series of empires, each vying for dominance in the region. In the sixteenth and seventeenth centuries, Transylvania was situated at the literal crossroads of the three conflicting empires that dominated East-Central Europe: the Habsburg Empire, the Ottoman Empire, and Poland-Lithuania. The Ottomans, under the rule of Suleiman I, engaged in an extended global conflict with the Persian Empire and the Spanish Empire in two parts of the world, conquered Buda in 1526. The Hungarian Kingdom, which at the time included Transylvania, was incorporated into the Ottoman Empire. Levantine trade, which had a global reach, enlisted Greek, Armenian, and Jewish merchants; their interests often collided with the commercial interests of the Transylvanian Saxons.[72] In an inter-imperial spirit, the nobility of Transylvania maneuvered its claims to autonomy between the Habsburg and Ottoman Empires, gaining significant freedom in the process.

After the failure of the Ottoman siege of Vienna, the Habsburg Empire—a reduced version of the imperial power that had colonized the Americas a century earlier—reconquered the pre-Ottoman territory of Hungary, including Transylvania. For almost two hundred years, Transylvania was administered by a governor sent by Vienna. As such, it was part—albeit a unique part—of an expansive imperial formation in competition with the Ottoman Empire; the Russian Tsardom and, later, Russian Empire; and the imperial ambitions of Prussia.[73] As the eastern border of the Habsburg Empire, Transylvania would be both peripheral vis-à-vis Vienna and of critical importance to the management of the empire's eastern frontier.[74] The German-speaking population of Transylvania would be targeted by Prussia's efforts to promote national unity under the umbrella of empire, although the interests of both Austrian Germans and Germans in East Europe remained secondary to the interests of the German Reich.[75] This position enlisted Transylvania's participation in an enduring discourse of border zones, one that remains a major historiographical factor today.[76]

The year 1848 was paradigmatically inter-imperial in Transylvania. Hungarians claimed that 1848 was the moment they asserted their independence from the Habsburg Empire and declared their right to establish a constitutional republic. With the help of the Russian Empire, which was vying for increased influence in the region, the Habsburgs squelched the Hungarian revolution and returned the region to Habsburg absolutism. Thus, Transylvania's three large ethnic groups, each now developing its own nationalism, were reminded of the might of the two conflicting empires dominating the region. By this time, Hungarians and the Hungarian-speaking Szeklers had formed one group. The three Transylvanian nations now claiming nationality—Hungarian, German, and Romanian—were doing so in an increasingly modern sense that linked rights to a newly constructed ethnic identity. The year 1848 also became a symptom of a problem that would haunt Transylvania: how would the issue of national self-determination play out in a region with at least three cohabitating populations with national ambitions (Romanians, Hungarians, Saxons) and at least three additional minority groups (Jewish, Romani, Armenian)?[77]

In 1867 Transylvania became part of the Hungarian portion of the newly constituted Austro-Hungarian Empire, a dual monarchy with a complex network of economic and political cores and peripheral regions.[78] Hungary's successful claim to equality with Austria, which resulted in the 1867 compromise, was a claim for equality with European imperial nations. The two parts of the empire developed parallel imperial ambitions and infrastructures. Austria aimed to be a multicultural empire, and Hungary wanted to be a strong republican state. While Austria entered a competition with Prussia, Hungary defended itself again Russian pressure. This period witnessed a developed discourse on the Hungarian Empire and its ambition to expand into Southeast Europe.[79] Hungarians became the "political nation" of a multiethnic, multilingual, and multiconfessional Transylvania. Against the perceived effort to Germanize the top levels of the Habsburg bureaucracy, Hungarian gradually became the language of state education in Transylvania. The other "minorities"—strategically named because, together, they constituted the majority—were given nominal educational and religious autonomy that, in practice, was selectively implemented. A largely unsuccessful process of enforced cultural and political Magyarization followed. This period saw a wave of migration as Transylvanian Romanians and Transylvanian Hungarians headed to Romania, which had been constituted as a state in 1859 and had its own expansionist ambitions. An even larger number of Transylvanian migrants fled to the United States and Latin America—two-thirds of them were nonnative Hungarian speakers. In these new settings, Transylvanian migrants, like others from East Europe, hoped to become white Americans, positioning themselves within a complex ethnic and racial field against the anxiety that they might replace freed slaves on southern plantations.[80] Immigrants to South America were encouraged to think of themselves as colonial actors, as were Jewish immigrants with Zionist ambitions.[81] Importantly, some migrants reversed course and went back to Transylvania.

To this complex history of empires and migrations we need to add another imperial layer that sits awkwardly with the previous ones. Since the eighteenth century, Romanians' claim to Transylvania had been anchored in a forceful and influential national narrative of territorial and linguistic continuity in the land since the Roman province of Dacia.[82] According to this narrative, the modern state of Romania was a continuation of the Latin-speaking territory of the Roman Empire. As Transylvania became a semiperipheral inter-imperial space, the Transylvanian Romanian national narrative embraced the classicist, Occidentalist *longue durée* of Roman imperiality and claimed kinship with the cradle of European Romance languages. Latin kinship was anchored in a range of translation projects. Like "New Romania," as Latin America was known, this Romania never quite made it into the Occidentalist club of European Latinity. The latter was increasingly restricted to Western Christianity and thus excluded Orthodox Romanians.[83] Within our analytical framework, this historical and linguistic node witnesses coloniality vying with inter-imperiality. The invention of Latin America as "New Romania" was an ideological move by which France—having lost its most prized possession in the Caribbean through the Haitian revolution of 1791–1804 and being forced to sell Louisiana to the United States as a result—tried to maintain political control in the American colonies and thus partake of coloniality.[84] In the process, Latinity was gradually displaced from the center of Christianity and increasingly equated with Catholicism. A classical entity like the Roman Empire is not part of the concept of inter-imperiality as we employ it in this project—namely, to elucidate the dynamics of Eurasian empires in the modern/colonial world-system. Yet the fact that modern nations in East Europe claimed allegiance with classical empires from the eighteenth century onward constitutes an attempt at trans-imperial negotiation in a world-system increasingly dominated by West European colonial powers.[85] Tracking Romanian history back to the Roman Empire was a way of enlisting the Romanian nation in the Occidentalist narrative promoted by late-eighteenth-century German romanticism—the supposed unilinear sequence tracing modern Europe back to a Greco-Roman and Christian past while obscuring both the Phoenician mythology of the birth of Europe and the influence of the Arab Muslim world in classical Greek.[86] By claiming continuity with the Latin-speaking territory of the Roman Empire, Romanian nationalism opted for a whitewashed notion of Europe and rejected a creolized one.

Four empires were dismantled at the end of World War I. The Austro-Hungarian Empire ceased to exist in November 1918, and Transylvania gained its independence—for a month. The Transylvanian Romanian gathering in Alba Iulia/Gyulafehérvár/Karlsburg on December 1, 1918, voted for Transylvania's union with Romania. This mythical event for Romanian Transylvanian nationalism gave voice to an anti-imperial majority. A Hungarian assembly in Cluj/Kolozsvár/Klausenburg on December 22, 1918, opposed the union. In 1920, the Treaty of Trianon, aiming to give each ethnic group in the ex-Habsburg territories the right to self-determination, recognized the incorporation of an enlarged Transylvania into Romania.[87] The interwar period also saw an attempt to assimilate Transylvanian ethnic groups into the Romanian population. Romanian replaced Hungarian as the state language. Antisemitism increased during this period and took three interrelated forms corresponding to Transylvania's three large ethnic groups—Romanian, Hungarian, and Saxon.[88] With this union, Transylvanians became acquainted with Romania's inter-imperial history, which involved the Ottoman Empire, the Russian Tsardom, the Russian Empire, and a semicolonial cultural relation to France. Transylvanian Saxons increasingly became the target of Prussia's imperial ambitions. Having "lost" its colonies at the end of World War I, the German Empire remapped the reach of its nation to include both the German-speaking populations in East Europe ("the German ethnic and cultural lands") and those who had settled in the Americas ("the overseas Germans"), thereby providing a transcontinental and transatlantic arc for the imbrication of coloniality and inter-imperiality.[89] The notion of *Kulturboden* (cultural territory), coined by geographer Albrecht Penck in 1925, gradually gained wider currency and was used to legitimize German territorial claims to expand the German "nation" as far east as possible.[90]

Between 1940 and 1944 part of Transylvania was once again included in Hungary. A period of Soviet administration of northern Transylvania followed at the end of World War II.[91] Transylvania was subsequently reannexed by Romania in 1945. From 1945 to 1989 Transylvania, now a historical province within the Socialist Republic of Romania, was, like the rest of East Europe, subjected to unevenly distributed Soviet hegemony, itself a function of Soviet-style imperial ambition. As such, Transylvania was part of the socialist semiperiphery that had emerged through a partial withdrawal from the world-economy to prevent a decline into peripheral status.[92] After 1989 the region entered a neoliberal period, becoming part of the European Union's periphery but remaining semi-peripheral at the global level. This period saw the largest wave of migration to West Europe, the United States, and Canada.

Transylvania has long been a spatial node of inter-imperial relations, with the region's empires in tension with other world empires and state formations on a global scale: the Hungarian Kingdom at odds with Bohemia-Moravia and Venice; the Ottoman Empire in global conflict with the Persian and Spanish Empires; the Ottoman Empire at odds with the Habsburg Empire; the Habsburg Empire confronting the Russian Empire; Austria and Hungary in tension within the Austro-Hungarian Empire; Austria-Hungary and Romania in conflict during the global conflagration of World War I; Hungarians and Romanians struggling over the region; Jewish, Romani, and Armenian minorities negotiating their position within a series of imperial entities. These imperial layers coexist, with varying degrees of impact at any given moment: the narrative of resistance to the Ottoman Empire does not disappear when the Habsburgs dominate Transylvania; the conflict between Vienna and Budapest over Transylvania continues to influence Hungarian claims to the region; Romanian nationalism cannot erase centuries of Hungarian and Saxon presence. The relational racialization of Jewish and Romani minorities straddles these imperial and national shifts.

We thus derive Transylvania as a unit of analysis from its inter-imperial condition. The region serves as our unit of analysis not because it was a historical province, a principality, or is now part of a nationally conceived state, that is, not because of a predefined regional or national categorization. Rather, it is necessary to analyze Transylvania as a coherent sociopolitical and economic unit in a world-historical perspective because the space emerging from and shaped by these inter-imperial dynamics and transnational shifts is what made the region the center of various territorial claims, religious and national identities, land rights, and political regimes. In world-historical terms, Transylvania's inter-imperial history suggests that the coloniality that gradually engulfed the world after 1492, the year Christopher Columbus landed in the Americas, constituted a late moment in a larger inter-imperial configuration of power that predated the emergence of Western Atlantic expansion and vied with it. That same year, the Spanish Catholic monarchs conquered Granada, the last Muslim state in West Europe, attesting to inter-imperiality's role in the emergence of coloniality. Also in 1492, Jews were expelled from the Iberian Peninsula by royal decree, and their confiscated wealth was used to finance Columbus's first voyage. The deported and dispossessed Sephardic Jews took many routes, some of them traveling through the Balkans and the Ottoman Empire before settling in Transylvania.[93] Transylvania's history of settlement and migration, partition and annexation, multiconfessionalism and multilingualism at the crossroads of Eurasian empires and Western colonial powers reveals that inter-imperiality both precedes coloniality and coexists with it, while it outlasts imperialism. As such, in contradiction of the conventional divide between premodern and modern European empires, it testifies to the modernity of the Western and Eastern imperial formations contesting and coproducing each other well into the twentieth century. Their artificial separation into modern and premodern empires proceeds along the lines of the Occidentalist discourse that gradually defined regions and populations constructed as nonwhite, non-Western, or non-Christian as outside of Europe, modernity, and the West. Inter-imperial formations such as Transylvania defy these categorizations and reveal them to be politically charged constructs emanating from hegemonic locations. We therefore view a detailed engagement with Transylvania's inter-imperial history as one of the many necessary contributions to the larger project of creolizing the modern as featured in and endlessly reproduced through the prevailing conceptions of modern Europe, modern empires, the modern nation-state, the modern world-system, and modernist literature.

THE FACE OF LAND

Peasants, Property, and the Land Question

The opening of Rebreanu's 1920 novel *Ion* sets the stage for the novel's plot through the use of surveying and mapping. The text begins with a camera's eye view of a rural landscape, following a road to a small village. The survey moves from the scale of the region, named Someş/Szamos/Somesch after its river valley, to that of a small village, Pripas—modeled after two Transylvanian villages where Rebreanu grew up. A cross unmistakably marks the landscape. The narrative seems to filter the point of view of a nonhuman narrator on an exceedingly hot day, scanning the landscape with a matter-of-fact gaze, as if assessing the temperature. An old woman (*o babă*) on a porch appears "crooked as a camp-iron, frying in the sun . . . she looked as if she were made of wood [*ca o scoabă, prăjindu-se la soare, nemişcată, parc-ar fi de lemn*]" (10, 13).[1] This description suggests a timeless, natural sense of belonging that is often associated with the rural, the primordial, and tradition. Soon, two animals on the scene are described as "Hungarian cows [*vaci ungureşti*]" (10, 13). Through this detail, the text announces its use of the Romanian language as a formal choice. The nonhuman third-person perspective cracks as the narrative voice slips unnoticeably into the filtering consciousness of the old woman (or perhaps another villager). This person is not marked racially or ethnically, a sign that she has an organic relation to the language of composition and can note the difference of the cows.

Having surveyed the yard with the old woman and the two cows, the narrative eye lingers on an encounter between two dogs.[2] One is a "shaggy sheep-dog [*un dulău lăţos*]"; the other is "a dirty little mongrel, carrying his tail high [*un căţel murdar, cu coada în vânt*]" (10, 13). The latter, a small, seemingly "mixed-race" dog, starts to sniff the former, presumably a "purebred" Carpathian shepherd dog, which "bares his fangs threateningly and continues his journey with suitable dignity [*îi arată nişte colţi ameninţători, urmându-şi însă calea cu demnitatea cuvenită*]" (10, 13). The distinction between the two dogs functions similarly to the distinction between the old woman and the Hungarian cows. The sheepdog belongs to the space, organically. The little dog claims intimacy with the sheepdog but is immediately and violently reminded of its mongrel status. The sheepdog cannot possibly allow sexual intimacy with the mongrel. The sheepdog trots down the road, dignified; the mixed dog returns to its place in a ditch. There is no doubt which perspective the narrative embraces, as it too follows the winding road. The opening of the novel thus announces a story about how things mix—or do not. This book collects such instances under the umbrella term *creolization*. The racial overtones of this impossible mixing remain eloquent throughout the novel: creolization, an everyday reality, is deemed undesirable.

Having set up a seemingly objective survey that nonetheless striates the land along lines of "organic" and "mongrel," the novel continues with this sentence: "There are signs of life in the village only after you reach Avrum's pub [*De-abia la cârciuma lui Avrum începe să se simtă că satul trăieşte*]" (10, 13). The aerial survey, the increasingly alert reader is told, constitutes a background for the real signs of life the novel will trace. This first section of the novel, however, has just taught the reader to be mistrustful of such statements. Just as the reader of Franz Kafka's *The Castle* knows that the village at the foot of the castle only passes for an immemorial space and that the land surveyor is a modern profession with colonial investments, Rebreanu's reader knows that Pripas is a modern village. The background (the landscape) is just as important as the narrative foreground, if not more so. Behind the modern camera eye surveying the landscape is a camera operator who sees not just two cows but two Hungarian cows, not just two dogs sniffing each other but a purebred dog and a mongrel. The ethnic and racialized imagery of the modern world-system has long shaped this small village in Transylvania. Hence, the modern camera operator, filtering one or more characters, knowingly identifies the pub around which village life revolves as Avrum's—a Jewish man.

Edward Said has argued that postcolonial literature is engaged in the reimagination of space. About Irish literature, he writes: "If there is anything that radically distinguishes the imagination of anti-imperialism, it is the primacy of the geographical element. . . . Because of the presence of the colonizing outsider, the land is recoverable at first only through the imagination."[3] Literature, Said adds, participates in a process of spatial recovery: "One of the first tasks of the culture of resistance was to reclaim, rename, and reinhabit the land . . . a sense of land reappropriated by its people."[4] Rebreanu's novel belongs on the same shelf as other works of literature around the world that dramatize what Said calls "the

imagination of anti-imperialism." Modernism globalizes this imagination in relation to multiple heterogeneous empires. Rebreanu's *Ion* stages its title character's
hyperbolic desire for land in an attempt at spatial recovery. The question of the
people—or, more appropriately, peoples—who claim the right to reappropriate the
land is in Rebreanu's case a function of inter-imperiality, a world-historic category
emplotted locally as place and language particularity. For Rebreanu's text, the implication is that literary ownership anticipates legal and political ownership. In
this case, the novel published in 1920 retrospectively projects such anticipation
onto the turn of the century.

The inter-imperial and trans-imperial modernism of *Ion* is unmistakably spatial and geographical.[5] The opening of the novel creates a literary map. Rebreanu
uses mapping—a colonial tool—to locate the village of Pripas in an inter-imperial
region of East-Central Europe. During the writing of the novel, Rebreanu compiled multiple lists of geographical toponyms, some historical and some fictional,
and drew maps of both the region and the village of Pripas (figure 1.1). For a novel
concerned, centrally, with the question of land, the literary representation of
space is paramount. Mapping, as Anne McClintock argues, has been deployed in
colonial contexts as a technology of knowledge doubling as a technology of possession. Its tacit power rests in the promise that "those with the capacity to make
such perfect representations must also have the right to territorial control."[6] In
Rebreanu's text, this tool is redeployed to claim literary ownership of the Transylvanian land through the use of the Romanian language and the astute use of
Romanian-language place names.

The geographical sites in Rebreanu's novel have multiple toponyms in multiple languages. The city of Cluj, invoked in the first sentence of the novel, was
known in medieval Latin as *Castrum Clus*. The Saxons settled there in the twelfth
century and gave it a German name, *Clausenburg*. At the time of Rebreanu's
novel, it was largely a Hungarian city, *Kolozsvár*. It is known in Yiddish as *Kloyzen-
burg*. Referring to the largest city in the region as *Cluj* is thus a consequential
and formal choice. So is Rebreanu's decision to name streams (*Râpele Dracului*)
and forests (*Pădurile Domnești*) in largely untranslatable Romanian-language
idioms.[7] A reading of the novel's opening becomes a case study of how inter-
imperial literature filters space into a language-specific place. It is also instrumental to an assessment, neglected by Said, of how the imagination of anti-imperialism
works in *inter-imperial* situations in which the colonizing outsider is not an overseas outsider, or not an outsider at all, or in which multiple languages are at stake,
yielding anti-imperial horizons articulated not just as polyglot but as interglot (as
discussed in chapter 4).

Glossing Said's work on Irish literature, Jahan Ramazani reminds us that
place names function as signifiers of native ground: "the recitation of place names

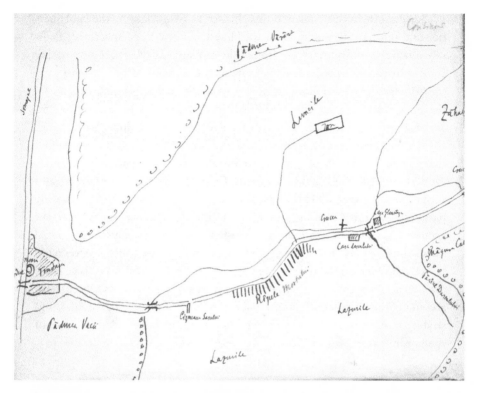

FIGURE 1.1.   Map of the Someş/Szamos/Somesch valley drawn by Liviu Rebreanu. Courtesy of the Romanian Academy.

represents a double decolonization: of the geographical place long under the physical occupation of an imperial power and of the literary space."[8] As Rebreanu's text enthusiastically sprinkles place names associated with geographical sites in the Romanian language, they indeed come across as recitations or even incantations. In an inter-imperial context, this strategy amounts to what Martina Tazzioli and Glenda Garelli call "counter-mapping," a reflexive practice that unsettles the spatial assumptions on which imperial maps are crafted.[9] For countermapping to act as a decolonial strategy against the essentialization of nation-states and world regions (rather than as anti-imperial or anticolonial resistance with its own nationalist agenda, which is always a risk), it must be coupled with a global perspective on place making.[10] As one strategy of creolizing the modern, such relational counter-mapping ideally uncovers the colonial and imperial entanglements between as well as within the peripheries and semiperipheries of the world-system, commonly constructed as fixed and unrelated locations on imperial maps. How does this work in Transylvania's case?

Our premise in this book and this chapter, as we interrogate the land question and agrarian economies in the world-system from the perspective of Transylvania, rests on an understanding of the modern and the rural as mutually constitutive on both conceptual and concrete socioeconomic levels. Rather than opposite ends of a continuum ranging from traditional to global, the rural and the modern are inherent, coimplicating heirs of imperial, colonial, and postimperial as well as postcolonial matrices of power. We are in dialogue with a range of theoretical approaches, from world-systems analysis to decolonial thought, that emphasize the role of colonial expansion in the emergence and functioning of the modern/colonial world-system. These analyses rarely consider regions such as Transylvania, other than as examples of the incorporation of increasing parts of a declining Habsburg Empire into the capitalist world-economy. We supplement these perspectives by proposing a sustained analysis of imperial formations such as the Habsburg and Ottoman Empires, which are too often perceived as premodern. In this chapter, we argue that an analysis of Transylvania's turn-of-the-century agrarian economy yields a quintessentially modern account of the intersections of colonial and imperial interests, hierarchies, and strategies of control. This account charts a hitherto neglected dimension of capitalism: its inter-imperiality.

The Land Problem: Landownership in Transylvania

Following its opening exercise in spatialization, inherent to both coloniality and capitalist expansion and their attending counter-mappings, Rebreanu's novel sketches a portrait of its titular character, Ion. Central to this literary portrait is Ion's desire for land. Ion is born into a poor Romanian family in the village of Pripas. His family used to own some land, which had come into the family as his mother's dowry, but his father squandered it, largely as a result of his drinking. The Romanian word Rebreanu uses to refer to Ion is *calic*, a condescending term for the poor that can also mean beggar (23, 32). Ion's family has two small plots of land left, but they are not enough to make a living in the local agricultural economy, so Ion works as a hired hand for landowning peasants. As an agricultural laborer who is not completely landless, Ion aspires to attain the status of landowning farmer.

What prompts Ion's desire for land? What is the nature of the affective bond between Ion and the land, which Rebreanu refers to as "almost pathological [*aproape bolnăvicioasă*]"?[11] It is clear that Ion's relationship to land exceeds individual desire, that it has collective and historical weight—with both local and global resonance. Rebreanu wrote about the genesis of *Ion*:

> The land problem appeared to me as bigger, more varied and more enduring than it seemed as I sketched the story of Ion Glanetaşu. The land problem appeared then as the very problem of Romanian life, of the existence of the Romanian people, a problem meant to always be newsworthy, regardless of the solutions it might receive in certain conjuctures. . . . Now I was thinking of a novel that would encapsulate the whole land problem.
>
> [*Problema pământului mi se arăta mai vastă, mai variată şi mai trainică decât o privisem schiţând povestea lui Ion Glanetaşu. Problema pământului mi-a apărut atunci ca însăşi problema vieţii româneşti, a existenţei poporului românesc, o problemă menită să fie veşnic de actualitate, indiferent de eventualele soluţii ce i s-ar da în anumite conjuncturi . . . Mă gândeam acum la un roman care să cuprindă întreaga problemă a pământului*].[12]

Rebreanu hoped the land question would endure, along with the novel dramatizing it. In addition to its narrative structure, the novel's modernism (Rebreanu's version of "make it new," the mantra of modernism) is anchored in the enduring novelty of the land question. The canonical status of the novel confirms Rebreanu's intuition.[13]

What, then, is the inter-imperial history of the land question? Transylvania's medieval history consists of a long series of heterogeneous migrations, for which land was not a problem in a modern sense. Only when Transylvania became an estate-based principality in the sixteenth century did land become a problem. The estates, anchored in the dialectic of noble ownership of land and serf labor, created the land problem, making it inseparable from the history of serf labor and revolts against this labor regime. This led to tension between a labor regime and a property regime. This tension is often described as a dialectic of labor and capital that originated in advanced "centers" and gradually incorporated a largely passive "periphery."[14] The Transylvanian landowning nobility, which was largely Hungarian speaking in the early modern period, maintained rights to land and tax exemptions through a series of imperial and protostate formations—the Hungarian Kingdom, the Ottoman Empire, and the Habsburg Empire. The estate system survived for two hundred tumultuous years on account of tight controls restricting landownership. Rules of entail, in particular, ensured that land was not "alienated" from the estates—in other words, redistributed across the social body. Until the nineteenth century, as Katherine Verdery emphasizes, peasants' nonownership of land constituted the structural infrastructure for the exploitation of their labor.[15]

Serfdom was abolished in the Habsburg Empire in 1785, but this shift had a limited impact in Transylvania, where the practice continued until 1848, when both serfdom and entail were abolished.[16] World-systems scholarship's central contribution to an understanding of transformations of production under capitalism has been to analytically disentangle what Friedrich Engels termed "the rise of the second serfdom" from its feudal counterpart in medieval Europe and to draw attention to the capitalist features of renewed enserfment. In 1974, Immanuel Wallerstein coined the term *coerced cash-crop labor,* with the explicit goal of addressing both the orientation toward the world-market and the coerced character of the "second serfdom."[17] His was the most explicit—as well as the most consequential—conceptualization in a series of attempts to capture the increased commodification of agricultural labor occurring throughout Central and East Europe.

In Transylvania, the agrarian reforms of 1848 were followed by the patents of 1854, which abolished serfdom and confirmed peasants' property rights by offering former serfs small parcels of land.[18] But the reforms had limited effects. Peasants who had not been serfs were excluded from the land offerings, and those who did receive land often could not sustain themselves off the small plots they owned and continued to work as hired hands for landowning nobles or wealthy peasants. The land owned by emancipated serfs was also generally too fragmented to be used efficiently. One modest peasant landowner in the region might have owned up to twenty small parcels of land but could barely make a living.[19] Fragmentation of the land was exacerbated by significant population growth (increasing 47.4 percent in the second half of the nineteenth century), which meant that the land of one household would be divided among more siblings through inheritance.[20] One of the major figures of the Romanian Transylvanian Enlightenment, George Barițiu, addressed the problem of land fragmentation regularly in his journalism, which captured both the shift from customary to commodified land rights and the related move of landlords from the countryside to the cities after selling their land.[21] The modernization Barițiu envisioned was anchored in peasant ownership of land.

Landownership was distributed unequally among an inter-imperial rural population consisting of Hungarian, Saxon, Romanian, Armenian, Jewish, and Romani peasants. After the 1867 Compromise, Jörg Hoensch reports, "Although 99 per cent of Hungary's landowners were peasants, they owned only 56 per cent of cultivable land. . . . The state owned between 6 and 7 per cent of the land, but 33 to 35 per cent of cultivable land remained in private or church ownership, estates sometimes equaling whole English counties in their extent."[22]

The Hungarian nobility remained the major landowners in Hungary, according to Iván Berend and György Ránki: "Prince Esterházy owned 300,000 hectares, Prince Schönborn 150,000, Count Károlyi 100,000, Prince Festetich 100,000 hectares."[23] In Transylvania, noble estates were not as large as those in Hungary, but they made up a significant portion of landed property. As a result of pressure from the owners of large estates and increasing land fragmentation, peasants in Transylvania who had received land through imperial decree after the 1848 revolution found themselves indebted to large estate owners in less than two generations. In 1895 half of Transylvanian peasants owned less than two hectares of land, and more than a million day laborers who lived on landowners' estates had become economically dependent.[24] As late as 1915, 25.3 percent of privately owned land in Transylvania consisted of the estates of the largely Hungarian upper classes.[25] The abolition of serfdom had created paupers.

Rebreanu's character Ion thus belongs to a class of Transylvanian Romanian peasants who, by the turn of the twentieth century, had been promised land for generations. This is why Rebreanu considered the land problem to be perpetual. Ion's desire for land is born from a history of serf exploitation. This is a narrative of class deprivation, but it is imbricated with race, ethnicity, religion, and language in an inter-imperial framework. Ion's memory of the land problem is extended in time. Though not a serf himself, Ion carries the memory of his ancestors' living in the long shadow of serfdom. In an inter-imperial framework, he does so in relation to Hungarians and Saxons, who own proportionally more land than Romanians, and in relation to Jews and Roma, who each, in their own way, have historically been at times excluded from landownership.

From the perspective of Transylvania's inter-imperiality, however, the story of the land problem is more complicated. Rebreanu's fictional village of Pripas is a composite of two real villages where Rebreanu grew up, Maieru/Major/ Meierhof and Prislop/Priszlop. They are located in the region of Năsăud/Nassod/ Naszód, which is part of historical Transylvania but has a parallel history within it.[26] The region constituted the eastern border of the Habsburg Empire and functioned as a separate administrative unit between 1762 and 1851. Empress Maria Theresa offered land to Romanian Transylvanian villagers on the border, and they became free on the condition that they defend the border and convert to Greek Catholicism. In this border region, land was collectively owned by peasant households and could not be alienated. Schools were opened for the children of soldiers on the border—the first schools where lessons were taught in the Romanian language in Transylvania. After the 1867 Compromise, the former border region was reconfigured administratively, and former soldiers had to renegotiate their land rights.

There are at least two major long-term echoes of the history of Năsăud/ Nassod/Naszód as a border region in Rebreanu's novel: Transylvanian Romanian peasants in this pocket of Transylvania have a recent memory of landownership, and they belong to an emancipated Romanian-language culture cultivated through the Uniate Church and its schools.[27] Ion's desire for land constitutes a revolt against the long history of exclusion from landownership in Transylvania, but it also carries echoes of a strategic nostalgia for the Habsburg border regiment and the land provisions for peasant-soldiers. The history of imperial dualism in Transylvania creates the trans-imperial agency of peasants, who pit one imperial power against the other. In this case, they strategically invoke nostalgia for Austrian dominance, which is posited as preferable to Hungarian domination.[28] The peasants are negotiating their options trans-imperially, maneuvering for agency between vying imperial powers. The concepts of inter-imperiality and trans-imperiality allow for complexity and ambivalence: they help explain both oppression (Ion's ancestors did not own land) and change (some of Ion's ancestors on the border *did* own land). Both sides of this history explain Transylvanian Romanians' connection to the motto "We want land [*Noi vrem pământ*]."

At the same time, the peasants' trans-imperial negotiations looked ahead, toward yet another imperial power looming to the east: Soviet Russia. In 1917 Romania's King Ferdinand promised land to all peasant-soldiers willing to fight the "godless Soviets."[29] He invoked the collective identity of a "bulwark of Christianity," which, since the Crusades, had entailed land or freedom from serfdom as a reward for peasants defending the faith. Rebreanu's novel, written after the author migrated to Romania, both refracts this history and implicitly advocates for land reform. Land reform would occur in the 1920s, after Transylvania was incorporated into Romania and inter-imperial agency shifted once again. After six million hectares of land were redistributed to 1.4 million Romanian and Hungarian peasants in 1921, it was expropriated Hungarian landowners' turn to negotiate jurisdiction inter- and trans-imperially. Transylvanian Saxons likewise attempted to renegotiate their historical privileges.[30] By opting for Hungarian citizenship under the terms of the Paris peace treaty on minority rights, they argued—ultimately unsuccessfully—that the Romanian law of nationalization should not apply to them.[31] Ironically, in 1927 the Romanian prime minister would admit to the League of Nations that the decision regarding land redistribution had been less about defending Christianity and more about "safeguarding the principle of private property as such," which the Soviet Union now endangered.[32] The addition of Russian and Soviet interests in the adjudication of the land problem in Transylvania enlarged the sphere of trans-imperial negotiations while confirming the inter-imperial dimension of the land problem itself.

The Desire for Land as Eroticized Affect

Against the historical background of serfdom, which was abolished slowly, piece-meal, and asymmetrically in the Habsburg Empire, Ion's desire to own more land translates into a bodily and affective relationship to the land he already owns:

> The land was the apple of his eye. . . . Ion scanned the whole lot with a thirsty gaze, weighing it. His pleasure at the sight was so intense that he felt like dropping to his knees to embrace it. It was ever more beautiful because he owned it. The thick lush grass, sprinkled with clover, was swaying languidly in the cool air of the morning. He could not restrain himself. He tore up a handful of grass and rubbed it passionately between his palms. (41)
>
> *Iar pământul îi era drag ca ochii din cap. . . . Cu o privire setoasă, Ion cuprinse tot locul, cântărindu-l. Simțea o plăcere atât de mare, văzându-și pământul, încât îi venea să cadă în genunchi și să-l îmbrățiseze. I se părea mai frumos, pentru că era al lui. Iarba deasă, grasă, presărată cu trifoi, unduia ostenită de răcoarea dimineții. Nu se putu stăpâni. Rupse un smoc de fire și le mototoli pătimaș în palme.* (58)

Ion has an exaggerated, intimate relationship to land, anchored in a notion of ownership that is particular to global capitalism.[33] To Ion, the land is beautiful—as long as it belongs to him. If, for Iberian colonizers in the Americas, conquered land represented virgin land to be penetrated with sword in hand (as McClintock shows), in the inter-imperial context of early-twentieth-century Transylvania, Rebreanu depicts land in an eroticized key. Ion's heart stirs at the sight of his beloved land, which he desires to embrace. A thirsty gaze holds the land in view. Through the device of prosopopoeia, a central figure of speech in colonial as well as postcolonial and inter-imperial literature, the land is in one breath anthropomorphized and gendered feminine. In literary terms, land becomes face.[34] A seduction scene develops, with Ion and the feminized land entering a dramatic, intense love story. As discussed in chapter 5, the implication is not only that land is feminized but also, conversely, that woman is treated as land.

Hyperbole of feeling is a sign of the pastoral, as we know from Raymond Williams, who dwells on situations in which hyperbolic feelings toward nature are often put to counterpastoral uses. As Rebreanu's twist on the counterpastoral genre meets naturalism, Ion cannot control the urge to touch and squeeze the land in his hands. The scene anticipates a consequential naturalist leitmotif for the novel as a whole: Ion is not fully the actor behind his actions. Prompted by an overwhelming desire for land, motivated by a long inter-imperial history of landownership, he commits acts for which he is not fully responsible. The land itself becomes the agent; once facialized, it acts. The outcome is a vicious circle in which it is no longer easy to tell who owns whom.

Clearly, Ion's desire for land is strongly gendered:

> The voice of the land pierced the lad's soul, like a call, overwhelming him. . . . He felt he was strong enough to rule over the whole land . . . his whole being burned with the craving for land, ever more land. . . . The love of land dominated him since early childhood. He had always envied the rich and had armed himself with a passionate determination: he must own a lot of land, he must! Since then, he loved the land more than a mother. . . . (43)
>
> *Glasul pământului pătrundea năvalnic în sufletul flăcăului, ca o che-mare, copleşindu-l. . . . Se simţea atât de puternic încât să domnească peste tot cuprinsul . . . toată fiinţa lui a1rde de dorul de a avea pământ mult, cât mai mult. . . . Iubirea pământului l-a stăpânit de mic copil. Veşnic a pizmuit pe cei bogaţi şi veşnic s-a înarmat într-o hotărâre pătimaşă: trebuie să aibă pământ mult, trebuie! De pe atunci pământul i-a fost mai drag ca o mamă. . . . (61)*

Sirenlike, the land sings an irresistible song. The novel frames a call-and-response game; the voice of the land calls, and Ion inevitably responds. Ion's desire creates the desirability of the land, which in turn yields his dogged determination to own more land. The text is performative: it foreshadows the fact that listening to the siren's song leads to Ion's undoing. Psychoanalytically, as the feminized land stands in the structural position of the mother, who is later replaced by a lover, Ion cannot help answering the call—picking up the phone, as it were. Land becomes, in Neelam Jabeen's formulation, woman-land, a leitmotif of the colonial imagination.[35] As Jabeen emphasizes, the connection between woman and land in such situations is not metaphorical but material: woman and land are instrumentalized as fertile through reproduction. Rebreanu's text flips the colonial implication but retains the framework of an erotics of conquest.

The story is deceivingly simple: Ion does not have enough land. Where there is lack, there is desire. Ion needs land for survival; peasants live off the land. Ion and his family eat exclusively what the land produces, and they live day in and day out with the worry of not having enough food.[36] They count the mouths they have to feed and calculate food needs against how much land they own. There is a perceived sense of scarcity in terms of resources drawn from the land. Ownership of land promises to resolve the issue of scarcity and thus of food anxiety. If only Ion had more land, according to this logic, there would be plenty of food.

Ion also needs to own land because property establishes a relationship with the imperial state. Since the French Revolution, Western liberalism has considered the property-owning citizen to be the subject of the state—subjected to the state and beneficiary of the rights granted by the state. More important, however, property distinguished passive citizens, who could enjoy natural and civil rights, from active citizens, whose contribution to and participation in the social enterprise entitled them to political rights (suffrage). An important milestone in this history is a legal decree proclaimed by the French National Assembly in October 1789 that defined active citizens as French nationals who paid a minimum of three days' wages in direct taxes and could not be defined as servants. The decree effectively restricted political rights to property-owning white French males and excluded women, foreigners, Black people, and workers from active citizenship.[37] This distinction ensured not only that the universal notion of citizenship produced particularisms from the moment of its emergence but also that such particularisms kept being reproduced in and across different imperial contexts. As Napoleon reintroduced slavery in the colonies in 1802, all enslaved people and servants were forbidden both entry into continental France and citizenship rights. In Ion's case, within the Austro-Hungarian dual monarchy, and despite claims to the contrary, equal rights, especially voting and language rights, were often denied to non-Hungarian Transylvanian populations (we develop this argument in chapter 4). In 1894 French prime minister Georges Clemenceau wrote in the newspaper La Justice that "the Romanian schools in Transylvania have to be maintained by private subsidies while the instruction is mandatory in Hungarian. The 3.5 million Romanians who form the majority of the population are deprived of any political rights."[38] Because of his lack of landed property, Ion is a second-class or passive citizen in Transylvania. This predicament means that his wife, Ana, is even further away from claiming citizenship rights, as her second-class status is compounded by her gender (see chapter 5).

To be a citizen (in the reigning Western liberal sense, a person), Ion needs property, with land being the paradigmatic property. Due to a differential voting system for Transylvania within Hungary, only a small percentage of Transylvania's male population could vote at this time. Historian Zoltán Szász writes: "The proportion of enfranchised male adults was 25 percent among Saxons, 20 percent among Hungarians, and only 9 percent among Romanians." He adds: "There were no such variations in inner Hungary. Thanks to the bias of the electoral law and to the comparative affluence of burghers, the proportion of voters was higher in the towns than in rural areas, and the main beneficiaries were once again the Hungarian and Saxons."[39] Peasants like Ion know that, although there are many propertied Transylvanian Romanian peasants who cannot vote, the future of voting rights rests with ownership—landownership in particular.[40] Without the right to vote, Ion belongs to a disenfranchised population, and the disenfranchised are patronized by both imperial and nationalist elites, with the latter including Romanian religious leaders (see chapter 7) as well as the small Romanian industrial and banking bourgeoisie that operated alongside the German and Hungarian bourgeoisie in Transylvania's cities.[41]

Ion also needs land to gain social capital among the men of the village. Property encodes a set of hierarchical social relations. Landownership, in particular, functions as a status symbol. At the beginning of the novel, despite his good looks, intelligence, and work ethic, Ion is a nobody in the village's social hierarchy. Once he is propertied, he becomes a leader among the villagers. Drawing on John Locke, Verdery reminds us that property implies morality—one is not only a citizen but also a *proper* citizen.[42] The irony, of course, is that Ion compromises his morality through his marital scheming, but at another level, he acquires propriety and social capital through landownership. As a propertied citizen of the village, Ion acquires power within a very complex landscape. To be sure, he is not a powerful actor in a broader Transylvanian sense, but he becomes as powerful as the other male villagers in Pripas.

Importantly, Ion wants more land than he needs—always more land. In fact, Ion wants all the land his eyes lustfully appraise. He fantasizes about dominating the land: "All the land bowed low before him. . . . And it all belonged to him; it was his now [*Pământul se închina în fața lui tot, pământul. . . . Și tot era al lui, numai al lui acuma*]" (305, 429). The feminized land submits, welcoming Ion's dominance, or so he imagines: "And the land seemed to reel, it bowed low before him [*Și pământul parcă se clătina, se închina în fața lui*]" (306, 430). Projecting himself as a combination of king and saint, Ion feels "proud and elated like every conqueror [*mândru și mulțumit ca orice învingător*]" (310, 435). This is the meeting point of an inter-imperial desire for land and an emerging anti-imperial nationalism, itself an inverted story of domination and virile conquest. The novel registers the seemingly paradoxical situation of an inter-imperial peasant's desire for land redistribution that degenerates into a claim to dominate all land. Through the gender dynamics at work in Ion's eroticized relationship to land, one can witness McClintock's theory of the feminization of land in colonial contexts echoed in the inter-imperial context of Europe's eastern periphery.

How can Ion, a poor but ambitious and highly intelligent young peasant, acquire land? The novel exaggerates Ion's physical strength and work ethic. He works all the time, passionately. His dedication to work is widely acknowledged and admired in the village. Although, in the novel, it is possible to purchase small plots of land through hard work, it seems impossible to buy enough land to make a living. There is no labor-based social mobility that leads to landownership. Alternatively, Ion can steal some land, which he does. He pinches a strip of land from a neighbor and serves time in jail for the initiative. A third option for Ion is immigration, which was driven by the promise of land. Peasants were enticed to immigrate by the prospect of making a thousand dollars working in the United States, which they could then use to purchase land upon their return. According to Sorina Paula Bolovan, 17 percent of the population of a village in the region immigrated during the first decade of the twentieth century; destinations were Romania (21.4 percent) and the United States (65.2 percent).[43] Although this was a historical reality during the novel's time frame, with more than 200,000 Romanians immigrating at the beginning of the twentieth century, Rebreanu's novel does not consider this possibility.[44] While the character Titu moves to Romania, and other members of the Herdelea family move to the nearby city, Rebreanu's peasants are ideologically immobile, rooted.

Having exhausted or bracketed these possibilities, Rebreanu employs the classic novelistic solution to Ion's path to social mobility: marriage. For those lacking access to the economic resources or information necessary to migrate, marriage has long offered the means of obtaining residence or citizenship in a spouse's better-off country or region. The poorest strata—the unskilled, the racialized, women, and feminized others—often employ marriage as a risky strategy to achieve upward mobility anchored in the body.[45] As a man, Ion is not at the most precarious end of this hierarchy, but as a poor Transylvanian Romanian peasant in Austria-Hungary, marriage into a landowning family constitutes for him the fast track to the acquisition of both land and citizenship rights. In this process, Ana is exchanged between her father and Ion, cementing marriage as one type of the "traffic in women" theorized by Gayle Rubin in 1975 (an argument developed in chapter 5).[46]

As a reminder that we are on the terrain of a twisted pastoral, we should recall Williams's analysis of "the country and the city" predicament, in which "the problems of love and marriage, in a society dominated by issues of property in land," become the stakes of a counterpastoral plot. What such texts dramatize, in Williams's words, is "the long process of choice between economic advantage and other ideas of value."[47] The other idea of value here, as elsewhere, is love. Rebreanu titled the first half of his novel "The Voice of the Land" and the second "The Voice of Love." This structure frames a tension between two perfectly symmetrical parts. Custom requires one to marry someone at the same level of wealth, or here, at the same level of landownership.[48] Although Ion is in love with Florica, a poor and landless young woman in the village who would be an appropriately horizontal match for him, he seduces Ana, whose father, Vasile Baciu, owns land. Marriage to Ana solves Ion's land problem, in the blink of an eye transforming him into a landowner. This solution translates into upward social mobility while exacerbating the choice between land and love.

Since Ion—figured as a conqueror—cannot seize land by force, his marriage to Ana represents a different form of masculine conquest that literally en-titles him to land. At the same time, it reduces Ana, through whom he acquires the land, to a subordinate position in a love triangle that initially includes Ion, Ana, and the land. Following his marriage, Ion visits his newly acquired plots, which he encounters "as if they were faithful mistresses [*ca pe niște ibovnice credincio-ase*]" (305, 429). What ensues is an actualized sexual encounter with the gendered land, transformed into a naked girl. Functioning as a nuptial (Ion marries the land), the scene ends on an orgasmic note:

> His eyes laughed and his whole face was bathed in a warm horny sweat. He was overcome with a wild urge to embrace the soil, to crush it with kisses. He stretched out his hand towards the straight furrows, cloddish and damp. The pungent smell, raw and fertile, stirred the blood in his veins. . . . And then slowly, devoutly, unconsciously, he dropped to his knees, lowered his head and lustfully pressed his lips upon the wet soil. And in the thrill of this quick kiss, he felt a cold intoxicating shiver. (305)
>
> *Îi râdeau ochii, iar fața toată îi era scăldată într-o sudoare caldă de patimă. Îl cuprinse o poftă sălbatecă să îmbrătișeze huma, să o crâmpoțească în sărutări. Întinse mâinile spre brazdele drepte, zgrunțuroase și umede. Mirosul acru, proaspăt și roditor îi aprindea sângele. . . . Apoi încet, cucernic, fără să-și dea seama, se lăsă în genunchi, își coborî fruntea și-și lipi buzele cu voluptate de pământul ud. Și-n sărutarea aceasta grăbită simți un fior rece, amețitor.* (430)

This is arguably one of the most influential passages in Romanian-language literature. An enraptured, flushed peasant passionately embraces and kisses his beloved land. His lustful mouth voluptuously, uncontrollably reaches for the moist, pungent soil. Rebreanu titled the first section of the novel "The Voice of the Land," but he could have called it "The Face of the Land," since prosopopoeia comes into play in this crucial scene as well. Rebreanu claimed that he witnessed an actual scene of a Transylvanian peasant kissing the land as if it were a lover, and this is what moved him to write *Ion*, "the first Romanian modern novel" and a testament to Transylvanian peasants' love of land.[49]

The fictional and the documentary intertwine in this instance to produce a hybrid event with consequential ideological overtones. Ion's love of land is compulsive, in a naturalist vein; yet there is a sense that the peasant also chooses this compulsion. The body of the peasant and the land share an implacable attraction, as if made of the same clay. Rebreanu is framing not only a struggle over land but also a struggle over the very meaning of both land and property. The scene of Ion having sex with the land encodes an alternative relationship to land suggested by the framework of legal property. This is a notion of property anchored in the flow of both affection and bodily fluids between Ion and the land. The anthropomorphizing of land renders it an active actor in the struggle over property. What does the land want? In Rebreanu's writing, it wants to submit to Ion's virility. Among many inter-imperial suitors, the land chooses Ion.

Enlisting peasants into a 1920 literary project with anti-imperial implications has resonance in world history: globally, peasants often become the bearers of claims to organic connections to land.[50] Various indigenous populations around the world create accounts of property as alternatives to the global imposition of a Western, legalistic notion of property rights. It is these contestations of commodification that Rebreanu's novel productively counter-maps as not only anti-imperial but also decisively inter-imperial and thus highly modern—rather than traditional—processes in the context of Transylvania's land problem.

The Land Problem and the Commons

Rebreanu's novel dramatizes the land problem in its two interrelated forms: individual ownership, made possible through capitalist property rights, and collective ownership, anchored in customary rights, themselves under attack after the advance of the commodity frontier into the region. The two forms correlate, imperfectly, with two uses of land: fields and commons. Fields are used for agricultural production; commons are used for animal grazing and wood. Rebreanu depicts Ion's desire for land as primarily a desire for agrarian land; in fact, it seems that Ion wants to transform all or most land into individually owned agrarian land. Given geographical and historical limitations, as well as ideological implications for inter-imperial nationalisms, the novel portrays Transylvanian peasants as equally invested in acquiring or maintaining rights in the commons. Through an episode that Rebreanu's notes refer to as the "Romanian-Saxon conflict [*conflictul româno-săsesc*]" (594), the novel dramatizes the Transylvanian version of the modern struggle over the use of the commons. In the last section of this chapter, we examine the implications of the struggle over the commons for the inter-imperial land problem.[51]

In addition to tracking Ion's individual desire for land, the novel has a subplot concerned with the collective use of the commons—forests and pastures. This subplot is crucial to an understanding of the land problem, since the balance between agrarian land and the commons is tilted toward the latter in Transylvania, which has a large forested mountainous area. In the Năsăud/Nassod/Naszód region, pastureland constituted 20.36 percent of all land, while forests constituted 52.92 percent, a proportion that fluctuated from village to village.[52] This distribution is crucial to an understanding of the debate over the commons in relation to inter-imperial nationalisms, since it involves a romantic investment in Transylvanian mountains. Wallerstein reminds us that holders of titled land rights have helped create spatial pockets of political resistance: "These same zones, however, are considered zones of libertarian resistance by those who have thus escaped. These zones are as doubtfully 'traditional' (that is, pre-modern) as most other phenomena we like to brand negatively as traditional."[53] Wallerstein cites high mountainous areas as prime examples of zones to which people retreated to fight the demand to create titles on land they customarily used. These zones of resistance are discursively reconfigured as traditional and primitive, although they are radically modern in terms of the challenge they pose to the advancing capitalist logic. At stake in Rebreanu's dramatization of the struggle over the commons is the question of who owns the western Carpathian Mountains, which gave Transylvania its name ("the land over the mountains"), and the Transylvanian forests, which served as places of refuge during wars and revolutions.[54]

We know that the global history of land overlaps with coloniality. The colonial process saw whole regions of the world become the "country" for other regions, which became "metropolitan" in relation to these sources of raw materials. Williams writes: "The traditional relationship between city and country was then thoroughly rebuilt on an international scale. Distant lands became the rural areas of industrial Britain, with heavy consequent effects on its own surviving rural areas."[55] We focus here on the consequent effects on areas that were considered backward vis-à-vis Britain, including the British countryside.[56] The concept of inter-imperiality is necessary to an assessment of how the formalization of land rights unfolded in a region like Transylvania, which, although it had fairly well developed cities, functioned as the country vis-à-vis metropolitan Vienna and Budapest—and the core of the world-system.

In Rebreanu's novel, the young poet Titu discovers the Romanian-Saxon conflict after moving to the village Luşca, modeled after the real village Nepos, previously known as Vărarea. Legend has it that the village took the name Nepos from a statement uttered by Joseph II during a visit to Transylvania at the end of the eighteenth century. The emperor reportedly welcomed Romanian villagers by saying, "*Salve, parvae nepos Romuli!* [Salve, you grandchildren of Rome!]." In recognition of the emperor's acknowledgment of their Latinity, which the villagers craved (for reasons described in the introduction), four villages changed their names and became Salva, Parva, Nepos, and Romuli. The name Nepos itself is thus a literal imperial inscription on the land—the language of the Austrian emperor translated into place name and superimposed on the peasants' desire for the recognition of their relation to the Roman Empire.

It is here that Rebreanu places the Romanian-Saxon conflict over the use of the commons. The character of Titu describes the village as economically prosperous: "a large, rich village, with lush pasture-land and numerous cattle herds [*sat mare și bogat, cu pășuni grase și vite multe*]" (263, 369). The Romanian-Saxon conflict concerns the pasture used by these herds:

> The Lușca people had had a lot of trouble with the Saxons of Păuniș on account of the pasture-land. For the last fifty years they have been wrangling about it before the Court but they had not reached a final settlement. In the course of the last spring, the Păuniș people had obtained an award in their favor, which the Lușca people had opposed on the grounds that they had had the use of this common since time immemorial. (297)
>
> *Lușcanii sunt în conflict cu sașii din Păuniș din pricina imașului. De cincizeci de ani se judecă și tot n-au ajuns la o hotărâre definitivă. Astă-primăvară păunișenii au dobândit o sentință în favoarea lor, dar Lușcanii au atacat-o, căci ei au folosința imașului din moși-strămoși.* (417)

The literary dispute penned in 1920 glosses a real historical dispute concerning pastures held by peasants in common ownership. This conflict (*cearta de hotar*) would have been known to Rebreanu's contemporaries, which is why he offers only a brief historical sketch. Two kinds of Transylvanian commons became the object of dispute at this time. One was the commons belonging to former serfs, who had the right to use, under certain conditions, pastures and forests formerly owned by nobles. The second, in the Năsăud/Nassod/Naszód region, concerned the commons on the border held by former soldiers. When the military administrative unit on the border was dissolved, the peasants' relation to common land was redefined. A process of modernization as commodification ensued, which attempted to formalize and legally encode peasants' rights to the commons. The agent of this formalization process was the imperial state working through a complex bureaucracy that, after the compromise, was largely made up of Hungarian-speaking functionaries. They regulated the land owned, individually and collectively, by Romanian, Hungarian, and Saxon peasants. The same bureaucracy regulated the inclusion and exclusion of Jewish and Romani minorities from the institutions of formalization. Far from being a strictly economic development, formalization was deeply politicized.

Romanian Transylvanian peasants resisted the perceived injustice of formalization. As Rebreanu's novel describes it, the struggle over ownership of the pastures in Lușca/Nepos lasted fifty years (in fact, it continued, on and off, for a century). The Transylvanian press covered the dispute and debated it extensively. It involved the border between commons belonging to four Romanian Transylvanian villages (Ilva-Mică, Feldru, Nepos, Rebrișoara) and three Saxon villages (Iaad, Pintac, Mettesdorf).[57] The line separating the commons had been drawn in the 1830s, when the villages were militarized. Villagers on both sides fought this line with renewed force starting in 1840, employing various political and juridical strategies. The Romanians accused the Saxons of moving the signs (*movila*) delineating the border between the commons, thus claiming a large area that historically belonged to the Romanian villages. Romanian peasants sent numerous petitions to the emperor, and they repeatedly sent a representative to Vienna to argue their case.[58] The matter was discussed in the Transylvanian Diet, and the peasants fought about it among themselves, sometimes violently.[59]

Paramount to the process of formalizing rights to the commons, which started in the eighteenth century, was surveying the land, measuring and quantifying its dimensions in modern units, and then recording those findings in administrative documents. This process yielded state documents (*cartea funciară*) and individual ownership documents (land titles). The modernization-cum-commodification of the land question meant that papers granting and regulating land titles mediated between the land and the peasants. Kafka gave this reality an ironic twist in the context of the Austro-Hungarian Empire as depicted in *The Castle*: K.'s job is land surveyor, and the text suggests that for something to exist, it first has to exist on paper—that is, factual existence is derivative of paper existence. This modern reality was perhaps most shocking when it came to the land on which peasants stood and on which their livelihood depended.[60]

Formalization involved common land being divided into quota shares according to an algorithm that translated old servitudes into rights to land—a process retraced by Monica Vasile.[61] Peasants were not allowed to enclose their shares in the commons, but this provision was not always respected.[62] The shares were inheritable and could be sold to other members of the landholding association. Prices varied widely, based on how the land could be used.[63] Peasants thus entered a property regime in which they could sell and thus lose their rights to common land. In theorizing the commodification of land, Wallerstein notes that in most cases, "mandated privatization of the property created multiple small owners who, however, were unable to maintain the property in a market situation. They thereupon sold their rights to some larger entrepreneur. At the end of this process, they had lost all rights within the erstwhile collective property, and economically were likely to be worse off than before."[64] In Transylvania, too, the value of land changed irrevocably with this development, while some peasants were increasingly pauperized.

To receive the shares owed to them according to the formalization formula, peasants had to prove ancestral ownership of the land. Everybody in the village knew that a certain peasant owned a certain parcel of land, the memory of which was secured through a complex and nuanced toponymical practice of recording ownership as well as use.[65] It was often difficult for Transylvanian peasants to navigate a bureaucratic system functioning in imperial languages (first German, then Hungarian, sometimes Romanian). The process of formalization was therefore rife with legal battles. An 1871 law regulated disputes related to formalization. Vasile estimates that 30 percent of Transylvanian households were involved in legal battles over land.[66] Judges became arbiters of formalization laws—in the dispute described by Rebreanu, adjudicating between Romanian and Saxon peasants. In this predicament, new forms of inequality were produced, intersecting with entrenched forms of injustice. Land often ended up in the hands of large landowners, old and new, who could purchase small parcels from peasants in times of crisis.[67] Ownership of forests, in particular, was adjudicated to the benefit of owners of large properties.[68]

Saxons had arrived in Transylvania in the early modern period, invited by local rulers who were taking advantage of the population surplus in regions that are now Germany. They accepted the invitation because they had been promised land. Known as "colonists," they enjoyed significant economic and legal autonomy through the period of Ottoman dependence and during the Habsburg Empire. The terms of the initial invitation to settle in Transylvania were renewed twenty-two times.[69] Saxons renegotiated their autonomy, including their rights to land, after 1848. After 1867, they found their historical autonomy severely curtailed.[70] They tried to negotiate their agency trans-imperially, drawing on their connection to the German-speaking empires—Austria and Prussia. Thus, at the time of Rebreanu's novel, Saxons, too, could claim ancestral rights to the commons—rights anchored in the terms of their initial invitation to colonize the border regions of Transylvania. The courts adjudicating formalization conflicts at the end of the nineteenth century were asked to decide which notion of ancestral rights was more forceful. In Rebreanu's version of this narrative, Hungarian authorities sided with the Saxons. At least, that is what the Transylvanian Romanian peasants were likely to believe, given the long and tense inter-imperial struggle among Hungarians, Romanians, and Saxons. One can see how the dispute over the commons, involving the juridical invocation of ancestral land rights, overlapped with the region's nationalisms, which themselves were ideologically anchored in a primordial claim to land. The literary, pastoral invocation of mountains, forests, and pastures served multiple disjunctive purposes.

In Rebreanu's novel, once the struggle over the commons de-escalates, an old man in the village explains to Titu: "Yes, sir, they have beaten us and tortured us, they have admitted the Saxons' right, but the common is still ours and no man from Păuniş dares set foot on our land [*Ei, domnişorule, ne-au zdrobit ei, ne-au chinuit, au dat dreptate saşilor, dar imaşul tot al nostru a rămas şi azi nu mai calcă picior de păunişan pe pământul nostru!*]" (300, 422). Ironically, the Romanian word for the quintessentially Romanian commons, *imaş*, is derived from the Hungarian *nyomás*. Likewise, the word the Romanian peasants use to refer to the Saxon peasants, *sas*, comes from the Hungarian *szász*. The possessive phrase "our land" in the Romanian language is inextricably bound with these linguistic connotations in the Hungarian language. Etymology functions as a reminder of inter-imperial traces, contributing to the creolization of a modern economic predicament intertwined with its inter-imperial yet equally modern history.

Crucial is the attitude Titu attributes to the old man in the scene: determination or doggedness. Peasants had fought for the commons for a century. A naturalist leitmotif, the old man's doggedness reminds the proto-intellectual Titu of another peasant—Ion. In Titu's mind, the two peasants constitute a collective, a "they" that slides into a "we":

> Titu suddenly felt like hugging him. The doggedness he could feel in the peasant's voice seemed to lift him and at the same time anchored his feet in the land, like roots no power could crush. . . . Only peasants know how to sacrifice themselves for the land, because only they intuit that land is the ultimate foundation. (300)
>
> *Lui Titu îi veni deodată să-l îmbrățişeze. Încăpățânarea ce-o simțea în glasul țăranului parcă-l înălța şi-n acelaşi timp îi adâncea picioarele în pământ ca nişte rădăcini pe care nici o putere nu le poate nimici. . . . Numai ei ştiu să se jertfească pentru pământ, căci numai ei simt că pământul e temelia.* (423)

Like Ion, the old man displays what Titu imagines is a primordial, bodily relationship to the land. Titu envisions the peasant's tenacity (*încăpățânare*) giving him roots—roots that Titu himself can use as an anchor. Titu is somewhat repulsed by Ion's naturalist perseverance in pursuit of land, as well as the gender implications at work. In contradistinction, the old man's conflict with the Saxons and the Hungarian authorities serves as an alternative model of determination. *Ion* dramatizes the old man's doggedness as the Romanian Transylvanians' structure of feeling. The novel suggests that this attitude—rather than the official papers produced by the imperial state—binds peasants to the land. Through his gesture toward the old man, Titu, the emerging intellectual, invents his own organic relationship to the land.[71] The scene depicts Titu growing the roots he posits as the dialectical counterpoint to the various routes he pursues. It is important that the man in the scene is old—ancient even—as his age offers Titu a narrative of endurance in the land. The old man allows Titu to both recall the history of serfdom and fantasize about a golden age when the man and his ancestors were collective masters of the land (Nepos). The legal struggle over the use of the commons slides unnoticeably into another form of ancestral collectivism. The time immemorial (*din moşi-strămoşi*) invoked by the old man suggests yet another notion of property—property as justice. In this sense, the right to use the commons can be seen as a form of inter-imperial reparations, returning the land to its rightful owners, who had used the land since time immemorial. An analysis of the naturalist framing of the novel teaches us that invoking immemorial roots in the land constitutes an inter-imperial mode of historicism.[72]

Rurality and Inter-Imperiality

World-systems and decolonial perspectives fasten their analysis on the constitutive relation between European colonial expansion and capitalism. Central to this analysis is the articulation of labor control based on the interests of European wage labor production. Aníbal Quijano coined the phrase "coloniality of labor control" to account for the possibility of maintaining the coloniality of power in the capitalist world-economy. Quijano views this articulation as "constitutively colonial, based on, first, the assignment of all forms of unpaid labor to colonial racialized groups (originally American Indians, blacks, and, in a more complex way, mestizos) in America and, later on, to the remaining colonized groups in the rest of the world. . . ."[73] In this chapter, with this framework in mind, we asked several questions: Where are Europe's peripheries, such as Transylvania, in this picture? What modalities of labor control operate in a region like Transylvania? If, as Wallerstein submits, classes belong to the world-economy as a whole, what is Ion's class status in the world-economy?[74]

Wallerstein points out that, whereas land in the Americas was characterized as virgin, whole areas of early modern East Europe were described as vacant.[75] Both discursive maneuvers camouflaged the expansion of the commodity frontier in the Americas and in East Europe.[76] The overwhelming scholarly spotlight on the Americas as the primary arena where these processes took place (despite Wallerstein's focus on East Europe starting in 1974) leaves processes occurring in East Europe and in the context of imperial rather than colonial dynamics largely unaccounted for.[77] The case of Transylvania offers a telling illustration of the importance of the advancing commodity frontier in the region, while adding nuance to the account of dialectical developments in Europe to include the imperial alongside the colonial dimensions of capitalism. After the sixteenth century, much of Europe's east gradually entered a quasicolonial relationship vis-à-vis the European core, providing raw materials by using labor-intensive technology and state-enforced, labor-exploitative social systems that involved most of the local agricultural population.[78] These regions became "internal Americas," to use Fernand Braudel's phrase. Andrea Komlosy refers to the Habsburg regions that followed this logic as "internal peripheries," analyzing the role Bukovina and Galicia played in the Habsburg monarchy's efforts to compensate for a lack of external colonies in its competition with Great Britain.[79] In the Habsburg monarchy, this internal expansion meant that already existing systems of bondage were juxtaposed to the prebendary economy of Bukovina and to serfdom in Galicia to serve the agricultural export economy. After the core regions of the empire abolished bondage in the 1780s, new forms of servitude and forced market-oriented labor arose in the zones of expansion, ensuring unequal exchange between the industrial production of the western lands and the agricultural production of the eastern lands of the crown.[80] As Komlosy succinctly puts it, "With regard to their territorial gains from eastern and south-eastern expansion and the decimated Ottoman Empire, Central Europe was made up of imperial core regions that created their own peripheries in order to develop peripheral procurement and export markets for industrialization in the core."[81] Transylvania was part of this economic dynamic until the last decades of the nineteenth century.

In this chapter, we traced Rebreanu's commentary on the processes of formalizing land rights, including rights to common land. In their introduction to a special section on land rights in the world-system, Araghi and Karides emphatically state the issue's centrality: "From a world-historical standpoint, the history of capitalism begins with the transformation of land rights."[82] This transformation was accompanied by centuries of struggle for and against the massive social transformation it implied: "the modern concept of land rights denotes the establishment of bourgeois land rights in the countryside (leading to export-led commercial agriculture) and in the city (as real estate)."[83] Likewise, for Wallerstein, the establishment of a legal basis for what became known as "title to the land" represents "the single most important change imposed by the modern world-system."[84] Although different customary rules concerning the right to utilize the land existed prior to the capitalist world-economy (though seldom in written form), the acquisition of a written title meant that land could be bequeathed to heirs or sold. The common

denominator in these transcolonial and trans-imperial processes of land commodification was a loss of the right to inhabit the land for many indigenous populations and an inability to use land for subsistence agricultural production by
farmers. This revised narrative concerning the commodification of land compli-
cates the classic capitalist dialectic between capital and labor. In Fernando Coronil's words, a "shift from a binary to a triadic dialectic"—that is, from capital
versus labor to capital versus labor versus title to land—reveals that linear accounts
of the gradual incorporation of passive peripheries into the dialectical logic of capital fail to track the massive transformation in the dynamics of both capital and
labor resulting from the commodification of land.[85]

We have argued that these processes followed an outward colonial movement,
but they also looked inward, toward parts of East Europe. Although, as Wallerstein points out, legitimating ownership of land by legal title is a fundamental
process of the capitalist world-economy, it typically occurred globally through
the seizure of land from those who previously had rights to it—either through
authorization by a monarch or conquest. In Araghi and Karides's view, however,
the global history of primitive accumulation and the transformation of land
rights starting in 1492 must include both an outward expropriating movement—
involving the conquest and separation of indigenous populations from the land
and the alienation of their customary land-use rights through massacre or
enslavement—and an inward movement of racialized land seizures and population displacement in Castilian Spain.[86] The subsequent reorganization of world
trade in accordance with the law of value around colonial land grabs and the
enforcement of racialized and gendered regimes of forced labor on monoculture
plantations links the commodification of land rights to the rise of industrial capitalism in the nineteenth century. That this inward movement happened not
only in colonial empires but also throughout Europe's imperial formations such
as the Habsburg Empire remains one missing piece in this global puzzle that
Transylvania's agrarian history can provide.

In world-systems analysis, the division of labor in which the emerging early
modern world-economy was anchored enlisted slavery in the Americas and serfdom in East Europe as modes of forced labor (a division we complicate in chapter 3). Wallerstein provides an indelible image: at the time the empires of West
Europe started the colonial project, they were feeding their own populations with
grains produced by serfs in East and Central Europe, while the ships that crisscrossed the Atlantic were likely built using wood extracted from East Europe.
This was possible only because of the way the land problem was articulated in
regions like Transylvania. By the turn of the twentieth century, the title character
in Rebreanu's novel, having lived in the long shadow of serfdom underlying

these global processes, displays a pathological desire for land. The gendered themes that depict Ion as a conqueror flip the colonial horizon in favor of an inter-imperial nationalism that works to transform a peasant's legitimate desire for land-use rights into a nationalist claim to an essentialized relationship to Transylvanian land.

TRANSYLVANIA IN THE WORLD-SYSTEM

Capitalist Integration, Peripheralization, Antisemitism

How is Transylvania's turn-of-the-century economy integrated into the modern/colonial world-system? The agrarian economy depicted by Rebreanu's novel does not *seem* modern. The peasants use antiquated technology to work the land, they consume what they produce, and they work for the teacher and the priest without pay. Katherine Verdery identifies feudal elements in the Transylvanian economy, rejecting Immanuel Wallerstein's premise of a capitalist world-economy that, by the end of the nineteenth century, had engulfed the globe. Zoltán Szász describes the Transylvanian situation, within a narrative of progress, as a form of "backward capitalism."[1] In this chapter, we argue that, at the turn of the twentieth century, Transylvania was fully—if asymmetrically—integrated into a structurally unequal capitalist world-economy. Within our analytical framework, imputed "backwardness" represents the outcome of the inter- and trans-imperial integration of this agricultural region into the capitalist world-economy's semiperiphery.

At the turn of the century, voices in Hungary complained about the country's marginal status within the Austro-Hungarian Empire. Austria-Hungary itself was in an uneven economic competition with the British Empire and in economic decline with respect to imperial Germany.[2] Located on the eastern border of Hungary, Transylvania was peripheral in three ways: within Hungary, as part of Austria-Hungary, and in terms of its structural position in the world-system. There is no doubt, however, that the economic goods produced in the region traveled on both imperial and trans-imperial routes. Despite a prevalent rhetoric of modernization-as-progress, integration into the capitalist world-economy often proceeded as a method of de facto peripheralization across empires that frequently involved pitting one empire against another. Transylvania's integration occurred in this way. As a result, various economic actors negotiated their economic and political agency trans-imperially, whether through alternative trade routes, labor migration, or civil resistance. Rather than mere remnants of an era in decline, early-twentieth-century empires were vigorously vying with the expanding capitalist world-economy. The analytical task of this chapter is to assess what integration meant for regions situated at the crossroads of capitalist expansion and ongoing imperial projects and impacted by both.

The notion of inter-imperiality highlights the fact that the agent of capitalist integration is not some generic state but a series of imperial and state formations, alongside a variety of other heterogeneous actors, including religious institutions.[3] States participate in integration, but overall integration occurs at a scale larger than the state. At the juncture of regional integration and nation building through empire, the textbook narrative about the emergence of sovereign nation-states in a post-Westphalian Europe becomes porous. The linear trajectory from empire to nation-state relegates both multinational polities and multiethnic empires to a past that (West) Europe had supposedly overcome by the end of the nineteenth century. Critical works in global history, international relations, and the sociology of globalization, however, have long insisted that, despite the prevailing rhetoric, West European states of the nineteenth and twentieth centuries were not nation-states.[4] Rather, they were imperial polities in a global system dominated by empires, in which imperial elites actively lobbied for national minorities to assimilate into dominant imperial nations.[5] As Andrea Komlosy points out, nation building became part of "a strategy for survival against the challenges of national movements within the empires as well as of inter(-imperial) state rivalry."[6] This reconceptualization serves as a framework for a much-needed reevaluation of the regional division of labor in the imperial formations of turn-of-the-century Central and East Europe. Although there were some forms of attachment to imperial institutions, the imperial entities of the region, and the Austro-Hungarian Empire in particular, produced multiple forms of quasi-belonging, exceptionalism, and unevenness. Transylvania's integration into the world-economy thus needs to be analyzed in relation to the imperial formations in the region and across a number of imperial technologies.

Four Modalities of Capitalist Integration

The fight between the Romanian and Saxon peasants over the use of the commons discussed in chapter 1 became acute because the cattle that roamed the pastures were likely destined for imperial markets. One form of capitalist integration hinged on world market trade—in this case, trade in agricultural products. The German-speaking lands of the Habsburg Empire had been excluded from the Prussian customs union founded in 1834 and thus, in effect, had been treated economically as a foreign country. This marked the gradual distinction, in Stefan Berger's words, "between a [German] national core, which excluded the Habsburg Empire, and a German-speaking periphery in southeastern Europe, for which Vienna was to become the core reference point."[7] The cattle invoked by Rebreanu's scene belonged to a capitalist economic framework for which Vienna constituted the main reference point. This market was itself mediated by the Austro-Hungarian customs union.[8] The union, which Transylvania joined alongside Hungary in 1850, included "one of the largest areas of free trade in Europe."[9] Agricultural products, especially flour, were the main objects of trade in Hungary. This flour was bought and sold within a commodity chain with global dimensions.[10]

From a West European perspective, East Europe as a whole functioned as a German breadbasket and a provider of vital commodities such as oil and ore. Economic expansion eastward gradually replaced agricultural colonization of overseas territories, prompting today's historians to refer to imperial Germany as having colonies in East Europe *and* overseas. Both were seen as "laboratories of modernity" where, as Berger argues, "a range of things, from gun boats to steam ships, from the telegraph to electrical technology, and from transport networks to drainage systems, were tried out before they were adopted for and in the national core."[11] Yet, although colonial and imperial interests were clearly juxtaposed, the decision for imperial outstretch into the European east rather than overseas marked a decisive difference between imperial Germany and the Habsburg monarchy on the one hand and colonial France and England on the other. In David Blackbourn's account, the actual German and Austrian "counterpart of India or Algeria was not Cameroon—it was *Mitteleuropa*."[12] A region like Transylvania was thus integrated into the world-economy via imperial routes meant to compensate for an inexistent colonial empire overseas. Importantly, this mode of integration-as-peripheralization was contested trans-imperially by groups disadvantaged because of their class, race, and ethnicity, as well as by individual actors. Peasant revolts, usually understood in a nationalist framework, were also revolts against this global predicament, which local elites often condoned.

In Rebreanu's novel, Ion is repaying a mortgage loan from the Someşana Bank, the name of an actual Romanian bank in Transylvania, which ties the local peasantry to an international financial system. The middle-class Herdelea family uses the same bank. After trade, finance functions as a second modality of capitalist integration. In the early nineteenth century, Vienna was the financial capital of the region, lending money and, beginning in 1855, offering credit.[13] Transylvanian

Romanian banks opened with the aim of sustaining investment and serving a growing Romanian middle class. Such historical Romanian banks were Albina in Sibiu/Hermannstadt/Nagyszeben, Economul in Cluj/Kolozsvár/Klausenburg, Aurora in Năsăud/Nassod/Naszód, and Victoria in Arad.[14] These banks, many of which had a co-op structure, had numerous branches across Transylvania, creating a financial network that included most villages. Some of them had global branches as well; Albina, for example, planned to open a branch in New York, which was meant to facilitate the movement of money immigrants sent home.[15] The founding of Transylvanian Romanian banks constituted a form of economic nationalism that evolved in reaction to an uneven capitalist integration.[16]

One of the most prominent Romanian Transylvanian politicians, Alexandru Mocioni (who appears again in chapter 4), advocated for political and linguistic rights, but he also used his family's considerable wealth to sponsor the Albina bank. He considered his political and banking activities to be closely intertwined. Likewise, priests and members of the two Romanian church administrations doubled as banking elite.[17] As nationalist leaders, they considered it their duty to support and invest in Romanian banks. This situation was based on their perception that if Transylvanian Romanians were to overcome their status as second-class citizens in the Austro-Hungarian Empire, they, like the Saxons, needed to have their own banks.[18] Most important, credit was needed to purchase land—often from Hungarian landowners. There was an ongoing debate about the lack of sufficient credit, and there were calls for a more balanced financial integration. But it is clear that Transylvania was part of a complex network of international financial institutions, to which local banks reacted with a strategy of financial nationalism.

A third modality of capitalist integration involved an elaborate imperial bureaucracy oriented toward the world-market, with the aim of modernizing state operations to align with developments in other imperial situations. This bureaucracy simultaneously provided an infrastructure for capitalist integration. The novel's village of Pripas belongs to an Austro-Hungarian bureaucratic network that serves political as well as economic needs. There is a notary in every village in Transylvania, as well as other imperial clerks. The word Rebreanu uses for clerk is *salgăbirău*, from the Hungarian *szolgabiró*, a reminder that most imperial clerks spoke Hungarian. A large part of the former landowning nobility entered the imperial bureaucracy.[19] The benefits of the ensuing integration, facilitated by the imperial state machinery, clearly echo this administrative hierarchy; its benefits accrue to some actors more than others.

Imperial functionaries recorded major events in people's lives—a process through which the *population* was created as an administrative unit. They recorded births, marriages, and deaths. The use of the census as a colonial and imperial technology, first introduced by the British in India, reminds us that colonial and imperial populations are also biopolitical units. The census measures the population as a labor force, and it tracks immigration. It also freezes nationality and religion into irreconcilable differences. If the British census made the Indian population more easily governable by rendering it impossible to declare one's inclusion in more than one caste or in a caste different from that recorded in the census starting in 1881, the imperial census in Transylvania clearly delimited Germans, Hungarians, Romanians, Roma, and Jews according to their mother tongue.[20] In a region with high rates of intermarriage and complex interglottisms, one could have only one mother tongue—and therefore one identity—for purposes of the census. As they do in other parts of the world, such measures reinforced ethnic and racial categories of identity.[21] It is clear that the census constituted one technology through which the imperial bureaucracy doubled as a mechanism of uneven capitalist integration.

A fourth mode of capitalist integration involved mobility—of people, goods, and information. People moved in search of labor—they immigrated to the United States, Latin America, and Romania, and sometimes back again. As noted in chapter 1, immigration offered a path to social mobility for peasants who did not own land and were considered second-class citizens in the empire. Working in mines offered an alternative, but not a sustainable one. High levels of mobility testified to the increased globalization of the labor force. Peasants were inducted into the global division of labor that undergirds the world-economy through local channels of marketing. The flow of information (and disinformation) concerning job opportunities was itself a sign of capitalist integration. At the time that Karl Marx and Friedrich Engels, extrapolating from the British context, were identifying class struggle as the primary conflict of the modern European bourgeois society—and proletarianization as its outcome—immigration to Europe's colonies in the Americas provided an escape from poverty for 12 percent of the continent's population.[22] Reinscribing the large-scale immigration of East Europeans to the colonies into the story of how modern society came about and how capitalist integration occurred allows us to creolize a significant component of the modern by weaving its colonial as well as its imperial dimensions into the narrative.

Overseas migration was more important in Hungary than in the Austrian half of the empire. From 1870 to 1910, some 3.5 million people emigrated overseas from Austria-Hungary, 3 million of them to the United States.[23] Among them, 1,422,205 Hungarian citizens immigrated to the United States, 6,056 to Canada, 264,460 to Argentina, and 8,500 to Brazil.[24] The Brazilian government was looking for white settlers to populate its vast domain and to "whiten" the predominantly black and mestizo population, so it offered free transportation to migrants from East Europe. The response was overwhelming; more than 100,000 citizens from Russia and Austria-Hungary left for Brazil starting in 1890, prompting the Hungarian government to ban immigration to Brazil altogether at the end of 1900.[25] The mobility of labor testifies to a capitalist logic that was fully at work in Transylvania at the turn of the twentieth century and in which whiteness became a currency for trans-imperial negotiation.

The mobility of both people and goods was facilitated by a developing rail system. As Berger notes with regard to Germany, the ability to define a national core by incorporating some layers of the imperial periphery while excluding others relied heavily on effective means of transportation and communication.[26] Railways brought the provinces closer to the centers of political power, but they also revealed tensions within the German confederation. Multiple train connections existed between Saxony or Bavaria and Austria, yet only one railway connected Austria with Prussia. The Austrian railroad and shipping companies that sought to open Hungarian coal mines to replace coal from Bohemia with a nearer and cheaper supply began extracting iron ore at Resicabánya/Reșița/Reschitz in southern Transylvania during the 1850s. The significant ironworks and steelworks they built soon attracted Hungarian entrepreneurs, and by the 1880s, they were producing railroad tracks. As Iván Berend notes, during the second half of the nineteenth century, Hungary was able to supply and expand its large network of railroads with coal, rails, and locomotives without resorting to imports.[27] It is therefore not surprising that the debate about the development of the railroad system in Transylvania was also symptomatic of its position within the world-system. The rail brought Transylvania closer to Budapest and Vienna to the west, as well as to Bucharest to the east, and it opened global trade routes. At the same time, it revealed economic, ethnic, and linguistic fractures within the Austro-Hungarian Empire. The region's integration into economic routes was facilitated by the railroads, but this integration happened slowly and in inter- and trans-imperial terms.

Iosif Marin Balog contends that the Transylvanian road system divided space into three kinds of routes: imperial, provincial, and local.[28] The absolutist imperial state of the mid-nineteenth century invested in roads with the goal of bringing order and discipline to a system perceived within an Occidentalizing discourse as backward and "Oriental." Local politicians petitioned Vienna to improve Transylvanian roads so that local economic agents could participate in broader trade. Nonetheless, the attention of the state—first the absolutist state and then the dualist one—slowly moved away from the task of improving roads and focused on the railroad system. The debate over the rail was one of the most resonant of the period and echoed other colonial and imperial contexts around the world, where the introduction of railroads helped siphon off resources in an extractive economy.

Globally, the accumulation of British capital provided the impetus for the expansion of railroads. One of the main sources of this capital was the unparalleled growth of the world sugar market during the first half of the nineteenth century. The increased production and consumption of sugar, which had gradually transformed from a luxury good into an item of mass consumption, prompted the sugar frontier to advance to new areas such as Cuba.[29] A mere thirteen years after the first steam-driven railway linked the slaving port of Liverpool with the industrial center of Manchester in England, the first Latin American railway, built with British capital and North American technology, began to operate in Cuba, linking Havana to the sugar plantations of Güines.[30] As Dale Tomich notes, for the next fifteen years, the railroad "followed" sugar, facilitating the geographical expansion of the sugar industry.[31] At the same time, railroads connecting industrial centers with rural areas started to transport staples and raw materials throughout Europe. Among the many small states in Germany, the railroad became a source of prestige and competition among princes and rulers. The first railroad in Austria linked the city of Linz/Linec to České Budějovice/Budweis (now in the Czech Republic) to facilitate the transport of salt between the Danube and the lower stretch of the Vltava (Moldau in German).[32]

The railroad came to Transylvania in 1868. The economic dispute over the rail system became a heated political debate in three languages and on behalf of a variety of economic interests. All Transylvanian groups supported the railroad, but for different and often opposing reasons, and therefore they did not advocate for the same rail routes. Paramount was a negotiation with Romania over a point of entry that would open a Balkan market for Hungarian products—considered essential for the Hungarian semiperipheral empire.[33] In addition to the conflict with Bucharest, there was a conflict between the warring interests of Budapest and Vienna. Transylvanian Romanian nationalists had their own interests.[34] There was a dispute among the three major cities in Transylvania (Sibiu/Nagyszeben/Hermannstadt, Cluj/Koloszvár/Klausenburg, and Brașov/Brassó/Kronstadt) over which cities the rail would connect to Budapest, Vienna, and Bucharest. If the railroad was associated with industrial modernity and a rhetoric of progress, the debate revealed that modernity meant different things to different actors.[35]

The railway system constituted an infrastructure of mobility with world-historical dimensions. The debate over the rail system was symptomatic of a region deeply aware of the global transformations related to industrialization, communication, and transportation technologies. The promise of agricultural modernization was tied to the possibility of export. The impact of the debate over the rail system was economic, but also cultural and psychological. Like Ana in Rebreanu's novel, peasants might be selling their products in the market in the nearby city, but the railroad opened other possibilities for them as both producers and consumers. Peasants' agency belies the linear accounts of global capitalism that tended to restrict production to the peripheries and consumption to the cores of the world-system. Instead, as Fernando Coronil points out, capitalism itself is the product of human activity, and the people affected by the capitalist transformation were not just another commodity—that is, labor power.[36] Once the railway existed, peasants' relation to the world-system changed. Regardless of whether their products actually circulated in the world market and whether they consumed products available in that market, they became tied to it at the level of desire. It is not a coincidence, then, that Transylvanian immigrants on their way to North and South America, in pursuit of their desire, reached the ports in Fiume/Rijeka, Hamburg, and Amsterdam by taking the train. In fact, Fiume/Rijeka (Sankt Veit am Flaum in German) was built by the British-American Cunard Steamship Company precisely to offer emigrants in Hungary an alternative to the ports of Hamburg and Bremen at the turn of the century.[37]

Finally, in terms of mobility, Rebreanu's novel reminds the reader that mail and newspapers arrive in Pripas through a modern postal system—a system that integrates the smallest village in Transylvania into a global information network. The World Postal Union was founded in Bern, Switzerland, in 1874, connecting the world through the circulation of the post. In addition to the railroad and the post, the telegraph brought modern communication to Transylvania; it ushered in trans-imperial connections on a large scale, starting with the first transatlantic cable connecting Ireland to Newfoundland in 1858.[38] Among other things, literary production thrived in the age of the postal system, which created the communication infrastructure for world literature as the literature of the world-system.[39]

Though often presented as premodern or even feudal, Transylvania's economy at the turn of the twentieth century was thus fully integrated into the global capitalist economy—but in a particular way. The Warwick Research Collective scholars explain the semblance of backwardness in similar areas of the world: "the multiple forms of appearance of unevenness—are understood as being connected, as being governed by a socio-historical logic of combination, rather than being contingent and asymmetric."[40] We traced four modalities of peripheralizing integration: trade, finance, bureaucracy, and mobility. Another sign of integration is the resistance to some of its consequences, evidence that integration into the capitalist system is complete and is already generating antisystemic movements.

Antisemitism on the Peripheries of European Empires

Capitalist integration-as-peripheralization met resistance in Transylvania and globally. Peasants revolted. Cultural elites mobilized. Nationalism acquired an important economic dimension. Religious elites enlisted their capital to create a resistance movement. So did local feminist organizations. In this section, we address the often antisemitic aspects of resistance to capitalist integration.[41] The association of Jewish commercial activities with capitalism and urbanization constitutes a long-standing, antisemitic "habit of thought" with world-historic resonances.[42] At the end of World War I, the Jewish minority of Transylvania accounted for 2.4 percent of the total population.[43] David Nirenberg's question, posed in a different context, resonates here: "How could that tiny minority convincingly come to represent for so many the evolving evils of the capitalist world order?" His explanation cites "a heightened resistance to reflection about the gap between our ideas about Jews, Judaism, or Jewishness, and the complexity of the world."[44]

The concept of inter-imperiality and the scale of the historical *longue durée* promise to do more justice to Transylvania's complex world. The Jewish population of Transylvania included descendants of Sephardic Jews. Some of them had traveled through the Balkans and settled in various places along the way. For a long time, Greeks, Armenians, and Jews constituted a merchant class engaged in a Levantine trade with global dimensions.[45] Armenians and Greeks were often discriminated against, but this discrimination was not premised on a history of antisemitism. The Romanian word for banker, *cămătar*, is of Greek origin, but in the late nineteenth century it was applied primarily to Jewish financial speculators, a process solidified by the reproduction of this stereotype in literature.[46] *Armenian* and *merchant* were likewise used as synonyms for a long time, but by the late nineteenth century, only Jewish merchants were considered "foreigners" engaged in trade.[47] In this section, we explore the development of this inter-imperial habit of thought, its complex relation to capitalist integration, and its resonances in Rebreanu's novel.

There is a long and convoluted history underlying Transylvanian antisemitism, as documented by historians such as Moshe Carmilly-Weinberger, Ladislau Gyémánt, Ezra Mendelsohn, Victor Neumann, and Attila Gidó. In the early modern period, Jewish inhabitants of Transylvania were not allowed to own land, and initially they could settle in only one city, Alba Iulia/Gyulafehérvár/ Karlsburg. For a while, they had to pay a "tolerance tax." Given the limitations on landownership and mobility, they often leased taverns and distilleries from the landowning nobility. The right to distill and distribute alcohol was a matter of dispute throughout the history of Transylvania.[48] In the eighteenth century, as part of the Habsburg Enlightenment, attempts were made to assimilate the Jewish population. As Pieter Judson notes, Joseph II issued edicts for each Habsburg territory with a significant Jewish population—Bohemia, Galicia, Hungary, and Moravia—between 1781 and 1785. These edicts removed several restrictions on Jewish life; opened commercial professions, artisanal crafts, and government service for the Jewish population; and required them to obtain a secular education.[49] Jewish people were also asked to eliminate differences in their appearance, and they had to take German names. Schools were opened for Jewish children to teach them the languages of the region where they lived. In Hungary, Jewish children could be taught in German, Hungarian, or another local language.[50]

After 1844, Jewish people were gradually granted equal citizenship with other citizens of Transylvania. József Eötvös wrote a highly resonant text titled "The Emancipation of Jews."[51] Throughout the debate on Jewish emancipation, Thomas Macaulay's 1833 intervention in the British Parliament was invoked as a stand applicable to Transylvania.[52] Yet the process of emancipation was not linear.[53] After 1848, a collective penalty was levied against Jewish participants in the revolution; it was later reimbursed in the form of a fund for Jewish schools and charitable organizations.[54] On the progressive side, the years 1853–1854 regulated agrarian relations, allowing the lease and purchase of property, as well as participation in trade. In 1860 all restrictions on Jewish acquisition of property were removed.[55] A law proclaiming Jewish emancipation was passed the same year as the 1867 Compromise. By the turn of the century, the Jewish population of the region had thus been emancipated for thirty years—roughly one generation.

What happened during this generation? How does the history of Jewish emancipation correlate with the narrative of capitalist integration-as-peripheralization traced in the first part of this chapter? In struggles over the economy, the old landed nobility continued to exert power, both economically and politically, and many members of the nobility migrated into the imperial bureaucracy. Meanwhile, capitalist integration and mobility created a new bourgeois class that, because of limitations on landownership, niche economic trajectories, and education-based social mobility, was perceived as consisting largely of Jewish people. As Berend notes, this highly urbanized Jewish population accounted for more than 53 percent of the clerks and employees in banking and trade and 43 percent in industry.[56]

It is crucial to place this situation within a world-historical framework. This type of social stratification was specific to peripheral and semiperipheral areas. Core states such as England, whose trade in the late Middle Ages was handled mainly by Italian and Hanseatic merchants, transitioned to a so-called indigenization of commercial networks (turning trade over to English merchants). By contrast, in Europe's eastern periphery, the emergence of such a bourgeoisie was politically threatening to the old elite. Trade therefore remained the purview of merchants who were perceived as foreign—Jewish, as well as German and Armenian in Poland, and Bulgarian and Greek in Romania. Wallerstein notes that, for East European peripheries specializing in the production of cash crops, "the issue . . . was not the existence or nonexistence of a commercial bourgeoisie. . . . The issue was whether this commercial bourgeoisie was to be largely foreign or largely indigenous. If it were indigenous, it added an additional important factor in internal politics. If it were foreign, their interests were linked primarily to those of the emerging poles of development, what in time would be called metropoles."[57] The emergence of the so-called Jewish question around the turn of the century was thus a reaction to the rapid rise of an urban, bourgeois class perceived to have a nonindigenous origin. This class was often seen as displacing the "indigenous, patriotic gentleman-entrepreneur" idealized in Polish and Hungarian literature throughout the nineteenth century, making it the target of nationalistic sentiment couched in anti-imperial terms.[58] In an inter-imperial context in which social stratification was systematically based on race and ethnicity, antisemitism was therefore often enlisted in the class struggle. The attitudes and policies inflected by this situation often borrowed from the repertoire of Western antisemitism—another meeting point of inter-imperiality and coloniality.

The old Hungarian nobility and the new bourgeoisie formed an uneasy alliance in Transylvania as well. Both were perceived by the disenfranchised classes as either winners or supporters of the emergent economy, but attitudes toward the two groups differed. Romanian Transylvanian peasants resented the Hungarian Transylvanian nobility and their descendants in the imperial bureaucracy. Many of them, however, came to express their resentment racially, as a form of antisemitism—distinct from but compatible with the religiously inspired anti-Judaism of premodern times (see chapter 7).[59] The Jewish population, which for a long time could not own land and was excluded from merchant and trade guilds, was through this process scapegoated as quintessentially capitalist—an emerging bourgeoisie in a peripheralized agricultural society.[60]

There is a crucial linguistic component to Transylvanian antisemitism. Post-1867 emancipation brought a new wave of Jewish assimilation. On the Hungarian side of Austria-Hungary, adoption of the Hungarian language was central to this process—a little-known fact in English-language historiography, which usually focuses on the Austrian side. Ladislau Gyémánt refers to this assimilation as "Magyarization in exchange for emancipation."[61] He notes that, in the process of fighting for their emancipation, Jewish people in Transylvania "pledged to set up national schools and other useful institutions and promised to submit to the process of Magyarization like all the other inhabitants of the country." According to Gyémánt, an 1860 initiative created an Association for the Promotion of Hungarian: "This language was to replace German in the communal, family and everyday life of the Jews, in order to persuade the public to have a more favorable attitude to Jews."[62] To be sure, Transylvanian Jews were profoundly multilingual. They spoke a number of "Jewish languages"; in addition to Yiddish and some Hebrew, they spoke two or three of the major languages of Transylvania (Romanian, Hungarian, and German).[63] Magyarization entailed a willingness to replace German with Hungarian in many spheres of life in which the Jewish people had been speaking German since the time of the Habsburg Enlightenment. As part of the emancipation process, Hungarian largely became the language of the Jewish religion and Jewish culture.[64] Some Transylvanian Romanians and Transylvanian Saxons resented Jewish adoption of the Hungarian language. Among other things, the census allowed an individual to identify with only one language, so Jewish transition to Hungarian contributed to the growth of the population identified as Hungarian—from 25.2 percent in 1880 to 31.6 percent in 1910.[65] In a situation of minority-majority political debate, the concern was that Jewish assimilation solidified an imperial claim to Transylvania.

Antisemitism among Transylvanian Romanians was related to antisemitism in Romania, inflected by its own inter-imperiality.[66] In 1866 the first Romanian Constitution stipulated that non-Christians could not be naturalized as Romanian citizens, effectively barring the path to Jewish emancipation and making the "Jewish question" inseparable from the emerging "national question" for decades to come.[67] Rebreanu, who moved to Bucharest during the writing of *Ion*, likely borrowed some of the text's antisemitism from Romania. In fact, many Transylvanian writers and politicians self-servingly emphasized the "imported" nature of antisemitism, which they contrasted with Transylvania's history of tolerance toward Jews. They pointed to parallels between the history of Transylvanian Romanians being treated like citizens without a country and the history of Jewish discrimination.[68] Despite claims to the contrary, antisemitism traveled between Romanian-speaking populations on the same routes that allowed other forms of mobility.

Antisemitism unfolded within a broad Transylvanian ethnic and racial field. Focusing on the post–World War I period, Attila Gidó invokes three forms of Transylvanian antisemitism: Romanian, Saxon, and Hungarian.[69] The largely Protestant Saxon population, attempting to protect its economic and political interests during an age of both Magyarization and increased Romanian nationalism, cultivated its own antisemitism. During the years 1828–1829 and again in 1859, the Transylvanian Saxon Trade Society called for the expulsion of the

Jewish population of Transylvania. They were not allowed to settle in Saxon towns such as Bistritz/Bestrecze and Sibiu/Hermannstadt.[70] Saxon traders resisted competition from Armenian traders as well, but not with the same passion directed against Jewish traders. This form of antisemitism developed not only in relation to the other ethnic and racial groups in Transylvania but also in relation to the broader German-speaking world, mediated by a thriving German-language print culture. Economic overtones shifted but remained resonant on this arc.

The Transylvanian racial and ethnic field becomes even more complex when one factors in relations between the two racial minorities—Jewish and Roma. Although both were considered foreigners in Transylvania, there was a lack of solidarity between the Jewish and Romani populations. Jewish leaders fighting for emancipation did not specifically seek rights for disenfranchised Roma. In a scene from Rebreanu's novel (analyzed in chapter 3), the Jewish pub owner closes the door on Romani characters who are being discriminated against—factually, but against an inter-imperial background, also symbolically. The situation reveals an ethnic and racial field where anti-Jewish and anti-Romani sentiments were produced relationally, through the stereotypical comparison of the two groups. As discussed in the next chapter, Franz Liszt described Jews as too materialistic within the narrative of capitalist integration, while Roma as not materialistic enough; Jews as too religious, and Roma as not religious enough; Jews as not artistically inclined, and Roma as quintessentially artistic.[71] This relational racialization symbolically and materially pitted one minority against the other and created the perceived impossibility of Jewish-Romani solidarity in the face of racism.

The unbridgeable gap between these two racialized groups, which neither comparison nor relationality could erase, had to do with the overlap of coloniality and inter-imperiality. The history of Romani enslavement in neighboring Moldavia and Wallachia and the Habsburg Empire's complicity with it in Transylvania created a colonial difference from the aspiring Romanian nation, making the Roma an internal colonial Other whose humanity was denied (see chapter 3). Roma claims to rights and political participation were therefore as unthinkable in turn-of-the-century Transylvania as the revolution of the enslaved in St. Domingue/Haiti was more than a century earlier. In turn, the history of discrimination against Jewish people in the region translated into an internal colonial difference anchored in religion, resulting in the racialization of religious customs and economic and social characteristics. Racialization of the Jewish population threatened their equality with other ethnic groups and their political claims, which had to be negotiated in the emerging secular state (see chapter 7). Against this background, Jewish solidarity with the Roma would have upended both the colonial and the imperial matrix of power into which all groups were woven at the time—making cooperation seem impossible. What is clear, however, is that capitalist integration reshuffled the ethnic and racial field in Transylvania, producing, among other things, a modern form of antisemitism that drew on coloniality as much as on inter-imperiality.

Avrum, the Jewish Pub Owner

How does this complex history resonate in Rebreanu's novel? The inter-imperial resistance to capitalist integration that enlists antisemitism in its project is also a mode of resistance to the transformation of peasants into consumers. Because there are severe limits on peasants' consumerism, they resist (or are encouraged to resist) one of the only forms it takes in the rural world: the consumption of alcohol. The competition between the church and the pub—one standing for the traditional spiritual life of the people and the other for the impinging economic order—yields antisemitic effects. In Rebreanu's novel, as the village priest scolds Vasile Baciu for drinking too much, he invokes the Jewish pub owners: "An honest man does not waste his time doing nothing but make the Jewish innkeepers richer and poisoning himself with their devilish draughts [*Omul de treabă nu se ține toată ziulica numai să îmbogățească pe jidovi și să-și otrăvească trupul cu hâlbăriile lor drăcești*]" (23, 31).[72] Drinking is a sin, in the eyes of the priest, because it enriches the Jewish pub owner. The association with the devil constitutes a religious antisemitic leitmotif, and the stereotype of poisonous drinks is a metonym for racial elimination.[73] The priest tells Ion "don't act like a Rom," but he also tells him "don't give your money to the Jews." The racialization of the two groups is produced through such discursive mechanisms. Gyémánt reports that the Transylvanian clergy was asked to "preach abstinence and set up anti-alcohol associations all over the country, which would counteract the effects of the Jewish tavern owners' activity."[74] The cautionary tale in the novel belongs to Ion's father, who lost his cherished land because of his drinking, the racialized implication being that the Jewish pub owner "stole" his property. As a reaction to capitalist integration, economic nationalism prescribes the injunction not to buy from Jewish merchants—neither alcohol nor other goods and services.[75]

Nirenberg explains the dimensions of the worry associated with capitalist integration, which "threatened to dissolve the bonds of love and obligation that tied man to man and (for the more conservative) man to God." The concern was that "the result would be an egoistic, materialistic world of self-love and self-interest in which only the desire for property and the circulation of money linked man to man." The dangers of such a world, Nirenberg concludes, was defined in terms of

"Judaism."[76] In Rebreanu's novel, the character of Laura deplores an increasingly materialistic world, in contrast to values associated with nation and family. Rebreanu's positioning of Avrum's pub at the very center of the village suggests a competition between the pub and the Transylvanian Romanian church, the self-appointed custodian of spirituality and family values. The implication is that the pub and its owner threaten both the spirituality and the national feeling associated with the church. In the racial imaginary of the novel, Avrum represents the threat that might destroy the moral fabric of the village.

The antisemitic imagination was associated with another aspect of capitalist integration: financial speculation and banking. In Rebreanu's novel, as a conflict erupts among the young male villagers, Titu goes to the pub to collect the gossip: "He shook hands with Avrum, as he always did when he wanted something on credit, and asked for a packet of tobacco, telling him to write it down on his account. Then, to justify his delay, he exchanged a few words with the Jew [ovreiul]" (30, 43). The fact that Titu, a young Romanian, buys tobacco on credit from Avrum is framed as an injustice. Credit is racialized—on a global arc—as Jewish.[77] As mentioned earlier, Ion's family borrows money from a Romanian bank, which is not viewed as problematic. In contrast, the Herdelea family buys furniture on credit from a Jewish company, and that ruins them. The underlying racial implication is that the Jewishness of the company's owner should have been a warning. In this literary archive, one witnesses nationalism taking a consequential antisemitic dimension. Ironically, in the process, the global capitalist enterprise—represented by the bank—wins the day.

In an eloquent conclusion of this narrative, midway into the novel, Avrum loses his wealth on account of a financial transaction with another Jewish character, who tricks him. Trickery embeds an antisemitic leitmotif, often lodged in linguistic idioms, in Romanian and Hungarian languages alike.[78] In neighboring Romania, national poet Mihai Eminescu enlisted this stereotype.[79] In Rebreanu's novel, Stoessel tricks Avrum in a deal presented as a paradigmatic capitalist transaction: "The business had appeared quite profitable, as the clerk claimed to have found a buyer to whom they would pass over the contract with a large profit for them, without needing to fork out a single penny; all he had to do was to sign the deed and cash the difference [*Afacerea părea bună, deoarece notarul spunea că a găsit un muşteriu căruia să-i revândă îndată contractul cu un câştig mare, încât ei n-au să scoată nici un ban din pungă, ci doar să iscălească şi să ia diferenţa*]" (270, 379). Although the villagers mourn Avrum's death, the episode seems to imply that he deserved to die on account of his thirst for labor-free financial gain. A peasant like Ion is described as hardworking but unable to earn a decent living, while the implication is that Avrum, who is seen working hard in his pub, would prefer easy work or no work at all. Along the lines of an inter-imperial class struggle, the sharp distinction between would-be hardworking Transylvanian Romanian peasants and would-be labor-free Transylvanian Jewish speculators morphs into an antisemitic stance. Avrum is punished for his desire—which is never actualized—to become a small-time real estate speculator.

Romanian-language criticism has often downplayed the racializing logic at work in such circumstances. It is clear, however, that Rebreanu's peasants see Avrum in racial terms. The text refers to Avrum using the archaic word *tartan*, an antisemitic term derived from the German *Untertan*, "an Austrian subject." Regardless of how long they have lived in a community, peasants like Avrum remain foreigners. Avrum's presence in the village remains tied, in the minds of his Romanian Transylvanian neighbors, to Habsburg and Austro-Hungarian imperial history, which gave Jewish citizens economic, political, and social rights. Significantly, another word used in Rebreanu's text is often deployed as a racial slur. The name of a village close to Pripas is *Jidovița*, a Romanian-language version of "Jewville." Rebreanu modeled this village after the historical village of Tradam/ Emtrádám or Unterdam (Yiddish), settled by Galician Jews in the seventeenth century.[80] In a short story called "Zestrea [The Dowry]," which preceded the writing of *Ion*, Rebreanu described the village's economic predicament in hyperbolic terms: "all houses in Tradam are pubs [*fiecare casă în Tradam e cârciumă*]."[81] The association with alcohol leads to the prejudicial description of Jewish characters. When the text tries to be complimentary toward a Jewish character, for example, it mentions that the villagers like him *despite* his Jewishness (288, 405). This strategy normalizes antisemitism as the default attitude toward Jewish characters.[82]

As Iveta Jusová writes, in the Czech context, "nationalism became an ally to racial hatred."[83] In Transylvania, Jewish people participated in a complex racial and ethnic environment tied to an even more complex confessional network. In exchange for Hungarian patriotism during the 1848 revolution, Jewish men were given voting rights—even though voting was severely restricted in Transylvania (only 9 percent of Transylvanian Romanian men could vote). Jewish emancipation functioned as a test of secularity for the Austro-Hungarian Empire, which professed to be not only a multicultural but also an enlightened, religiously neutral state (see chapter 7). Elections were, however, often rigged to benefit Hungarian or Magyarized candidates. In Rebreanu's novel, electoral success for a Transylvanian Romanian candidate depends on a calculation of Jewish votes: "in our villages there are few who have the right to vote, while the Jews are all voters! [*în satele noastre sunt puțini cu drept de vot, pe când ovreii sunt toți alegători!*]" (231, 324). When the Romanian candidate loses the election and Transylvania sends a Magyarized Saxon to the Budapest parliament, the racialized implication is that Jewish voters, though small in number, are partly to blame for the electoral outcome. The Romanian disenfranchised would-be voters thus "hooted the Hungarians and the Jews, as they walked up towards the town hall [*huiduiau pe ovreii și ungurii care se îndreptau spre primărie*]" (248, 348).[84] Within the Transylvanian debate on the complex electoral system, Hungarian and Jewish voters were perceived as forming one unit. Transylvanian Romanian nationalists resented Transylvanian Hungarians, but they resented Transylvanian Jews just as much on account of a racialized perception as traitors.[85] The tacit implication was that if Jewish people were willing to assimilate, they could have assimilated into the majoritarian Transylvanian Romanian population. The Armenian population in Transylvania had followed a similar path to Jewish assimilation, including linguistic assimilation to the Hungarian language, but no such implication was at work in their case. Rebreanu's novel reveals the profound and multidirectional implications of inter-imperiality, capitalist integration, and antisemitism.[86]

The Commodification of Literature

What does literature, read in an interdisciplinary analytical framework, tell us about the land question and its relationship to integration into the capitalist world-system, including its antisemitism? Many components of Rebreanu's novel are straightforwardly historical: the priest Belciug is based largely on the local priest in the village of Prislop/Priszlop, and the character Herdelea has many features in common with Rebreanu's father. The novel, in turn, had a palpable effect on the real world. Today, the village of Prislop/Priszlop is named Liviu Rebreanu. Even more insidiously, the village of Tradam/Emtrádám/Unterdam was renamed Jidovița (its name in the novel) in the 1940s—an example of antisemitism in fiction playing out in the real world and a reminder that countermapping can become self-defeating when it is enlisted in a nationalist agenda.[87]

Rebreanu's novel sold well and quickly became famous. Villagers in Prislop/Priszlop knew that Pripas represented their village. Ion Boldijer found out there was a novel circulating in which he was the main character, named Ion Glanetașu. So he wrote a letter to Rebreanu and asked for, in the author's words, "half of my profit from the novel, to which he thought he contributed with his personality [*jumătate din câștigul meu de la romanul la care credea el că contribuise cu persoana sa*]" (717). The letter, written in an oral language rife with grammatical and spelling mistakes, did not sound threatening, and yet Rebreanu rejected its premise: "Obviously, I did not respond to his request, since I knew myself to be innocent of personality theft [*Dar, natural, nu i-am răspuns la cerere, deoarece mă știam nevinovat de furt de personalitate*]" (717).[88] In Don Quijote mode, Ion Boldijer wanted the fictional character to be recognized as a historical person with financial needs. The metalepsis (a leap from one narrative level to another) involved a move from historical context to text. As if alluding to J. M. Coetzee's novel *Foe*, a quintessential postcolonial text, Boldijer wanted the author to pay his dues. Perhaps Rebreanu should have considered paying him a dividend, given Boldijer's quixotic gesture. Besides, the novel sold well and endured over time because of the historicity of the narrative. Rebreanu presented the anecdote about Boldijer's letter as the stuff of comedy, an effect often associated with metalepsis. How funny is it that Ion Boldijer, the actual historical carrier of the history of serfdom, the land problem, and peripheralization, would want the middle-class intellectual to share his profits from the novel-turned-commodity?

Ion Boldijer's request to Rebreanu functioned as another confirmation that the village of Prislop/Priszlop was not only integrated into but also integral to the capitalist world-economy, where personalities sell and where a peasant knows enough about its workings to claim copyright over his own life story. Boldijer might have also claimed intellectual property because he intuitively anticipated that, in the future, it might matter more than land. Readers who doubt the force with which literature participated in turn-of-the-century social life might find Gérard Genette's reminder convincing: "The most troubling thing about metalepsis indeed lies in this unacceptable and insistent hypothesis that the extradiegetic is perhaps always diegetic and that the narrator and the narratees—you and I—perhaps belong to some narrative."[89] The blurry line between inside and outside a text (the diegetic and extradiegetic) worries many readers. The underlying concern, of course, is that we might all belong to this narrative.

THE *LONGUE DURÉE* OF ENSLAVEMENT

Extracting Labor from Romani Music

We have argued that a history of land ownership in Transylvania is concomitantly a history of labor and that the division of labor that underwrites these histories belongs to the world-economy. For centuries, the regime of landownership in Transylvania was anchored in serfdom. Far from being feudal or premodern, serfdom belongs to a modern matrix of labor that is both colonial and interimperial. Within this matrix, serfdom exists in relation to waged labor, but also to enslaved labor. For five centuries, Romani laborers in the neighboring Danubian principalities of Moldova and Wallachia were legally enslaved, and their labor in agriculture, the trades, and the arts accumulated as wealth for enslavers. And yet Romani populations in East Europe remain a paradigmatic and often neglected example of a double practice of erasure and appropriation. Labor history, largely concerned with the working classes, has long focused on urban industrial workers rather than rural laborers in agrarian societies. Until recently, enslaved rural populations outside the industrial world played only a marginal role in labor histories of modernity and were depicted as abject in artistic and literary representations, even when their art was foundational to dominant aesthetic practices. Although historians have foregrounded the labor of the enslaved in the transatlantic trade and different forms of indentured labor that were enmeshed with it globally, enslaved rural populations rarely appear in labor histories of modern East Europe.[1] In this chapter, we place the history of enslavement in Moldova and Wallachia in relation to the regulation of Romani populations in Transylvania and trace a relational arc between these labor regimes and the status of Romani labor at the turn of the twentieth century. Throughout, we position the history of enslavement and its aftermath within the inter-imperiality of the region.

Naming conventions are central to the narrative we track in this chapter, revealing a complex politics of language. Instead of the available racialized designations—whose racial connotations are even more pronounced in the Romanian-language equivalents—we use the autonym *Rom* (plural, *Roma*) and the adjective *Romani*.[2] The lack of a linguistic connection between the terms *Romani* and *Romanian*, despite the phonetic similarities, has provided justification for Romanian nationalists to racialize Romani citizens to this day.[3] We place the linguistic confusion over the Rom/Romani designation in relation to the Romanian language within Transylvania's inter-imperial predicament, which is conducive not only to an ethnic field, as critics most often assume, but also to a complex racial field.[4] Within this racial field, as we have seen in the previous chapter, the racialization of Jewish and Romani populations is produced relationally, within a dynamic that inflects all other subject positions.

One of the strategies deployed in the erasure of Romani labor history is the cyclical deployment of the trope of idleness, which forecloses the recognition of Romani labor as labor. Although the racialized trope of the idle Rom appears throughout heterogeneous discourses in East Europe, most consequential for the Transylvanian situation was its dramatization in composer Franz Liszt's 1859 book *The Gipsy in Music* (*Des bohémiens et de leur musique en Hongrie*). Hungarian born and Paris based, Liszt ventured to explain the mythologized relation between the region's Romani population and its music. Whereas he racializes the Jewish minority of the region as too invested in work and material gain, he describes Romani populations as adamantly resistant to wage labor and essentially lazy. Having invoked "this audacious defiance," which he romanticizes, Liszt writes a section of his book about "the Gypsy at work," describing Romani laborers as blacksmiths, gold washers, and musicians.[5] In such accounts, Romani laborers are depicted, unproblematically, as both working and idle.

Here, we are concerned with the imbrication of material histories and textual strategies that place Romani labor, especially as aesthetic performance, outside the purview of labor histories. After a section on the history of the enslavement of Romani populations in Moldova and Wallachia, we return to the first scene in Rebreanu's *Ion*. That scene—and the novel in general—enlists Romani characters and tropes associated with Romani life in the service of a narrative describing the struggles of Romanian nationalism within the Austro-Hungarian Empire.

Mobility functions as a mode of labor for the Romani characters in the novel, who are modeled after the musicians Rebreanu knew in his childhood. These rural musicians traveled on foot from village to village in search of work. Our attention to Romani music supplements James Clifford's understanding of the link between culture and travel, where travel and cultural exchange risk being romanticized in a cosmopolitan spirit, reminiscent of the history of romanticizing Romani travel.[6] The Transylvanian village in Rebreanu's text aligns with Clifford's argument, in that it is a complex node of multiple scales of travel relations. These travel relations are highly heterogeneous; the cultural exchanges involved pivot on the coercion of labor shaped by the larger history of slavery, capitalism, and geopolitics. As Katie Trumpener emphasizes, Romani mobility and the highly heterogeneous Romani diaspora (extending from the Middle East to Transylvania to North Africa to Brazil) need to be understood in relation to the history of enslavement—in the *longue durée*.[7]

There are multiple scales of mobility in relation to which we can understand Romani musicians' labor. Zooming in from the global to the local, we get a map of labor mobilities that underscores both global labor histories and imperial formations. On a global scale, there was the relocation of Romani populations from northern India to Europe. On an inter-imperial scale, Roma traveled through the Ottoman Empire and the Balkans. On an interregional scale, Roma traveled from Moldova and Wallachia to Transylvania during and after their emancipation from slavery. Urban Romani musicians traveled across Europe to play in various capitals as well as at a series of world fairs.[8] Finally, on a local and regional level crisscrossed by inter-imperial relations, they traveled from village to village, as invoked by Rebreanu's novel. These large- and small-scale circuits of Romani music were instrumentalized by imperial or nationalist elites (similar to other folk art elsewhere in the world) and the "surplus profits" of subaltern art were absorbed and sublated in literary texts such as *Ion*. Romani artistic practices thus formally shaped the very art that denigrated them. At the same time, Rebreanu's novel reveals how Romani cultural and artistic production operated subtextually as a counterpoint to the narrative of Transylvanian Romanian nationalist aspirations.

Rebreanu's *Ion* received a lot of attention from Romanian literary critics. Yet these critics did not analyze the racialization of the Romani characters in the novel's opening scene. This episode includes an altercation between the main characters and three Romani musicians at a rural dance (*hora*) in Transylvania—a setting that positions the three Romani musicians within the story's imperial and nationalist political drama. Their presence invites us to reconsider the modernity of the novel and to rewrite the underlying history from the perspective of abject laborers in the region. This scene constitutes a minor plot involving three minor characters, but we argue that it is crucial to the construction of the novel's narrative arc and, more broadly, to a particular configuration of Transylvanian Romanian nationalism in an inter-imperial framework.[9] Returning to the argument proposed in the introduction, we frame the literary details provided by Rebreanu's narrative as consequential to the ethnic and racial configuration we interrogate. Importantly, one of the Romani musicians pleads to be paid for his labor. "'Didn't you hire me? [*Nu m-ai tocmit tu?*],'" he asks. This question is followed by the deprecating addition: "huffs the gipsy sensing that he might remain unpaid [*se zborși țiganul presimțind că va rămâne neplătit*]" (32, 46).[10] The plot device of nonpayment of Romani labor constitutes a formal element of the novel that not only registers a history of enslavement but also subtextually exposes the constitutive role of unpaid aesthetic labor—here and globally.

Enslavement in Wallachia and Moldova

We position the study of Romani labor at the intersection of labor history and the study of enslavement. Neither field has a lot to say about Romani labor. Labor history tends to be place specific, focusing on the factory, the workshop, the office, and, more recently, the household. When labor is spatialized in this way, it obscures itinerant and street-based labor. In turn, the study of slavery has focused on the Atlantic and the global South. Slavery scholarship almost never includes the enslavement of Romani populations in East Europe.[11] It is at the juncture of these two fields that the Romani people come into focus as "the European minority par excellence," profoundly unsettling Europe's self-congratulatory narrative of having adequately addressed its violent past.[12] Present *in* Europe for centuries but not considered *of* Europe, the Roma have not been part of Europe's reckoning with either racism or enslavement. Such reckoning happens less systematically than is often proclaimed, but when it does, it routinely restricts European racism temporally to the Holocaust, conflating racism with antisemitism, and it relegates enslavement spatially to Africa and the Americas, equating enslavement with the transatlantic trade. The Roma fall through these temporal and spatial cracks in Europe's politics of memory, which remains incomplete without a consideration of anti-Romani racism and the legacy of Romani enslavement in Europe.[13] When Romani history is approached as European labor history, it illuminates both the parallels with the enslavement of Africans in the transatlantic trade and the racializing tropes and attitudes that make both African Americans and European Roma more vulnerable to unequal treatment than other groups.[14]

Slavery (*robia*) was practiced in what is now Romania for more than five hundred years as part of a labor regime with an elaborate infrastructure. Its origins can be traced to the Mongol invasion of 1241–1242.[15] The practice of enslaving prisoners of war throughout the European East initially applied to Tatars. After large numbers of Roma settled in the newly created principalities of Wallachia and Moldova in the fourteenth and fifteenth centuries, enslavement became widespread in the Danubian principalities and sometimes crossed into Transylvania. In these regions, slavery was distinct from serfdom; it developed alongside serfdom and in some cases continued after serfdom ended.[16] There were three kinds of enslaved people: those belonging to the prince or the state, those belonging to monasteries, and those belonging to nobles or boyars.[17] This division indicates the entrenchment of the institution of slavery at multiple levels of society. Enslavement defines not only the enslaved-enslaver relation but also, more generally, the relation between free and enslaved persons. The meaning of freedom is enmeshed with enslavement.

In this section, we trace the nineteenth-century legislation concerning the enslavement of Roma in Moldova and Wallachia, both of which had majority Romanian-speaking populations and were vassal principalities that paid tribute to the Ottoman Porte. We argue that these laws established state-sponsored enslavement as a racial institution. As in other historical situations of enslavement, legal documents offer a limited but valuable archive for research but must be supplemented with social histories.[18] In the following section, we track the link between enslavement and the regulation of Roma in nineteenth-century Transylvania and the racializing practices associated with this regulation. Throughout, we position the enslavement of the Roma inter-imperially—between multiple conflicting empires (Ottoman, Russian, Austrian) and their ethnic and racial fields—in a period of rising nationalist struggles.

In the seventeenth century, laws in Moldova and Wallachia began to be codified. These laws recorded the "old way," the "old custom," or the "law of the land."[19] Under the influence of the French Enlightenment, but also as a function of reforms in the Ottoman Empire, Moldova and Wallachia continued this project at the beginning of the nineteenth century, collecting varieties of customary law and proposing modernizing legislative initiatives. Such initiatives were part of an effort to leave behind an "Oriental" past and position the two principalities in the Western sphere, both institutionally and economically. The tension between customary and modern was most apparent in laws addressing the institution of enslavement. The existence of slavery was regarded as an old custom; it was accepted as an ancestral fact, but, invoking the spirit of the times, new laws tried to improve the condition of the enslaved. Similar contradictions were evident in the writings of West European Enlightenment thinkers, who often condemned slavery philosophically but justified the enslavement of black Africans on "practical" or racial grounds.[20] As in the Americas, the enslaved resisted the institution of slavery in a variety of ways, predominantly by escaping.[21]

In Wallachia, the Ottoman-imposed Greek ruler Ioan Caragea initiated legal reforms through *Legiuirea Caragea* (in effect from 1818 to 1865).[22] Written in Greek and translated in parallel into Romanian, the document classified legal

personhood by gender, into men and women; by birth, into natural sons and il-
legitimate sons, biological sons and stepsons; by age and mental capacity, into
of age and underage, wasteful and mentally incapacitated; and by chance or fate
(*noroc*) into free, enslaved, and freed (*slobozi, robi şi sloboziţi*).[23] According to
this last distinction, "Free are those who are not owed to another [*Slobozi sînt
aceia care nu sînt dobîndă altuia*]."[24] A section titled "Of Slaves and Gypsies [*Despre robi şi ţigani*]" followed. The conjunction *and* suggested that not all enslaved people were Roma, but all Roma were currently or formerly enslaved.
Thus, "Slaves are those who owe another; the Gypsies in Wallachia are in this
way [*Robi sînt, cîţi sunt datori altuia; acest fel sînt ţiganii în Ţara Rumănească*]."[25]
Race and social position overlapped in these formulations. Slavery as a racial institution was anchored in the positing of the difference-as-inferiority of the enslaved. The threefold distinction of free, enslaved, and freed proved highly
consequential; when freed, the formerly enslaved did not enter the population
at large but constituted a separate category that, owing to the experience of enslavement, brought into question future inclusion in the body politic.

This definition of enslavement belonged to a clear economic framework: the
enslaved owed themselves to enslavers. They owed their "life," though not in its
entirety: "The master of the Gypsy does not have power over the life of the Gypsy
[*Stăpînul ţiganului nu are putere asupra vieţii ţiganului*]."[26] The enslaved owed
their labor lives to enslavers. Theoretically, they could become free if they bought
themselves (that is, their labor) from enslavers. In a capitalist situation of freedom,
wages would be owed in exchange for labor, but in this case, payment could be
made to the enslaver in exchange for future labor owed. The life of the enslaved
constituted labor *in potentia*. Thus, if a person used someone else's enslaved property, that person would be obliged to return the enslaved person, with interest for
potential labor lost—40 *taleri* for a skilled enslaved man, 20 for an unskilled enslaved man, 30 for a skilled enslaved woman, 15 for an unskilled enslaved woman.[27]

The legislation of enslavement in Moldova functioned along similar lines.
Codul Calimach (1817) was authorized by another Ottoman-imposed Greek
ruler, Scarlat Calimach.[28] It is important to point out that both sets of laws in
Moldova and Wallachia were instituted under the aegis of empire and in the context of competing claims to modernity among the empires of the period—yet
their effects persisted long after these peripheral principalities gained independence. Calimach's code was written in Greek and subsequently translated, over
the years, into Romanian. In cases for which the law had no stipulation, "custom" was the deciding principle. The code nonetheless presented itself as a modernizing law inspired by West European legislation, especially the Austrian
code. This legislation remained in force through 1865; its 1831 revision (*Regula-*

mentul Organic, written under Russian occupation) contained a note that maintained its validity.

Having established what constitutes a law and who counts as a legal subject (a man endowed with language, who undertakes legal actions using his free will and without being forced by circumstances), Calimach's code proceeded to define slavery (*robia*). First, it acknowledged that slavery goes against the natural order of things. However, because the unwritten "law of the land" concerning enslavement had been in effect for a long time, it remained in force. The law insisted that slavery in Moldova was different from Roman slavery, in that the enslaver's power did not extend over the life of the enslaved or even over his or her property: "the slave is not in all ways a thing, because in those acts, relations, rights and duties that concern others and not his master, he is considered a person subject to the law of the land and protected by it [*robul nu se socoteşte întru toate ca un lucru, ci în cît faptele, legăturile, driturile şi îndatoririle lui privesc pe cătră alţii, iar nu cătră stăpînul sau, se socoteşte el ca o persoană drept aceia este robul supus pămînteştilor legi şi se apără de cătră ele*]."[29] In areas that concerned the enslaver, however, the enslaved were thing-like: they could be bought and sold, gifted, bequeathed, offered as dowry, or exchanged for debt. As in Wallachia, the enslaver did not have power over life and death.[30] In the absence of a death threat, the Moldovan law required that the enslaved owe labor as well as obedience.[31]

Wallachia's *Legiuirea Caragea* included a chapter on sales, which divided things into moving and nonmoving. Tellingly, in terms of parallels with the West European trade in enslaved Africans, who were listed as cargo, one category of the Wallachian law consisted of "unmoving things and Gypsies [*lucruri nemişcătoare şi ţigani*]."[32] Obviously, enslaved people moved—they were valuable precisely because they moved as they worked; when they were hired out, they had to travel to work. The enslaved were legally defined as unmoving—often considered part of a labor unit (*sălaş*)[33]—because they belonged to an estate, just like other kinds of property the estate owned, such as land, built environments, tools, and animals. An article of *Codul Calimach* regulating the inheritance of an agrarian estate stipulated: "The inventory of an estate consists of those things necessary for working the land, like slaves, cattle and tools, as well as those needed for harvesting, transporting and conserving the harvest [*În legatum de înarmarea moşiei se cuprind cele trebuincioase pentru lucrarea pămîntului, adecă robii, vite şi unelte, precum şi cele pentru adunarea de roduri, pentru cărat, aşezat şi păstrarea lor*]."[34] Based on this logic, the enslaved could be offered as dowry, along with animals and unmoving things.[35] The revision of the Moldovan code in 1831 and 1835, *Regulamentul Organic*, described the enslaved as "family property

[*proprietatea familiilor*]" and "private property [*proprieta a particularilor*]"—
historically covered by the legal principle of *protimisis*, in an attempt to keep
land in the hands of a few families.[36]

The early-nineteenth-century legal codes of both Wallachia and Moldova regulated the marriage of enslaved people to each other and to free people. Thus,
much like the regulation of plantation slavery in the American colonies, Wallachia and Moldova legislated sexuality and reproduction.[37] In Moldova, the
main principle read as follows: "There can be no legal marriage between free
people and slaves [*Între oameni slobozi și robi nu se poate alcătui însoțire
legiuită*]."[38] The law detailed a number of situations; for example, financial com-
pensation would be owed to an enslaver in the event of a marriage that led to the
loss of potential enslaved labor, and there were stipulations as to the status of
children born to such marriages. This attention to marital arrangements indicated the centrality of the perceived need to manage the reproduction of labor
power over time and to prevent racial mixing.[39] Another article stated that
"children born to a female slave add to the wealth of her owner at the time of the
birth [*Copiii care se nasc din roabă, sporesc în folosul aceluia care în vremea
nașterii lor este proprietariul ei*]."[40] The next article used the same vocabulary to
legislate the reproduction of animals (*sporirea dobitoacelor*). Since marriage between enslaved people often involved replacing one enslaved person with another
or paying for the loss of one, the law addressed prices: "The price of slaves will be
decided by a judge according to their age, skill and occupation [*Prețul robilor să se
hotărască de cătră judecătorie după vrîsta, iscusința și meșteșugurile lor*]."[41] Here,
too, value was determined by the labor of the enslaved; a distinction was made
between various forms of skilled labor and nonskilled labor. Importantly, musical
performance was not considered skilled labor, a provision with long-term consequences for Romani musicians.

The Moldovan *Codul Calimach* acknowledged the frequency of sexual relations between enslavers and enslaved women by including an article that read:
"If someone keeps a slave mistress until the end of his life and has not freed her,
she will be free and, if they had children, they will be free as well [*Dacă cineva,
avînd roabă țiitoare pînă la sfîrșitul vieții sale, n-au slobozit-o pre ea din robie,
atunce să rămîe slobodă și, dacă au făcut copii cu dînsa, să rămîie și ei slobozi*]."[42]
Historians of enslavement have pointed out the circularity of the argument that,
since an enslaved woman owes herself to an enslaver, she cannot make sexual
choices, leading to a situation of statutory sexual exploitation.[43] If an enslaved
woman had children with a man other than her enslaver, that was legislated differently: "Children born out of the whoring of the female slave, after the law,
follow the fate of their mother [*Copiii cei din curvie a roabei, după legi, urmează
soartei mamei lor*]."[44] *Curvie* referred to out-of-wedlock sexual activity; since the

marriage of the enslaved was heavily regulated, sexual activity often fell under the rubric of *curvie*. In the long term, this legislation created the racialized perception that enslaved women and their descendants were sexually promiscuous, in another global comparative arc with unfree women laborers on Caribbean plantations. As was the case with enslaved and, later, indentured African women in the Americas, the trope of sexual availability and promiscuity both added to Romani women's racialization as inferior, uncivilized beings and, in a circular logic, justified their unfree status.[45]

Who accumulated the surplus value extracted from the unpaid labor of the enslaved? One answer is the Moldovan and Wallachian boyars. The enslaved worked in the fields and in households. Boyars lived in relative luxury supplied, at least in part, by this unpaid labor. Their status—which translated into political, social, and cultural capital—accrued according to the number of enslaved people they owned. A second answer is the Romanian Orthodox Church, which acquired large estates as gifts from princes and boyars; these estates often came with enslaved people who worked the land. The wealth of the Orthodox Church—material and symbolic—is tied up with the history of enslavement. A third answer is the Ottoman Empire. The Phanariot rulers sent by the Porte to administer Moldova and Wallachia came from a handful of Greek families in Istanbul. The administration of these principalities was extremely lucrative. Agricultural products from Moldova and Wallachia were sold in the Ottoman Empire at prices imposed by the empire. The right of free export was regained from the Ottoman Porte in 1829, at which time both principalities became agrarian suppliers for West Europe and markets for Western industrial products. They maintained their inter-imperial condition as they continued to play the role of buffer between the Ottoman, Habsburg, and Tsarist Empires.[46] The modern Turkish state often draws on the glory of the Ottoman Empire but largely refuses to acknowledge responsibility for the empire's participation in and facilitation of a long history of enslavement. Some of the labor of the enslaved translated into built environment in Istanbul and other cities in the Ottoman Empire.[47] Finally, a fourth answer is the Romanian state. Romania was founded in 1859 through the union of Moldova and Wallachia, three years after the last legislation abolishing enslavement was passed in the two principalities. The Romanian state in many ways remained a racial state. It condoned and sometimes prescribed segregation in both communities and schools. It accepted and reproduced institutionalized racialized language. The agrarian reform of 1864, which marked the end of legal serfdom, made no provisions for the Romani population and contained no references to enslavement. Reparations for wealth lost through enslavement would need to work through this complex constellation of at least four heterogeneous beneficiaries of the unremunerated labor of the enslaved.[48] An opportunity to make reparations was missed in the post-1989 period, when property nationalized by the Romanian socialist state was returned to its pre-1945 owners, including the descendants of boyars and churches. Once again, no provisions were made for descendants of enslaved Roma.

The enslaved were fully emancipated in 1855–1856. A rhetoric of forgiveness was deployed throughout the emancipation period—that is, the enslaved were forgiven what they owed. As occurred after the abolition of slavery in the Americas, the two principalities offered to compensate enslavers for their economic loss but offered nothing to the enslaved. *Uncle Tom's Cabin* was translated into Romanian in 1853 from the French edition published the same year; it included a censored introduction by one of the leaders of the emancipation movement, Mihail Kogălniceanu. He used the opportunity to place the enslavement of the Roma in a world-historical framework, where it indeed belonged.[49] Significantly, Kogălniceanu advocated for both the abolition of slavery and the emancipation of peasants from serfdom. In 1855 writer and politician V. A. Urechia published several installments of his unfinished novel *Coliba Măriucăi* (Little Mary's cabin) in the abolitionist journal *Foiletonul Zimbrului*, drawing inspiration from Harriet Beecher Stowe's novel. Other abolitionists pointed to the end of slavery in non-Western, non-European locations, such as Egypt in 1855, to argue, in an inter-imperial framework, that its preservation in the Romanian principalities was a sign of backwardness, even with respect to former Ottoman possessions—thus enlisting Orientalism to profess a will to Occidentalize.[50] A wave of migration followed emancipation. Freed Roma moved across Europe; some crossed the Atlantic, but others moved across the mountains to neighboring Transylvania.[51]

Regulation of the Romani Minority in Transylvania

How does the history of enslavement in Moldova and Wallachia relate to the land problem and the inter-imperial history of labor in Transylvania? Enslavement existed in some pockets of Transylvania, albeit with a different juridical framework. The historical archive includes a few reference points but remains painfully limited. George Potra mentions a 1585 document from Alba Iulia/Gyulafehérvár/Karlsburg that reports a donation of two enslaved persons.[52] Adalbert Gebora traces a number of eighteenth-century sale contracts involving enslaved Romani people.[53] Achim documents the presence of enslavement in regions of Transylvania bordering Wallachia and Moldova.[54] Enslavement was formally abolished in the Habsburg Empire in 1783, yet the empire had a border agreement with Moldova that guaranteed the return of runaway enslaved people in exchange for imperial army deserters who had fled to Moldova.[55] In other words, the Habsburg Empire not only tacitly tolerated enslavement in some of its territories but also helped Moldova and Wallachia manage their enslaved populations.

Historians often posit a rigid distinction between the principalities of Moldova and Wallachia, on the one hand, and Transylvania, on the other hand, at the beginning of the nineteenth century. In an Occidentalist gesture anticipating Samuel Huntington's "velvet curtain of culture" across Europe, historian Neagu Djuvara places Moldova and Wallachia in the Orient and Transylvania in the Occident.[56] Yet Romanian nationalism in the nineteenth century was premised on contact among Romanian-speaking populations across the Carpathians. There were linguistic, religious, and cultural exchanges between Romanian-speaking populations in the three principalities. There were economic exchanges, and there were migration flows. What historians of nationalism rarely acknowledge is that racial prejudice stemming from the history of enslavement traveled on some of the same routes. One can find enslavement-related racial prejudice in Transylvania as well.

That being said, Romani populations in Transylvania have a different history from those in Moldova and Wallachia, framed by institutions of the Habsburg Empire. In the early modern period, Roma enjoyed some freedom in Transylvania; their itinerant labor was often protected. Gold washers in particular benefited from a high degree of independence. At the end of the eighteenth century, however, under Maria Theresa and Joseph II, the Habsburg Empire tried to assimilate its Romani population as it engaged in its own version of the Enlightenment, anchored in a project of state consolidation.[57] As part of this "civilizing mission," a long list of measures was proposed, including a ban on speaking the Romani language, wearing traditional clothes, and marrying other Roma. A major initiative undertaken by Maria Theresa imposed a fixed dwelling place on Roma and attempted to integrate them into the agricultural economy, a process referred to as colonization (*colonizarea țiganilor*). Roma were supposed to follow church rituals and become "new Christians"—the same label that had been used in Habsburg Spain to refer to converted Moors after the Reconquista. These measures were only selectively implemented, and Maria Theresa's son Joseph II felt the need to reenergize the project. *De regulatione Zingarorum* (The regulation of Gypsies) was issued in 1782, after a series of other such decrees; once again, it attempted to integrate the Romani population but limited the number of Roma who could settle in one place.[58] One of the most important long-term consequences of these Enlightenment-era policies was the segregation of Romani communities, paradoxically advocated as a form of integration.

Habsburg policies attempted to standardize some of the same aspects of Romani life that had been regulated in Moldova and Wallachia through enslavement—marriage and child rearing in particular. The obligatory education of Romani children sometimes led to them being taken away from their families and placed in foster homes. This was a common practice of imperial and colonial rule throughout the world, aimed at disrupting the ethnic, religious, and family ties of imperial and colonial subjects. In his widely circulated and, in Transylvania, well-known *Dissertation on the Gipseys* (1787), Heinrich Grellmann argued for the forced education of Romani children. The circulation of this text in the region was a function of the Transylvanian Saxons' relation to the broader German-language European culture, its various Orientalist discourses, and its inter-imperial networks.[59] Grellmann deployed an analogy between the practice of forced education and the colonial civilizing process, including its racializing dimensions. Furthermore, Grellmann repeated the rumor, widespread across Europe, that Roma might be cannibals.[60] He also invoked the European civilizing effort in Africa: "Perhaps it is reserved for our age, in which so much has been attempted for the benefit of mankind, to humanise a people who, for centuries, have wandered in error and neglect: and it might be hoped, that, while we are endeavoring to ameliorate the condition of our African brethren, the civilisation of the Gypseys, who form so large a portion of humanity, will not be overlooked."[61] Similarly, he cited the colonial project in India: "We send apostles to the East and West, to the most distant parts of the earth, and, as will be hereafter shewn, into the very country whence the Gipseys migrated, in order to instruct the people who know not God. Is it not inconsistent for men to be solicitous for the welfare of their fellow-creatures in distant regions, and to throw off and leave to chance those who, equally wretched, have brought their errors home to us?"[62]

How to proceed? Grellmann wondered: "Banishment was not the proper method to be adopted; nor would it have been adviseable to make them penitentiaries or galley-slaves: but care should have been taken to enlighten their understanding, and to mend their hearts."[63] Grellmann's *Dissertation* offered a vocal critique of both the enslavement of Roma in Moldova and Wallachia and practices of banishment and extermination across Europe. Yet it is clear that Grellmann was developing his arguments *in relation* to the institution of enslavement and its attendant racializing practices—regionally and globally. He was aware of enslavement as a worldwide system; he considered the *possibility* of present or future enslavement. Subsequent plans for the internment of Romani populations in the Habsburg and Austro-Hungarian Empires offered the blueprint for placing a minority deemed undesirable in camps.[64]

Grellmann liberally compiled research on the Roma of East-Central Europe conducted by a number of philologists and would-be historians in the eighteenth

century. His text belonged to an Orientalizing racial discourse that, like all Ori-
entalisms, created the need for a civilizing project.[65] The contours of a project of
emancipating the Roma and turning them into useful citizens had been sketched
by Samuel Augustini ab Hortis in the first ethnographic monograph about the
Roma in Europe, *Zigeuner in Ungarn* (Gypsies in Hungary), written in 1775.[66]
Augustini had launched the hypothesis, later taken up by Indologists such as
J. Ch. Rüdiger and Grellmann, that, based on linguistic evidence, the Roma's origin could be traced back to India.[67] While linguists emphasized the Indo-European
connection as a way of including the Roma in a "European family," locating the
start of the Romani migration in India often further Orientalized them.

With their Oriental origin thus documented, Grellmann described the Roma
as having an unchanging essence anchored in race: "Let us reflect how different
they are from Europeans: the one is white, the other black;—this clothes himself, the other goes half naked;—this shudders at the thought of eating carrion,
the other regales on it as a dainty. Moreover these people are famed, and were
even from their first appearance in Europe, for being plunderers, thieves, and
incendiaries: the European, in consequence, not merely dislikes, but hates
them."[68] Grellmann exaggerated the number of Roma in different parts of Europe, deploying the colonial trope of animality to describe "hordes" that "rove"
and "swarm" the continent. In terms of religion, they were below heathens, a
"savage people."[69] Especially notorious, for Grellmann, was the depravity of
women. The *Dissertation* described "the refuse of humanity" in Europe, descendants of the lowest caste of India, "the dregs and refuse of all the Indians."[70] The
tropes of animality, savagery, and cannibalism stemming from colonial discourse
placed the construction of the Roma as Other on the side of the colonial difference. In Sylvia Wynter's terms, colonial Others who were classified as subhuman
or nonhuman, such as indigenous peoples and the enslaved, were the physical
referents of the revamped and modified untrue Christian Other of medieval Europe, who had been Jews and Muslims.[71] Although Grellmann's book constitutes a symptom of a particular form of Habsburg-era racism, his racializing
formulations were not independent of the Roma's enslavement in Moldova and
Wallachia, which deployed some of the same essentializing and othering
maneuvers.

The long-term effects of this discourse were most enduring in the world of
labor. A long chapter of Grellmann's *Dissertation* titled "Their Occupation and
Trades" began with a statement about idleness: "the reason why poverty and want
are so generally their lot; namely, their excessive indolence, and aversion from industry."[72] The ensuing description of various skills and occupations was followed
by a reminder that Romani work was often a ploy. The aim of the Enlightenment project, as conceived by Grellmann, was to help Roma become industrious

subjects and useful citizens. This is a familiar refrain: render racialized populations serviceable to capitalism. The project helps enlist their labor into the particular mode of peripheralization analyzed by Immanuel Wallerstein. Grellmann recommended the measures implemented by Maria Theresa and Joseph II, among them the attempt to placate laziness by permanent surveillance. He saw no contradiction between his description of a primordial laziness and his reporting that Roma were often not paid for their work.[73] Roma both worked and did not work; as a result of this rhetorical paradox, their work was not considered worthy of remuneration. The nonpayment of Romani labor in the Habsburg Empire echoed the institutionalized nonpayment of enslaved Roma in Moldova and Wallachia.

Written out of Labor History: Romani Musicians

By the mid-nineteenth century, Liszt was telling a romantic story, different from Grellmann's but retaining the racial framing of the discussion. Comparing Roma to Jews, to the disadvantage of the latter, Liszt posits "an invincible dislike for work" as integral to the Romani essence. In search of a romantic mix of nature, feeling, and artistic egoism, Liszt finds it in "the figure of the Gypsy."[74] This figure would multiply and travel; much of the criticism that purports to take Romani history as its object is in fact concerned with this figure.[75] To produce his romantic theory of music, Liszt must bracket the assumption that music making constitutes a form of labor: "For the Gypsy, art is not a science that one might learn; or a trade which one may practice; or a skillfulness which may be imparted by dint of certain procedures and expedients. Nor is it an industry which may be cultivated according to the lessons of experience. . . . It is a mystic song."[76] Liszt critiques the initiatives of Maria Theresa and, implicitly, Grellmann's argument on the Roma's behalf, but he reproduces the myth of idleness, which, for different reasons, still places the Roma outside the purview of labor. Liszt posits that the collection bowl at the end of a Romani musical performance measures the quality of the emotion produced; it does not function as financial remuneration for the musicians' efforts.

We know that, over time, racialization transforms into stereotypes and idiomatic language. Heinrich Wlislocki, who claimed that he lived temporarily with a group of Roma in Transylvania at the end of the nineteenth century, wrote articles on Romani life for the first journal of comparative literature, which appeared in Transylvania in the 1880s. He was following in the footsteps of George Borrow, whose book *The Zincali: An Account of the Gypsies of Spain* was also purportedly based on direct observation. Importantly, Wlislocki invoked the stereotype of Romani servility, which he portrayed as a body posture—a bent spine and a lowered head.[77] Aside from stereotypes pertaining to the body, Transylvanian languages carry the racializing baggage of this history. Emily Gerard, who was married to an Austro-Hungarian officer and briefly lived in Transylvania, wrote in 1888: "The word Tzigane is used throughout Hungary and Transylvania as an opprobrious term by the other inhabitants whenever they want to designate anything as false, worthless, dirty, adulterated, etc. 'False as a Tzigane,' 'dirty as a Tzigane,' are common figures of speech. Likewise, to describe a quarrelsome couple, 'They live like the gipsies.' . . . To call anyone's behavior 'gipsified' is to stamp it as dishonest. 'He knows the Tzigane trade' is 'he knows how to steal.'"[78] If, as indicated in the previous chapter, racialized language depicts Jewish merchants as financial speculators, it also creates idioms that stereotype Roma as thieves. Gerard offered her interpretation of this use of language: "These phrases must not, however, be taken to express hatred, but rather good-natured sort of contempt and indulgence for the Tzigane as a large, importunate, and troublesome child, who frequently requires to be chastised and pushed back, but whose vagaries cannot be taken seriously, or provoke anger."[79] This is a familiar attempt to deflect the possibility of linking racism (hatred) to this use of language. In fact, we know that good-natured contempt toward a marginalized group is the textbook definition of racism. Although there were no enslaved people in Transylvania at this time, the figure of an adult child in need of patronizing indulgence is clearly an inheritance of enslavement.

At the turn of the twentieth century, Transylvania's Romani population was 4.67 percent of the total population.[80] Many Roma were musicians. Why? Aside from being agricultural servants, many Roma worked as itinerant laborers. A nineteenth-century Romani song lists various occupations: "some blacksmiths, / some sieve-makers, / some shoe-makers, / some musicians [*care fierari, / care ciurari, / care cismari, / care lăutari*]."[81] As the local agricultural economy was incorporated into the capitalist world-economy, the work performed by blacksmiths, for example, was less in demand.[82] In Transylvania, where this shift occurred earlier than in Moldova and Wallachia, blacksmithing as a way of life was no longer feasible, and music grew in importance as an alternative craft. Yet the entertainment provided at various communal events was not always considered labor in need of remuneration. The tradition of hiring Romani musicians to play at various celebrations was inherited from the Ottoman Empire, and this inter-imperial background served as the basis for confusion over payment.[83] Viorel Cosma describes the practice, traces of which survive in Romani songs, of musicians begging for payment before 1900, followed by the practice of collecting money (*chetă*) from dancers and listeners.[84] Nonetheless, music was an attractive form of culture making, as well as a path to social mobility. In many regions, Roma acquired a monopoly on musical performance. Some Romani musicians became famous and traveled the world. One of them was Barbu Lăutaru, who was born enslaved in Moldova and used his music to buy his freedom. He was greatly admired by Liszt and by Moldovan literary personalities of the time, such as Vasile Alecsandri.[85]

The Romani Musicians in the Opening Scene of *Ion*

We foreground aesthetic labor as an overlooked dimension of diasporic mobility, one that has shaped the ideological and material economies of Central and East Europe and the inter-imperial field. Romani musical skill and performance emerge as sites of extracted labor whose surplus profit is channeled into dominant nationalist struggles. Ultimately, we suggest that, given the influence of Romani music on Europe's celebrated musical innovations in the Romantic period (as evidenced by Liszt), and given the incorporation of Romani musical labor into Rebreanu's novel, the histories of empire and nationalism and their implications for enslavement need to be rewritten as coconstitutive with the histories of music and literature.

Throughout Rebreanu's novel, Romani people appear as either minor characters or reference points—in both cases, as othered presences, defining and enabling the pursuits of the main characters. In the opening dance scene, the young peasants dance and flirt, the elderly watch, while the middle-class teacher and priest meditate on Romanian national culture in the Austro-Hungarian Empire. Rebreanu claimed he wrote the episode that became the first chapter of *Ion* during one sleepless night. Here is the crucial scene:

> The three fiddlers play by the shed, stretching their strings to the breaking point. Briceag—foot on a log, left elbow on his knee, cheek caressing the violin, eyes shut—sizzles his fingers on the strings and the fiery wild song leaps forth. Holbea is blind in one eye, has one leg shorter than the other and a violin with only three strings, but he seconds with the same passion with which Găvan, an ugly Gypsy, black as an Arab, bows his bass fiddle. (11)
>
> *Cei trei lăutari cântă lângă șopron să-și rupă arcușurile. Briceag, cu piciorul pe o buturugă, cu cotul stâng pe genunche, cu obrazul culcat pe vioară, cu ochii închiși, își sfârâie degetele pe strune și cântecul saltă aprig, înfocat. Holbea e chior și are un picior mai scurt, iar la vioară numai trei coarde, dar secondează cu aceeași patimă cu care*

Găvan, un țigan urât și negru ca un harap, apasă cu arcul pe strunele gordunii. (14)

The three Romani musicians have been hired to perform at the village event. The name Briceag means "pocketknife" in Romanian, implying a criminal past. Holbea—derived from *a se holba*, "to stare"—seems to be a nickname acquired after the second musician lost an eye, presumably in a violent incident. Găvan's name is less suggestive, but it may relate to his thinness. Rebreanu offers a musical tableau of the three Romani musicians passionately playing their instruments.[86] The tableau is equipped with vivid visual and auditory details (note the precise description of Briceag's body position and the onomatopoeic sound of fingers on violin strings: *sfârâie*). The reader is encouraged to hear the Romanian folk music played by the Romani musicians. The narrative voice, echoed by the implied reader, expresses admiration for the quality of the music as well as the passion (*patimă*) with which the musicians perform.

The scene makes it clear that musical performance involves physically strenuous labor. The dancing goes on for a long time, a function of rolling one dance song into another, yet the musicians are not allowed to rest. The music requires the performance and display of high emotion. It requires travel. The musicians are abused verbally and physically. On the one hand, the scene depicts intense labor—"stretching strings to breaking point." On the other hand, then, words like *sizzling*, *fiery*, and *passion* accord with Liszt's rejection of musical performance as labor.[87] The description of Găvan as "black as an Arab [*negru ca un harap*]" installs the inter-imperial racialization that rhetorically resolves the contradiction.[88]

In this section, we analyze six modalities through which Rebreanu's text renders legible an arc between the history of enslavement and the labor of the Romani musicians. We engage Rebreanu's text to show how it enlists Romani characters, associative language pertaining to Roma, and the history of enslavement into its project.[89] These six modalities are (1) the invocation of Roma in the framing of the question of freedom, (2) the production of abject status as a marker of social mobility within the struggle for landownership, (3) the framing of poverty within a racialized economic hierarchy, (4) the sketching of Romani characters as stereotypical servants, (5) the reproduction and reinforcement of the spatial segregation of Romani communities, and (6) comedy as a mode of abjection. Although these modalities are structurally interlocked and are constellated differently in different contexts, such that racialization serves different ideological purposes, we separate them for heuristic purposes. The distinct functions they play—in Rebreanu's novel and elsewhere—in linking the *longue durée* of enslavement with the labor of Romani musicians warrant their point-by-point analysis.

The first modality concerns the novel's framing of freedom. Slavery yielded, in the long term, a distinction between the enslaver and the enslaved, but also between the free and the unfree. Rebreanu's text draws on this history to emphasize that its titular character is free; he cannot be treated "like a Gypsy." *Free* here implies both labor freedom (Ion is not a serf) and national freedom (a claim to rights within the empire). All ethnic groups in Transylvania are implicated in this logic, but it is most crucial for Romanian Transylvanian peasants, who are positioned at the bottom of the social, political, and economic hierarchy. Romanians' claim to freedom, in particular, is anchored in the Roma's position below them. In the dance scene, the Transylvanian Romanians are Romanian not because they are not Hungarian—the most common dichotomy in the context of Transylvania within the Austro-Hungarian Empire—but because they are not Roma. This is a story that Romanian literary criticism, centered on the national Romanian-Hungarian narrative, has not told. The Hungarian state's oppression of the Romanian population in Transylvania, which it sometimes triangulates with the German minority, is usually the focus of analysis. Rarely considered is the larger ethnic and racial field formed by Hungarians, Romanians, Germans, Roma, Jews, and Armenians. Race is most often subsumed under discussions of nationalism and therefore not theorized as such. Rebreanu's Romani characters, however, radically trouble the narrative of Romanian oppression at the hands of the Hungarian state. However oppressed Rebreanu's Ion is, he can be violent, both physically and verbally, to the Romani musicians. Unlike Indian modernism, where claims to postcolonial modernity were often coupled with calls to dismantle the caste system, Rebreanu's brand of modernism fails to recognize the contradiction between modernity and the "tradition" of racializing Roma and, in fact, seems to dwell in the contradiction.[90] At the same time, in making this reading possible, the scene encodes, more or less self-reflexively, its own conditions of production, opening them up to critical evaluation.

The Romanian folk music provided by the Romani musicians does not merely entertain the Transylvanian Romanian peasants; it is necessary to the production, through a very particular rhetorical gambit, of their Romanianness and their implicit whiteness. It is important to remember that this was a period of massive migration to the United States, which created widespread anxiety that, in Tara Zahra's words, "East European men and women would be treated like nonwhite colonial labor, Chinese 'coolies,' or enslaved Africans." [91] In a report on his visit to the Austro-Hungarian Empire, African American reformer Booker T. Washington described a blurry category he refers to as "Slavs" as the "inferior race" of the region.[92] To minimize the possibility that migrants from Transylvania would become a racialized labor force on US southern plantations, local immigration advocates insisted on the whiteness of peasants like Ion.

The racialization of the Romani musicians in this scene helps to produce Ion's whiteness.

At the end of the novel, the same musicians play a song that would become the Romanian national anthem, "Romanians, Awaken! (*Deșteaptă-te, române!*)." The two scenes that bookend the novel can be seen as unwitting reminders of the event that functions as the retrospective inaugural moment of Romanian national discourse: the entry of Wallachian prince Mihai/Michael the Brave into Alba Iulia/Gyulafehérvár/Karlsburg in 1599.[93] Briefly uniting the three regions with Romanian-speaking populations (Moldova, Wallachia, Transylvania), this event prefigured the Romanian state established in 1918.[94] It thus acquired mythical dimensions in the nationalist discourse. The city of Alba Iulia/Gyulafehérvár/Karlsburg has gradually been reconfigured to reflect this discourse.[95] Importantly, this event unfolded with music provided by Romani musicians in the background. Mihai the Brave reportedly made his triumphal entry into the city (figured as a proto-Romania) surrounded by Romani musicians, whose music heralded his triumph.[96] Embedded in the narrative as minor details but echoing this historical background, the scenes that spotlight Romani characters in Rebreanu's novel (village dance, middle-class ball, marriage, church inauguration) provide a much-neglected but consequential arc for a narrative concerned with the staging of freedom. The minorness of the Romani characters is essential to the construction of this arc.

If lack of freedom, for both serfs tied to the land and enslaved Roma, means immobility, the utmost expression of labor freedom is social mobility. A second, related modality of linking Romani labor to the history of enslavement ascribes social mobility to Romanian Transylvanian peasants through a mechanism that relegates the Roma to social stagnation. In a statement that functions as the crux of the novel, Ion declares: "If it hadn't been for you, advising me what to do, master Titu, I should be worse off now than a gypsy! [*Dacă nu m-ai fi învățat dumneata, domnișorule, rămâneam mai rău ca țiganii!*]" (304, 428). Ion's desire for land is dramatized as a question of justice in the context of the Austro-Hungarian Empire. He wants to have his own land so he will not have to work for others. He laments: "So he would have to be someone's *slugă* forever—work only to enrich others! [*Va să zică va trebui să fie veșnic slugă pe la alții, să muncească spre a îmbogăți pe alții?*]" (66, 93). The word *slugă* refers to a person hired to work in someone else's household and, by extension, a social subordinate. In the context of Rebreanu's text, this word is crucial because it functions as a reminder that Roma and the history of enslavement appear in the conversation about landownership, capitalism, and modernization obliquely but consequentially. According to the logic of Rebreanu's text, Ion should have the opportunity to move up in the world. Indeed, once he acquires land, Ion becomes a leader

among the young men in the village. The Romanian word the novel uses is
vătaf; one of its historical meanings is "supervisor of the enslaved."[97] Ion's right
to social mobility is predicated on his presumed racial superiority vis-à-vis
Roma, the internal colonial Others whose geographical mobility after emancipation did not lead to social mobility.

Unfreedom and social stagnation translate into low social status. The third
modality the novel uses to link enslavement and Romani labor is thus an economic hierarchy anchored in the essentialized poverty of the Roma. As preparation for the novel, Rebreanu wrote a short story dramatizing an important
village ritual, the slaughtering of a pig before Christmas. He describes the title
character's poverty as follows: "in the whole village, only Glanetașu and the gypsies could not do the *bojotaia*, in fact even some of the gypsies tried hard and
managed to be like other people and slaughter at least a piglet. It was at such times
that Ion cursed the life that destined him to such shame in the village. [*în tot
satul, numai Glanetașu și țiganii nu sunt în stare să facă bojotaia cuvenită, ba
încă și unii țigani se sileau și izbuteau să fie în rândul oamenilor și să taie barem
câte un mascur. Atunci își blestema viața care-l sortește să rămână de rușinea
satului*]" (138, 196). It is a most unfavorable comparison. In the economy of the
novel, the fact that Ion cannot perform a ritual that *even Roma* can execute renders his situation tragic and in need of correction. The phrase "even some of the
gypsies" functions as a forceful rhetorical strategy, resulting in the creation of
what Toni Morrison calls "hierarchical difference" and what we have referred
to here as colonial difference.[98] Ion is not necessarily compared with other villagers (the reader never finds out whether Roma in the village perform the ritual);
rather, he is compared to a structural position, the lowest rung of the economic
ladder, simultaneously an epistemic and racial relegation to abject, subhuman
status. The outcome of the comparison is shame (*rușine*). To be worse off than
Roma, if only rhetorically, is to be not "in line with other people" (*în rândul
oamenilor*)—a literal, ontological fall from humanity into what Wynter terms
"the coloniality of being."[99] The novel is invested in righting a wrong, that is,
landless Ion's position below other peasants—Romanian peasants and, in a larger
inter-imperial framework, German, Hungarian, and Jewish peasants and landowners. The novel is not, however, invested in questioning the Roma's position
below "people" or the existence of the racialized hierarchy itself. This predicament becomes even more evident in the way Romani employment is depicted in
the novel.

The stereotypical portrayal of minor Romani characters who work as servants
represents the fourth modality of linking the history of Roma enslavement with
Romani labor. Morrison reminds us that servants often belong to "an economy
of stereotype," whereby a writer deploys "a quick and easy image without the

responsibility of specificity, accuracy, or even narratively useful description."[100] In one scene in the novel, the character of the priest is accompanied by a servant: "Mrs Herdelea opened the door and saw, standing behind the priest a bearded old gypsy, hat in hand [*D-na Herdelea deschise și văzu la spatele preotului un țigan bătrân, bărbos, cu pălăria în mână*]" (223, 313). On this occasion, the servant's presence is required so he can carry a table the priest is repossessing from the teacher. The teacher's wife gets angrier and angrier, and she attacks the old man: "As the priest was not within her reach, she brought the broom down upon the gypsy's back, howling. . . . The gypsy dashed through the gate. [*Fiindcă preotul nu-i era la îndemână, croi pe țigan, țipând. . . . Țiganul o zbughi pe poartă*]" (224, 314). The scene invokes a racialized occupation. The fact that the priest comes with "his" servant points to the long history connecting religious institutions to enslavement. To insult the priest, the teacher's wife beats his servant, a reminder that such actions would constitute an honor affront under enslavement law. Although Transylvanian Romanian peasants in Pripas are given names, the old man appears in the novel as only a racialized character, the hat-in-hand gesture a symbol of a presumed humility reminiscent of the bodily posture described by Wlislocki. The beating he endures, without any consequences for the teacher's wife, echoes the beating of the enslaved.

Romani laborers do not inhabit the same space as other villagers. The fifth modality that connects the history of enslavement and Habsburg Enlightenment regulations to turn-of-the-century labor hinges on the production and reproduction of the spatial segregation of Romani communities. In a central scene in Rebreanu's novel, as Ion scans the village landscape from the vantage point of his cherished small plot of land, his gaze traces a village road: "The back lane started from Vasile Baciu's new house, swept round to the church, passed it and plunged again into the main lane, just beyond the priest's orchard, amidst the hovels of the gypsy quarter [*Lângă casa nouă a lui Vasile Baciu pornește Ulița din dos care face un ocol mare ca să treacă prin fața bisericii și să se arunce iar in Ulița Mare, dincolo de grădina popii, printre bordeiele țigănimii*] (42, 59). Roma live in a corner of the village, not on the back street, which, in Rebreanu's description, reconnects with the main street, but segregated on its right edge, likely since the time of Habsburg "integration." The fact that the Romani quarter is referred to as *țigănime* (a derogatory collective noun connoting an undifferentiated, presumably disorderly Romani neighborhood) is not uncommon. Cosma compiled a three-page list of villages named Țigănești, Țigănia, and variations thereof.[101] In the nearby city of Bistrița/Bistritz/Beszterce, one neighborhood is called *Țigănime*. The phrase *bordeiele țigănimii* echoes the enslavement-era grouping of families as a labor unit, often referred to by the name of their shelter (*sălaș* or *bordei*). On the map of Pripas that Rebreanu drew, each house is marked with the name of the family inhabiting it.[102] On the edge of the map, marking a spot slightly larger than one house, Rebreanu wrote not the name of one or more Romani families but *Țiganii* (figure 3.1).

The musicians who play at the Sunday dance in Pripas live in a similar integrated-yet-segregated hamlet on the edge of another village, Lușca. They likely do not own the land on which their houses are built; rather, they are "tolerated" on communal land.[103] Rebreanu's novel dramatizes a Romanian peasant's desire for land, and the Romani quarter is tethered in a very particular way to that desire. The land question is filtered through the national question, which itself is racially configured. Ion's desire for land therefore comes across as a project for justice, whereas the question of Romani landownership resonates throughout the novel as an eloquent silence. No provisions for Romani landownership were made either

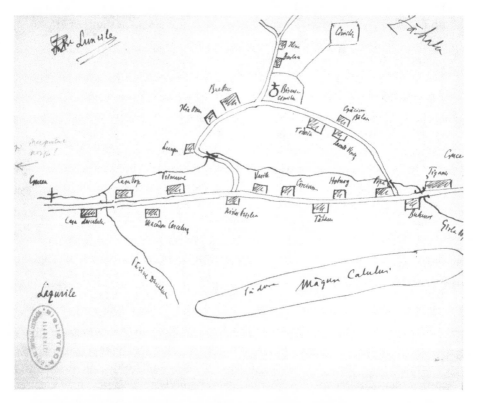

FIGURE 3.1. Liviu Rebreanu positioned the Romani quarter on the right edge of a map he drew of the village of Pripas. Although all other houses in the village have a name attached to them, the Romani people in the village remain nameless. Courtesy of the Romanian Academy.

after their emancipation in Wallachia and Moldova or after their enforced settlement in Transylvania. What ensued was a long process of spatial segregation that predetermined labor trajectories. The musicians in Rebreanu's novel travel in search of labor because of historical restrictions on their settlement. Their mobility implies that they do not belong to the village or national community; they are only inserted into village events when they can serve the community's needs through their labor.

Accordingly, the sixth modality is the use of stereotypes associated with Roma in the production of comedy, used to solidify a sense of national community that excludes Roma. In the novel, a middle-class Romanian dance is prefaced by a curious performance: "The performance had already begun. . . . A lanky, weedy-looking schoolboy was reciting a gipsy anecdote, grimacing all the time, rushing up and down the stage, changing his voice constantly, rousing boisterous guffaws at the back of the hall and discreet smiles among the chairs in front [*Spectacolul începuse. . . . Acuma un elev lung și slab declama o anecdotă țigănească, strâmbându-se într-una, repezindu-se încoace și încolo pe scenă, schimbând mereu glasul și stârnind râsete zgomotoase în fund și zâmbete discrete pe scaune]*" (117, 167). The student is mimicking Romani stereotypes—exaggerated facial expressions and the inability to control one's body or voice. He is likely telling a joke about the Roma, a genre in itself, in which they usually come across unfavorably. The other students, seated at the back of the room, respond with loud laughter. Middle-class young women, eager for the dance to start, restrain their laughter and respond with discreet yet eloquent smiles. The community gathers and collectively mocks a racialized minority. A child, a member of the majority, mimics racial stereotypes attached to a minority. The spectacle reinforces a sense of community. It is followed by other recitations, all "relished with the proper national satisfaction [*gustate cu cuvenita plăcere națională]*" (117, 167). The implication is that there are no Roma among either the student population or the dancing lower middle class. But they are, of course, present; a group of Romani musicians led by the famous Carol Goghi, who reportedly played for Franz Joseph and whose music was acclaimed as far away as Berlin, provides the music for this event.[104] The novel, however, does not linger on the Romani musicians' reaction to this Transylvanian version of a minstrel show.[105]

Romani Literature

In Rebreanu's scene, the dancers stop intermittently to pressure the musicians: "'Go on, gypsy! Come on, crow!' [*Zi, țigane! Mai zi, cioară!]*" (11, 15). The Romani word *cioară* is deployed as a racial slur.[106] Even though the musicians claim fatigue, they are forced to play on. When they become angry, they are careful not to show it: "Only when the lad moved away mumbling does he and the other fiddlers allow themselves to show distress again, in the Romani language [*Numai după ce flăcăul se îndepărtă bodogănind, începe iar să se necăjească cu ceilalți lăutari, pe țigănește*]" (15, 20). The musicians switch languages, from Romanian to Romani, the latter being used only at a distance from the Romanian characters, in their visual and auditory blind spots. The modernist narrator, who slips in and out of various characters' consciousnesses and has visual access to the Romani characters, does not have access to the Romani language beyond its sound. The narrator can discern, at the level of tone, that the Romani words communicate Romani suffering (*se necăjească*), but the words themselves cannot be understood. Unlike Hungarian and German, the two imperial languages, as well as the occasional French phrase, which the narrator comprehends and often quietly translates into Romanian, the Romani language is rendered untranslatable.[107] The Romani characters switch to Romani knowing that their complaints cannot be understood by the Romanian characters. They remain lost on the narrator, too, who is thus identified as *gadje*, or non-Romani. The implied reader is likewise unequivocally positioned as non-Romani. The Romani language, despite its untranslatability, nonetheless remains "stitched" to the fabric of the text.[108] The very word for *musician* used by Rebreanu, *lăutar*, constitutes such stitching, carrying resonances of the Arabic *al 'ūd* and the Turkish *laut*, a reminder of the history of Roma migration and the interimperial framework within which Romani musicians are positioned in the text.[109]

The music performed by the Romani musicians in Rebreanu's scene cannot be seen as an extension of Romani music, which enters the purview of World Music in various forms. Rather, it is as a sublated trace of Romani literature, which remains outside the purview of the modern, an oral tradition in a "less spoken language."[110] This exclusion is reproduced by Romanian-language literary criticism, but also by studies of international modernism.[111] Romani arts belong to a political economy of differently remunerated labor, which they enter as the most profitable form of labor for capital: one that can be paid so little as not to be paid at all, and therefore denied the status of labor altogether.

COUNTING AND DISCOUNTING LANGUAGES

Transylvanian Interglottism between
Hugó Meltzl and Liviu Rebreanu

One character admonishes his wife in German, which he learned while serving in the Austro-Hungarian army and to which he switches when he is drunk. Another character struggles to say something in Hungarian, which she speaks haltingly. One proudly declares that he does not speak Hungarian, even though he does, perfectly. Another stretches her words, as is presumably a typical characteristic of Saxon German. Two other characters switch between Romanian and Yiddish. Others communicate in the Romani language, on the side of a dialogue in Romanian. French phrases are sprinkled into some Romanian-language conversations. Accents, intonations, and proficiencies in all these languages are described throughout. We seem to be in a Transylvanian Babel. The language characters choose to speak at any given time is as important as what is being said, if not more so. What linguists describe as the metalingual function of language is often what is communicated, in an inter-imperial key.

In previous chapters, we noted that the languages in *Ion* (Romanian, German, Hungarian, Yiddish, Romani, French) are traces of Transylvania's inter-imperial history. Each of these languages is actually more than one. There are at least three kinds of Hungarian: the language developed as the Hungarian literary language, its Transylvanian regional variant, and Szekler/Székely Hungarian. German, in this context, is also at least three languages: Transylvanian Saxon, Austrian German, and the German literary language. Transylvanian Romanian is, at this time, a regional variant of the language spoken in Romania. Yiddish is a composite language, and so is Romani. The French spoken by Romanian would-be elites is Francophone French. These languages and their multiple variants have complicated relationships to one another, all participating in a complex language field within ethnic, racial, and religious hierarchies. Borbála Zsuzsanna Török offers one linguistic map: "Conforming to the anthropological vision of the Enlightenment, *Landeskunde* [German-language regional and cultural studies] casts distinctions between the 'civilized German,' the 'less cultivated Hungarian,' and the 'uncivilized' Romanian, Slav, Roma, etc."[1] As a Transylvanian novel in the Romanian language (among the "uncivilized" on this map), Rebreanu's *Ion* is itself an inter-imperial statement. It is written against the presumed superiority of the two asymmetrical imperial languages of the Austro-Hungarian Empire, German and Hungarian; in an ambivalent relation to French and the Paris-anchored world republic of letters; and in a tense relation to the "smaller" languages of the region (Romani, Yiddish, Armenian). Rebreanu's choice of language (and it *is* a choice) constitutes one of the novel's most important formal elements. In this chapter, we discuss the linguistic dimension of Transylvania's inter-imperial condition, developed through the related concept of interglottism. As Mary Louise Pratt asserts, "Inter-imperiality and the *longue durée* intersect in the concept of imperial afterlives, and language is one of that concept's most enduring manifestations."[2] We argue that Transylvanian interglottism constitutes the most central manifestation of the region's inter-imperial afterlife in the *longue durée*.

It is not coincidental that Transylvania is considered the birthplace of the discipline of comparative literature and thus of a particular notion of comparatism. According to a narrative most recently traced by David Damrosch, comparative literature was born in 1877 in Cluj/Kolozsvár/Klausenburg, the capital of Transylvania, with the publication of the first comparative literature journal, *Acta Comparationis Literarum Universarum* (*ACLU*).[3] *ACLU* was edited by Sámuel Brassai and Hugó Meltzl between 1877 and 1888.[4] The first issue of the journal listed its place of editorial production, in an eloquent mix of Hungarian and French, as "Kolozsvár (Clausenbourg), Transylvanie (Hongrie)." The editors proposed two principles for what they imagined, in 1877, would be an influential discipline in the future: translation and polyglottism.

In this chapter, we present a case study in linguistic inter-imperiality. We read the interglottism at work in Rebreanu's novel *Ion* against the polyglottism theorized and performed editorially by the journal *ACLU*, which we examine against the background of post-1867 Austro-Hungarian policies for the use of languages. An analysis of the linguistic dimension of Rebreanu's novel helps clarify the politics of polyglottism at stake in one origin story of comparative literature, which is intimately and ambivalently implicated with its inter-imperial moment. Unlike a polycentric mix of multiple but equal languages, the polyglottism at work in Rebreanu's text mirrors inter-imperial conflicts, inequalities, and hierarchies. We therefore refer to it as *interglottism*—not a random Transylvanian Babel but a mode of connecting the linguistic with both the political, social, and economic imperial order *and* its contestation. The unequal power relations at work in this and other inter-imperial contexts and the corresponding linguistic hierarchies echo but are not the same as or reducible to the creolization of languages in the colonial context of enslavement and the plantation economy. We contend that, while the notion of creolization is helpful in analyzing both contexts, the way it is deployed accounts for the significant differences between coloniality and inter-imperiality.[5] We conceive of interglottism as the central mode of creolization analyzed in this book.

A Brief History of Transylvanian Interglottism

Imperial states use language as an imperial technology. Because Transylvania's inter-imperial history includes multiple empires, its linguistic landscape involves multiple languages—both multiple imperial languages and multiple and unequal local vernaculars. As Pratt writes, "By their very formation, empires are trans-linguistic force fields: the language of the imperializing power lands on spaces already territorialized by other languages, perhaps other imperial languages."[6] The result is often an inter-imperial linguistic force field, with its associated multilingual cultural production, as occurred in places like the Caribbean or the Indian Ocean. The modality by which the Austro-Hungarian Empire—specifically the Hungarian side of the empire—deployed language as an imperial tool differed dramatically, however, from its use by the British, the French, or the Spanish Empire.

As part of the Habsburg Enlightenment and its project of centralized state consolidation, emperor Joseph II introduced a number of language reforms at the end of the eighteenth century, in a declared attempt to modernize education and fight illiteracy in the empire. Most consequentially, in 1784 he issued a decree replacing Latin with German as the official language of communication, education, and the judicial system. Few scholars know that Latin was the written language of science and philosophy and the oral language of institutionalized political debate in this region of East-Central Europe until the nineteenth century.[7] Joseph's modernizing language reforms aimed to displace Latin. German was already in use in the western part of the Habsburg Empire, and Joseph wanted to streamline its administrative use in the eastern parts, in the name of efficiency and practicality. German had emerged over the course of the eighteenth century as a vernacular (Goethe deplored its belatedness), and it was now considered "developed" enough to export in the name of enlightenment.[8]

The strategy was to introduce the use of German slowly and flexibly. Other local languages would be allowed in certain areas, but only in the Latin alphabet.[9] Although Joseph's decree had limited immediate effects in Transylvania, it constituted the beginning of a successful effort to give the German language ascendancy not only over Latin, which had functioned as the lingua franca of the educated nobility and remained in use throughout the nineteenth century, but also over other languages in the region. In particular, Joseph's decree concerned the languages of ethnic groups with emerging nationalist ambitions: Serbian, Croatian, Ruthenian, Romanian, Slovakian, and Hungarian. Note that this list doubly minoritizes the languages of groups seen as lacking such ambitions: Yiddish, Romani, and Armenian.[10] The lack of nation-building prospects was tied to what Max Weinreich called the "social plight" of Yiddish globally, summed up in the now famous formulation: "A language is a dialect with an army and a navy."[11]

The decree of 1784 prompted resistance. Latin was celebrated as a linguistic equalizer—among other things, it was the language in which the nobility participated in political debate and the language of science and culture. Most consequential was the resistance of the Magyar nobility, which perceived the decree as an attempt to Germanize Hungary.[12] They initially defended Latin against accusations that it was a dead language and thus unable to support an Enlightenment project, but they subsequently started a process of introducing Hungarian as an alternative imperial language. It is worth mentioning that this shift in position vis-à-vis the Hungarian language was often produced via texts written in Latin.[13] In 1843 the Hungarian parliament abolished the use of Latin in its deliberations and imposed Hungarian as the language of parliamentary communications. In 1847, in opposition to the replacement of Latin with Hungarian, the Croatian parliament declared Croatian to be the official language of Croatia. In 1847 Hungarian became the language of the Transylvanian Diet, a move that prompted opposition from the local Saxons, who were allowed to keep administrative documents in German.[14] These developments were both in sync and in tension with a European current linking nation to territory to monolingualism. The very idea of what we call *language* today was consolidated through this process.[15] The outcome was that some languages, including local languages, became *foreign* languages.

Before his death, Joseph II withdrew his language decree, but, by then, the process had become irreversible. Latin was now twice dead. After the events of 1848, when Hungarians revolted against Austrian domination (including perceived linguistic domination) and were defeated, emperor Franz Joseph reinstated German as the official language. He changed course by 1860, when he passed the so-called October Diploma, which allowed communication with the administration in local languages. Theoretically, this should have included all the languages of the Habsburg Empire. In fact, the diploma functioned as an early compromise with Hungary, anticipating 1867. As a consequence, Hungarian became the language of the administration in multilingual Transylvania; other languages were tolerated locally, largely at village level, for limited use. At the same time, the October Diploma was interpreted as a shift away from Habsburg centralization toward more regional autonomy, offering linguistic rights to what were now called the "nationalities" of the empire. Emboldened by this implication, the Transylvanian Diet declared in 1863: "The three languages of the country, Hungarian, German, and Romanian, share equal rights in official public communication."[16] The very idea of declaring the equality of three languages was particularly Transylvanian: equality in Transylvania has historically been tied to the right to use one's language or languages. It remains a useful reminder today: how does multilingualism address the issue of equality?

This period of posited equality was short-lived. The 1867 Compromise led to an arrangement between Austria and Hungary and the formation of the Austro-Hungarian Empire. Transylvania was incorporated into Hungary. The compromise functioned as an implicit linguistic compromise: Austrian officials accepted the Hungarian monolingual paradigm as equal to the German paradigm.[17] Linguistically, this meant that, while the new Austrian constitution guaranteed equal linguistic rights for nationalities in the western part of the empire, Hungary developed its own linguistic policies in the eastern part. Austria and Hungary drastically differed over linguistic and cultural rights for nationalities and minorities. On one side of the empire, there was a claim to imperialist cosmopolitanism; on the other side, there was an ambivalent and largely unsuccessful effort at enforced Magyarization. When scholars invoke the famed multiculturalism of the Austro-Hungarian Empire, often with a focus on Jewish authors who wrote in German, they generally have the Austrian side in mind, and Galicia is often considered a limit case. But Hungarian policies, especially Hungarian policies in Transylvania, could hardly be described as cosmopolitan or multicultural.[18] The specific forms of anti-imperialism developed in Transylvania were closely intertwined with resistance to the gradual imposition of Hungarian as the language of imperial administration and education.

Three laws were passed the year after the 1867 Compromise: the law of Transylvania's union with Hungary, the law of nationalities, and the law of education. The heated debate around the law of nationalities revolved around its invocation of a unitary and indivisible Hungarian political nation. Supporters claimed it was a progressive law that included all citizens in a political community and aimed to work in an Enlightenment spirit toward political inclusion and centralization. A distinction was drawn between Magyars—an ethnic group—and

Hungarians—members of a nation composed of many ethnic groups. József Eötvös, the Hungarian minister of religion and education at the time and an advocate of the law, famously believed that nations were slowly becoming anachronistic.[19] The unitary nation was meant to placate the spread of nationalism. What ensued, in fact, was a tension among various understandings of *Kulturnation* and *Staatsnation*, or, in terms proposed by Susan Gal, between authenticity and universalism.[20]

Regardless of how we interpret the 1868 law of nationalities and dissect its asymmetrical implementation, one consequence was crucial: a unitary nation needed a language.[21] On the Hungarian side of the Austro-Hungarian Empire, this language would be Hungarian. The possibility of a tyrannical majority nation oppressing linguistic minorities would be minimized through local autonomy and the use of other languages at the local and confessional levels (Tocqueville's study of the United States served as a model for Eötvös).[22] The question of majority and minority was flipped, however, because the Magyars were not the majority in post-Compromise Hungary; they constituted about 40 percent of the population, but they owned much of the land and were the dominant political group within a retrograde electoral system. In Transylvania, according to the 1850 census, Magyars constituted 26 percent of the population, Romanians 59.5 percent, Germans 9.3 percent, Roma 3.8 percent, Jews 0.8 percent, and Armenians 0.4 percent.

Within the contemporary debate on the 1868 law of nationalities, which included important dissident Magyar voices, the position of the non-Magyar population of Hungary, including Transylvania, was represented in the Hungarian parliament by Alexandru Mocioni/Mocsonyi Sándor, a descendant of a wealthy and illustrious Macedonian-Romanian family based in Budapest. Mocioni studied law in Budapest, Vienna, and Graz, and he traveled through Europe and learned about the interglot and polyglot regions of Switzerland and Belgium. He spoke Romanian, Hungarian, German, French, and English. A member of the Budapest parliament between 1865 and 1874, Mocioni participated in the heated debates of 1867–1868. In a speech he delivered on November 24, 1868, in collaboration with Serbian representatives, he proclaimed the sovereignty of the peoples of Hungary, in the plural. He claimed there were six nationalities in the territory of Hungary within the Austro-Hungarian Empire, each with its own language and cultural traditions: Hungarians, Romanians, Serbs, Slovaks, Ruthenians, and Germans. The Hungarian state thus had to be polyglot; there could be no one state language. The law should recognize the *existence* of these nations as juridical and political actors, the premise for equal rights. When it came to linguistic rights, Mocioni posited the principle of the equality of languages (*egală îndreptățire a limbilor*). He envisioned two possible methods of implementation: The first, based on the Belgian model, was to use all languages everywhere and at all times. The second possibility, which Mocioni explained against the background of booing in the Budapest parliament, was the use of language territories—the languages spoken in each administrative unit would be official languages.[23] Mocioni's arguments for multilingualism were dismissed. Mocioni adhered to a strategy of political passivity, drawing attention to the fact that people who did not legally exist could not be active in parliament. His observations echoed similar debates taking place in St. Domingue at the close of the eighteenth century, according to which the unfree and non-whites were not part of "the nation" and could therefore not become citizens (see chapter 5). Retrospectively, Mocioni's strategy comes across as an extended piece of performance art. It was, of course, a linguistic statement as well: since they could not use their own languages, these politicians decided to use no language at all. The question of what a region with six equal languages would look like resonated back then and still resonates today; it is one of the questions that prompted this book.

It was over education that the perceived "linguistic war" was largely fought. The law of education, also sponsored by Eötvös, created nondenominational schools funded by the state, with mandatory attendance for children up to age twelve. The language of these state schools was Hungarian. In 1869 the much-debated national history of Hungary became a compulsory subject in school curricula. The Treford law of 1879 required that all teachers be able to speak and write in Hungarian. An 1882 law mandated the teaching of the Hungarian language and Hungarian literature in secondary schools. In 1905 the Berzeviczy law was proposed, requiring the use of Hungarian in confessional schools and the centralization of all curricular and textbook decisions. In 1907 the Apponyi laws instituted a disciplinary system for teachers, including the dismissal of those deemed not to be linguistic "patriots." In response to this series of laws, which were thought to contradict both the theoretical openness of the 1868 law of nationalities and the spirit of an inclusive political nation, nationalism congealed among Transylvanian Romanians and Transylvanian Saxons, especially with claims to linguistic freedom.

In 1892 a document titled *Memorandum of Romanians in Transylvania and Hungary* protested "the legal domination of one language in a polyglot state [*asigurarea legală a dominaţiunii exclusive a unei limbi într-un stat poliglot*]."[24] Hoping, in a trans-imperial spirit, to pit Hungarian and Austrian interests against each other, organizers sent the document to Franz Joseph. Famously, in his own piece of performance art, the emperor refused to read the memorandum. In support of their claims, Transylvanian Romanian nationalists cited other anti-imperial struggles around the world. In the mid-nineteenth century, the Irish struggle against empire—well covered in the international media—had served as a foil for Transylvanian struggles.[25] Continuing this line of argumentation, on May 27, 1904, Transylvanian Romanian religious leader Ioan Meţianu gave a speech in the Hungarian parliament drawing a comparison between Transylvanian Romanians in Hungary and the Irish under English domination.[26]

The comparison of the Romanian Transylvanian linguistic plight to that of the Irish remains highly eloquent. Edward Said revised his account of postcolonialism to include the postcolonialism of the Irish and Irish postcolonial nationalism. In this way, Said acknowledged and theorized intra-European imperial and anti-imperial predicaments, which other scholars later extended to an analysis of East Europe.[27] Spatial politics tied to the use of place names was central to the anti-imperial imaginary theorized by Said. The uneasy postcolonialisms of Ireland and East Europe straddle conventional categories of analysis, prompting the development of new comparative frameworks and concepts. Tracing the imperial difference that distinguished the Hungarian use of language as a technology of domination from the British use, while at the same time acknowledging nationalist trans-imperial negotiations of language rights, results in the creolization of the modern conception of language as national language—with important consequences for both multilingualism and comparatism.

Comparative Literature: In Search of a Transylvanian Origin

In 2003 Gayatri Spivak's field-defining *Death of a Discipline* issued a call to "open up, from the inside, the colonialism of European national-language based Comparative Literature and the Cold War format of Area Studies."[28] But how should the project of decolonizing the endangered discipline of comparative literature be undertaken? One answer was provided by David Damrosch's 2006 essay "Rebirth of a Discipline: The Global Origins of Comparative Studies," which advocated a return to two globalizing moments in the history of comparative literature as *alternative* genealogies for the discipline. Damrosch identified one such moment as the creation of *ACLU*, the first comparative literature journal, as described by one of its editors, Hugó Meltzl. Can a return to *ACLU* and to Meltzl function as an alternative to what Spivak called "the colonialism of European national-language based Comparative Literature"? In this section, we retrace Meltzl's advocacy of polyglottism as a foil to Rebreanu's interglottism, which we understand as a symptom of the linguistic afterlife of Transylvania's inter-imperiality.

In Meltzl, one finds an editor with a polyglot education and scholarly career.[29] He was born in 1846 into a wealthy German-speaking family in Transylvania. Having attended the Hungarian-speaking Unitary Collegium in Cluj/Kolozsvár/Klausenburg (where his future coeditor, Brassai, was a teacher), he continued his studies in Leipzig, Heidelberg, and Vienna. He worked in German, Hungarian, Italian, French. Once he completed his studies, he returned to Transylvania in 1872 to teach German literature at the Hungarian Royal University, founded the year of Meltzl's return and later named after the Austro-Hungarian emperor. Meltzl served as chair of the German Literature Department, dean of the Faculty of Philosophy, and rector of the university. One of his scholarly projects was a short study of Dante, which he published in French. Another project was a bilingual collection of Romani folk poetry, which *ACLU* published in Romani and in German translation; parts of it were subsequently translated into English in the United States. These are some of the biographical features that make Meltzl such a fascinating figure for contemporary comparatists.

In his theoretical writings for *ACLU*, Meltzl emphasized the principle of polyglottism, intertwined with an unusual mix of both antinationalism and anticosmopolitanism. Meltzl wrote a series of three articles in German, titled "The Present Tasks of Comparative Literature [*Vorläufige Aufgaben der vergleichenden Litteratur*]," articulating *ACLU*'s mission.[30] In 1878 Meltzl published, in French, a text titled *La reforme litteraire en Europe*, making a case for the existence of alternative literary journals (such as *ACLU*) in a modern literary world dominated, in his view, by populism, mercantilism, and nationalism.

Meltzl's writing constituted a breath of fresh air at a time and in a region defined by accelerated nationalism. He proposed a revision of literary history (*Litteraturgeschichtsschreibung*) through comparatism, positing the joint principles of translation (*Übersetzungsprinzip*) and polyglottism (*Prinzip des Polyglottismus*) as a foundation for the discipline of comparative literature: "the *principle of translation* has to be not replaced but accompanied by a considerably more important comparative tool, *the principle of polyglottism*."[31] The first principle yields a large body of literature Meltzl called translation literature (*Übersetzungslitteratur*). The second principle remains to this day one of the only methodological anchors for the discipline of comparative literature: "True comparison is possible only when we have before us the objects of our comparison in their original form (*vergleichenden Objecte in möglichst unverfälschtem Zustande vor uns haben*)."[32] Meltzl was invested in polyglottism as the study of literary texts in their original form—that is, a contribution to the criticism of Cervantes should be published in Spanish. He was equally interested in polyglot production (*polyglotte Originalproduction*), texts that, in one way or another, were polyglot at the moment of their writing.[33] He argued for the need to engage with languages under the threat of extermination (*Ausrottung*) and for the study of literatureless peoples (*litteraturlosen Völker*), the latter under the onslaught of uninvited missionary zeal (*mit missions-süchtiger Unberufenheit*).[34] The discipline of comparative literature could only be interdisciplinary, as it was already entangled with history, anthropology, and philosophy. Meltzl was interested in analyzing the material infrastructure that facilitated the circulation of literature (the world postal system), and he argued for the inclusion of new technologies (e.g., the phonograph) into methodologies of literary study.[35] He supported the career of one of the first female comparatists—Dora d'Istria (*die geniale Dora d'Istria*).[36] Following in Goethe's footsteps, Meltzl proposed a normative ideal: "True 'world literature' (*wahre 'Weltlitteratur'*), therefore, in our opinion, can only remain an unattainable ideal (*unerreichbares Ideal*) in the direction of which, nevertheless, all independent literatures, i.e. all nations, should strive."[37]

Meltzl was an ardent advocate for the study of small European languages and literatures. In the third article in his series, he nonetheless proposed that, for the time being, polyglottism be supplemented by the principle of "decaglottism (*Dekaglottismus*)." This principle referred to the ten European languages that had made important contributions to world literature (*zehn moderne Litteraturen mit wahrhaft weltlitteraturischen Erscheinungen*) and achieved a certain classicism: German, French, English, Italian, Spanish, Portuguese, Dutch, Swedish, Icelandic, and Hungarian.[38] Meltzl emphasized that he invoked decaglottism in the interest of economy and with reservations (*nur im Interesse einer weisen Ökonomie u. Beschränkung übernehmen, ohne dabei die mindeste Auszeichnung zu prätendieren*). Icelandic was represented by medieval epics and supplemented by the invocation of Steingrímur Thorsteinsson, the prominent nineteenth-century Icelandic translator and Meltzl's partner in comparatist dialogue.[39] As for Hungarian, which was the literature to which the journal belonged (*unser Litteraturblatt in allererster Linie angehört*), it was represented by two figures: József Eötvös and Sándor Petőfi.

In its editorial practice, *ACLU* largely worked with the two imperial languages, German and Hungarian. Since the ideal was to publish criticism of any given text in the language of that text, Meltzl argued that this should at least be the case for German and Hungarian literature, given that they corresponded to the journal's own neighborhood (*Cultivierung der deutschen Litteratur, nächst der magyarischen, welche übrigens auch der geographischen u. ganzen culturellen Nachbarschaft entspricht*). To this imperial diglottism (*Diglottismus*), the journal added three European languages: English, French, and Italian. English and French were, of course, colonial languages, but Alfred J. López draws attention to the fact that comparative literature, as imagined by Meltz in 1877, did not engage with literature in English, Spanish, or French outside of Europe. Most relevant for purposes of this book is the fact that, though based in Cluj/Kolozsvár/Klausenburg and surrounded by a majoritarian Romanian-speaking population calling for linguistic rights, Meltzl did not include Romanian on the list of *ACLU*'s languages; nor did he address the debate on polyglottism traced in the previous section of this chapter. Theo D'haen writes in response to this eloquent omission: "The fact is that not only did Meltzl not include Romanian as one of the working languages of his journal, but he also excluded all other languages of all other minorities in the Austro-Hungarian Empire." D'haen continues: Meltzl "needs to defend polyglottism as a defense against the encroachment of German, yet he also needs to raise Hungarian above the status of other minority languages in the Austro-Hungarian Empire, particularly Romanian."[40]

Meltzl was interested in the literatures of Transylvania, plural; when it came to Romanian-language literature, however, he relegated it to the weaker side of the imperial distinction between literature and folklore.[41] "Folklore is not literature, just as myth is not history," writes Walter Mignolo. Insisting on this distinction, Mignolo adds, yields "a hierarchy of cultural practices parallel to economic and political regulations."[42] To be sure, Meltzl challenged the superiority of the "large" European languages and cherished "small" literatures' contributions to the literary circuit (*Litteraturverkehr Europas*), even if they did not achieve the neoclassicism he admired aesthetically. He noted that the minor folk traditions (including Romani, Jewish, and Armenian in Transylvania) were in need of asylum (*Asylbereithalten*) against the racial hatred displayed by major European cultures. But in Austria-Hungary in the 1870s and 1880s, the very terms of the debate, *Kunstlitteraturen* and *Volksliederlitteraturen*, which *ACLU* tried to rewrite but nonetheless reproduced, were intimately entwined with inter-imperial politics. Meltzl's inclusion of Hungarian in *Dekaglottismus* resonated locally as an ideological position—indicating that Hungarian was more developed than other languages in the region. This claim resonated in the political sphere, supporting Hungarian's ascendancy to the status of imperial language. Meltzl's plea for polyglottism was inter-imperial and interglot, echoing underlying political hierarchies.

Meltzl's journal first appeared in 1877, nine years after the law of nationalities spearheaded by Eötvös. The first issues of *ACLU* included a motto from Eötvös.[43] Meltzl had encountered Eötvös's writing as a student in Heidelberg, where he befriended Eötvös's son, a fellow student and future mathematician.[44] Eötvös did not become fluent in Hungarian until late in life; his first written language was German. He was the author of the novel *The Carthusian* (1839–1841), which Meltzl praised for one chapter in particular. Eötvös's fiction created a quasimythical figure of a suffering Hungarian peasant.[45] Eötvös was also the minister of religion and education and the initiator of reform in higher education, which led, among other things, to the founding of the University of Kolozsvár. Eötvös died in 1871, and Meltzl was hired by the university in 1872. Importantly, Eötvös was a liberal supporter of nationalities and their languages and a proponent of Jewish emancipation. But his institutional position and the faulty implementation of the law of nationalities led to his name being associated, in the eyes of minorities, with imperial policies, including linguistic policies. These were very tense years, during which the issue of polyglottism, as a corollary to the nationalities problem, constituted *the* major political debate in Transylvania. In this context, Meltzl tied his name to Eötvös.

During Meltzl's tenure at the university in Kolozsvár/Cluj/Klausenburg, his colleague Gregoriu Silaşi/Szilasi Gergely taught Romanian literature. The language of instruction was Hungarian.[46] Silaşi was at the center of a public scandal, having been accused of using the Romanian language to explain Romanian literary texts to students, a charge he vehemently denied.[47] Meltzl participated in faculty meetings during which the Silaşi affair was discussed.[48] It is believed that he warned Silaşi that students would storm his course and interrupt his teaching. The affair concerned one of the tenets of Meltzl's program for *ACLU*: the correspondence between language and literature. In what language should Romanian literature be analyzed and taught? In 1886, the year of Silaşi's early retirement, *ACLU* published Silaşi's reflections on Romanian folk traditions in German and Hungarian.[49] Dora d'Istria's studies of Romanian folk songs were published in French.[50] The principle of polyglottism, which Meltzl passionately advocated, had a clear limit.

Meltzl believed the Hungarian language lent itself to world literature. The first issues of *ACLU* started a project of translating Petőfi, Hungary's national poet. Meltzl commissioned translations of Petőfi's work in more than thirty languages.[51] He was engaged in a heated dispute over Petőfi's oeuvre, aiming to denationalize its framing and focus instead on its regional and global dimensions.[52] In contradistinction, for Meltzl, Romanian was an oral language. He admired and collected folk songs in the Hungarian, Romanian, and Romani languages. He placed Romanian and Romani literatures, however, strictly within the framework of folklore, mirroring colonial and imperial differences as well as the geopolitics of knowledge production at work globally. The developmental model of language and literature underwriting *ACLU*, whereby literary cultures develop over time from folklore to world literature, reproduced marginality within the local literary system. In 1880 the journal started listing two places of production—Kolozsvár and London. Meltzl moved the printing of *ACLU* to London, following his collaboration with *Trübner's American and Oriental Literary Record*, known for its Orientalist interests, including folklore.[53]

Meltzl's theoretical writings were receptive to a number of local and regional political debates. His exile of Russian literature from *Decaglottismus* was a reaction to the banning of Ruthenian in the Russian Empire, a situation decried in the first issue of *ACLU* and described as a concern for the emerging discipline of comparative literature. Meltzl's advocacy of Romani language and folk traditions was a response to the long history of discrimination traced in chapter 3. His silence on the Transylvanian linguistic struggles in the 1870s and 1880s is even more eloquent, given these engagements. Importantly, the Hungarian-language press, invested in an inter-imperial narrative of the vindication of Hungarianness on the European stage, found Meltzl's journal not Hungarian enough.[54] In response, Meltzl tried to negotiate a position between Hungarian literature and a polyglot, transnational literary sphere.

Meltzl's advocacy of polyglottism should be filtered through what Rebecca Walkowitz calls "comparative audiences," including late-nineteenth-century Transylvanian comparative audiences: Saxon, Romanian, Hungarian, Jewish, and Romani.[55] His list of languages for *ACLU* was comprehensive but highly selective, embedded in a history of interglottism.[56] In the midst of a heated Transylvanian debate on polyglottism, Meltzl's notion of decaglottism promoted Hungarian as a classical language and Hungarian literature as world literature. Hungarian literature is indeed "small," and in other contexts, the Hungarian language functions as a minority language, but in this space and time, Hungarian literature was written in an aspiring imperial language, sustaining a semiperipheral empire attempting to extend its sphere of influence over an Orientalized Balkan region. Meltzl's *ACLU* obliquely, if ambivalently, participated in this project.

We return to Meltzl to frame our reading of Rebreanu's interglottism because, following Spivak's challenge, we agree with Aamir Mufti that "any conception of world literature (or culture) must now confront the legacy of colonialism."[57] And the legacy of colonialism we have framed in Transylvania's case is an entangled legacy of coloniality and inter-imperiality. In Istanbul/Constantinople, which Mufti invokes as the second birthplace of the discipline of comparative literature, this means confronting the legacy of the Ottoman Empire in its relation to other world empires.[58] In Cluj/Kolozsvár/Klausenburg, it means confronting the legacy of the Habsburg and Austro-Hungarian Empires and their particular place in the world history of empires, including in relation to the Ottoman Empire and the Russian Empire. To return to Spivak's second wager, largely forgotten by the critics who participate in the comparative literature debate, *ACLU*'s location in Cluj/Kolozsvár/Klausenburg also allows us to challenge "the Cold War format of Area Studies," which would place the study of Transylvania and of *ACLU* in a Slavic languages department and in a field called East European studies, although none of the languages at play in Transylvania are of Slavic origin. Once we both confront the legacy of colonial and imperial rule and de–Cold War the format of area studies, Meltzl's polyglottism resonates somewhat differently.[59] If Transylvania is to function as an origin for comparative literature, as we believe it can, and if this origin is strategically based on *ACLU*'s polyglottism, this polyglottism needs to be put in relation—however complex—to the region's inter-imperiality and its associated linguistic hierarchies.

Rebreanu's Interglottism

As a child, Rebreanu spoke Romanian at home. He started his formal education in Romanian (his father was a teacher), and his first readings were of Transylvanian fairy tales—in Romanian.[60] Rebreanu soon learned Hungarian and German, the languages of the Austro-Hungarian Empire after 1867. The study of Latin remained central to the curriculum in the region.[61] Rebreanu continued his education with six years in military school, first in Sopron and then in Budapest (for part of this time, he went by the name Rebreàn Olivèr). In addition to Romanian, Hungarian, and German, Rebreanu studied French, and he later added English and Italian to the mix.[62] His early writing exercises were in various languages—Hungarian, German, and French—and his first publications were in Hungarian.[63] Rebreanu later self-translated some of his early drafts written in Hungarian into Romanian.[64] Only later in life did Rebreanu start writing in Romanian. While it is important to acknowledge that Rebreanu's first language, Romanian, was a subaltern language in Transylvania during his formative years, it is equally crucial to note that it was a creolized language. When Rebreanu revised his first drafts of *Ion*, written in a language closer to the Transylvanian Romanian dialect, he edited them to remove "impurities."[65] This situation raises the question: has Rebreanu's writing always been "born translated," in Walkowitz's vocabulary? Although he appears to be moving between distinct languages, he is engaged in the practice of interglottism—a practice with world-historical resonance.

Rebreanu's predicament should teach us to ask another important question: on what historical infrastructure does one learn five or six languages? Meltzl spoke German in his family and then learned Hungarian in school. Coming from a privileged background, he traveled across the German-speaking educational and cultural sphere and, in the process, acquired other European languages. This is not, however, the infrastructure of Rebreanu's "interlanguage trajectory," to use Mignolo's phrase.[66] Rebreanu's childhood interglottism was very much a function of survival and aspirational social mobility in an inter-imperial local situation shot through with the possibility of social mobility on a worldly scale. Born into a modest Romanian-speaking family in Transylvania, he needed to learn both Hungarian and German to acquire a basic education. Once he pursued a more advanced education, he learned the "foreign languages" taught through the imperial school system. To become a Romanian-language writer, he needed to relearn Romanian. Translations from other languages helped with this project: Rebreanu translated Russian and English works, which he accessed in German, into Romanian. Importantly, he had asymmetrical skills in these languages. Both Meltzl and Rebreanu were therefore situated at the periphery of empires, but their respective interglottisms were influenced differently by class, a category defined through its intersection with race, ethnicity, and religion.

Both Meltzl and Rebreanu produced lists of the languages they spoke. Such lists constituted a metalingual genre in the region. They have also become a leitmotif of comparative literature scholarship. Reflecting on his own childhood, Elias Canetti, who acquired his *Bildung* (education/formation) in an adjacent inter-imperial space, writes about the gesture of counting languages: "People often talked about languages; seven or eight different tongues were spoken in our city alone. . . . Each person counted up the languages he knew; it was important to master several, knowing them could save one's own life or the lives of other people." The logic of the list should not, however, preclude an account of linguistic hierarchy. Most important, Canetti stresses the fact that, during his education, his mother privileged "languages with literatures attached to them."[67] The eloquent *counting* of languages thus follows heterogeneous imperatives.

Here, we focus on a young, Transylvanian Rebreanu—before his entry into Bucharest-based literary institutions. This Rebreanu is a multilingual migrant writing in a hybrid language and functioning in translation. We place him in the context of his intellectual formation—interglot Transylvania during the last decades of the Austro-Hungarian Empire. Rebreanu started writing *Ion* in 1913 and worked on it, on and off, until 1920. Thus reframed, Rebreanu's novel becomes legible, centrally, as a dramatization of the inter-imperial linguistic policies implemented through an education system anchored in the post-1868 laws described earlier. At the same time, this is a defamiliarizing interpretation of the novel's modernism, where modernism is tied to the formal use of the metalingual.[68]

An important but neglected narrative thread in Rebreanu's novel traces a young man named Titu through his inter-imperial *Bildung* as a function of the languages he learns and uses in different spheres of life. Titu goes on a pilgrimage through the educational institutions of Transylvania, noting and commenting on the linguistic politics of each.[69] A foil for young Rebreanu, Titu's first language is Romanian, which he learns at home in his family. After attending elementary school and part of secondary school where lessons are taught in Romanian, he goes to a Hungarian-language high school in Bistrița/Bistritz/Beszterce. Titu's father rationalizes the move: "because these days you can't do anything unless you speak the language of the masters [*că-n ziua de azi nu faci nimic dacă nu rupi limba stăpânirii*]" (50, 72).[70] And the language of the masters in Transylvania is, at this time, Hungarian, proclaimed the state language by laws passed in 1868. Rebreanu frames what purports to be an enlightened official language—and a would-be imperial language backed by a world literature—as the language of domination (*limba stăpânirii*).

In Rebreanu's novel, young Titu learns Hungarian in high school and prides himself on his ability to speak the language better than any Hungarian. This is a familiar leitmotif in postcolonial literature (theorized most influentially by Salih's *Season of Migration to the North*)—with resonance in an inter-imperial context. Titu also needs to speak Hungarian if he is to work in the imperial administration. Hungarian is the key to inter-imperial social mobility.[71] The word Rebreanu uses to refer to an imperial functionary is *solgăbirău*, derived from the Hungarian *szolgabiró*. Rebreanu's novel asks the reader to learn such words in order to understand the text—a modality of creolization lost in translation. Rebreanu tells the reader in passing that there is only one Romanian speaker working in the post office and one Romanian-speaking clerk at the courthouse. In one episode, Titu encounters a man who works for the railroad who had to Magyarize his name to get his job: "he dances to the master's song, otherwise he would be left on the streets [*că joacă şi el cum cântă cei mari, altfel ar rămâne pe drumuri*]" (375, 525). Throughout, the novel refracts debates in the Budapest parliament, where representatives of minorities lament that Transylvanian citizens are divided into two classes: those who speak Hungarian (first class) and those who do not (second class).[72] These debates even mention the Romanian railroad worker who had to change his name to get a job.[73]

Having learned Hungarian to perfection, Titu transfers to a Saxon school and learns German. His father explains why Titu needs German: "If you speak German . . . you can travel the whole world [*Cu limba nemţească . . . poţi umbla toată lumea*]" (50, 72). The aspirational world striated by the German language is the world of the Austro-Hungarian Empire and Germany but also the German-speaking world invoked by proponents of *Kulturboden*—and, in Rebreanu's youth, of regional higher education.[74] By learning German, Titu becomes worldly, a provincial cosmopolitan. This aspiration is apparent visually, in an inter-imperial key, as Titu claims that the styling of his facial hair follows "the Anglo-American fashion [*după moda anglo-americană*]" (50, 71). That the emerging inter- and anti-imperial intellectual strives to appear modern, whether through clothing or hairstyle, should sound familiar.[75] Linguistically, the character of Titu is a textbook example of an emerging anti-imperial intellectual, necessarily male, passing through the dominant language and cultural norms before he rejects them and returns to his mother tongue. Ironically, and similar to other colonial and inter-imperial situations, the schools that were meant to produce a Magyarized managerial class for the Hungarian semiperipheral empire simultaneously supplied leaders for anti-imperial nationalist movements.[76]

In a crucial episode in the novel, while passing by a school Titu overhears a teacher scolding a group of children: "Only Hungarian! . . . Hungarian! . . . Speak Hungarian! [*Numai ungureşte!. . . Ungureşte . . . Trebuie ungureşte!*]" (175, 249). The scene functions as an epiphany for the young poet, who understands the scolding of the children as a form of linguistic oppression and takes it upon himself to resist it. This scene had echoes in the Hungarian parliament, where Transylvanian representatives compared the imposition of the Hungarian language on Transylvanian Romanian children to the imposition of Latin on Hungarian children before 1784.[77] They argued that children learn better in any subject if they are taught in a language they understand.[78] In another scene in *Ion* echoing the Apponyi laws, Romanian-speaking students are required to recite prayers in Hungarian, to the dismay of the Transylvanian Romanian priest. The scene functions as a dramatization of the relation between language and religion, the latter considered the epitome of affective intimacy.[79] The violent intrusion of the Hungarian language into the religious sphere registers as an attack on one's soul: "'The heathens don't even spare our God! . . . They want to kill our soul, it's not enough that they chained our tongue!' [*'Nici pe Dumnezeu nu ni-l cruţă, păgânii! . . . Vor să ne ucidă sufletul, nu le ajunge că ne-au încătuşat limba!'*]" (347, 486). The way to chain a people is to subordinate their culture and especially their language. Note that in 1784 Hungarians claimed that the German language was killing their soul; one hundred years later, Transylvanian Romanians claimed that Hungarian was doing the same thing to them. The inter-imperial dynamics at play in the imposition of different languages is one of the characteristics of regions crisscrossed by conflicting imperial interests.

In Rebreanu's novel, events considered to be ethnographic milestones in one's life occur in the Hungarian language. Ion's marriage ceremony, for example, is conducted in Hungarian: "After writing down their names in the register and reading it out, in Hungarian, the due paragraphs of the law . . . [*După ce îi însemnă şi le citi pe ungureşte cele cuvenite . . .*]" (213, 301). To emphasize the alienation of the Romanian peasants, the narrator, who is otherwise polyglot, does not translate the words of the marriage ceremony. The ubiquitous apposition "in Hungarian [*pe ungureşte*]" functions as a reminder of the impenetrability of the Hungarian language to the Transylvanian Romanian peasants. Such scenes illustrate the metalingual function of language, moving it from the intralinguistic to the interglot.[80]

The debate over the use of Transylvanian languages in the justice system serves as a platform for the novel—*as* a novel—to demonstrate that linguistic justice has a metonymical relation to justice *tout court*. The right to use one's language in the justice system was guaranteed by the law of nationalities, but it was not always respected, and the issue became a matter of intense dispute. In

Rebreanu's novel, when Ion gets into legal trouble, he receives a series of official communications from the court that are written in Hungarian, which the peasant cannot read: "When, next day, the guard brought him the subpoena, Ion shrugged his shoulders indifferently and asked what day the trial was, because he could not read the Hungarian text [*Când, a doua zi, straja îi aduse citația, Ion strânse din umeri nepăsător, întrebă în ce zi e judecata, căci nu pricepea scrisul unguresc*]" (99, 141). On account of this linguistic predicament, Romanian Transylvanian peasants needed mediators between them and the justice system: translators.[81] In the novel, both the village priest and the teacher serve as translators, and in fact, they acquire their power in the village through their translation activities.[82] One scene depicts two Transylvanian Romanian peasants, plaintiff and accused, listening to court proceedings but not understanding what is being said. Before entering the courtroom, the two peasants had resolved their dispute according to old village rules, with the help of an elder from a neighboring village. One agreed to return the land he stole, and the other agreed to withdraw the charge. In other words, there is no legal dispute to resolve. The scene frames a justice system that insists on imposing its verdict in a nonexisting case. The verdict represents the weight of the law embodied in the Hungarian language. The justice system turns out to be a place of punishment for plaintiff and accused alike. Scenes like this help us reread, comparatively, Franz Kafka's narratives of entanglement in the Austro-Hungarian legal system; the famed opacity of the law is often a function of inter-imperial language policies.

Aside from its role in education and the justice system, language is instrumental to the production of space, the Transylvanian dynamics of which we analyzed in chapter 1. Most importantly, Transylvanian inter-imperial language hierarchies are at work in the distinction between the country and the city. Toward the end of the novel, Titu decides to immigrate to the Romanian capital; this decision, plotted by Rebreanu in a novel published in 1920, foreshadows Transylvania's incorporation into Romania. On his way to Sibiu/Hermannstadt/ Nagyszeben, Titu scans the landscape:

> Titu could not get enough of the Transylvanian landscape—which ran, folded, fell behind, stretched out into the distance, moved closer again. . . . And the train passed haughtily past Romanian villages, splitting some like a merciless tyrant, rarely stopping here and there for a moment, marking every halt with the sound of harsh Hungarian words, forever hurrying and scolding the traveling peasants or the servants. . . . Then came the large stations, ante-chambers of cities, and the peasants could no longer be seen. In their stead, there appeared noisy, impatient,

bustling townsmen, speaking commandingly only in a foreign language. (373–74)

*Titu nu se mai putea sătura privind pământul Ardealului care fugea,
se îndoia, rămânea în urmă, se întindea departe, se apropia iarăşi. . . .
Şi trenul trecea trufaş pe lângă satele româneşti, pe unele spintecându-
le chiar ca un tiran neîndurător, şi doar pe alocuri se oprea câte-o clipă,
însemnându-şi oprirea cu vorbe aspre ungureşti care zoreau sau huiduiau veşnic pe ţăranii drumeţi sau slujitori. . . . Pe urmă veneau gările
mari, anticamerele oraşelor, şi ţăranii nu se mai zăreau. În schimb,
apăreau surtucari grăbiţi, gălăgioşi, nerăbdători, vorbind poruncitor numai în grai străin.* (523)

The landscape unfolds as a sequence of villages and small towns inhabited by
peasants and townsmen (the latter are referred to as *surtucari*, after their urban
jackets). Viewed from the train, the Transylvanian landscape maps itself neatly
as either the country or the city.[83] What the novel adds to this dynamic is a strong
linguistic dimension: most inhabitants of the country speak Romanian, while
city dwellers speak mostly Hungarian and Saxon (and occasionally French).[84]
The Transylvanian railway system striates the land, offering trajectories of travel.
Importantly, this is also a literary landscape within the inter-imperial parameters
reproduced by *ACLU*: the country is largely illiterate, the producer of folklore;
the city is literate in Hungarian and German, the producer of literature. The tension is mediated by the character of Titu, who belongs to the rural world of the
peasants but is also an aspiring writer; he would go on to transform the world
of the peasants into the stuff of his literary projects. But to become a writer, Titu
must first travel to the large Romanian-speaking city, which provides the necessary literary institutions. From the vantage point of the train window, Titu
struggles to rewrite the land, country and city, in the Romanian language—in
the process, rendering all other local languages foreign.

There is a clear linguistic division of labor underwriting the language regime
in Rebreanu's village. Titu's father strategically "passes for Magyarized [*face pe
unguritul*]" (631) by speaking Hungarian in public, while at home he plays the
Romanian nationalist. Slowly, however, this division of labor translates into comprador complicity: "moving to the state school was like deserting to the enemy.
A Romanian who had to teach Romanian children to speak only Hungarian is
no longer a Romanian, but a renegade proper (*Apoi a trece la stat însemna într-
un fel o dezertare la vrăjmaş. Românul care trebuie să înveţe pe copiii români să
vorbească numai ungureşte nu mai e român, ci renegat sadea*)" (69, 97). Accusing someone of being a *renegade* constitutes a most injurious insult. Within a
symbolic linguistic war, a renegade is a deserter, a traitor; *dezertare la vrăjmaş*

means "to cross over to the enemy."[85] Aside from Titu's father, who is presented as a sympathetic character because of his generational position and gendered family obligations, *Ion* offers a gallery of minor characters who function as despicable renegades.

The Invention of Monoglottism

Meltzl's theoretical writings strongly opposed nationalism: "every nation today insists on the strictest monoglottism (*starrsten Monoglottismus*), by considering its own language superior or even destined to rule supreme (*Allein-Herrschaft*). This is a childish competition (*kindischer Wettlauf*) whose result will finally be that all of them remain—inferior."[86] Meltzl strongly opposed the linguistic competition and the ensuing hierarchy. Yet the editorial politics of *ACLU*, especially the theory of decaglottism, did not fully placate nationalism. By promoting the duo Petőfi and Eötvös as authors of world literature and relegating the literary production of other Transylvanian groups to the category of folk literature (even a folk literature with literary dimensions), *ACLU*'s editorial politics exacerbated nationalism. In the next generation, Rebreanu tried to redress this perceived injustice.

In resistance to the Transylvanian inter-imperial linguistic hierarchy, numerous characters in Rebreanu's novel proudly declare, in Romanian, "I don't speak Hungarian!" On his way to Romania, Titu declares his independence the same way (374, 525). Clearly, Titu does not mean "I cannot speak Hungarian," since he has spent most of the novel bragging about his proficiency in the Hungarian language; instead, he means "I won't speak Hungarian any longer." Monolingualism has become an agenda. Note the irony of a trajectory from multilingualism to monolingualism as a return to one's native language in an inter-imperial context. As postcolonial theorists such as Ngũgĩ wa Thiong'o have argued, because language functions as one of the most important vehicles of domination, a return to the native language and its transformation into a literary language are perceived as necessary.[87]

After Titu's sister Laura visits Cluj/Kolozsvár/Klausenburg, she writes a letter to her family: "I liked Cluj very much, a big and beautiful city, but it seemed strange not to hear one word of Romanian [*Mi-a plăcut mult Clujul, oraș mare și frumos, dar mi s-a părut straniu că n-am auzit nici o vorbă românească*]" (256, 359). Later in the novel, echoing his sister's letter, Titu fantasizes about a future Cluj: "He already pictured it, his imagination taking him on its stormy wings. . . . Here he is in Cluj, where he had been once, years ago. Everywhere, one could hear only Romanian [*o zugrăvea de pe acuma și închipuirea îl ducea pe aripi furtuno-*

ase. . . . Iată-l în Cluj, unde a fost o singură dată cu câţiva ani în urmă. Pretutindeni numai grai românesc]" (265, 372). Titu dreams of modernity as urbanization, which, ironically, would occur through the migration of Romanian peasants and the lower middle classes to the largely Hungarian, Saxon, and Jewish cities, aiding his own ascent to the status of Romanian Transylvanian bourgeoisie.

Whereas Rebreanu's peasant character Ion fights for land redistribution, his intellectual counterpart Titu wants everyone—Hungarians, Saxons, Jews, Armenians, and Roma—to speak Romanian. The irony is that Titu wants to hear only *grai românesc* in Cluj/Kolozsvár/Klausenburg, a majoritarian Hungarian city. The suggestion is that the path to political sovereignty necessarily passes through linguistic sovereignty, which in turn is conceived as national monolingualism. This argument resonates in a speech by Ioan Meţianu in the Budapest parliament, in which he stated, "individuals can speak perfectly two or even more languages, but history knows no nation with two languages [*Indivizi pot să vorbească perfect două, ori chiar mai multe limbi, dar popor cu două limbi nu cunoaşte istoria neamurilor*]."[88] It is a striking aphorism, giving voice to a monolingual imperative. The outcome of the Transylvanian linguistic conflict would seem to demand multilingualism and translation, in the spirit theorized by Gloria Anzaldúa in another border region of the world.[89] In this case, however, the outcome is not the overcoming of Magyarization and the return to a multilingual Transylvania, but a reversal. Having been Germanized and then Magyarized, Transylvania would now be Romanianized.[90] Hungarian would be replaced by Romanian as the state language of a projected unitary people. "In the sea of Romanians, foreigners disappeared [*În marea de români, străinii dispăruseră*]" (378, 531), Titu reflects in the largely Saxon city of Sibiu/Hermannstadt/Nagyszeben.

After 1918, this desideratum led to Romanian migration to Transylvanian cities and new educational and linguistic reforms. The university in Cluj/Kolozsvár/Klausenburg, the site of Meltzl's *ACLU*, reopened in 1919 with a new Romanian-language professoriate. In a reversal of "Only Hungarian! Only Hungarian!" posters admonished students to "speak only Romanian."[91] The university would become a home for intellectuals working, among other things, to create a national literature aligned with the literature across the Carpathians—and with the world literature *ACLU* cultivated.[92] The inter-imperial history of Transylvania would now be filtered through the lens of a majoritarian Romanian nationalism. This nationalism imagined itself as anti-imperial, but it acquired its own imperial dimensions in its claim that Romanians were "the worthy descendants . . . of the world's masters [*urmaşi vrednici ai stăpânilor lumii*]" (247, 346). Framing themselves as descendants of the Romans, Romanian nationalists aimed to turn the situation upside down—making themselves the masters (recall that we saw Ion represented as a conqueror in chapter 1).[93] The Roman

Empire was invoked in the colonization of the Americas, and the legacy of that same empire, particularly the Latinity of the Romanian language, served the nationalist needs of Transylvanian Romanians. This was an oxymoronic form of nationalist anti-imperial historicism, with its own imperial undertones.[94] Its goal was the recovery of preimperial times (all the way back to a mythical Roman Empire) that were currently being devalued (debates in the Budapest parliament regularly mocked the premise that Romanians were descendants of Romans). A parallel narrative of worthiness and continuity in the land was traced through religion (see chapter 7).

Niculaie Gheran's biography of Rebreanu parallels Titu's development in *Ion*. Gheran argues that Rebreanu found his identity as a writer through the Romanian language. According to this narrative, Rebreanu's "spiritual maturity coincides with his abandonment of foreign languages." Gheran's idea that Rebreanu had to "unburden" himself of "foreign languages" goes hand in hand with a quasi-religious revelation that "darkness became light," leading to the "miracle" of Rebreanu's writing in Romanian.[95] Against this narrative, widely reproduced by Romanian literary criticism, we believe that Rebreanu chose to write in Romanian not because he found his soul and the soul of his nation reflected in it but as a response to what Jahan Ramazani calls "linguistic estrangement"—as an inter-imperial literary gesture.[96] Rebreanu's literary monolingualism is an inter-imperial invention.[97]

The Romanian language was claimed by Transylvanian Romanian nationalists through its association with Romance languages. Therefore, the learning of Romance languages, especially French but also Italian, was cultivated. The inter-imperiality of Transylvanian Romanians cross-pollinated with that of Romanians in Wallachia and Moldova—and Romania after 1859. The latter had a different imperial history that involved the Ottoman Empire, the Russian Empire, and a semicolonial cultural relation to France.[98] Most important for Rebreanu's text was the regular use of French in Romanian public spaces and the arts. In an inter-imperial spirit, Titu resists the use of the French language as well. He immigrates to Romania not because it is a monoglot haven but because he believes it, too, needs reform. A friend who recently visited Romania describes to Titu "towns poisoned by luxury and debauchery, serfs wriggling in the dark, townsmen ashamed to speak Romanian and proud to be chatting in French, smug upstarts who know neither God nor law [*orașe otrăvite de lux și desfrâu, clăcași ce se zvârcolesc în beznă, surtucari cărora li-e rușine să vorbească românește și se fălesc sporovăind franțuzește, ciocoi spilcuiți care nu cunosc nici Dumnezeu, nici lege*]" (193, 274). If Titu resists a Transylvania where Hungarian is the language of the land, he also resists a Romania where Romanians chat in French—a sin akin to depravity and lawlessness.[99]

As the novel progresses and Titu encounters renegade characters, speakers of either Hungarian or French, he experiences an awakening and grows increasingly disenchanted with his multilingual prowess. His sister reports that "[Romanians] are forced to say in Hungarian that they are Romanian [*sunt siliți să spună pe ungurește că sunt români*]" (144, 205), an existential impossibility in the age of nationalism. As a result, Titu decides to become a writer, a poet. He wants to help the nation through his writing, deploying the Romanian language as a symbolic weapon. In the Budapest parliament, Transylvanian Romanian representatives used Romanian literature as evidence of not only equality with European nations but also superiority over Hungarian literature.[100] Rebreanu posits Titu and, by extension, his own novel as necessary ingredients in the nationalist struggle. At the same time, the novel frames the *youthfulness* of Titu's hyperbolic nationalism. The novel placates its overflowing nationalism with a sustained, implacable irony that often renders Titu's rhetorical flourishes ridiculous.[101] Arguably, this irony—worthy of the Hero of Solferino in Joseph Roth's *Radetzky's March*—constitutes one of the text's most legible signs of modernism.[102] Without its irony, the novel would risk foreclosure of the realization that vernacular authenticity constitutes the other face of Orientalism.[103] Most importantly, irony seeps into the novel's metanarrative: the thematic case for monolingualism is made through a Romanian-language text that enlists the other languages of Transylvania in its composition.

The novel, published in 1920 and rewritten between 1918 and 1920, offers a retrospective explanation of why linguistic Magyarization did not have the desired effect. Keith Hitchins reports, "In 1880 the number of Romanians who indicated they knew Magyar was 5.7 percent: in 1900 it has risen to 8.7 percent and in 1910 to 12.7 percent."[104] Although the linguistic laws that attempted to force the population of Transylvania to learn Hungarian worked in the case of Armenian and Jewish minorities, they ricocheted when applied to Transylvanian Romanians and produced, among other things, Romanian linguistic nationalism—a claim to monoglottism.[105] In light of this new Romanian nationalism, the polyglottism advocated by Mocioni in 1868 fell out of favor. Transylvanians would continue to be multilingual, but they would not necessarily learn one another's languages.[106] Instead, in their march to modernity mediated through coloniality, they would learn West European languages such as French, Italian, and, once again, German—languages of knowledge production on a world-systemic scale. As interglottism spurs monoglottism, regional inter-imperiality breeds nationalism and spurs global coloniality.

If Meltzl's *ACLU* and its principle of polyglottism are to function as a foundation for a reimagined comparatism, they must be rehistoricized within the Austro-Hungarian situation in conversation with other Transylvanian figures, including Rebreanu. To celebrate *ACLU*'s polyglottism, as we should, we need to acknowledge that its desire for the global also yielded a failure to engage with the contemporary debate on Transylvanian interglottism. In light of this recontextualization, comparatism could develop a much-needed typology of heterogeneous poly- and interglottisms. As we proposed in the introduction, this project can be conceived only through the creolization of theory, including the theory that underwrites the narratives we tell about the foundation of the discipline of comparative literature.

THE INTER-IMPERIAL DOWRY PLOT
Nationalism, Women's Labor,
Violence against Women

In previous chapters, we linked the struggle over land to Transylvania's inter-imperial history and argued that this history must be understood in terms of a global framework within which Transylvania was slowly and unevenly integrated into the capitalist world-economy. Chapters 2 and 3 traced the racializing dimensions of this process, while chapter 4 unpacked the complex linguistic politics attending it. This chapter analyzes the gender dynamics at work in inter-imperial nationalisms and in the trans-imperial agencies of nationalist actors. Violence against women often sustains inter-imperial nationalisms, even as they draw on the invisible labor of women. Returning and adding to the analysis of Rebreanu's novel in previous chapters, we argue that the portrait of the novel's main female character constitutes a symptom of an inter-imperial predicament that sidelines projects of gender emancipation in the service of prioritizing anti-imperial struggles.

Rebreanu's novel creates an intricate Transylvanian social universe—a miniature rural world situated in a complex network of asymmetrical global relations. Class divides this world into peasants and the rural lower middle class; each group has its own echelons and hierarchies that intersect with other group-building distinctions—ethnicity, race, language, religion. Equally consequential is the place-specific mode by which gender crisscrosses this rural world and inflects these categories. The plot concerning inter-imperial landownership is gendered, and so is the anti-imperial nationalist narrative; capitalist integration, secularisms, and romantic plots are gendered. So is violence. This chapter examines the gender configurations underpinning one of Rebreanu's female literary portraits: Ana, the young peasant woman in *Ion* and the title character's wife.

We place our analysis against the background of a developed women's movement globally and in the Austro-Hungarian Empire and an emerging women's writing tradition.[1] In the Austro-Hungarian Empire, these movements congealed in Vienna, developed in parallel in Budapest, and remained largely urban and bourgeois. On account of his rural location at the periphery of the Austro-Hungarian Empire, the young Rebreanu might well have been unaware of some of the permutations of the global debates about gender. It is hard to visualize Rebreanu reading Mina Loy's "Feminist Manifesto" (1914), for example. It is difficult to imagine Rebreanu as Sigmund Freud's contemporary (*Beyond the Pleasure Principle* was published in 1920, the same year as *Ion*). In matters of gender and sexuality, a metropolis like Vienna (not to mention Paris or New York or Shanghai) and a small village in Transylvania are separated by a distance that in some respects feels like an abyss. But it is clear that Rebreanu, who lived in Budapest for a short time (1903–1906) and then in Bucharest, must have encountered these cities' diverse networks of women's organizations, but chose not to acknowledge their concerns. Rather than address modern gender dynamics, we argue, his text mandates their silencing. In this chapter, we make a case for the legibility of layers of gendered silence. How does the inter-imperial method help us read the scale and hybridity of this silence?

The fact that Rebreanu's novel is in dialogue with global modernism when it comes to gender and sexuality does not mean that it features modern female characters or explores women's desires, or that it experiments with alternatively gendered literary forms. One of the methodological insights of feminist criticism since the 1980s, especially postcolonial feminist criticism, hinges on a premise that we propose to return to and develop: the critic needs to analyze both what texts articulate and what they mute or outright suppress. The latter task, resulting in the reading of a range of heterogeneous silences, is crucial when working with difficult archives—in this case, texts written by interested male authors in an inter-imperial, semiperipheral space.[2] In this chapter, we divide gendered silence into five modalities: (1) the silencing of female characters' speech, (2) the silencing of narrative outrage over sexual violence, (3) the rendering of women's labor invisible, (4) silence as a form of piety, and (5) the naturalist deployment of female suicide as fate. We argue that the framing of silence constitutes one of the text's most forceful signs of semiperipheral modernism. To stage this discussion, we first unpack the relation between the land question and gender as produced by the paramount modern colonial institution of citizenship.

Gender, Property, and Citizenship

The social status of Transylvanian women is a function of uneven access to the institution that mediates relationships with the imperial state: citizenship. Critics usually position the question of Transylvanian citizenship in an ethnic frame of reference (Romanian and Saxon Transylvanians have fewer rights than their Hungarian counterparts). We deploy a world-historical perspective that considers race, ethnicity, and gender as they relate to Transylvanian Romanian women's access to citizenship. Citizenship rights emerged in the immediate aftermath of the French Revolution, at which time rights were granted to male property owners, whose ability to pay taxes and contribute to the maintenance of social order qualified them as "active citizens." Women, foreigners, and children were defined as "passive citizens" and denied political rights.[3] This distinction was colonially and therefore racially inflected: in the case of white West European women, their status as passive citizens was considered a temporary circumstance that would be remedied by educational measures. The French constitution of 1793 extended active citizenship to all adult (not necessarily propertied) males, leaving women to derive their membership in the social community from their relationship to men.

In the colonial context, the reduction of enslaved Africans to commodities deprived them of any gender status comparable to that of citizens. In the French colony of St. Domingue, where the revolution led by Toussaint-Louverture resulted in the abolition of slavery in 1794, the racially constructed notion of skin color took precedence over property as a criterion for the granting of citizenship. Not all whites were property owners, but many free mulattos were, so the colonial assembly gave nonpropertied whites the right to vote even before this was accomplished in France. However, both enslaved people and mulattos were excluded from the franchise after a series of heated debates.[4] The argument used by both white planters and poor whites at the close of the eighteenth century was that the unfree and nonwhites were not part of the nation and therefore could not become citizens. The debate over citizenship in St. Domingue resonated globally. The question of who is considered part of the nation—materially and symbolically—has remained one of the tests for citizenship.

After the end of the enslavement trade, plantation owners increasingly depended on the natural reproduction of the enslaved population to maintain the necessary labor supply. Enslaved women's birth strikes—documented in the British Caribbean at the beginning of the nineteenth century and in German Southwest Africa at the turn of the twentieth century—seriously affected planters' plans to ensure a sufficient supply of cheap labor. At the same time, laws against racially mixed marriages, which varied widely in scope across the colonial world, included the loss of citizenship and voting rights for both partners and their offspring in Germany's African colonies in the early twentieth century. In turn, informal sexual relationships between white male colonists and black women were encouraged as long as they did not produce children.[5] In the process, the notion of Europeanness as whiteness was reinforced not only in relation to the colonies but also in terms of the racialization of European Others through citizenship laws.[6] The institution of marriage, which granted citizenship rights to white European women through their husbands, was enlisted to deny citizenship to racialized populations. These measures were aimed primarily at preventing the nonwhite population from acquiring property and thus achieving voting rights.

Such measures were echoed in the European east by similar attempts to deny rights to local racialized populations, especially those with a history of enslavement—the Romani people. Seen as a threat to the social and political order of enlightened European states on account of their nomadism, Roma were supposed to be "civilized" into European citizenship through settlement, compulsory labor, conversion, and military service. As of 1863, legal residence in a community of the Habsburg monarchy could be acquired only through birth or marriage, yet Romani births and marriages were often unregistered, making it impossible for them to prove citizenship. In 1890 the Austrian Interior Ministry demanded that local authorities register all people of Romani descent in their districts. Six years later, local authorities were prohibited from furnishing Roma with passports allowing them to travel abroad.[7] Citizenship was thus withdrawn from racialized populations in East Europe against a background of enslavement and regulation. This legacy disproportionately affected Romani women's citizenship rights, whose racialization, as discussed in chapter 3, was tied to gendered stereotypes of sexual availability and promiscuity.

Scholars in the diverse fields of the sociology of inequalities and legal studies have recently redirected attention to the key role citizenship has played in the unequal distribution of opportunities on a global scale. Legal scholar Ayelet Shachar traces the Western institution of citizenship back to the feudal *entail*, a legal means of restricting the succession of property to descendants of a designated estate owner, as practiced in medieval England.[8] The land regime in Transylvania has likewise been anchored in entail—to the benefit of Hungarian owners of large estates. The entail of property kept land in the hands of dynastic families by entrenching birthright succession and forbidding future generations to alter the estates they inherited. It was this institution that, according to Shachar's analysis, shaped the modern principle of determining West European citizenship based on jus soli (right of soil) and jus sanguinis (right of blood, or descendance from citizen parents). The entail of citizenship helped preserve the state's wealth in the hands of designated "heirs of membership titles"—the state's citizens—by allocating political membership at birth and excluding noncitizens from the same opportunities.[9]

Similarly, Roberto Korzeniewicz and Timothy Moran's *Unveiling Inequality: A World-Historical Perspective* argues that national citizenship has been the best indicator of an individual's position in the world income structure for the past two centuries.[10] The two scholars trace the high rates of inequality in most of Latin America, the Caribbean, and Africa back to systematic exclusion based on ascriptive criteria such as race, ethnicity, and gender, all of which historically limited access to economic, social, and political opportunities to a tiny elite. In turn, low inequality rates in all of West Europe and parts of East Europe, as well as in Australia, Japan, and Canada, can be attributed to the relatively widespread extension of property and political rights derived from achieved characteristics, such as education, which has facilitated the development of redistribution regimes. Thus, for Shachar as well as for Korzeniewicz and Moran, the institutionalization of citizenship ensured the social and political rights of the populations in West European nation-states, while selectively excluding colonial subjects and populations racialized as nonwhite, non-European, or non-Western from those same rights.

The reconceptualization of citizenship illuminates the workings of the institution from its emergence in the context of the French Revolution. On the one hand, the gradual extension of citizenship rights from propertied white males to all white males and then to white women accounted for the gradual development of low inequality in continental France by the eighteenth century. On the other hand, the categorical exclusion of St. Domingue's black and mulatto population from French citizenship, irrespective of their property status, ensured the maintenance of high inequality between France and St. Domingue/Haiti, as well as between other Western colonial powers and their colonial possessions. It becomes clear that the entail of property on which Shachar based the entail of citizenship was a colonial entail. Both the entail of property and the colonial entail of citizenship helped preserve inherited property, in the form of material goods themselves and the *right to* such goods—state support, social services, and infrastructure—in the hands of the (racially, ethnically, and geopolitically) designated heirs to the colonial enterprise.[11]

In a crucial decolonial reversal of terms, St. Domingue's first constitution after it became the independent republic of Haiti in 1805 aimed to erase the differences that had made a racial hierarchy possible. To that end, it ruled that all Haitians, including white women and members of naturalized ethnic groups such as Germans and Poles living on the island, would be referred to by the generic term *black*. Gerald Horne describes the crafting of a "radically new concept of citizenship: that only those denoted as 'black' could be citizens, revalorizing what had been stigmatized. Yet 'black' was defined expansively—unlike 'white'—to mean those that rejected both France and slavery, meaning that even a 'white' could be defined as black as long as he or she repudiated the logic of racial slavery that intended that only 'whites' should rule and Africans should serve."[12]

In the following, we ask how this global history of citizenship, anchored in coloniality, played out in an inter-imperial situation in a particular region of East Europe. Landownership in Transylvania was regulated by entail, which kept land in the hands of a small number of families throughout the early modern period. These families negotiated their privileges (most importantly, their tax exemptions) with a number of conflicting imperial formations—the Habsburg Empire, the Ottoman Empire, the Russian Empire, and the Austro-Hungarian Empire. The rise of nationalism at the end of the eighteenth century brought the convergence of ethnos, language, and land—and the realization that Transylvanian land was largely in the hands of the Hungarian nobility (with exceptions, and in a complex asymmetric dynamic with the Transylvanian Saxon and Romanian populations) and that the two racialized groups of Transylvania have been excluded from property. Despite claims of a widespread Enlightenment project, this nobility preserved a serfdom-based labor structure well into the nineteenth century. Serfs spoke Hungarian, Saxon, and Romanian. This was a complex ethnic *and* racial field, as it operated through the racialized exclusion of both Jewish and Romani populations from property ownership until the late nineteenth century. In this chapter, we trace the turn-of-the-century imbrication of the dowry plot with the de facto exclusion of Transylvanian Romanian women from citizenship through the silencing of their claims to both property and labor.

Modernist Naturalism on the Periphery of European Empires

One influential narrative of metropolitan global modernism revolves around the figure of the so-called New Woman. At the turn of the twentieth century, white European women started to enter the labor force in large numbers; they rented their own spaces and began to move away from the family household, and they plotted courses that did not necessarily end in marriage. Women become artists, and female writers around the world entered the literary professions. This last development is perhaps most influentially captured by Virginia Woolf's novel *To the Lighthouse* (1927), which sets up a tension between a Victorian mother (Mrs. Ramsey) and a modernist female artist (Lily Briscoe). "I did my best to kill her," Woolf writes of the Angel in the House, the Victorian model of femininity ambiguously embodied by Mrs. Ramsey.[13] The symbolic killing of the Angel in the House is undertaken by a text that experiments with and develops innovative literary forms attuned to the shock of this modern turn in gender roles.

For the most part, the New Woman makes her appearance in urban literary settings, which allow anonymity and thus gender experimentation. This chapter is concerned with the question of how modernist global debates about gender resonate when viewed through the country v. city lens in an inter-imperial framework (there is no anonymity in the countryside). How does a young peasant woman in a semiperipheral region participate in the global modernist phenomenon? How do changes in gender dynamics become legible when women do not leave patriarchally conforming roles behind, given that anti-imperial nationalism often cohabitates with and cultivates hegemonic forms of masculinity?[14] What is at stake when modernism enacts the fate of a peasant woman apparently stuck in tradition? What literary forms are deployed in the service of such representations? And how do they help us creolize the modern in both modernity and modernism?

Departing from conventions of periodization that pit realism and naturalism against modernism (such that modernism comes after and supersedes realism), we read Rebreanu's novel as a text that, as a sign of its semiperipheral condition, registers the convergence of naturalism and modernism. The Warwick Research Collective drew attention to the fact that Theodor Adorno's defense of modernism is a defense of its realist inclinations, insofar as "modernist techniques are affirmed not for their own sake but because they are taken to register and resonate with the systemic crisis of European modernity in the late nineteenth and early twentieth centuries."[15] They thus reframe the contours of modernism to include literary phenomena that mix modernist experimentation with realist forms, including naturalism. The authors conclude: "To read modernist literature in the light of combined and uneven development is then to read it with one eye to its realism."[16] The critical task becomes to describe the workings of realism *within* modernism.

Rebreanu's use of modernist naturalism in 1920 has world-historical resonance. Jennifer Fleissner argues consequentially that the figure of the New Woman enters the international literary scene much earlier than the high modernist moment, certainly earlier than Woolf, starting in 1890s naturalism.[17] The modern anxiety concerning changes in gender dynamics found its first literary representations in naturalism. This insight is even more forceful in a global modernist context.[18] The global dimensions of naturalism include its popularity in Brazil and Argentina in the 1880s and 1890s, opening a comparative arc between Transylvania and the South American countries where many East Europeans migrated in the nineteenth century. It also includes the convergence of literature and the social sciences enlisted in the study of modernity. Rebreanu's naturalism draws from psychology and criminology, and it imagines itself as a companion project to the ethnography and sociology of the region. Confirming the novel's own framing, the Romanian-language reception of *Ion* insisted on both its modernity and its objectivity.[19] This mix of impulses invites a critical collaborative reading across the humanities and the social sciences that reconfigures our "stagist accounts of realism and modernism."[20]

If naturalism often gives voice to modern anxieties about gender through the theme of prostitution (Émile Zola's *Nana*), Rebreanu's text, though receptive to debates about prostitution in the Austro-Hungarian Empire, dramatizes such anxieties through the rural dowry plot.[21] The dowry plot involves negotiations by which women are bartered into marriage as a means of transferring land. At the turn of the century, feminists explicitly compared marriage based on economic interests to prostitution.[22] Rebreanu gives this naturalist plot an inter-imperial trajectory. The question of landownership is imbued with Transylvania's history: land was historically owned primarily by Hungarian and Saxon nobles and urban merchants, while Transylvanian Romanians, predominantly a population of peasants, were excluded from ownership, alongside Jews and Roma. Land thus became the primary object of desire for the Transylvanian Romanian nationalist struggle. The dowry plot, a profoundly gendered transaction, concerns the transfer of land from one generation to the next and, with it, the transfer of citizenship rights by which landownership is secured.

Dowry and Virginity

Rebreanu's novel introduces the character of Ana in the opening scene, the Sunday dance described in chapter 3. Ana, who has a relatively large dowry (consisting of land), appears in the novel as the object of the main character's highly choreographed, economically motivated seduction. From the beginning, Ana seems destined to suffer: "Ana's elongated, sunburnt face, a signboard of much suffering, saddened [*Fața Anei, lunguiață, arsă de soare, cu o întipărire de suferințe, se posomorî*]" (18, 24).[23] Ana's physiognomy (destiny made face) carries traces of her outdoor labor and her past and future trauma. Both the novel and its reception translate the facial imprint of suffering into the language of ugliness. Ana, the text tells the reader, is simply and factually ugly. The implication is that the only thing Ana has to offer is a dowry.

Repeatedly, Ana is compared to plants and animals: "she drifted like a sickly reed, lifeless, scrawny [*se legăna în mers, ca o trestie bolnăvicioasă, fără vlagă, slăbănoagă*]" (45, 64). This sustained comparison to animals belongs to the woman-land connection analyzed in chapter 1. Ana does not resist or otherwise fight this characterization. She waits patiently for a series of blows to fall: "The girl crouched on the oven, like a guilty dog, eyes to the ground [*Fata se ghemui pe vatră, ca un câine vinovat, cu ochii în pământ*]" (151, 215). The reader recognizes the aesthetics of naturalism in Ana's gesture-turned-body and the idiom of fate. Empathy with Ana's suffering is out of the question. The emotion produced by the text is repulsion.

An ambitious and upwardly mobile young peasant, Ion attempts to convince himself that he loves Ana, despite her ugliness. Marriage to Ana would bring Ion land and, possibly, access to the institutions of citizenship in the Austro-Hungarian Empire. His attempts at self-persuasion are unsuccessful, however: "How frail she looks and ugly! . . . How can one hold her dear? [*Cât e de slăbuță și de urâțică! . . . Cum să-ți fie dragă?*]" (44, 63). Initially unaware of his economic motives, Ana loves Ion. She misreads the nature of the plot: while Ana functions in a romantic scenario, Ion and her father, Vasile, operate in the economic framework of landownership, itself linked to inter-imperial pressures. Ana desires Ion, but Ion desires Ana's land.

Ana's love for Ion is daring, a sign of a modern aspiration to marry for love rather than to fulfill a parental economic arrangement. The novel's text registers a mutation in the rural discourse on love.[24] Ana knows that she belongs to her father, but she desires and pursues Ion anyway. What the father claims, in particular, is Ana's virginity, which will be transferred through marriage. Vasile tells George, Ana's other suitor: "I'll give you the girl and you'll take your whip and get the crazy ideas out of her head! [*Io-ți dau fata, iar tu să ai bici, să-i scoți din cap gărgăunii!*]" (23, 32). Note that the father encourages his potential son-in-law to beat Ana into submission using a whip, otherwise reserved for disciplining animals in the household. The word Rebreanu uses, *gărgăuni*, means "poisonous wasps"; the idiom refers to the action of driving poisonous wasps out of a rebellious woman's head, a version of the taming of the shrew. The modernity of Ana's desire rests in the whims she hopes to embrace, against all odds. Such whims have global resonance in 1920. They are discernible in Rebreanu's text, but not as a full-fledged female revolt. There is a sense that such whims constitute luxurious indulgences in a world that has real problems to deal with—the anti-imperial struggle. Nineteenth-century socialism relegated both nationality and gender to side issues (*Nebenwidersprüche*, in Marxian terms) with respect to the international class struggle, while the anti-imperialism at work here recenters nationality but forfeits gender as secondary or even irrelevant.

With the unwitting help of Titu, the would-be nationalist intellectual, Ion concocts a strategy so that Vasile will give Ana to him, not to George. This plan, a game of give-and-take, involves three possible actors—Ion, George, and

Vasile—and, symbolically, Titu. Ana, who is one with the land, is the object of the transaction. Her agency consists of stealing her own virginity from her father and fraudulently giving it to Ion—a form of property theft. In other words, Ana revolts against the discourse of virginity in which the dowry plot is anchored by denying virginity its economic value and gifting it instead. All parties punish her for this act. When her father discovers that Ana is pregnant, he sends her to Ion, who declares: "I have nothing to settle with you, but I will talk to him and come to some arrangement [*Că eu cu tine n-am ce să mă sfătuiesc, dar cu dumnealui om vorbi și ne-om chibzui*]" (168, 238). Although she is not an agent in either the economic or the linguistic transaction, Rebreanu relentlessly foregrounds Ana's silence as a form of eloquence: "Ana alone never uttered a word, sighing like a criminal waiting for a verdict [*Numai Ana tăcea mâlc și suspina ca o osândită care-și așteaptă verdictul*]" (189, 268); "Ana, who had not spoken a word and of whom neither side took the slightest notice [*Ana, care nu rostise nici o vorbă și pe care nici n-o luaseră în seamă potrivnicii*]" (227, 318). Through these formulations, Rebreanu frames one modality of inter-imperial silence as the muting of women's speech.

The negotiation of landownership through marriage constitutes a version of what Gayle Rubin has called "the traffic in women"—a system in which men exchange women among themselves on a continuum ranging from prostitution to marriage.[25] Other male characters in the novel have obtained their land through marriage, including both Ana's father and Ion's father. The traffic in women is the law of the land, as implacable as the weather. Ion therefore thinks he is justified in treating Ana as a means to an end, "as if she did not come with the dowry [*parcă ea n-ar fi ținut de zestre*]" (212, 300). For her part, Ana eventually realizes that "she was nothing but a tool in man's hand [*o unealtă în mâinile bărbatului*]" (280, 394). The child born to Ana is likewise instrumentalized: "he was carrying in his arms all the land he had won [*duce în brațe tot pământul câștigat*]" (327, 458). We know that the traffic in women, metonymized in the dowry plot, is a familiar literary theme—across period and region. The challenge here is to assess its resignification as a function of an inter-imperial force field.

Rebreanu initially called his novel *The Dowry* (a more eloquent title than *Ion*). The word *dowry* (*zestre*) appears in the novel thirty-eight times. The issue of dowry is raised on both sides of the class structure. The two main female characters, peasant Ana and lower-middle-class Laura, both need a dowry, but different norms are in play, yielding a distinct transactional dynamic. Ana has a dowry and suffers the consequences of being transacted alongside it. Laura has no dowry, so she compensates for this lack by her middle-class, nationalist feeling. The conversation about the dowry hides the fact that, as Raymond Williams puts it, rural courting is "no more evidently moral than the advantageous sex of the town."[26] Prostitution is on the margins of the narrative, as both a dreaded possibility and a symbolic implication. Wrapped up in nationalist ideology, the economic transaction that puts women in circulation through marriage acquires a veneer of respectability, consecrated by religion. Rebreanu's modernist text dwells in the abyss between the claim to the nation's modernity and the apparent nonmodernity of gender oppression.

Rebreanu's Ana does not consent to the violent sexual act that determines her fate. Ana invites Ion into her father's house, which consists of one room, where her drunken father is snoring on one side. Most rural houses at this time had only one room, so it was common for sex to have a fairly public dimension.[27] Ana leads Ion to her bed on the built-in oven (*vatra*). She clearly desires Ion: "each night she felt a wild urge to melt away in the lad's arms, to give him the full proof of love [*simțea în fiecare seară tot mai nebună o pornire de a se topi în brațele flăcăului, de a-i da dovada întreagă a iubirii*]" (134, 191–92). It is equally clear, though, that the sexual act that follows is not a function of Ana's desire. Ana does not desire *this* sexual act. The sex scene is rapelike: "Then Ana began to whisper many complaints, to lament and to beg him to behave [*Apoi Ana începu să-i șoptească imputări multe, să se jelească și să-l roage să fie cuminte*]" (135, 193). As Ana cries and implores, afraid of both Ion and her father, Ion "shut her mouth with a kiss [*și-i astupă gura cu o sărutare*]" (135, 193). Ana continues her pleas: "'what do you want to do … what are you doing? … No … no … [*ce vrei să faci … ce faci? … Nu … nu …*]'" (136, 194). The narrator quickly dismisses Ana's pleas: "she blabbered in his ear, crying without resisting [*și-i lihăi în ureche, plângătoare dar fără împotrivire*]" (135, 193). This sentence is filtered through a narrator who claims access to characters' actions, thoughts, and emotions. Victims of sexual violence are expected to resist, and crying *is* a mode of resistance. Therefore, the rendering of Ana's pleas as "crying without resisting" constitutes an eloquent narrative strategy. It anticipates and placates a future charge of sexual violence. A second modality of silence thus diffuses the possibility of narrative outrage over sexual violence.

Ana initiates the sexual encounter, but she seems to have something other than penetrative sex in mind. When Ion initiates penetration, she begs him to stop. In Rebreanu's erotic universe, however, *no* often means *yes*. Later in the novel, Florica struggles against Ion's sexual advances as well, and *no* is again interpreted as *yes*. The text immediately refers to Ana and Ion as "the lovers [*îndrăgostiții*]" (136, 194). Rebreanu downplays Ion's sexual aggression, which he describes in his notes as a "deflowering [*deflorarea*]" (592), placing the event in the framework of virginity, with voyeuristic resonances.[28] In Rebreanu's aesthetic universe, the violent deflowering of Ana is part of the naturalist plot; it is dramatized as a form of nature (Ana as a flower), only vaguely in need of a responsible agent.[29]

Rebreanu deploys ellipses throughout the novel, to varying effect. The ellipses following the words *no* in this scene are perhaps the most consequential. What is being left unsaid? Or, rather, what do the ellipses articulate? What is the reader asked to infer when faced with this series of ellipses? These questions call for a return to Wolfgang Iser's reader-response theory, with an eye to its implications for situations of sexual violence. Echoing the gendered metaphorics of Iser's theory, the text plays with the reader, "revealing" or "concealing" things through its blanks, as if in an erotic game.[30] It is important to foreground the fact that Rebreanu's ellipses are not mere "gaps of indeterminacy" (Iser's phrase) to be filled in by the reader's desire. Ion's sexual violence against Ana occurs in the gaps between the words on the page. In these ellipses, the text structurally frames sexual violence as an unnamable secret shared by text and implied reader. That there is sexual violence is one of the text's "horizons of expectation." The text thus renders the reader an accomplice in the sexual violence. What happens, then, when we move from the implied reader, the reader in the text, to actual historical readers—and from reader-response theory to reception theory? Simply put, readers experience this scene in *Ion* differently because they relate differently to the reader implied by the text. They cannot help but accommodate some of the text's structuring mechanisms, including its blanks, but they might refuse others, as a function of their own heterogeneous histories. If the critic is a version of the reader, the same applies to the figure of the literary critic. It says a lot about Romanian literary criticism and its attending professoriate that this scene in Rebreanu's *Ion*—arguably the most canonical text in Romanian literature—has never led to a discussion of rape.[31]

Ana "loses" her virginity. The language of loss endures idiomatically, detracting from the fact that the loss is not Ana's but her father's—that is, his loss of leverage in the land transaction. Regardless of this distinction, Ana is now guilty within a religious narrative. A register of sin becomes operative. Shame and its affective responses take over (a novella Rebreanu wrote as a precursor to *Ion* was titled *Shame*). Ana, who has had sex once, having been coerced into it, becomes a "slut [*rapandulă*]" (163, 232). She has now been "defiled [*a pângărit-o*]" (160, 226). The implication is that Ana should have safeguarded her virginity, and her failure to do so renders her sinful.[32] Her body, displaying signs of pregnancy, becomes a target of abject interest in the village. The community participates in her ritual shaming. The site of this ritual is the main street in the village, where a visibly pregnant Ana walks when Ion refuses to welcome her into his house and sends her back to her father.

We have argued that the dowry plot belongs to an inter-imperial bind. Most immediately, Transylvanian inter-imperiality involves a tension within the Austro-Hungarian Empire—between Vienna and Budapest. Peasants negotiate their rights—their access to citizenship—trans-imperially, often claiming that their dependence on Vienna before the 1867 Compromise was more desirable than their current dependence on Budapest. Inter-imperiality also involves the Russian Empire, which intervened in the Hungarian revolution of 1848 and became a threatening presence in the region. But it is important to note that the inter-imperial nature of Transylvania at the turn of the twentieth century involves older imperial histories as well. Ana's walk of shame echoes an Ottoman-era custom in Romanian culture of sending a bride who turns out not to be a virgin back to her parents, as the community watches and throws abusive slurs at her.[33] This custom is highly resonant for the inter-imperial narrative. Rebreanu turns to "rural virtues" as custodians of the Romanian language and the Romanian culture within a nationalist, Occidentalist narrative that traces these virtues to the Roman Empire and thus to Latin Europe.[34] But he shows that the same village is also a custodian of Ottoman legacies. The text stages a tension not between empire and anti-imperial nationalism; rather, it pits multiple imperial histories, with heterogeneous temporalities, against one another. Gender is thus negotiated across empires and within multiple temporalities, between an Oriental (Ottoman) and an Occidental (Habsburg, Austro-Hungarian) empire and against the distant background of an ancient empire (Roman).

Rebreanu's text stages Ana's premarriage pregnancy as exceptional, although it is not historically uncommon. As the novel itself acknowledges, women in the region sometimes married while pregnant or after giving birth. It is, in fact, likely that many women had sexual relations before marriage, especially with their future husbands.[35] What is being invoked in Ana's case is a discourse on virginity, not the region's common practices. As we know from Michel Foucault, the more forceful the discourse prohibiting certain forms of sexuality, the more suspicious we should be of its success.[36] In other words, rules related to virginity exist because they are regularly transgressed. There is, however, a twist here as well, whereby the discourse on virginity intersects with inter-imperiality: if virginity is needed to guarantee paternity, in an inter-imperial space with a racially and ethnically mixed population, it is also needed to guarantee that reproduction happens within the ethnic and racial group. It is one thing for a man to be unsure whether a child is his biological offspring (this is Ion's ploy: Ana's child might or might not be his—who can be sure?). It is a different thing altogether to worry that one is raising a child fathered by a Hungarian, Romani, or Jewish man.[37] Only by surveying a woman's past (her virginity) can a man ascertain that he is the father—and the father of a Transylvanian Romanian child. The closedness of the virgin female body metonymically stands in for the closed nature of the ethnic and racial group.[38] In the *longue durée* of the coloniality of entail, virginity assures that property (land) is not alienated from the group, thus politically and symbolically tying threats to the imagined national body to women's bodies, consequently understood as in need of supervision and control. Simply put, virginity safeguards against the threat of creolization.

In the economy of the novel, therefore, only the immediate marriage of Ion and Ana can solve the problem of Ana's pregnancy. And if Ion is to marry a now-defiled Ana, a substantial dowry is needed to compensate for the loss of her virginity. An extravagant dowry makes up for a subpar bride. It materially and symbolically atones for the loss of pride associated with the failure to display a stained sheet after the wedding night. As in other parts of the world where civil and religious notions of marriage significantly overlap, marriage to the perpetrator of sexual violence solves the religious problem.[39] The gendered violence attached to this social mechanism is reenlisted in the acknowledgment that marriage constitutes the infrastructure for the inheritance of both property and citizenship—for the men of the ethnic and racial group. Women's complaints against this predicament register as whims (*gărgăuni*).

Dowry Lists

The dowry conflict is resolved through the negotiation of a marriage contract, mediated by the village priest and recorded by an imperial clerk. Eventually, the negotiators agree on the terms:

> He [Vasile] consented to give him [Ion] as dowry all his plots of land and both houses, on the sole condition of having them entered, after the wedding, in both Ion and Ana's name. For the time being, after the marriage, Ana would move into Glanetașu's house, together with a team of oxen, a horse, a cow with a calf, a sow with seven piglets, a new wagon and other sundries to which a young bride and wife is entitled. The same day they went together to the village clerk for the legal forms and then to the priest to have the banns put up, so that the wedding should be celebrated the second Sunday after Easter. (191)
>
> *Primi să-i dea zestre toate pământurile și amândouă casele, cerând doar să fie scrise, după cununie, pe numele amândurora. Deocamdată, după cununie, Ana se va muta la Glanetașu, împreună cu o pereche de boi, un cal, o vacă cu vițel, o scroafă cu șapte purcei, un car nou și altele mai mărunte ce se cuvin unei mirese și neveste tinere. În aceeași zi se duseră la notar pentru înștiințările legale și pe urmă la preot să facă strigările de cuviință așa fel ca nunta să se serbeze chiar a doua duminică după Paști. (271)*

Rebreanu's text dramatizes a crisis in the property culture of a Transylvanian village. At the time, most legal conflicts among peasants involved negotiations over the passing of land from one generation to the next.[40] Weaving documentary detail into its fictional fabric, the novel aspires to sociological relevance. The negotiations over Ana's dowry (*tocmeala*) require multiple meetings between the two families, one side represented by the bride's father and the other by the groom himself (his father is not considered manly enough).[41] They also involve the imperial state, which demands a marriage contract and a public record of the event. They implicate the church and the priest, who needs to publicly announce the wedding, which can happen only during certain times of the year (in this case, after Easter). And they marginally involve an old woman (*o babă*) in the village, representative of an older custom, who specializes in matchmaking and dowry negotiation. The negotiations thus engage a heterogeneous mix of secular-imperial and nationalist-religious interests (we complicate this distinction in chapter 7).[42]

Women in the Austro-Hungarian Empire could own property—insofar as they belonged to the same class, ethnic group, and racial group as male property owners. They could inherit family property.[43] Theoretically, this legal provision should have made them strong economic agents. Women's right to own property also should have opened avenues for citizenship. In practice, however, female ownership was selectively implemented at the edge of the empire, or it was implemented as a maneuver in negotiations between men. Vasile does not want to give his property to Ion as dowry, and he uses the law that allows women to own property as a ploy. As for Ana, she is not an active citizen; in fact, she belongs on a list of goods. In assembling this list of property, an inventory of sorts, Rebreanu's novel aspires to documentary status.[44] Foremost on this list is the land Ana's father reluctantly passes on to Ion. This land is rendered in the plural (*pământurile*), given the reality of land fragmentation. Next come two houses, a sign of significant wealth; a variety of animals, with their reproductive prospects; household tools, such as a new wagon; and sundry necessities for a young wife, including her clothes, bedding, and kitchen tools. At the scale of a small Transylvanian village on the eastern edge of the Austro-Hungarian Empire, the property recorded as dowry anchors the owner's claims to subsistence, but also to the voting rights coveted by male peasants in this part of the empire. The novel's list appears to suggest that Vasile and subsequently Ion should have voting rights—but not Ana.

Crucially, Ana does not belong to this list in the same way that enslaved people belonged to lists detailing the holdings of estates until the mid-nineteenth century in neighboring Moldova and Wallachia. Unlike the enslaved, Ana is a legal subject, even though the law is not invested in protecting her rights. The rhetorical analogy to enslavement implied in the trope of the list foregrounds Ana's oppression, at the cost of erasing the regional history of enslavement traced in chapter 3. This is another juncture where Ana's lack of citizenship becomes inter-imperially inflected: if the text's silences frame Ana's lack of citizenship rights, the absence of any Romani women limits the novel's engagement with gender and race as they pertain to women's access to citizenship. The category "Transylvanian women" is crisscrossed by ethnic, racial, linguistic, and religious differences, yielding hierarchical access to citizenship rights. On account of her class, ethnicity, and language, Ana is close to the bottom of this hierarchy. Race, however, a neglected category of analysis in this context, places Romani women in an even more precarious predicament—a reality that, rather than framing as an eloquent silence, the text suppresses.

Women's Labor

Within the logic of the naturalist text, Ana's silence leads to her comparison with animals: "Ana was as humble and meek as a dog [*Ana era umilită și tăcută ca un câine*]" (251, 353). This proximity to animal abjection risks rendering Ana's endless, inherently human labor invisible: "She drudged like a servant-girl.... Ana alone had to carry the household load on her back [*Robotea ca o slujnică.... Ana singură trebuia să ducă in spinare toată gospodăria*]" (258, 363).[45] The Romanian word *slujnică* refers to a woman hired to do the housework—a maid or a servant. In her husband's household (*gospodărie*), Ana functions like an unpaid maid. She is not used in the land transaction and is subsequently discarded; she is put to work first in her father's household and then in Ion's. The narrative that renders women's strenuous labor invisible constitutes a third modality of silence with world-systemic dimensions, characterized by Maria Mies as "housewifization."[46] The term refers to the generalization of housework as women's work alongside the generalization of nonwage labor at the level of the world-economy. Both mechanisms reduce overall labor costs for global capital. As an unpaid housewife who systematically performs both productive and reproductive labor, Ana exemplifies the definition of women's subsistence labor.

It might seem that the novel limits Ana's spatial movements to the household. She cooks and takes food to family members working the land. The novel does not show Ana working in the fields, but it mentions a gendered division of labor pertaining to the fields as well: "work women generally did: hoeing, haymaking, carrying, and sowing [*lucrurile muierești: săpatul, pologul, căratul, semănatul*]" (39, 56). It is likely that, in addition to her housework, Ana attends to these tasks in the fields. But Ana also crosses the country-city divide through weekly trips to the city: "on Thursdays, when she went to the weekly fair in Armadia, with eggs, hens, cheese and butter [*Joia, ducându-se la bâlciul săptămânal în Armadia, cu ouă, păsări, brânză, lăptării*]" (97, 138–39). Most cities and small towns in Transylvania featured these markets, such as the one in Beiuș/Belényes/Binsch. Women's market activities functioned as a linchpin between an agricultural economy with a misleading feudal feel and world-market integration.[47] Ana sells largely what she produces herself—dairy products, in particular—but she also organizes and manages her work as a salesperson. This is income-generating labor. To keep this labor unpaid and not translate it into either status or rights, Ana's work is described as an extension of her domesticity, a natural propensity. Women field laborers in the British colonies were paid lower wages than men by virtue of the same assumption of domesticity and despite their higher survival rate and equal efficiency at estate work when compared to men.[48] Tellingly for these global connections, in his search of the most downtrodden man in Europe to compare to black laborers in the U.S. South, Booker T. Washington arrived at the conclusion that "the man farthest down in Europe is woman."[49]

The dowry plot is thus closely intertwined with Ana's invisibility as an economic agent: because the value of her labor is not recognized as either subsistence or wealth producing, the dowry compensates economically for her upkeep.[50] Her father has to pay an excessive dowry as if Ana were a parasite, as if she were just another mouth for Ion to feed. Rebreanu's novel registers this structural contradiction by meticulously recording Ana's work in ethnographic detail. One passage describes her laundry routine, which involves a complex sequence of activities: soaking the wash, boiling it, beating it with a wooden hammer (*cu maiu*), rinsing it in an ice-cold river, wringing it, and drying it. This is strenuous, time-consuming labor that stretches over several days. But to ensure that her labor remains invisible, Ana is repeatedly accused of laziness. Through this mechanism, the value extracted from Ana's unpaid and unrecognized labor accumulates into wealth that her father and then Ion claim for themselves. It also accumulates into capital within the inter-imperial narrative of economic nationalism traced in chapter 2.

Ana's birthing of her child is likewise framed as a mode of invisible labor. In that scene, Ana has just brought food to Ion's family, who are working the land that came with the marriage and harvesting wheat.[51] As Ana's labor pains start, the parties witnessing the scene are inconvenienced, worried that their food might be delayed. They continue to work while Ana shrieks in the background. "What, this is woman's fate! [*Ei, așa-i soarta femeiei!*]" (260, 366), Ion declares, as he continues to harvest. The almost cinematic juxtaposition of the birthing scene and the field work tracks another gendered distribution of labor: men work the fields, and women produce the children (despite sufficient evidence of women's work in the field). This is Rebreanu's novel at its most naturalist, staging the most implacable inertia, the cycle of biological reproduction. Two forms of fertility (woman and land) come together in the "editing" of this scene. The natural process of birth once again denies its status as work (despite the double meaning of *labor* as both productive and reproductive). This cycle is narrativized through a rhetoric of animalization, as Ion describes Ana's delivery as an inopportune act of "dropping her litter [*să fete*]," her cries of pain only briefly enlisting his empathy (*mila*) (260, 365). The naturalist text is descriptive and prescriptive at the same time: her whims notwithstanding, this is Ana's destiny, as it should be, give or take a few shades of trauma.

Violence against Women

Alongside sexual violence and in conjunction with it, Rebreanu's text traces the domestic violence rampant in the village of Pripas. Through brute physical violence, Ana's father imposes his will concerning his daughter's marital prospects. Rebreanu lingers extensively on this violence, at times describing it as a form of enjoyment, a "blood-thirsty pleasure [*plăcerea sângeroasă*]" (163, 232). The only other mode of masculine gratification is drinking, so these beatings come across as the *only* pleasure in the text. The novel itself often seems to take pleasure in recording violence. A structure of sadistic voyeurism is dramatized by the text, which inducts the reader into its gendered mechanisms.

Ana's beatings extend over time. Initially, Vasile Baciu beats his daughter for three days, as if part of a ritual, then every day for three weeks: "no day passed without his beating her, until he tired [*nu trecea zi să n-o bată, până ostenea*]" (168, 239). Once Ana moves into her husband's household, Ion starts to beat her, at first on rare occasions and then regularly: "since he could not calm down otherwise, he often beat Ana. . . . When he saw her crying, he got some relief [*neputându-se potoli altfel, bătea deseori pe Ana. . . . Numai când o vedea plângând, se mai răcorea*]" (258, 363). The novel suggests that Ana's humility (and sometimes her ugliness) triggers the violence, leading the men to beat her passionately. They find palliative relief in the pleasure of beating her. Repetition, a naturalist leitmotif, is deployed in the beating of women's flesh. The reader joins the villagers in watching the spectacle of violence, dutifully filling in the gaps framed by the numerous open-ended ellipses.

Domestic violence infiltrates every corner of Rebreanu's universe. Women are violent, too. Ion's mother, who is described as overly masculine, is violent toward Ana. Nor is violence limited to the world of the peasants; for example, the teacher's wife slaps a Romani servant (as detailed in chapter 3). When Laura, the lower-middle-class woman in Rebreanu's gender scheme, revolts against her marital prospects, her father (whose own father beat his mother daily) raises his fist to strike her. In this last context, across class, physical violence functions more as a threat than reality, but it is certainly palpable. Women and racial minorities suffer both physical blows and the psychological terror (*groaza*) that accompanies their possibility. Rebreanu's biography reports that his own mother used violence to discipline her children: "as she talks, she hits [*cum zice, cum lovește*]."[52] In the wider Romanian-language cultural context, domestic violence is often rationalized as a mode of pedagogy,[53] or sometimes love.[54]

When Vasile starts to beat Ana, the villagers gather, watch, and verbally entreat him to stop. With one exception, they do not interfere. Their explanation, stated aphoristically by the narrator, has the force of a proverb: "every man is master in his own yard and no stranger may interfere, regardless of what one is doing [*omul, orice ar face în ocolul lui, e stăpân și străinul n-are ce să se amestece*]" (164, 233). Vasile Baciu is the master of his house. In the context of a novel embedded in an inter-imperial struggle over land, one is reminded that a master needs property, including land, to become or remain a master. Once he is a master, he has absolute rights within his domain. Violence is claimed as such a right, parallel to a state's monopoly on violence as a guarantor of social order.[55] Anyone interfering in another man's house becomes a stranger (*străin*), a word otherwise used by Rebreanu to refer to non-Romanians in the inter-imperial space. Indeed, only the Jewish character Avrum intercedes on Ana's behalf, seemingly as a function of foreignness (as analyzed in chapter 2). The Romanian Transylvanian characters, their voices one with the modernist narrator, collectively accept and respect Vasile's mastery of his house. Violence is intimately linked to inter-imperiality: not allowing Vasile to be master in his own house would go against the collective desire for mastery of the land.

For all intents and purposes, Ana's beatings are public spectacles (there is no anonymity in the village). One reason Vasile beats Ana is to regain his honor among the men of the village, which he fears he lost on account of Ana's lost virginity. He beats her so they can hear her cries as confirmation of his mastery of his house. Foucault influentially argued that modernity brings, among other things, a shift away from corporal punishment and toward subtler forms of discipline, especially self-discipline.[56] In this framework, women become docile through self-surveillance, which is largely a psychological process; there is no need for public beatings and public shaming rituals. We have argued that Pripas is a modern village integrated in a global network, both economically and politically. It is tempting to think of domestic violence as an anachronism that a modern community somehow tolerates. But this is modern violence reintegrated into what Partha Chatterjee calls a "new patriarchy"—an anti-imperial patriarchal rule.[57] This is violence rerationalized as a by-product of the struggle for landownership against a range of inter-imperial strangers. As such, it reaffirms the status of gender struggle as a side issue to class struggle and conflicts in an inter-imperial context. This mode of gender oppression is far from being *not* modern.

Rebreanu's novel foregrounds the fact that women in the village entreat their husbands to help Ana. But this is the limit of female solidarity. Ana does not have a mother or any other knowledgeable woman who can teach her how to prevent pregnancy or how to deal with it if it occurs. One woman in the village tries to comfort Ana after one of the beatings: "'There now, sweet child! Shut up and endure, for it is the woman's lot to suffer, that is God's will. Hush now! Hush!' ['*Taci, draga lelii! Taci și rabdă, că femeia trebuie să sufere dac-așa a lăsat-o Dumnezeu. Taci mulcom, taci!*']" (236, 330). This is the kindest assistance Ana receives—an invitation to silence (*taci și rabdă*). It is crucial that it comes from another woman, who gives voice to a religious principle that twists the naturalist trope of fate: God sent women into the world to suffer. They are sinful and therefore guilty, always and with no recourse. Silence is ideologically connected to a sign of their piety. Toward the end of the novel, the other female peasant character, Florica, is found symbolically guilty of Ion's death. Although they are theoretically citizens of a modern empire, women are often abandoned by the state and thrust into an apparent religious anachronism. The secular justice system does not interfere with the violence perpetrated against women within the family. One explanation for this abandonment is that the imperial state tolerates this religious anachronism as a sign of its confessional modernity, which it uses to legitimize empire.

Inter-Imperial Suicide

Like other silenced women in imperial and inter-imperial contexts, Ana eventually commits suicide: "the thought of death descended into her soul like a happy escape [*gândul morții i se coborî în suflet ca o scăpare fericită*]" (243, 340). The decision reveals a rift in Ana's subjectivity: "'I will kill myself. . . .' But she did not even recognize her own voice ['*Am să mă omor. . . .*' *Dar nici nu-și mai recunoscu glasul*]" (313, 440). The distance between Ana and her voice allows the emergence of a minimalist form of agency; seemingly, the only act possible is the taking of one's own life, the writing of one's own death. Importantly, Ana's death wish constitutes a refusal of motherhood. Aside from being a religious sin, Ana's suicide is "unnatural" because she should want to be a mother. Yet the control of women's reproduction capacity in colonial and imperial contexts was often met with resistance, as shown by the enslaved women's birth strikes mentioned above. "Love of motherhood was neither natural nor universal," Rhoda Reddock concludes from Caribbean women's resistance to pronatalist policies during and after slavery—but also from European and South African women's rejection of similar measures in the twentieth century that only further the dominant class' economic interests.[58]

Ana is not loved by her husband, she is beaten by her family, she has no community of women, and she is convinced there is no escape. What the modern nation dictates in these circumstances is for Ana to refocus on her child as a mode of reproducing the nation's body. Ana's suicide says *no* to this imperative, refusing both the redemptive claims of motherhood and complicity with a national project that does not take her struggles into account. This is the most eloquent act of resistance to Ana's co-optation by the nationalist inter-imperial narrative. The statement "Ana would glide along like a ghost [*mergea ca o nălucă*]" (319, 448) remains open ended. Our analysis is motivated by a desire to trace the specters of Ana and women like her.

Importantly, when Titu finds out that Ion raped Ana, he both condemns it and is awed by it: "it made him feel puny beside this peasant who strode steadfastly forward, sweeping aside every obstacle indifferently, fighting his way with unrelenting vigor, goaded by an overwhelming passion [*se simți mic în fața țăranului care a mers drept înainte, trecând nepăsător peste toate piedicile, luptând neobosit, împins de o patimă mare*]" (304, 428). There is an uneasy complicity between the inter-imperial intellectual and the peasant. The novel frames Ion's character traits as repulsive (he schemes, he manipulates) and his sexual drive as pathological (he has sex with the land). But Ion also displays masculine qualities of a vigorous fighter who plows forward at any cost. The nationalist intellectual believes the nation is in dire need of such masculine traits. Ion's passion for land travels across narrative levels, in a case of metalepsis, losing some of its naturalist coarseness along the way and becoming Romanian Transylvanians' "structure of feeling."[59]

Masculinism is sanctioned by the community: "all envied Ion for having got all that land through Ana [*toți pizmuiau pe Ion că s-a ales cu atâta pământ pe urma Anei*]" (364, 510). The sexual aggressor is enviable. His cunning and determination become allegorical signs that the nation can make progress too; it, too, can plow forward at any cost. Needless to say, the emerging nation would be a "gendered nation."[60] Ion's act renders him a hero among the young men of the village: "nearly all the village lads looked upon Ion as their leader [*mai toți flăcăii îl priveau ca pe un fel de vătaf al lor*]" (95, 136). His maneuver brings him symbolic capital among the other male villagers, who look up to him. The text stops calling Ion a *slugă* (an agricultural servant) and refers to himself as a *vătaf* (a supervisor). The envy his act inspires functions as a homosocial bond, creating a male alliance with nationalist flavors.

As Ana hangs herself, the narrative filtered through Ana's consciousness announces that she is first seized by terror, then by joy: "Then a thrill shot through her body. She felt a fierce and overwhelming joy and ecstasy, as if a long-awaited lover had clasped her in his arms with a savage, deathly passion . . . she let her body hang loosely [*Apoi un fior o furnică prin tot trupul. Simți o plăcere grozavă, amețitoare, ca și când un ibovnic mult așteptat ar fi îmbrățișând-o cu o sălbăticie ucigătoare . . . Se moleși, lăsându-se să atârne in voie]*" (323, 453–54). The possibility of female pleasure comes at the moment of death. We know from postcolonial novels (Salih's *Season of Migration to the North*) as well as postcolonial theory (Spivak's "Can the Subaltern Speak?") that female suicide often functions as a sign, a speech of sorts, that both imperial powers and nationalist discourses translate into their own terms. On the one hand, Rebreanu's novel registers Ana's suicide as a sign; on the other hand, it writes over that sign in the naturalist language of fate. The deployment of naturalism to this end constitutes the most consequential modality of inter-imperial silence.

Rebreanu declared that he wanted his novel to deliver a form of poetic justice: "aesthetic logic could not leave his trickery unpunished, however frequent such cases are in real life [*logica estetică nu putea admite înșelăciunea lui nepedepsită, oricât asemenea cazuri sunt frecvente în viața reală]*" (668). Yet Rebreanu's novel capitalizes on what it refers to euphemistically as a "trick," using it to sustain the reader's desire for the plot.[61] In the end, the novel punishes Ion without getting justice for Ana. Both the novel and its Romanian-language reception frame Ana as stuck in her destiny. Throughout the dowry negotiations, Ana cyclically moves between her father's house and that of her future husband: "Her feet carried her, like an abandoned dog [*Mergea cum o purtau pașii, ca un câine izgonit]*" (167, 237); "she found herself a moment later in the village lane, walking home, wearily, breathing heavily [*se pomeni curând în ulița, mergând spre casă, obosită, suflând greu]*" (168, 238). These walks illustrate that, until an arrangement is made, Ana can only move between the two households of her father and her would-be husband. Rebreanu's ideological world cannot create a path to emancipation for Ana. She cannot be economically self-sufficient. She cannot vote. She cannot pack her things and move to the city. She cannot divorce. Ana's cyclical walking back and forth, ironically, bespeaks her inertia.[62]

Our interdisciplinary collaboration teaches us that this literary world does not coincide with the historical and sociological realities of early-twentieth-century Austria-Hungary, including Transylvania. Young women in the eastern provinces did leave their villages, joining a growing proletariat in the empire's industrializing cities. Sex work was one option, leading to racialized worries about white slavery.[63] In migration, women found a route to freedom.[64] There were cases of single mothers who made a living and supported themselves. There were women who divorced on account of domestic violence. There were women who loved other women.[65] The novel's gender politics thus functions as a semiperipheral mode of inter-imperial *literary* modernism. Although Rebreanu claims documentary status for many aspects of his literary project, he fictionalizes on the margins of history so that he can exaggerate the Transylvanian Romanian peasant's virility. Ion works hard, mostly outdoors; he is strong and determined; he impregnates Ana through one sexual act. This portrait indicates an effort to remasculinize a culture thought to be at risk. In turn, this remasculinization registers as a promise of upward mobility for that culture within the trans-imperial hierarchies of the time. We know from Franz Fanon that imperial domination has a feminizing dimension; it emasculates its subjects.[66] In *Ion*'s inter-imperial predicament, we see this dimension in the impotence of old Herdelea, Titu's father, who cannot provide for his family and is regularly humiliated. Rebreanu's text aims to change this dynamic in Titu's generation by infusing Transylvanian Romanian men with a substantial dose of peasant virility, at the very moment in the region's history that the peasantry is being reinterpreted as the repository of Romanianness. The node at which the novel's documentary value is most consequential is in its dramatization of the uneasy complicity between an idealist anti-imperial intellectual and a determined but violent peasant. Given the weight of this inter-imperial history, Ana's modest desire for emancipation can only be fictionalized as a whim.

FEMINIST WHIMS

Women's Education in an Inter-Imperial Framework

We have argued that Transylvania's inter-imperiality yields, among other things, at least three conflicting nationalisms. In the previous chapter, we traced the overlap between violence against women and Transylvanian Romanian nationalism and argued that the naturalization of women's labor as an extension of their domesticity serves economic-nationalist ends. A multilayered reading of Rebreanu's novel has so far revealed nationalism's ambivalent reliance on the figure of a determined, passionate male peasant. Building on this argument, in this chapter we delineate one inter-imperial nationalism's investment not only in the male Transylvanian Romanian peasant but also in an unspoiled, *uneducated* lower-middle-class woman. We analyze women's education as a matter of intense trans-imperial debate.

In *A Room of One's Own*, one of the foundational texts of Western feminist literary criticism, Virginia Woolf quite literally addresses educated women and educational institutions. Thematically, this canonized feminist essay is concerned with the spaces of learning available to women and likely to lead to the possibility of women becoming writers. What do the great men of letters of the nineteenth century have in common? Woolf asks, creating an opportunity to provide an implacable answer: "nine out of those twelve were University men: which means that somehow or other they procured the means to get the best education England can give."[1] If a woman is to write, if she is to be "emancipated into intellectual freedom," Woolf knows, she needs to fight for her own admission into institutions of learning—whether in England or elsewhere.[2] The field of feminist modernist studies has been preoccupied with the figure of the New

Woman—tracing women who leave the family home, move to the city, take jobs, and pursue their desires—but it has paid less attention to the question of women's education. How does literary modernism interlock with the sociology of women's education? Furthermore, how is the convergence of modernism and women's education distributed globally? How does *global* modernism approach it?

We know that education stratifies the world-system, creating inequality, especially among women and racialized populations. That Woolf's *A Room of One's Own* solves its financial question in a colonial key is telling for the issue's global scope. The resources her fictional woman needs in order to write come from an aunt in India: "My aunt, Mary Beton, I must tell you, died by a fall from her horse when she was riding out to take the air in Bombay. The news of my legacy reached me one night about the same time that the act was passed that gave votes to women."[3] In search of material support for women's learning and writing needs, Woolf invokes capital extracted from empire's exploits. British women produce their emancipation, the convergence of educational opportunities and voting rights, by drawing on value extracted from the colonies. The aunt in Bombay dies, conveniently, at the right time; the "news" of this "legacy"—more appropriately described as material inheritance, that is, property—opportunely reaches Woolf's character at roughly the same time women receive legal recognition as political actors. We have seen how property is a prerequisite for citizenship. We now know that this is a structural relation, not a mere coincidence, as Woolf's text frames it. Nor is it a coincidence that this same legacy produces asymmetrical, unequal access to spaces of learning for non-British women in Bombay and elsewhere in the formerly colonized world.

This chapter takes up the question of modernism's engagement with women's education. How is women's education configured in an inter-imperial space like Transylvania? Building on the previous chapter's discussion of inter-imperial silence, we trace the selective muting of the issue of women's education. We argue that the ensuing belatedness of peripheral and semiperipheral feminisms vis-à-vis Woolf's project of emancipation through writing is structurally reproduced by such muting. Returning to Rebreanu's novel, we reemphasize that the text frames feminism as poison. What feminism threatens to poison is anti-imperial nationalism, which has its own plans for lower-middle-class women.

The novel develops on two parallel tracks, each revolving around a male character: Ion Glanetaşu, the peasant who schemes to own his own land; and Titu Herdelea, the emerging poet and nationalist intellectual. Two female characters sustain these narrative tracks: Ana, Ion's wife; and Laura, Titu's sister. The previous chapter drew Ana's inter-imperial portrait, while this chapter is concerned with Laura, a rural, lower-middle-class young woman in an inter-imperial predicament. In Laura, Rebreanu sketches a character tempted by feminism. However, she retrospectively describes her minimalist feminist inclinations as a youthful phase to be rejected by her mature self, who becomes a devoted mother and assistant to her husband in the nationalist cause. Toward the end of the novel, Laura reminisces about her youthful dreams: "I had bees in my bonnet and my heart [*aveam gărgăuni în cap și-n inimă*]" (278, 391).[4] The word *gărgăuni* means "poisonous wasps," used idiomatically to invoke extravagant, strange ideas in need of extermination. As noted in the previous chapter, the novel deploys the same word to describe Ana's rebellion against her father's control of her virginity and the idea of marriage as a transaction. In Ana's case, the feminist notions constituting such *gărgăuni* are driven out violently, through beatings inflicted by her father and her husband. This marks the class difference between Ana and Laura, who is gradually socialized into relinquishing her own *gărgăuni* rather than being corporally punished into obedience.

Once again, we place our encounter with Rebreanu's text against the background of a developed women's movement globally and in the Austro-Hungarian Empire. Our reading of the novel traces the Transylvanian debate on women's education, drawing out its connections to a world-historical predicament. We do so through a revised encounter with the scholarly literature on postcolonial feminism.[5] Although many postcolonial feminist theorists trace the development of women's movements in conjunction with nationalist movements in colonial and semicolonial spaces, the East that often constitutes their object of analysis rarely includes East Europe. The region is not mentioned in any of the case studies compiled by Chandra Talpade Mohanty and her collaborators in one of the foundational texts in the field of postcolonial feminist studies, for example.[6] This omission functions as a stark reminder of how the Cold War lens that relegated the European East to the Second World on political grounds simultaneously obscured parallels and entanglements with the so-called Third World, both economically and with regard to the processes of racialization and the ethnicization of religion. Yet, posing the "woman question" in an inter-imperial space like Transylvania fits a similar analytical framework developed by postcolonial theorists for the Third World.

Starting in the mid-nineteenth century, a number of Transylvanian voices, both men and women, debated the question of women's education. Foremost among them was Transylvanian Romanian writer and reformer George Barițiu, who wrote a series of articles on women's education. Proposing an analogy with Englishwomen's situation, he advocated for the modernization of the nation through the education of women. One article, "On the Education of Women of the Romanian Nation" (*Despre educațiunea femeiloru la națiunea românească*), published in 1869, proposed the benefits of a limited education for girls. Invoking the legacy of the French Revolution and the contemporary emancipation of women in Britain, the text worried about introducing venom into the na-tional body under the guise of a foreign education for girls.[7] The arc opened by Barițiu's ambivalence closed a few decades later when, on October 10, 1906, Alexandru Vaida-Voievod, a Romanian Transylvanian representative in the Budapest parliament, once again argued for women's rights, including the right to education.[8] Instead of a British comparison, however, he proposed a Japanese model of women's education, which he understood as an attempt to teach women those aspects of life that represented their calling: housework.[9] Once women were educated in this spirit, he argued, they would lose interest in feminism, which would cease to be a problem. Without such schools, Vaida-Voievod warned, sooner or later women would ask for rights.

Between Spinsters and New Women: The Construction of Female Authenticity

In the character of Laura Herdelea, Rebreanu sketches a young modern woman in a rural setting. The text teases the reader into anticipating that Laura might develop into a New Woman, only to shift gears and marry her off into a tradi-tional family tasked with meeting the reproductive needs of a Transylvanian ethnic group with national aspirations. The resonant muting of the question of Laura's education is instrumental to this project. Laura is nineteen, that is, of marriageable age. And the marital project is urgent so that Laura does not be-come a spinster, a frightening possibility embodied by a few minor characters, such as "the girls of the Jewish butcher, old and bitter, with nothing else to do [*fetele hahamului Cahan, bătrâne și înăcrite, neavând altă treabă*]" (156, 221). Spinsterhood, which the field of feminist modernist studies has recovered as a mode of feminism, signifies here a wasted, empty life—with antisemitic over-tones.[10] This view of spinsterhood constitutes a feature of a modern world-system in which the gendering of populations from the sixteenth century onward re-duced costs for capital by defining women's labor as nature and thus delegiti-mizing any occupation other than marriage and child rearing.[11] The stigma associated with spinsterhood functions as a reminder of the centrality of women's "natural" trajectory.

Laura strives to avoid spinsterhood—individual and ideological—without giving the impression that she tries too hard. In particular, she is not presented as a seductive, modern girl. In contrast, another minor female character is de-scribed as such: "Margareta Bobescu was the daughter of a clerk at Aurora Bank, a dark-haired, slim, cute girl, with penciled eyebrows, lots of powder, and lips painted a fiery red. Because she painted her face and went about in silk dresses, all of Armadia said she had a screw loose [*Margareta Bobescu, fata unui funcționar de la Banca Aurora, o brună înaltă, mlădioasă, drăguță, cu sprîncenele înnegrite, foarte pudrată și cu buzele vopsite roșu-foc. Pentru că se sulimenea și umbla cu rochii de mătase, toată Armadia zicea că-i lipsește o doagă]" (81, 115). Margareta's last name hints at a bob hairstyle, the most legible marker of a New Woman. She is conventionally attractive—dark-haired, tall, and slim, all signs of a modern woman.[12] She should be marriageable, except that she wears too much makeup and silk dresses. Her red lipstick stands out, a sign of excessive sexuality. The verb used for makeup application is *sulemeni*, from the Turkish *sülümen*, a linguistic choice that cites an Orientalizing approach to makeup and cosmetics, used here to pass judgment on a modern, Westernized girl.

The fact that Margareta Bobescu wears silk dresses adds to her offensiveness. The Austro-Hungarian Empire had a sophisticated textile culture, including a silk industry that flourished in Vienna after the incorporation of the Italian province of Lombardy in 1815.[13] Silk is traded around the world at this time and constitutes an object of women's consumerism. In 1912 economic historian Werner Sombart advanced the thesis that women's consumption of luxuries and their growing taste for expensive jewels and textiles (including silk) had supplied the decisive impulse for the emergence of the capitalist world-economy. For Sombart, the consumption habits of courtesans and mistresses of upper-class men were the driving force behind the display of luxury, which subsequently had to be extended to upper-class wives and bourgeois housewives.[14] This connection to silk is echoed in 1913 by Marcel Proust's Odette, a coquette turned bourgeois wife, who also paints her lips a deep red and wears silk.[15] In Rebreanu's text, the sexualized consumption of silk comes across as a betrayal of the nation, which in turn constitutes a form of madness.

The character of Margareta Bobescu functions as a foil and a warning to Laura. In contradistinction, when Laura attends a local dance, she wears a national folk costume. The literary strategy deploys dress as a political tool—with well-documented world-historical resonance.[16] Later in the novel, Laura makes her own wedding dress, presumably using local patterns and materials, thus assembling a second folk costume. As in other parts of the world, dress is a sign of local authenticity, and it is enlisted as such in Rebreanu's modernist project. Authenticity, of course, is a highly stylized construct, and it requires effort to create and maintain.[17] Laura's proximity to Margareta functions as a reminder that Laura's authenticity is a modern production; she is a modern girl in a folk costume. Rebreanu's text demonstrates familiarity with the global figure of the modern girl, her lipstick and her dresses, only to marginalize her as a flat minor character, mentioned once and quickly dismissed.[18] The fact that everyone in the village recognizes Margareta's madness is a function of a modernist narrator who acts as a conveyor of gossip.

Inter-Imperiality and Nationalist Feminism in the Semiperiphery

At the turn of the twentieth century, Transylvanian women's educational aspirations were caught between competing nationalisms responding to Transylvania's inter-imperial condition. In literary terms, Rebreanu does not send his female characters to school in order to retain their constructed ethnic and linguistic purity, which he then uses to limn the boundaries of the national community. The most important mechanism of such delineation is marriage. As we have seen in the previous chapter, the tacit (and sometimes not so tacit) assumption was that Transylvanian Romanian girls should not marry outside the ethnic group. However, strict endogamy was not a social reality in Transylvania at this time; between 1901 and 1905, 11.6 percent of marriages were mixed, and between 1916 and 1918, 19 percent were mixed.[19] Rebreanu's novel, published in 1920, offers a prescriptive narrative, a story of ethnic separateness for a border region with an ethnically mixed population. Laura becomes the site where the tension among inter-imperiality, nationalism, and women's education is negotiated.

One argument in postcolonial studies, made by Partha Chatterjee with regard to women in colonial India but with broader theoretical ramifications, has become highly consequential: in colonial contexts, nationalist ideology produces a separation between the material sphere and the spiritual sphere, claiming the latter as the realm of its self-identity and tasking women with its representation.[20] Whereas imitation of the imperial power in the material domain is desired, even when it leads to comprador compromise, the spiritual domain must be cultivated outside of this relation, in all its unique and autonomous authenticity. When it comes to women, therefore, anti- and postcolonial nationalisms selectively appropriate elements of modernity/coloniality. This does not mean that women remain defined by traditional norms; rather, they are enlisted into the modern world of the nation, which constitutes itself as a new patriarchy. The education of women consequently becomes a matter of intense negotiation: education can occur only when literature and pedagogical materials are available in the native tongue or tongues, and it must concentrate on housework and its virtues.

Chatterjee emphasizes that women in colonial India at the end of the nineteenth century propagated the nationalist ideal, embracing housework training and feminine virtues. Feminist postcolonial theorists suggest a slightly differ-ent but consequential emphasis, pointing to the emergence of nationalist forms of feminism. Mrinalini Sinha writes:

> The nationalist project both initiated women's access to modernity and set the limits of the desirable modernity for women. In this context, sev-eral early-twentieth-century feminists, such as Halide Edibe in Turkey and Hudá Sha'rawi in Egypt, constructed their dynamic public roles as a duty to the nation rather than as a right. As signifiers of the nation, women needed to be modern, but they could not mark a complete break from tradition. The woman of the anticolonial nationalist imagination, then, was not necessarily a "traditional" woman. She was more likely the "modern-yet-modest" woman who both symbolized the nation and negotiated the tension between tradition and modernity.[21]

In colonial and semicolonial situations, women's movements are often born with a strong nationalist flavor. The Transylvanian example suggests that this is often the case in inter-imperial settings as well. The demands articulated by women's organizations are thus often voiced from *within* the nationalist para-digm.[22] This does not mean, however, that all demands are nationalist in nature; feminists often use the nationalist paradigm strategically.

What happens in inter-imperial situations when we are dealing with multi-ple nationalisms, reacting to layers of imperial history, none of which corre-sponds to the model of the British Empire described by theorists like Chatterjee and Sinha? In Rebreanu's novel, Laura's access to modernity is indeed curtailed by the nation's semiperipheral modernity, which functions like an "ideological sieve" (Chatterjee's phrase), determining which of its components are not poi-sonous to the nation's soul.[23] As a discursive entity, Laura represents a "modern-yet-modest" Transylvanian Romanian woman. But she is not solely a symptom of the male author's desire to enlist women in the nationalist project. She is also a sign of an overdetermined local Romanian Transylvanian feminism that imag-ines itself as a corollary to the nation, defining itself in relation to and often in competition with at least two other local feminisms dedicated to two other na-tions. Rebreanu's novel invites the reader to contemplate Laura wearing her folk costume with a modern attitude; this attitude is not at odds with how local feminists discursively constructed the role of women like Laura.

Maria Baiulescu, a Romanian Transylvanian writer and journalist, endorsed a reproductive project as a form of nationalist feminism. In a speech she gave in 1914, she called on women to identify with "the mother of our people"; women's role, she said, is to keep "the language, the law, the traditions, and the whole national treasure holy and unshaken."[24] In 1920, the year *Ion* was published,

Constanța Hodoş, an outspoken Romanian Transylvanian writer and journalist, published a short manifesto advocating women's education. She rebuffed the perception that women act like "spoiled children" and praised reflexive and energetic mothers.[25] A pacifist document, Hodoş's manifesto called for women's economic independence, encouraging them to resist the stereotype of "kept women." Importantly, the manifesto also advocated change for peasant women, who suffered on account of beliefs "falsely legitimated by tradition." Despite these feminist additions to the political agenda, Hodoş's manifesto retained the nationalist framing of women's education, including its focus on motherhood. In documents penned by both Baiulescu and Hodoş, one witnesses Transylvanian Romanian women strategically navigating a discursive and material terrain on which women are expected to be modern and traditional at the same time.

Romanian Transylvanian feminism reacted not only to Austro-Hungarian imperial policies but also to other Transylvanian nationalisms, including other feminist nationalisms aligned with their own interpretations of inter-imperial history. Hungary had a developed and complex women's movement before World War I that included strands of liberal feminism, conservative nationalist feminism, and socialist feminism.[26] Much of this feminism was centered in Budapest. A major figure was Emma Ritoók, originally from Transylvania; she gradually became a vocal representative of a Hungarian nationalist brand of feminism with imperial flavors. In 1920 Ritoók coauthored a document with Charlotte de Geőcze titled, in French, *Le problème de la Hongrie: Les femmes hongroises aux femmes du monde civilisé*. As Hungary ceded a large part of its territory at the end of World War I, Ritoók and Geőcze called on women of "the civilized world," identified as "Femmes, Jeunes filles, Mères—nos Soeurs"—to defend Hungarians' millennial claims to Transylvania.[27] Hungarians, the two authors claimed, represented the most civilized ethnic group in the region.[28] The other ethnic groups, Balkan in origin, were immigrants, fugitives asking European Hungarians for hospitality, which, in the authors' opinion, had been largely granted.[29] One sign of Hungarian civilization consisted of the rights enjoyed by women in Hungary, including property rights and education. For these authors, the most feminist nation was the most civilized one, and the "woman question" buttressed the Hungarian semiperipheral imperial project. It should be clear that there could be little convergence between Hodoş's and Ritoók's feminisms, as they were aligned with conflicting inter-imperial nationalisms.

For their part, Saxon Transylvanian women reacted to yet another version of Transylvania's inter-imperial history. Following the 1867 Compromise between Austria and Hungary, Saxon Transylvanians switched from being an autonomous group with historical privileges to being a minority group. Their relation to the influential German-speaking world rendered their minority status highly visible, as Prussia claimed such minorities as part of a global German cultural world. Saxon Transylvanian women produced their own feminist nationalist discourse through a German-language publishing network and in relation to the women's movement in Germany.[30] Marie Stritt, one of the leading voices for women's suffrage and for women's educational and reproductive rights, was originally from Transylvania.[31] Saxon Transylvanian women thought it was their duty to support their ethnic group's struggle for minority rights. Their main goals were educational equality for girls and cultivation of the German language. Less nationalistic than their Romanian and Hungarian counterparts, they developed a separate path for emancipation. After World War I, Transylvanian Saxon author Mária Berde spearheaded a movement called Transylvanianism, an attempt to move away from conflicting nationalisms and imagine a multicultural, multilingual future for Transylvania.[32] Tracing the careers of Stritt and Berde, it becomes clear that although they nominally shared an investment in women's education with Transylvanian Romanian and Transylvanian Hungarian women's organizations, they participated in separate organizational and discursive networks.

The inter-imperial competition among these different feminisms resulted in a restricted focus when it came to justice. None of the three feminist groups fought the racialization of the Roma in Transylvania. They were sometimes antisemitic and found little common ground with Jewish women's organizations. They concentrated on women's education and gave less attention to domestic violence and poverty—issues that concerned the character of Ana. In fact, they often had a patronizing attitude toward peasant women. Their nationalist frame of reference was international, in the sense that many women's organizations around the world shared a nationalist investment. But the nationalist frame restricted the possibilities for other forms of internationalism, limiting solidarity with anti-imperial and antiracist struggles around the world.

One of the most immediate effects of the development of three separate women's nationalist movements was their failure to obtain voting rights in the pre–World War I period. At the time, Transylvanian Romanian nationalists were working to achieve what was called *universal* suffrage. Intellectuals like Laura's husband and brother struggled to obtain voting rights for Romanian men, historically disenfranchised in the Transylvanian electoral system. The call for universal suffrage, however, did not include women's voting rights. To be sure, each of the three feminisms advocated for women's voting rights, but only secondarily; their main project was each one's respective nation. The ongoing debate on voting rights for women peaked in 1913, when a congress of the International Woman Suffrage Alliance was organized in Budapest. Charlotte

Perkins Gilman was in attendance and gave a talk titled "New Mothers of a New World."[33] For the organizers, though, voting rights seemed less urgent than the chance to offer evidence of Hungary's modernity (examples included a telephone broadcast and tourist opportunities) as imperial vindication on a worldwide scale.[34] The hijacking of the issue of women's suffrage in Budapest helps explain why Rebreanu's novel, centrally concerned with universal suffrage, weaves a resounding silence on Transylvanian women's suffrage into its fabric.

The Lower-Middle-Class Marriage Plot

With a marital ideal as her horizon, Laura and her younger sister Ghighi engage in a number of highly gendered activities in their parents' household. Evenings are spent knitting and embroidering items for their future trousseaux, the usual accompaniment to (or in this case, a replacement for) a dowry, and "singing old Romanian romantic songs in cute soprano voices [*să cânte romanțe vechi românești cu niște voci simpatice de sopran*]" (55, 79). These activities demonstrate a caricatured femininity that the novel quietly mocks, but they socialize the Herdelea sisters into expectations of marriage and motherhood. To complete the picture, the family takes a loan and purchases new furniture for a salon—creating a stage for future courting. Rebreanu describes in detail an attempt at a rural, gendered bourgeoisification, with words like *salon* and *trousseau* borrowed from French to add some sophistication. The spatial distribution of Laura's mobility is anchored in this salon. As a young girl, she leaves it to go for a walk, visit friends, and attend a dance in a nearby city. As a married woman, she moves into a similar rural salon, which she leaves once to go to a resort for a meeting of the extended family. These routine activities severely restrict the female characters' mobility, which we know is increasing globally.

Choosing between two suitors, Laura rebels against her family, especially her mother, and advocates for love: "She would cross herself and swear that she preferred death to Pintea. She had plenty of time to marry, for nowadays girls no longer married as before at an age when they had not even opened their eyes [*Se închina și se jura că mai bine moartea decât Pintea. De măritat mai are destulă vreme, căci azi fetele nu se mai mărită ca altădată, înainte de a fi deschis bine ochii în lume*]" (75, 105). The formulation posits an earlier time when girls married early (sometimes as young as twelve), through arrangements made by their parents.[35] And it posits the present, when things have changed. Through these temporal markers, the novel displays familiarity with an Occidentalist account of the modernity of gender emancipation that it otherwise repurposes.[36]

In a familiar move, Laura rebels through. Husband hunting, a leitmotif of women's writing at this time, drives the plot.[37] Lingering on the margins of the text, however, is the barely articulated possibility that Laura might refuse to marry. This is the unnamed yet terrifying scenario Rebreanu's text works to prevent. Following a botched kiss with her crush, Aurel, Laura turns to Pintea and dedicates herself to the marriage plot. The risk, as articulated through Laura's parents, is too high: "If Laura hesitates and misses this lucky opportunity, she'll get old a spinster, like the unmarried Bocu women in Armadia, who turned fifty and are still looking for some fool to court them, although they have many thousands to back them. Besides, Laura was at the best age. After twenty, a girl starts to fade and uglify [*Dacă Laura se va codi și va scăpa ocazia norocoasă, va îmbătrîni fată mare ca și dominișoarele Bocu din Armadia, care au împlinit cincizeci de ani și tot mai așteaptă vreun nebun să le pețească, deși ele au la spate miișoare multe. De altefel Laura are vârsta cea mai frumoasă. Fata, după ce trece de douăzeci de ani, începe a se vesteji și urâți*]" (75, 105). Spinsterhood is posited as the outcome of a failed courtship; no woman could possibly choose to be single. With this warning on the horizon, and with the threat of fading feminine beauty after the age of twenty (the leitmotif of woman as flower), the novel solves Laura's rebellion conservatively. She agrees to marry, sobbing. The "I love you" that follows the marriage ceremony belongs to the matrimonial register. The possibility of passionate love, let alone sexual desire, has been left behind.

If it seems, at the beginning of the novel, that Laura could develop into a New Woman, by the middle of the narrative, with her engagement functioning as a pivot, a conservative shift is forcefully under way:

> Laura had, since her engagement, undergone a great change. She had always been a serious girl, but her gravity now suited her better. Though in the past she had generally disagreed with her mother in almost every respect, now the two of them chatted together like two friends and Laura never stopped asking her mother how a certain dish was cooked, how men's trousers were cut, how the pickles must be preserved. She was determined to be a perfect housewife, to prove to Pintea that, although she had no dowry, she possessed so many other precious qualities that she could compete with any young lady in Transylvania. (153)
>
> *Laura, de când se logodise, trecuse printr-o schimbare mare. Serioasă fusese ea întotdeauna, dar acuma parcă seriozitatea îi ședea mai bine. De unde până atunci nu se potrivise deloc în păreri cu mama ei, azi vorbeau ca două tovarășe și nu se sfia s-o întrebe mereu, ba cum se gătește cutare mâncare, ba cum se croiesc pantalonii bărbătești, ba cum se fac murăturile . . . Era hotărâtă să fie o gospodină desăvârșită, să vadă Pin-*

tea că, deşi ea n-a avut zestre, are în schimb atâtea alte calităţi preţioase
încât se poate lua la întrecere cu orice domnişoară din Ardeal. (217)

Laura starts acting with gravity; she wears her seriousness as a badge of honor. Instead of forming a unit with her rebellious sister, Laura now becomes a companion (*tovarăşă*) to her conservative mother, who transitions into her role as instructor in the subject of housework. In no time, Laura becomes the perfect housewife (*gospodină desăvârşită*), a quality meant to compensate for the lack of a dowry. A good bourgeois marriage is one in which the wife obeys the husband unconditionally: "She does not deviate from his wishes [*Nu-i iese din vorbă*]"; and anticipates his desires: "she has come to guess even his thoughts [*a ajuns să-i ghicească şi gândurile*]" (309, 435). On account of these qualities, Laura presents herself as a winner in an imaginary competition among young Transylvanian housewives.

These qualifications render Laura a legitimate partner in her husband's nationalist project. While on her honeymoon, she writes her family a letter from Bistriţa/Bistritz/Beszterce, where the newlyweds dine luxuriously at the *Gewerbeverein*. The text uses only the German name of a local trade and commerce club—a hint at the growing number of trade associations founded in nineteenth-century Germany and Austria-Hungary to protect the interests of the bourgeois middle classes from both big capital and the workers' movement. Military music is playing during dinner. Laura is wearing a "dress as blue as the sky [*rochia cea albastră ca cerul*]" (48). No longer a folk costume, Laura's blue dress is a reminder of the importance of blue print (*Blaudruck* or *kékfestö*) as an expression of nationalist sentiments in many rural communities in the Netherlands, Germany, the Czech lands, and Hungary.[38] Both the cotton and the indigo dye needed to make blue dresses—or the "sky-blue tie [*o cravată albastră-azurie*]" (28) Titu wears early in the novel—were imported from India by European colonial trading companies. They became more readily available and much cheaper after indigo started to be mass-produced across Central Europe and was finally replaced by synthetic indigo (aniline) in 1898. Whether knowingly or tacitly, the text reveals that nationalist sentiment in inter-imperial locales such as Transylvania is permanently enmeshed with coloniality, even at a time when Austria-Hungary is no longer a competitor among sea powers.[39]

Importantly, the plot does not end with Laura's marriage. Laura becomes a compulsive advocate for motherhood and identifies, seemingly without a crack, with the gendered script that writes women's nature as housewifery and motherhood. As discussed in chapter 5, on a parallel track in the novel, Ana commits suicide, refusing an implied narrative of redemptive motherhood. Laura's advocacy for motherhood is strengthened by this tragedy. The narrative of modern self-discipline does not apply to the peasant Ana, who is coerced into gendered submission through public beatings, but it applies to lower-middle-class Laura, who apparently internalizes a self-disciplining project of creating women for the nation. Laura thus comes to share her mother's "deep contempt for any woman who bore no children [*dispreț adânc pentru femeile care nu fac copii*]" (93, 132). The collectively despised childless woman is guilty on many fronts, but primarily she is guilty of not reproducing the nation in an imaginary demographic war (a majority-minority political debate). Rebreanu's text builds yet another resounding silence into its fabric at this juncture—women's global struggle for reproductive rights. Rebreanu must have been aware of the fact that contemporary women were fighting for the right to choose whether and when to reproduce—motherhood as a project for freedom, as Simone de Beauvoir would later put it, as opposed to a project for the nation.[40] Women's reproductive rights, however, are at odds with the goals of inter-imperial nationalism, which counts bodies in a symbolic demographic competition.

Reproduction has a serial logic. In time, Laura takes on the task of teaching her marriageable sister that "a girl does not even live until she gets married. That's why one must weed girls' whims. . . . Only now do I have a purpose in the world [*Fata nici nu trăiește până se mărită. De aceea trebuiesc stârpite fumurile din mintea fetelor. . . . Parcă de-abia acuma am și eu o țintă în lume!*]" (278, 391–92). The word *țintă* designates the target used in shooting or archery—symbolically, a fine-tuned goal or cause. The teleology of Laura's life becomes reproduction—biological reproduction (children) and ideological reproduction (helping her husband in the nationalist project). Unsurprisingly, having given birth to a girl, Laura now hopes for a boy. Laura's declamations align neatly with Mrs. Ramsey's statements in Woolf's *To the Lighthouse*, as they resonate in the female artist's head: "an unmarried woman has missed the best in life."[41] Except, crucially, Rebreanu's text does not feature a suspicious female artist like Lily Briscoe—a structural impossibility in the economy of Rebreanu's novel. It is only the text's iterative subtle irony that allows the reader some distance from what it frames as Laura's destiny.

One might be tempted to believe that a rural marriage of this kind might, in time, yield a Madame Bovary. This scenario is reserved for Roza Lang, a childless woman married to a Jewish man. Roza is sexually promiscuous and is severely judged for her promiscuity. Laura's brother Titu has an affair with Roza but gradually distances himself from her. Rebreanu's portrayal of Roza is aligned with the antisemitism analyzed in chapter 2. Aside from being racialized through their association with alcohol production and distribution, Jewish people in the Austro-Hungarian Empire were racialized through stereotypes of sexual deviance.[42] It is impossible for Titu to love Roza long term, and his sisters move as far from what Roza represents as possible. Among other things, Roza spends her time reading Hungarian-language romance novels. In contrast, the two Herdelea sisters are kept from attending school and groomed for youthful marriage.

Six priests and a bishop preside at Laura's wedding. Such impressive processions, accompanied by fanfare and bombastic speeches, celebrate the collective offering of women's emancipation on the altar of nationalism. Their hyperbolic dimensions awe young women into endorsing the naturalism of the nationalist narrative. An analysis of this dimension of the plot requires a mode of feminist secular criticism in an inter-imperial framework.[43] It is not some abstract tradition that modernity and its modernisms dialectically engage. This tradition often takes the form of a religious system, with a legible infrastructure and ideological framework. As they claim authority over the spiritual sphere, religious systems often interlock with inter-imperial nationalisms (see chapter 7), with important consequences for women's education.

Girls' Upbringing

We argued in chapter 4 that Rebreanu's novel is centrally concerned with the politics of education in an inter-imperial framework. Laura's brother Titu, the future poet, attends a series of schools, and the novel dramatizes an entire philosophy of education in relation to him. Paramount is Titu's polyglottism, which gives him access to educational institutions in the region. In contrast, Laura's education consists of learning how to perform household duties. Her teacher is her mother, even though her father is a teacher by profession. "Boys get education; girls get upbringing," local feminist voices emphasized.[44] The fact that the novel offers minute details of her brother's formal education only makes the absence of Laura's education more striking. Rebreanu's text goes to great lengths to *avoid* a parallel narrative of a female-centered Bildungsroman. This avoidance is not strictly a question of class. In Rebreanu's text, there are educational limits for young men as well. Titu's trip to Bucharest, for example, is beyond the means of his family; he has to save for months to afford it. But he "procures the means," as Woolf puts it, to attend schools in the immediate vicinity. If there were equal opportunities for young women, Titu's sisters could have attended schools—girls' schools or coed schools—in Năsăud/Nassod/Naszód, Bistrița/Bistritz/Beszterce, or Cluj/Kolozsvár/Klausenburg. Many educational institutions at this time took boarders and enrolled girls from a similar class background—daughters of teachers and priests—from across the region.

At least six languages were spoken in Transylvania: Romanian, Hungarian, German, Romani, Yiddish, and Armenian. Three of them—Romanian, Hungarian, and German—were languages of formal education. The inter-imperial history of the region yields a complex linguistic hierarchy and distribution of labor among these languages, as well as a long-standing struggle for linguistic equality. This linguistic war was largely fought over education—initially boys' education; then later, and with a twist, girls' education. It is against this background that Rebreanu *decides* not to send his female characters to school. This authorial choice is tied to the issue of interglottism: if women do not attend the various schools available in Transylvania, which would require them to learn Hungarian, German, or sometimes French, they can be claimed by the nationalist monoglot paradigm.

The Herdelea girls repeatedly express pride in their monoglottism. More than the future nationalist intellectual (Titu), Rebreanu fashions lower-middle-class women into custodians of the nation's spirituality: "If our aspirations have penetrated the souls of the finest women, then we are close to our goal [*Dacă năzuințele noastre au pătruns până în sufletul femeilor alese, înfăptuirea e aproape*]" (264, 371). These "finest women" become signifiers of the difference cultivated by the nation as a marker of its exceptionalism.[45] In one scene, an inspector visits the local school and realizes that the teacher's wife and daughters do not speak Hungarian, the state language, but the father defends the situation: "it would be rather difficult.... There is no place where women can.... But my son speaks it better than any Hungarian [*ar fi greu.... Femeile n-au de unde să.... Băiatul însă vorbește mai abitir ca un ungur*]" (345, 483). The excuse is that there is no school where women in the family can learn to speak Hungarian. But this is a *literary* statement; it is crucial to point out that it is not historically accurate. Rebreanu refuses to have his female characters attend school.

At the turn of the century, feminists in the Austro-Hungarian Empire advocated for women's access to education. They argued that education was an economic necessity; unmarried women should be able to provide for themselves, and married women should not be economically dependent on their husbands. Poverty could be avoided if both spouses worked. A hundred years after the publication of Mary Wollstonecraft's *Vindication of the Rights of Woman*, feminists in the Austro-Hungarian Empire followed in her footsteps—conceptually, rhetorically, and strategically. They argued that education would make women better wives and mothers. They used slavery as a rhetorical tool (women should not be treated like enslaved people).[46] Claims to modernity were anchored in the education of women: a nation could not be fully modern or economically prosperous if the women enlisted in the state's nation-building project were not modern. Modernity, however, was also figured as anti-imperial national emancipation that enlisted women to achieve its own ends. As Maria Mies argues, the naturalization of women, as well as that of peasants and enslaved people in the colonies, occurred in parallel, both temporally and ideologically, with the rise of the norm of the bourgeois housewife and the proletarianization of male nonwage workers in industrial centers. Both developments were conceived as dimensions of a larger civilizing process in which education played a central part.[47] In between the colonizing and the colonized positions were inter-imperial spaces such as Transylvania, where women's education was caught in the tension between anti-imperialist nationalism and the trans-imperial negotiation of political rights. The latter can be granted to some groups, but not all. And such rights are rarely—and selectively—granted to women.

We can identify the educational opportunities available to Transylvanian women at this time by examining the biographies of female writers and female teachers in the region.[48] If the Herdelea sisters had gone to school, what would they have learned? What type of education would they have experienced? In Cluj/ Kolozsvár/Klausenburg, Antonina De Gerando was the director of a girls' school starting in 1880. Born in Paris to French and Hungarian noble parents, she received a privileged education (studying under Jules Michelet). In 1882 she published, in Hungarian, a text titled "A Woman's Life." She made the case for women's education so they could better serve their traditional roles but also, in the spirit of Wollstonecraft, advocated for marriage as a union of equals. Students at De Gerando's school learned to perform gendered activities such as sewing and cooking, but they also studied languages and read literature. Baiulescu articulated the regulations and curriculum of another girls' school opened by the Association of Romanian Women in Braşov/Brassó/Kronstadt.[49] This school taught students to cook, clean, and sew; girls also learned the theoretical side of cooking, tailoring, and accounting, plus religion and music. To this list of academic subjects, Baiulescu added three languages and literatures: Romanian, Hungarian, and German. In the curricular documents developed by both De Gerando and Baiulescu, one can see echoes of the kind of education traced by Kumari Jayawardena in colonial contexts: "Modernity meant educated women, but educated to uphold the system of the nuclear patriarchal family."[50]

We know, however, that when girls attend school, any school, they learn things beyond what the institution intends to teach them. If the Herdelea girls had attended school, they might have developed dreams of higher education—an impossibility within Rebreanu's text. The university in Budapest started enrolling women in 1896; the university in Vienna, in 1897; and the university in Cluj/ Kolozsvár/Klausenburg enrolled its first woman in 1895. Once women were educated, multiple and globally expanding higher education opportunities opened for them. Ritoók studied in several universities (Budapest, Leipzig, Berlin, Paris) and earned a doctorate in philosophy.[51] She studied with Georg Simmel in Berlin and was a friend of Ernst Bloch. She was one of the founding members, alongside György Lukács and Béla Balázs, of the Sunday Circle in Budapest. A New Woman herself, Ritoók wrote novels dramatizing the predicament of New Women in the region. For her part, Berde studied in Aiud/Nagyenyed/Straßburg am Mieresch, spent time in Munich, and received a doctorate in German literature in Cluj/Kolozsvár/Klausenburg. She went on to become an accomplished poet and one of the main proponents of Transylvanianism. Trajectories like Ritoók's and Berde's would have extended the educational mobility of Transylvanian Romanian women beyond the control of men like Rebreanu. As a result, he put his nationalist faith in the male Romanian peasant and an unspoiled, *uneducated* lower-middle-class woman.[52]

The turn-of-the-century woman of the Romanian Transylvanian nationalist imagination needed to be protected from the "risks" of education. This impulse becomes even more apparent when one notes that all the educated women in Rebreanu's novel are minor characters. When Titu moves to Luşca, a nearby village with an ethnically mixed population, he falls in love with a teacher, Virginia Gherman. She is dedicated to her profession and has aspirations to become a poet. She nonetheless becomes a renegade when she marries a Hungarian gendarme. The novel implies that her education and her professional life are responsible for destroying her nationalist attachments. The wife of another minor character teaches at a German school for girls. She is German herself and, as a consequence, is not teaching the children to speak Romanian—one of the most acute risks for the nation's long-term reproductive potential. Women's education and the wage labor trajectories opened by education are thus present in the novel, but marginally. Having entered into mixed marriages and thereby literally embodying trans-imperial communication and negotiation, these two minor female characters become an obstacle to the nationalist struggle.[53]

In the economy of Rebreanu's novel, the marriage plot serves the wider inter-imperial nationalist plot.[54] The family of Laura's husband, Pintea, is spread across the regions claimed by Romanian Transylvanian nationalism. Each member of the family and his or her reproductive prospects are described in detail. If only the Pintea family can produce enough offspring, the fate of Romanian Transylvanian nationalism will be sealed. When Laura enters the picture, her job is to assist in the project of bringing Magyarized Romanians back into the national fold: "bring these lost sheep back to the flock [*reducem la matcă pe sărmanii rătăciţi*]" and undertake "the great work of reawakening these miserable Romanians [*marea operă de redeşteptare a acestor români nenorociţi*]" (257, 361). This formulation echoes the title and main message of the revolutionary anthem *"Deşteaptă-te, române!"* (Romanians, awaken!), composed during the

1848 Romanian revolution and intoned at symbolically significant events recalling nationalist sentiment (this is the same anthem performed by the Romani musicians who were the subject of chapter 3). Here, the sentiment attached to the song reinforces the selective muting of the issue of women's education.

Women's Writing: Between Nationalism and Cosmopolitanism

An engagement with Rebreanu's novel offers eloquent but limited insights into the convergence of modernism and women's education in Transylvania. The author function is clearly gendered in *Ion*. Titu describes one of his sisters' social events: "The girls finally began talking about literature, which means they exhausted all major topics of conversation [*În sfârșit fetele se porniră să vorbească despre literatură, ceea ce înseamnă că au sleit toate subiectele mai de seamă*]" (83, 117). Titu refers to his sisters and their friends as "the geese [*gâștele*]" (86, 122). When they attend a dance, they look "like dolls [*ca niște păpuși*]" (115, 164) or like "fairies [*zâne*]" (116, 165). These descriptions were penned by a male writer. Deprived narratively of an education, the two Herdelea sisters cannot develop into the kind of artist Titu becomes.[55] Pretty geese do not write literature. With Woolf, one can imagine the authorial voice of *Ion* whispering, "Women can't write, women can't paint," although, filtering Lily Briscoe, "clearly it was not true to him but for some reason helpful to him."[56] This narrative perspective is helpful to Rebreanu; it implicitly projects the author of the novel as superior to "the geese."

Feminist modernist studies have taught us to ask another question at this juncture: how would the narrative of *Ion* unfold if it were written by a female author? The female Transylvanian Romanian author most similar to Rebreanu was Hodoș. Her 1908 novel *Martirii* (The martyrs) could function as a companion to Rebreanu's *Ion*. Her novel is also about Transylvanian Romanians' struggle against the Austro-Hungarian Empire, but instead of being set at the turn of the century, it revolves around the events of 1848. The narrative follows two male friends, framing nationalism as requiring strong men. One obstacle to manhood is marriage to a non-Romanian, so the main character's wife, a Hungarian, needs to die for the masculinist nationalist plot to develop. His daughter falls in love with a Hungarian man, and she too dies to prevent her marriage outside the ethnic group. As in Rebreanu's novel, the nationalist claim is anchored in the presumed superiority of Transylvanian Romanians not over Hungarians and Saxons but over two racialized Transylvanian groups: "Romanians were not a small meagre nation, like the Gypsies or the Jews, they cannot be humiliated,—they are a great, old and glorious people [*Românii nu erau un popor mic, nenorocit, ca țiganii sau ca ovreii, după cum erau batjocoriți,—ei sunt un neam mare, vechiu, și glorios*]."[57] The juxtaposition of Rebreanu's and Hodoș's novels makes legible a comparative arc anchored in the risk of intermarriage and the protection of Romanian Transylvanian girls. Through such formulations, Hodoș's novel positions itself not only within a similar masculinist ideological narrative but also within the inter-imperial racial field described in chapters 2 and 3. Hodoș's female characters are more developed, but they are enlisted in the struggle for similar ideological ends. One character even kisses the cherished Transylvanian land.

Rebreanu left the Austro-Hungarian Empire during World War I and finished his novel in Romania. The first Romanian-language female modernist writer to enter the literary canon was Hortensia Papadat-Bengescu, whose 1919 debut novel, *Ape adânci* (Deep waters), was published by Alcalay Press, which also published *Ion* in 1920.[58] Papadat-Bengescu's writing implicitly engages Romania's inter-imperial history, but the modernity that corresponds to her work's modernism has other interests in women, including women's education. At a distance from the struggle for the nation in Transylvania, Papadat-Bengescu could develop a self-described feminine literary project and directly stage the issue of women's education. Not surprisingly, then, in Papadat-Bengescu's novel, as in countless works of global modernism, women read and write, they learn to swim, they speak about the desires of the flesh, and they dance to nontraditional tunes. Papadat-Bengescu's women profess their love for other women and invoke a suffering "without a name."[59] A chapter titled "Women among Themselves" dramatizes an encounter among four types of modern women, chatting and sharing intimate stories. One is childless, a predicament described as "consoling."[60] A modern girl, a tennis player with cigarette in hand, comes across as a New Woman. Her masculinity is ironized but not dismissed. Land is kissed in Papadat-Bengescu's novel too, but the female characters are dreaming of a country without end and without borders, inspired by a Rome that is not the ancestral home of Romanians but one where all peoples find a home. If Hodoș's novel is aligned with Rebreanu's ideologically, Papadat-Bengescu's dramatization of modern women's urban lives and desires offers a backdrop against which to understand Rebreanu's brand of modernism in a global framework. Papadat-Bengescu's modernism imagines itself as cosmopolitan in spirit.[61] She aspires to "the world republic of letters" through an attunement with both European modernist forms (especially Proustian) and the politics of (white) women's literature. In contradistinction, Rebreanu's *Ion* aims to enter the same republic of letters by sketching an altogether different global predicament: rural women on the periphery and semi-periphery of the world-system, tasked with embodying the nation for various inter-imperial nationalisms. In the latter case, women's struggles as women, including the struggle for education, are often delayed, redirected, or belittled.

GOD IS THE NEW CHURCH
The Ethnicization of Religion

An analysis of religion in conjunction with inter-imperiality is overdue. Religious experience often sustains the institutions supporting disenfranchised populations in inter-imperial spaces, where religious institutions often double as political and social institutions. A focus on religion provides an opportunity to unpack various forms of enchantment—including nationalism—that coexist with the specific rationality of modern social organization. Such a focus reveals the mechanisms through which religion cultivates emotions, including fear and hope, that can be enlisted in a variety of projects, both progressive and conservative. Studying religion, we often account for a moral system, which likewise travels from the religious to the social and political realms. A spotlight on religion can illuminate everyday experiences of spirituality, which might or might not overlap with institutionalized religion. An understanding of religion often gives us a model of community and its modes of attachment, including solidarity—especially relevant in a rural context. Finally, the power dynamic attached to religious experience is in need of interrogation. In this chapter, we analyze the relation between inter-imperiality and religion, as seen through the prism of Transylvania.

Depending on how one counts—as with languages, we encounter lists—there were at least seven organized religions (confessions) in Transylvania at the turn of the twentieth century: Greek Orthodox, Roman Catholic, Greek Catholic, Calvinist, Evangelical Lutheran, Unitarian, and Judaic. Two denominations served Transylvanian Romanians: Greek Orthodox and Greek Catholic. Transylvanian Hungarians were primarily Roman Catholic and Calvinist, with Lutheran and

Unitarian minorities. Transylvanian Saxons were primarily Lutheran, with a Calvinist minority. Within Judaism, there were Orthodox and Reformed Jewish communities, as well as a small number of Szekler Sabbatarians who practiced Judaism.[1] There were also significant atheist populations nominally associated with each of these groups.

Multiple threads come together in this last chapter. We return to the land problem and add a significant religious element to the discussion of landownership in chapter 1. We revisit the narrative of capitalist integration analyzed in chapter 2, with the reminder that priests constituted a financial elite and that antisemitism worked as a form of exclusion from groups whose nationalism was inseparable from religion. We remind the reader that the institution of enslavement analyzed in chapter 3 might not have endured for four centuries were it not for the complicity of religious institutions. The interglottism analyzed in chapter 4 finds a foil in Transylvania's multiconfessional culture, and a monoglot linguistic nationalism finds symmetry in the desire for a national religion. The gender dynamics traced in chapters 5 and 6 become inseparable from a religious ideology that tasks women with the life of inter-imperial nationalism while camouflaging patriarchal violence against women. In all these instances, we reinscribe the inter-imperial dynamics that institutionalized religion had unleashed on subaltern social strata, languages, and histories into the very concept of modernity. We thus creolize the prevailing understanding of the modern, rather than relegate religion to a traditional, premodern remnant of an obsolete past.

Multiconfessionalism, Conversion, and Toleration

Transylvania's history of multiconfessionalism is concomitantly a history of conversion—moving between religious options as subjects negotiate their identities vis-à-vis a number of inter-imperial power configurations. In the sixteenth century, the Reformation saw conversions from Roman Catholicism to Lutheranism, Calvinism, and Unitarianism. During the seventeenth and eighteenth centuries, the Counter-Reformation witnessed conversions back to Catholicism. In the eighteenth century, some Greek Orthodox believers converted to the Greek Catholic Church, also known as the Romanian Church United with Rome or the Uniate Church. Some converted back again. Some Roma assimilated into the Orthodox, Greek Catholic, and Roman Catholic Churches while maintaining elements of their own religious traditions. Orthodox Armenians—historically Coptic Orthodox—converted to Roman Catholicism. Some Szeklers converted to Judaism; when they were persecuted, they converted to Calvinism and then converted back to Judaism.[2] Many Jews converted to Christianity.[3] As in other parts of the world, conversions often went hand in hand with shifts in the power structure in general or state control in particular. Conversions constituted a type of agency that allowed inter-imperial subjects to position themselves within a structurally unequal field of alternatives and negotiate their options in a shifting terrain.[4] In Transylvania, the meanings of modernity were closely entangled with the politics of conversion, reflecting the role religion played in both inter-imperiality and coloniality.

Other than the number of confessions and cycles of conversion, Transylvania's status as a meeting place for three Christian churches—Catholic, Protestant, and Orthodox—makes it unique in religious history. Transylvania functioned as a venue for negotiations between the Reformation and the Counter-Reformation. Alongside Holland and England, Transylvania is considered the birthplace of the concept of religious tolerance that emerged at the time of the Counter-Reformation. Through the Uniate Church, Transylvania offered a meeting point for Eastern and Western Christianity, an attempt to overcome the 1054 schism that divided Europe in two, with long-term consequences.[5] Transylvania's history is therefore crucial to a relational, tripartite understanding of the global history of Christianity. At the same time, a creolized account of the role of modern religions weaves non-Christian beliefs and religious institutions into Transylvania's religious makeup to render this history truly global.

In the early modern period, Transylvania was known as the land of the "three nations": Hungarian, Szekler, and Saxon. Following the Reformation, these three nations had three "accepted" religions: Roman Catholic, Lutheran (since 1557), and Calvinist (since 1564). A fourth was added to the mix in 1568: Unitarian. Lurking on the margins of its early modern inter-imperial history, associated with the racialization of religion within modernity/coloniality, was Transylvania's claim to autonomy during Ottoman times, celebrated as helping to minimize the spread of Islam and its influence on other local religions. However, the relation between Christianity and Islam was much more complex. The Ottoman Empire, which gained influence after the conquest of Buda, developed a protectionist attitude toward the Reformation. Stephen Fischer-Galati argues that local Protestantism survived in part because of Ottoman protectionism.[6] The inter-imperial tension between the Habsburg and Ottoman Empires—one dedicated to self-serving religious homogeneity and the other to self-serving religious diversity—provided protection for Protestants.[7] Susan Ritchie argues that through the Edict of Torda/Turda (1568), which legislated universal freedom of worship, "Transylvania eventually became one of the safest places in Europe for the development of progressive Protestantism." She refers to the Edict of Torda/Turda as "a shared Islamic-Unitarian undertaking," acknowledging the role of the Ottoman Empire—and, in broader terms, the inter-imperial force field—in the emergence of toleration as a religious principle.[8] However, Europe's growing self-assertion as Christian and Western in the "long sixteenth century," following the conquest of Muslim Granada by the Catholic monarchs and the subsequent colonial expansion into the Americas, informed attitudes and policies toward religious others. As Charles V, head of the rising House of Habsburg and of the Spanish and German colonies in the Americas, strove to become the leader of Christendom, coloniality gradually overrode the Ottoman imperial policy of religious tolerance. As a result, the perceived threat of Islamification took hold in tolerant Transylvania as well and remained a leitmotif in the *longue durée*. The inter-imperial history of Transylvania thus offers a unique perspective on the history of Christianity, given its triangular complexity and its global relation to Islam.

Despite its reputation as a haven of toleration, Transylvania had its limits, both before and after being encroached on by coloniality. Greek Orthodoxy was not recognized as an "accepted" religion of the land, and its "tolerated" status led to long-standing struggles over religious rights. The religion of Orthodox believers was recognized in 1781, with Joseph II's Patent of Toleration.[9] For the Jewish population, the situation oscillated between periods of persecution and toleration. Judaism was granted legal status in Hungary in 1895. As noted in chapter 3, Roma in Transylvania were forced to assimilate—renounce their traditional dress and occupations and attend Christian churches. They were called "New Christians"—the same term used in Habsburg Spain to refer to the converted Moors. As elsewhere, the tolerated were conditionally accepted by the powerful, who chose *not* to act in situations when they could have used their power.[10] As Robert Stam and Ella Shohat remind us, tolerance reinforces a religious and social norm.[11] That Transylvania is considered the birthplace of toleration speaks to the tension among a hierarchy of inter-imperial religious options and, ultimately, to the imbrication of modernity with both coloniality and inter-imperiality.

Catholicization as Civilizing Mission

The church in Prislop/Priszlop, the village on which Rebreanu modeled his fictional Pripas, was Greek Catholic at the turn of the twentieth century. Rebreanu does not specify the denomination of the church in his novel, describing it simply as a Romanian church, a sign of the increasing ethnicization of religion in the inter-imperial field. English-language religious studies rarely focus on the Greek Catholic Church. This version of the Christian church was founded in 1701, following Transylvania's incorporation into the Habsburg Empire after the defeat of the Ottomans. Its founding was an attempt at Catholicization anchored in the

Habsburg project of confessional absolutism in a region known for its multilin-gualism and its confessional puzzle—both considered signs of backwardness. Catholicization often took coercive forms in the western parts of the Habsburg Empire (against Protestants and Jews), but with the founding of the Greek Cath-olic Church, the Habsburg project of Catholicization was negotiated differently on the eastern border of the empire—in Transylvania and Galicia.

A *longue durée* approach to the imbrication of religion, inter-imperiality, and coloniality provides the necessary context for understanding the Catholic mis-sion in Transylvania. As we mentioned, the Spanish Empire that conquered the Americas increasingly defined itself along religious lines. Following the 1492 conquest of the kingdom of Granada, the last Muslim state in West Europe, by the Spanish Catholic monarchs, Jews were expelled from the Iberian Peninsula by royal decree. Castilian Spain initially continued the project of assimilating the Moriscos—Moors who had been converted to Christianity. In 1609 the Moors too were expelled, while the remaining Jewish and Muslim converts were under constant suspicion of secretly practicing non-Christian faiths.[12] Early modern Spain distinguished between "old Christians" and "new Christians"—with mo-mentous consequences. The principle of "purity of blood" (in Spanish, *limpieza de sangre*) was gradually institutionalized, and all individuals considered of "impure" descent—that is, Jews, Muslims, and other non-Christians—were banned from holding public and religious office and any position of authority within the university, the army, or the municipality.[13]

Jewish people's expulsion from Spain in 1492 was followed by Christopher Columbus's "discovery" of the "New World" that same year.[14] Spain's conquest of more territories in the Americas and Charles V's rise to power over the first modern empire with colonies throughout Europe and the Americas strength-ened the belief in the "divine mission" of Christendom. This set the stage for a reconfiguration of West European Christian identity in the sixteenth century.[15] In turn, this reconfigured Christian identity provided a link between the reli-gious pattern in Spain (Christians, Jews, Moors) and that in the New World (Christians, Native Americans, enslaved Africans). The colonial reorganization of religious difference inaugurated a modern racial order, which in turn yielded the racialized division of labor undergirding the emerging capitalist world-economy. The Spanish Empire's colonization of the Americas produced a modern concept of race that shaped subsequent practices involving the production of dif-ference around a religious core. Importantly, both the imperial difference within Europe and the colonial difference in the conquered areas would define the racial Other through the possibility or impossibility of conversion.

This early modern history created a split between colonial difference and im-perial difference. Once it was defeated in the Americas, the Habsburg Empire turned east and expanded toward the eastern periphery of Europe. The central imperial difference that anchored the intra-European imperial project was religious: Christian Orthodoxy was Oriental, with that term's meaning caught between Hellenistic and Russophile connotations.[16] The other Oriental form of Eastern Christianity was Coptic, the target of colonial missionary zeal, especially in Africa, as documented by Saba Mahmood.[17] Importantly, the Orientalism associated with Orthodoxy was defined through its proximity to Islam, a function of its inter-imperial history of both dependence on the Ottoman Empire and resistance to it. A crucial dimension of the Habsburg expansion was therefore an effort to convert Orthodox Christians, perceived as "tainted" by Islam, to Catholicism—over time leading to a creolized form of modern religiosity. Like in the Americas, Catholicizing East Europe was considered a civilizing mission. To this day, the civilizational line drawn by Samuel Huntington through the middle of East Europe coincides with the religious line separating Catholicism, on the one hand, from Orthodoxy and Islam, on the other. Huntington merely reproduced the religious boundary anchoring the Habsburg discourse of a civilizing mission.

The Habsburg extension to the east happened at the same time as West Europe's Enlightenment, when the latter ostensibly embraced secularism. By the nineteenth century, West European empires claimed they were exporting secularism rather than Christianity. Populations around the world undergoing modernization on a European model were now being invited by modernizing elites to convert to secularism. We rarely consider the fact that this happened in both European colonies and East Europe—resulting in an extended period when secularism was almost synonymous with modern rationality. This brand of secularism was infused with Christian assumptions, anchored in the continuity between the Christian promise of redemption and a secular narrative of progress, but presented as a form of universalism.[18] The very terms of the debate derived from the language of Christianity, because *religion* rarely approximated experiences of the *sacred* around the world.[19] Far from being a religion, Hinduism, for example, was a colonial invention meant to give colonial elites an understanding of the range of spiritual experiences on the Indian subcontinent. In the context of India, where Hinduism was neither institutionalized nor based on a sacred text, the colonial introduction of the category "religion" was intended to group Hindus and Muslims under one label and delimit them from one another; the intervention created, to some extent, the modern interreligious conflict. Questions of secularism in India therefore concerned not the separation of state and religion but the state's relationship to religious minorities.[20]

The founding of the Greek Catholic Church in Transylvania occurred against this global background. It involved negotiations over religious dogma and concessions—such as marriage for priests. Romanian Transylvanians, who were largely Orthodox Christians at the turn of the eighteenth century, were encouraged to convert to Catholicism as a way to claim equality with other citizens of the empire. The long road to citizenship thus passed through the acceptance of Greek Catholicism. There was a world-historical dimension to this promise of social and political equality through conversion to a more powerful denomination—a phenomenon occurring on a global scale as a function of coloniality as well as inter-imperiality.[21] In the case of Transylvanian Romanians, this involved a conversion from an Oriental to an Occidental form of Christianity. In terms proposed by Peter van der Veer, such a move also constituted a necessary step toward a "conversion to modernity." Van der Veer considers the latter an "interplay between Europe and the colonized world," following a shift whereby "conversion of others is gradually marginalized in modern Europe and transported to the non-Christian, colonized world."[22] This chapter argues that the politics of conversion to modernity played out in East Europe as well, in an integrated relation to coloniality and the colonized world but inflected as inter-imperiality.

We know that Jesuits were enlisted in the colonial civilizing mission in the Americas. Before their suppression in 1773, Jesuits assisted the imperial project of Catholicization in Transylvania. They sometimes did so by drawing direct comparisons between their work in the Habsburg peripheries and in the European colonies. Resistant populations in Transylvania (Romanian and Romani) were Orientalized through such comparisons.[23] In the case of Eastern Orthodoxy, resistance to Jesuit missionary zeal constituted not a resistance to Christianity, as it was in other parts of the world; rather, it was an intra-Christian affair. To understand the interlinking of coloniality and the politics of conversion as a world-historical phenomenon, the history of Catholicization in East Europe must therefore be brought into this conversation. Tellingly for the inter-imperial predicament, Orthodox believers taunted the Uniates as papists, accusing the Catholic Church of imperial overreach, while the Uniates insulted the Orthodox as Muscovites, pointing to Russian Orthodoxy's imperial overreach.[24] Adding to the dynamic of inter-imperiality analyzed in previous chapters, we can now posit that inter-imperiality and its attending creolizations also played out between religious fields.

Secular Governance

According to the preeminent theorist of secularism Charles Taylor, Western secularity is "so new, and so unprecedented, that comparisons with other epochs and places will be misleading."[25] This anticomparatist perspective excludes the possibility of an account of secularity in relation to Eastern Christianity. And yet, a revised perspective that foregrounds comparative secularisms globally reveals that what happened in West Europe was not isolated; it developed in relation to the colonial project and impacted colonies, ex-colonies, and inter-imperial zones—outside of Europe and in East Europe.[26] Mahmood argues that "insomuch as secularism is characterized by a globally shared form of national-political structuration, the regulation of religious difference takes a modular form across geographical boundaries."[27] What does it mean to bring the question of secularity into a part of Europe that Taylor did not consider the purview of *A Secular Age*?[28] This multiconfessional Europe was not only slow and reluctant to secularize; it was also an unlikely combination (from Taylor's perspective) and a creole mix (from our perspective) that included the two elements that, for Taylor, propel secularism: Christianity and, in the case of Transylvanian Romanians, Latinity.[29]

Decolonial approaches to religion have critiqued Taylor's view and other Hegelian understandings of modernity as a linear sequence and a cumulative result of events, from the Renaissance through the Reformation and up to the French Revolution. In *The Underside of Modernity*, Enrique Dussel points out that this perspective obscures the fact that these landmarks of European modernity are but consequences of more decisive global events, such as the "discovery" of the "New World" and Europe's rise to the center of the world-system: "what was perhaps already the 'consequence' of the European centrality over a world periphery . . . was instead presented as the 'consequence' of rationalization, science, and the 'modern self.' Taylor may have been totally mistaken."[30] Thus, when Taylor writes, "In the nineteenth century, one might say, unbelief comes of age," we respond by drawing attention to the many manifestations of belief coexisting alongside unbelief in parts of East Europe.[31] As we will see, a critical reading of Rebreanu's *Ion* supports our reframing of modernity's relation to religion not only for non-European contexts but also for inter-imperial Transylvania.

The major figures on the Hungarian side of the Habsburg Empire in 1848 were Enlightenment thinkers. In their desire to build a secular state, they advocated religious pluralism and tolerance. József Eötvös (encountered in chapters 2 and 4) was a devout Catholic, but he firmly believed in the separation of church and state and called for the autonomy and equality of all religious institutions of the empire.[32] Jewish emancipation served as a test of secularity.[33] As the narrative went, all members of the polity, regardless of belief, were included in the political body. The state was purportedly neutral from a religious point of view. This narrative aligns with Taylor's understanding of secularism as a mode of accommodating pluralism. Since the Austro-Hungarian Empire imagined itself as a multicultural society (as we have seen, more so on the Austrian side than the Hungarian side), it also needed to imagine itself as secular. However, Catholicism was not one option in a plurality of religions; rather, it was the "civilized" form of religion in an inter-imperial order. Protestantism was a close second in an imagined civilizational competition. Far from being neutral, the secular state managed and participated in the production of this religious hierarchy. It thus reconfigured religiosity to suit its needs. In this kind of situation, Mahmood thus identifies a "generative contradiction" for modern secularism.[34] As we will see, this contradiction was fully at work in the Transylvanian context.

Within the Austro-Hungarian Empire, the Hungarian state's projects for secular governance were manifold. Most importantly, as noted in chapter 4, the imperial state was invested in secularizing education in Transylvania. State schools—by definition, secular—were meant to slowly replace religious schools. The process of Magyarization was understood as, essentially, a secular project; its claims to legitimacy in the Budapest parliament were made in the name of modern secular progress. Similarly, there was a sustained effort to secularize marriage, which was taken from the jurisdiction of churches. Bookkeeping was removed from the purview of religious institutions and transferred to that of the imperial bureaucracy. But if these were efforts at secularization, the imperial state also regularly interfered with the supposed autonomy of the religious sphere. The debate regarding the separation of Transylvanian Orthodoxy from an imperially imposed Serbian tutelage was symptomatic of the imperial state's investment in maintaining a denominational hierarchy at odds with the claim to coeval religious pluralism. Joseph II's 1783 decree placed the Transylvanian Orthodox Church under the jurisdiction of Carlowitz/Sremski Karlovci, a situation that lasted until 1864.[35] The struggle for separation constituted a claim to religious autonomy for Transylvanian Romanians, which further ethnicized religion. In contrast to the secular claim, this debate was witness to an imperfect differentiation between religious and political institutions. The multidimensional conflict, extending into multiple layers of society, testified to a religious predicament underlying the secular thesis. As Mahmood has argued, a religious hierarchy produced at least in part by the secular state exacerbates religious tensions in religiously diverse parts of the world, leading to renewed polarization of religious difference.

Postsecular Nationalism

The narrative of religious pluralism and toleration that developed in Transylvania during the Reformation and Counter-Reformation changed most consequentially in the nineteenth century, as it intersected anti-imperial efforts that enlisted religion in their projects. Benedict Anderson argues that nationalism is both territorial (requiring bordered land) and linguistic (requiring a national language). Anderson understands nationalism's modernity as entailing a progressive secularism; nationalism thrives in the woundlike void left by the waning of religion. The risk in this argument is that the secular standpoint characterizes religion as nonmodern, retrograde. This possibility is confirmed by Taylor's definition of secularity, which places societies where "religion was everywhere" not only outside the West (which, for Taylor, overlaps with Latin Christendom) but also back in time.[36] In a "country and city" framework, from this perspective, religion becomes a sign of backwardness, with peasants enchanted by religious belief and therefore lost to the modern national cause.

A reading of Rebreanu's *Ion* suggests that, in addition to its claim to land and language, anti-imperial nationalism mobilizes religion. There are multiple explanations for religion's centrality to the construction of nationalism. Religious institutions provided an infrastructure for cultural mobility, linking Romanian-language populations in Moldova and Wallachia. Keith Hitchins argues that the relationships among the three Romanian-language principalities (Moldova, Wallachia, Transylvania) in the eighteenth century were primarily religious.[37] Toward the end of the nineteenth century, there was a sense that nationalism could no longer accommodate the tension between the two Romanian Transylvanian churches, Orthodox and Uniate. If nationalism demanded one language mapped onto one territory, inter-imperial nationalism demanded one religion. Increasingly, anti-imperial leadership overlapped with religious leadership. This observation offers an important insight into ongoing debates about the postsecular: the *post* in postsecular is not temporal (it does not mark a time *after* the secular, which was never actualized); rather, it is critical (it places a question mark next to secularism). As a critical term, *postsecularism*, used selectively, offers a more rigorous historicism concerning this region's modernity, attentive to the multiconfessional inter-imperial dynamic. How, then, is this historicism related to a creolized notion of the modern?

To answer this question, we return to the inter-imperial notion of nationalism addressed in previous chapters. How do we explain the fact that many anti-imperial struggles around the world are religious? In colonial and postcolonial settings, secularism is often perceived as a Western ideology, an import from West Europe. Similarly, in inter-imperial situations, secularism often "(re)appears as a colonial vestige," an argument convincingly made by Piro Rexhepi in relation to Bosnia and Herzegovina.[38] In both contexts, therefore, religion continues to be a powerful force in projects of resistance to empire, creolizing a supposedly linear trajectory to a secular, rational modernity. Nationalist projects often attempt to rejuvenate precolonial or preimperial traditions, whether ongoing or newly reinvented. A variety of postcolonial and anti-imperial nationalisms around the world thus enlist indigenous religious traditions in their projects. This is often the case, with important modifications, in inter-imperial settings like Transylvania, where anti-imperial movements often mobilize around denominational identifications, which are then translated into broader markers of cultural identity. In these inter-imperial regions, the coming of the modern coincides with the coming of "courage" and "authenticity"—to use Taylor's terms—which in turn are inseparable from religion.[39] In chapter 5 we analyzed one aspect of inter-imperial, faith-based resistance, mobilizing around the spirituality of the women of the nation. In this chapter, we delve deeper into the religious matrix of Transylvanian Romanian nationalism as it reacts to and coexists with a very specific form of imperial secularity.

It is within the *longue durée* framework linking coloniality to religion that we come to understand that some of the most prominent leaders of nineteenth-century Romanian Transylvanian nationalism were religious figures. Inochentie Micu-Klein of the Transylvanian School (Şcoala Ardeleană), who advocated for political and linguistic rights at the end of the eighteenth century, was a bishop in the Uniate Church. In the mid-nineteenth century, Andrei Şaguna, an Orthodox bishop, took up the mantle. Education in the Romanian language was facilitated by religious institutions. Grigore Silaşi, a professor of Romanian literature at the University of Cluj/Kolozsvár/Klausenburg, was a Uniate priest. George Bariţiu, a prominent intellectual and journalist, was trained in theology. Alexandru Mocioni explained the link between the religious and nationalist spheres: "We understand, then, why the national church has been, is, and will forever remain the existential condition for the survival of the Romanian people. . . . The cultural role of the church is to moralize the people [*Pricepem deci, de ce biserica naţională a fost, este şi va rămânea în veci condiţiunea de viaţă a poporului român. . . . misiunea culturală a bisericei este moralizarea popoarelor*]."[40] One can discern echoes of the argument articulated by Partha Chatterjee in the Indian context: spiritual life (the moralizing of the people), which is used as a claim to sovereignty, is overlaid with religious life. Romanian Orthodoxy in particular functioned simultaneously as both religion and culture.[41] Although anti-imperial nationalism featured secularizing elites, especially in the latter part of the nineteenth century, it cannot be grasped outside its religious condition. Secularization is delayed when religion anchors cultural identity in the service of nationalism.[42]

Thus, when Aamir Mufti proposes that "the fate of the great secularization project of eighteenth-century Europe is being determined in the contemporary postcolonial world," we point to the related struggle over secularization in East

Europe.[43] Similarly, when Mahmood argues that postsecularism does not make sense in India, we caution that it does not make sense within an European East-West dichotomy and within a European empire like the Habsburg either. In Mufti's words, echoed by Rexhepi, secularism comes across "as a Western ideology, to be countered by the recuperation of truly indigenous lived traditions."[44] In a context in which the religious and the national codetermine each other, secularization and progress do not go hand in hand. To understand this predicament in an inter-imperial framework, we need a revised method of secular criticism.

On Literary and Religious Canons

The first modern Romanian-language novel begins and ends with a cross. What does it mean for a modern novel to be bookended by a religious sign? What kind of literary framing device is a cross? What does this cross tell us about the novel's canonicity? What does it tell us about the relation between religion and literature? In this book, we examined several aspects of the struggle over land as dramatized by Rebreanu's *Ion*: it is an ethnic struggle, a racial struggle, a linguistic struggle; it is a tension between the country and the city, between gender emancipation and conservativism. In this chapter, we add another, often overlooked dimension to this already complex dynamic: religion. Rebreanu's novel dramatizes the interplay between a heterogeneous mix of religions and secularisms in an inter-imperial framework.

In the opening scene of the novel (whose spatial dynamics we analyzed in chapter 1), as the narrative traces the road to the village of Pripas, it pauses to remark on a cross:

> At the left edge of the village you are welcomed by a crooked cross on which a Christ with a weather-beaten face is crucified, a wreath of faded flowers dangling from his legs. There is a faint breeze and Christ dolefully shivers its rusty tin body against the moth-eaten wood, blackened by time. (9)
>
> *La marginea satului te întâmpină din stânga o cruce strâmbă pe care e răstignit un Hristos cu fața spălăcită de ploi și cu o cununiță de flori vestejite agățată de picioare. Suflă o adiere ușoară, și Hristos își tremură jalnic trupul de tinichea ruginită pe lemnul mâncat de carii și înnegrit de vremuri.* (11–12)[45]

The crookedness of the cross, the discoloration of Christ's face, and the weathered flowers suggest that the inhabitants of the village pay little attention to these religious signs. The text naturalizes the presence of the cross at the entrance to the village. Like the village itself, the cross has seemingly always occupied this space. Time itself is being invoked through the cross. Hospitality—to visitors, to the narrator, to the text—coincides with a forceful insertion into a religious predicament. The cross marks the space, revealing that the novel's mapping involves a mode of spatialization filtered through religious difference. Having introduced the cross, the novel mentions an "old little church, sad and ramshackle [*bisericuța bătrână, pleoștită și dărăpănată*]" (10, 13). This unassuming church becomes a crucial actor in the inter-imperial drama.

Completing a perfect circular structure, the last scene of the novel returns to the cross that welcomed the reader: "Across the road, from his wooden cross, face gilded by a belated ray of sunlight, the tin Christ seemed to be caressing them, his body quivering in the autumn evening breeze [*Peste drum, pe crucea de lemn, Hristosul de tinichea, cu fața poleită de o rază întârziată, parcă îi mângâia, zuruindu-și ușor trupul în adierea înserării de toamnă*]" (409, 573). If the perspective in the opening scene of the novel was that of a visitor entering the village, now it is that of someone leaving, walking into the sunset invoked by the belated ray of sun. As the reader is exiting the text, the Herdeleas are moving to the city, concluding their narrative of inter-imperial bourgeoisification, which includes Titu's turn to literature. The novel Titu will write one day, the novel we are reading, is coming to an end. The Herdeleas look back on the village, surveying it, visually taking hold of its landscape. Filtered through their gaze, the village reassuringly seems as unchanged as the cross and its shivering Christ. The one visible sign of change is the tower of a shiny new church, which replaced the humble wooden structure encountered at the beginning of the novel. To a large extent, the reader now realizes, the novel has been about the building of this church. As if a gloss on Proust, the steeple of the new church reorganizes the landscape, functioning as its only vertical, erect symbolic reference. The cross that bookends the novel has done its job, overseeing a modern plot whose dénouement turns out to be the building of a religious edifice. In conjunction with nationalist historiography, such as the publication in 1908–1909 of Nicolae Iorga's *History of the Romanian Church*, the first modern Romanian novel stages an implacable and consequential meshing of inter-imperiality, modernity, nation, and religion. Aside from the land problem, which props Rebreanu's claims to the canon, this religious configuration reinforces *Ion's* enduring canonicity.

We know that criticism dedicated to an analysis of the coloniality/modernity/religion nexus needs to be attentive to practices of othering anchored in deep-seated, often tacit religious assumptions. In our case, Rebreanu's novel makes it clear that antisemitism cannot be divorced from religion. In one episode, Titu invites his lover, Roza Lang, and her husband to his parents' house on Christmas. Roza's husband is Jewish, and Titu's mother reacts:

The arrival of these guests disturbed Mrs. Herdelea's happiness, she was cross that Titu desecrated the holidays by bringing some Jews into the house, no matter how much the young man tried to explain to her that the Langs were in fact not Jewish, although he was a Jew, because they were not following the Jewish law, or any law for that matter. (141)

    Sosirea acestor mosafiri tulbură mulțumirea doamnei Herdelea, bosumflată că Titu i-a adus în casă niște jidani să-i pângărească sărbătorile, oricât se silise tânărul să-i explice că soții Lang, deși el e ovreu, nu sunt jidani, deoarece nu țin legea jidovească, ba chiar nici o lege. (200–201)

Titu goes to great lengths to explain to his mother that the Langs are secular Jews. He emphasizes that Mr. Lang is *evreu* (a generic term) but not *jidan* (a racialized term), because he does not practice Judaism. But in Mrs. Herdelea's world, Jews are Jews whether they practice, reform, convert, or are atheists. Coloniality has by now encroached upon an inter-imperial framing of religion, and the suspicion hovering over Jewish people remaining in the Iberian Peninsula has traveled to and taken hold in the European East as well. This form of racism is accordingly infused with religion, which is why the Langs' presence taints the sacredness of Christmas. The verb *pângări* is derived from the noun *păgân* (in Latin, *paganus*), a non-Christian. Historically, given the inter-imperial Ottoman history of the region, the word applied to Turks and Muslims. In time, its use became a generalized mode of othering and could apply to atheists as well. In Rebreanu's text, *păgân* attaches to secular Jewish characters who follow no religious law. The presence of these characters implies sacrilege and profanity vis-à-vis the Christian religious holiday. We are missing something important about the Transylvanian ethnic and racial field if we do not attend to the enmeshing of religion and inter-imperiality in such practices of othering—that is, if we do not creolize our understanding of the modern they embody.

The Comedy of Power

One area in which secular criticism imposes itself is in the analysis of power. Religion can be a very powerful force—within an already complex field of power relations. Hitchins writes about the politicization of the clergy in nineteenth-century Transylvania: "They [political elites] recognized the great influence that the clergy exerted, particularly among the peasantry, and they were eager to enlist both bishops and priests as regular participants in the national movement. . . . For some, he [the priest] was the chief defender of the nation at the grass roots level."[46] Returning to a "country and city" critical framework, we analyze the priest's role in the anti-imperial national movement at the grassroots level—among peasants.

One must read slowly and carefully to uncover Transylvania's multiconfessional history in Rebreanu's text, which presents the village of Pripas as ethnically and religiously homogeneous.[47] Other Transylvanian villages and cities invoked in *Ion* are, however, marked by multiple religious signs. Armadia, modeled after the Transylvanian city of Năsăud/Nassod/Naszód, features an Orthodox church and a small, old Catholic church (100, 143). Bistriţa/Bistritz/Beszterce, a real-life Transylvanian city, is dominated by a Saxon church tower: "the steeple of the Saxon church, a giant sultry sentry, clad in immemorial clothes, grey and age-worn [*turnul bisericii săseşti, un paznic uriaş şi ursuz, îmbrăcat în straie străvechi, cenuşii, mâncate de vreme*]" (272, 382). Readers are told that the courthouse in Bistriţa/Bistritz/Beszterce stands "between the Romanian and the Saxon churches [*între biserica românească şi cea săsească*]" (273, 383). The village of Gargalău, where Titu relocates, has two unequal churches: "In the middle of the village, the new Hungarian church rose haughtily, a white weathercock at the top of its steeple. . . . On the outskirts of the village, like hungry beggars, came humble, poverty-stricken hovels, thatched with sooty straw, and, hidden shyly in a corner, was the little Romanian wooden church, a ramshackle, with a small tapering spire of mouldy shingles [*În mijloc se înălţa trufaşă, cu un cocoş alb în vârful turnului, biserica ungurească nouă. . . . Pe la margini, ca nişte cerşetori flămânzi, se răzleţeau bordeie murdare, umile, învelite cu paie afumate şi, într-un colţ, ruşinoasă, se ascundea parcă bisericuţa românească de lemn, dărăpănată, cu turnuleţul ţuguiat de şindrilă mucigăită*]" (172–73, 244–45). Often, like in this last formulation, the text displays church envy: the Hungarian church's haughty demeanor humiliates the modest Romanian church. Inequality is measured through the size and state of an ethnic group's church. All in all, these religious signs write the landscape into an uneven multiconfessional script against an uneven inter-imperial background. The result is a network of religious institutions populated along ethnic, racial, and class lines, entangled with issues pertaining to language.

In Rebreanu's novel, there are two leaders in the village of Pripas: the priest (Belciug) and the teacher (Herdelea). Belciug is the name of a real-life priest in the village of Prislop/Priszlop, after which Pripas is modeled. Belciug served between 1896 and 1922.[48] Herdelea is a fictional name, and the character is a composite of teachers Rebreanu knew in his childhood, including his father. With the duo of Belciug and Herdelea, two village lower-middle-class intellectuals, Rebreanu creates a couple in the tradition of *Don Quijote*'s priest and barber. In literary history, once one has a priest, a barber, and a group of peasants, one has a village. The priest occupies a stable position from Cervantes to Rebreanu, raising questions about the centrality of the secular to the genre of the novel more generally. Rebreanu's text is ambivalent about the inevitability of the priest's presence. On the one hand, the priest represents a crucial point of reference for the community. On the other hand, in the tradition of Cervantes and Rabelais, he is an object of ridicule.

The novel's rural narrative track splits in two. One revolves around the conflict between Ion and Vasile Baciu over Ana's dowry: the land. The other revolves around Titu's development into a poet and nationalist intellectual. We analyzed the interglot plotting of Titu's development, which witnesses his turn to monoglottism, in chapter 4. A subplot on this second track concerns the conflict between the priest and the teacher, each aiming to garner more power over the villagers. The priest's name, Belciug, refers to a metal ring attached to an object so that a chain or a lock can be placed on it. Romanian-language idioms use the word to form constructions that suggest chaining or harnessing something for the purpose of trickery or control. For example, a *belciug* attached to an animal's nose implies physical manipulation. Flaubert-like, Rebreanu's use of the proper name Belciug is deeply satirical, pointing to the manipulative power of the priest. Most immediately, both the priest and the teacher maneuver to manipulate Ion.[49] If Ion's desire for land is framed as a naturalist tragedy, the drama between the priest and the teacher—read here as the dramatization of the secularization thesis—is played out as comedy.[50]

The priest and the teacher have authority over the villagers, and they are in competition over who yields more power. The novel refers to the mass of villagers as *prostime* (307, 432)—literally, the stupid masses—a term that invokes ignorant, uneducated peasants. The latter are ignorant on account of their illiteracy, but also implied in the term *prostime* is an assumption of naïve religiosity. The novel asks a crucial theoretical question: how do nationalist elites control the *prostime*? One global mechanism at play draws on religion: redirect peasants' religious devotion toward nationalism. This process necessitates the refashioning of figures like the priest into heroes of the national cause—that is, they become intellectuals. Once peasants believe in the analogy between nation and God, intellectuals like the priest can guide their political lives.

It is crucial to note that although they call the peasants *prostime* and take turns manipulating them, the priest and the teacher function as "sponsors of literacy."[51] Hitchins estimates that there were about 10,000 Romanians in Transylvania who could read and write in 1848; 4,250 were priests, and 1,000 were teachers.[52] In other words, priests accounted for almost half of the literate Romanian Transylvanian population in the second half of the nineteenth century. Both the priest and the teacher teach peasant children to read and write. But because their power in the village is anchored in the peasants' limited literacy, which necessitates translation, they restrict their investment in this project. The result is a profoundly condescending attitude toward peasants. Once the peasants get the vote, through the struggle over land analyzed in chapter 1, they are told how to vote. This is how we arrive at analogies like the one suggesting that Transylvanian Romanians go to the voting booth and to church with the same devotion ("*Românii merg la vot ca la biserică*"). Naïve peasants, as this inter-imperial classism has it, cannot be trusted to know what they want; they need intellectuals to whisper their own desires to them. In Marx's terms, with which Edward Said prefaces *Orientalism*: "they cannot represent themselves, they must be represented."[53] The possibility that peasants are not a mass at all and might want different things is out of the question. So is their full citizen status.

What does it mean to refer to the village priest as an intellectual? Intellectuals, historically, were a secular class. The term emerged out of the secular defense during the Dreyfus affair.[54] To this day, one mode of global secularity is represented by an international secular intelligentsia. And yet, as we have seen, leaders in inter-imperial spaces are often religious figures. Can they serve as intellectuals? Or is *intellectual* a misnomer here? Said has influentially argued that the role of the intellectual is to ask awkward, even embarrassing questions and to function as a contrarian in relation to the powers that be.[55] The priest in Pripas is certainly part of the resistance to empire, especially in relation to the use of language. But if the role of the intellectual is also, in Said's understanding, to reject orthodoxies of opinion, then the priest is often on the side of orthodoxy.

The priest in Rebreanu's novel is a power broker. The signs of his authority are ubiquitous. When he visits the Sunday dance, the villagers welcome him: "The pious old wives rushed up to kiss his hand. 'No, no! don't . . . please stop it!' murmured the priest holding his hand out nevertheless to be kissed with a contentment that enlivened his withered, parched countenance [*Babele cucernice se repeziră numaidecât să-i sărute mâna. Lăsați, lăsați! murmura preotul, întinzând însă dosul palmei spre sărutare, cu o mulțumire ce-i înviora fața tăbăcită de slăbiciune*]" (20, 27). The kissing of the priest's hand has religious connotations as part of ritual, but it is also a recognition of his power in the village. He is village royalty—with all the irony attached to it. The conflict between the priest and the teacher is a symptom of a growing, secularizing resistance to the priest's leadership role. The teacher, a more modern and more secular village leader, challenges the priest's authority, if only slightly and largely unsuccessfully. The priest would like to make claims to modernity, especially the modernity of the nation, but without relinquishing rituals such as hand kissing.

Most importantly, Belciug would like to present himself as a quasi saint. He is old, weak, and a widower. The priest is ill, having famously had kidney surgery in Cluj/Kolozsvár/Klausenburg. His weakness gives him an aura of sainthood:

> Widowhood and intransigence brought him the fame of a saint. People came to him from as far as five counties away, to have him read to them or to confess. The peasants especially respected the fact that, since his deaconess died on him, no one had the feeling he was chasing women. (64)
>
> *Văduvia și strășnicia i-au dobândit faima de sfânt. Veneau la dânsul oameni și din al cincilea județ, să le citească sau să-i spovedească. Țăranii îl respectau mai ales pentru că, de când i-a murit preoteasa, nimeni nu l-a simțit umblând după femei. (90)*

Greek Catholic priests, following a compromise inaugurated at the founding of the Greek Orthodox Church, could choose whether to be married or celibate, but celibacy retained its capital within the Catholic Church hierarchy. Belciug apparently chose marriage, but once his wife died, he returned to celibacy. In Rebreanu's text, the peasants find it surprising that the widowed priest is not harassing women in the village. This observation functions against the historical background of priests, especially widowers, sometimes doubling as village lovers. Gossip about lover-priests, especially Uniate priests, circulated freely.[56] Belciug's purported abstinence is thus unusual, almost heroic. Seamlessly combining Christianity and pre-Christian spirituality, the peasants transform Belciug into a saint and undertake pilgrimages to visit him. He is not, however, a Dostoyevskian saint, a would-be philosopher; Belciug is a clown-saint. The obvious pleasure he derives from hand kissing is an object of satire.

There are numerous other signs of pre-Christian spirituality in the novel. Ion's mother, Zenobia, believes that her son might have been bewitched and wants to prepare charms. George's mother goes to the fortune-teller, worried that Ana is under a spell. Another old woman in the village, Baba Firoana, is both an expert in charms and spells and a midwife of high repute. These signs, all archived as part of the comedic plot, confirm that the modern village analyzed in this book is not disenchanted, in Weber's sense.[57] Belciug condones these acts of deviance from the faith.[58] The peasants are in fact enchanted by a combination of Christianity and pre-Christian spirituality that testifies to a creolized, syncretic type of religious belief. It is crucial to emphasize that this double enchantment does not make the village less modern—rather, its modernity is a function of this constitutive contradiction. In terms proposed by Purushottama Bilimoria, if "secularism is born from the underbelly of modernity as the 'disenchantment of the world' (Weber), the postsecular marks the birthing of the 'disenchantment of secularity.'"[59] In this case, the peasants thus redeploy pre-Christian beliefs within a thoroughly modern environment, where pre-Christian practices signal their disenchantment with the secular promise.

It is equally important to emphasize that the priest's power has an economic dimension. In a village where the peasants complain of poverty, Belciug has a relatively prosperous household and servants: "To cook his food and tidy his rooms, Belciug had Baba Rodovica, so famously pious that she was always chosen to knead the dough for the communion bread. Apart from her, Belciug had two servants looking after the cattle and the yard [*Belciug, pentru a-i găti de mâncare și a-i deretica prin casă, avea pe baba Rodovica, atât de vestită ca evlavioasă încât ea frământa întotdeauna prescurile; încolo două slugi la vite și în ogradă*]" (64, 90). The novel depicts the effort to emancipate a *slugă* (Ion), an agricultural worker. These references to the priest's servants are therefore highly eloquent. The priest oversees work on church land, and the peasants' labor is apparently unpaid: "The priest had been out in the fields to supervise the pruning of an orchard belonging to the church [*Popa fusese la câmp să supravegheze munca la o livadă a bisericii*]" (58, 82–83). The priest functions as a supervisor, an overseer of unremunerated labor that harkens back to the time of serfdom, when serfs owed churches their labor. Historically, peasants engaged in debates about priests' salaries, which they posited as the modern alternative to owing labor.[60] An elderly Romani man also serves the priest (see chapter 3), so this unpaid labor echoes the enslavement of the Roma as well. The wealth of the church thus accumulates as a function of unremunerated labor solicited from pious peasants. Within the history of labor emancipation, then, and in accordance with the narrative traced in chapter 1, the church is a retrograde force. Since it serves the national cause, which itself is perceived as a modern cause, its economic excesses are nonetheless bracketed.

Tellingly, the novel makes it difficult to distinguish between Belciug's property and church property. The priest and the church are one, and they are both relatively wealthy. As the novel assesses the wealth of other villagers, it uses Belciug as a reference point: "Toma Bulbuc was the richest peasant farmer in Pripas, better off even than Father Belciug himself [*Toma Bulbuc e cel mai bogat țăran din Pripas, mai cu stare decât însuși popa Belciug*]" (96, 136). To be wealthier than the priest is to be exceedingly wealthy. Belciug's identifying property is his carriage (*brișca*, from the Russian *bricika*). While Titu must work for months to save enough money to take a train to Bucharest, and everyone else travels on foot, the priest is mobile, traveling in style, assisted by a probably unpaid peasant-driver (*vizitiu*, from the Hungarian *vezető*). The priest's mobility signals his claim to modernity, but the exploitation of peasant labor creolizes his claim by drawing attention to the centrality of nonwage labor in the modern world-system.

The religious dimension of inter-imperial Transylvania is thus caught in a series of juxtapositions of the prevailing norm and deviations from it.

Within the comedy of power plot, the powerful priest—powerful on account of a religious-political-economic mix—suspects that the teacher is working against him to "undermine and diminish his authority [să-i sape şi să-i ştirbească autoritatea]" (60, 86). How can one diminish the priest's authority? The game involves a competition in patriotism.[61] Who is more patriotic, the priest or the teacher? In an inter-imperial situation, the question becomes: who betrays the national cause more, the priest or the teacher? An entry in Rebreanu's notebook referring to the conflict between Herdelea and Belciug reads: "Their enmity is caused by nationalism, which of the two is more Romanian: Herdelea, who has become teacher in a state school, or the priest, who receives the congrua [Duşmănia e din pricina naţionalismului, care-i mai român dintre ei: Herdelea, ajuns dascăl de stat, sau popa, care primeşte 'congrua']" (594). Whoever claims more patriotism, or less of a comprador position, has more power over the peasants—a situation with world-historical dimensions.

The teacher, who works in a Hungarian-speaking state school, becomes a renegade the moment he teaches Romanian Transylvanian children the Hungarian language. Herdelea serves the assimilation project every day by teaching in broken Hungarian, however hesitantly. As a consequence of this betrayal, the priest, who teaches religion in the Romanian language, can claim superiority over the teacher—and thus more power in the village. But this is not the end of the story. The priest receives a salary from the imperial state, the congrua invoked in the passage above. The seeds of the congrua were planted in 1861, as a way to assist poor priests, and it was renewed in 1868.[62] By 1883, as part of a Magyarization project to decrease the power of Romanian churches, the Hungarian government claimed the right to distribute the congrua to priests it deemed worthy, rewarding them for patriotic behavior in the service of the Hungarian state. Rebreanu's novel echoes the intense debate over the implications of the congrua, especially as it developed in the 1890s. Going back to our argument about secular governmentality, the debate about the congrua testifies to the limited differentiation between the political and religious spheres, with the theoretically secular imperial state funding and otherwise interfering in the administration of religious institutions.

Belciug likely also receives an income from villagers, and possibly grains and labor time as well. These resources should allow him to forfeit the congrua, yet he holds on to it, at the risk of selling out the nationalist cause: "Belciug was a staunch nationalist, but he did not show it, for fear that he might lose the Government's subsidy, without which he could not live like other people [Belciug era mare naţionalist, deşi nu se prea arăta a fi, de frică să nu-şi piardă ajutorul de la stat, fără de care n-ar mai fi putut trăi în rândul oamenilor]" (90, 128). Belciug does not need the *congrua* to survive; he needs it to be the wealthiest man in the village, with the exception of Toma Bulbuc. Belciug reads newspapers so that he can keep up with the national movement, but also to keep up with the latest news about the *congrua* debate. In this comedic framework, the priest and, by extension, the church become exemplars of greed.

What *kind* of power does the priest and, by extension, the church have? The church has the power to accumulate land. It helps build and sustain communities through its religious schools. It prints and circulates books—often the only print culture that flows across inter-imperial borders. It has the power to influence elections. It has financial power. Most important, however, the church yields ideological power, rationalizing the peasants' status quo as God's will. A peasant declares meditatively: "What else can we do? . . . We work, of course, that's what God left us in the world for [*Apoi ce să facem? . . . Muncim, că de aceea ne-a lăsat Dumnezeu pe lume*]" (39, 55). When Ana is beaten by her father, as we have seen, a neighbor rationalizes domestic violence: "You must bear everything in silence, for God has willed it that women shall suffer [*Taci și rabdă, că femeia trebuie să sufere dac-așa a lăsat-o Dumnezeu*]" (236, 330). When the Jewish tavern owner Avrum hangs himself, another villager reflects: "When you're destined to die, you even die out of the blue, this is how God willed it [*Apoi când ți-e scris să mori, mori și din senin, c-așa a lăsat Dumnezeu!*]" (269, 378). When Ion's young son dies: "What can a doctor do when God's hand interferes? [*Ce să facă doftorul dacă-i mâna lui Dumnezeu la mijloc?*]" (340, 477). It could be argued that these formulations are rhetorical in their aphoristic qualities—they are just something one says. And yet they also paint a picture in which "God is everywhere," to use Taylor's phrase. Religion here is not one option among many, and it is incompatible with a self-sufficient humanism that sees the human being as the agent of his or her destiny (a doctor *could* save the life of a child). God is everywhere because the deity remains an a priori reference point for big existential questions. And yet this profoundly religious predicament coexists with the projects of a secular state, on the one hand, and the efforts of a modernizing secular nationalist elite, on the other. As we argued earlier in relation to other Transylvanian historical circumstances, the combination of secular and religious is a function of inter-imperiality, itself juxtaposed with and at times overridden by global coloniality.

"God Is the New Church"

Let us return to the humble wooden church the reader encountered at the beginning of Rebreanu's novel, which, by the end, has been replaced by a larger, more imposing building. The increasing power the church claims is reflected by the built environment—a shiny new church. Like the little wooden church, this one is a religious institution. The rituals performed within its walls remain largely the same. But the new church belongs to a new paradigm and therefore carries different meanings. The very construction of the church testifies to this shift. The priest Belciug manipulates inheritance law to convince the peasants negotiating Ana's dowry to donate their land to the church.[63] His rationale: "By this act, you would strengthen the Lord's dominion on earth so that the Lord should receive your souls for ever and ever! [*Făcând astfel, întăriți puterea Domnului pe pământ ca și Domnul să vă primească sufletele în ceruri în vecii vecilor!*]" (366, 512). Belciug is selling forgiveness for one's sins; the anti-Catholic theme functions as an inter-imperial, ironic motif. Of course, the inheritance will strengthen the church's and the priest's power in this particular world. Having planted the seed of this idea, the priest cunningly proceeds to draft a document, which he tricks the two illiterate villagers into signing. In a free, indirect style, the novel presents the priest as actively scheming toward Ion's death:

> Father Belciug saw the operation of God's mercy in this bloody occurrence. He felt sorry for Ion, but at the same time he rejoiced that the church would benefit by his death. He congratulated himself on the happy idea with which the Lord had inspired him for securing to the holy house of God so precious a fortune. (392)
>
> *Preotul Belciug văzu o milostivire cerească în întâmplarea aceasta sângeroasă. Îi părea rău de Ion, dar în aceeași vreme se bucura că biserica va câștiga prin moartea lui. Se felicita pentru norocoasa idee ce i-a fost inspirată de Dumnezeu de-a asigura pe seama sfântului locaș o avere atât de frumoasă.* (549)

The "poetic justice" Rebreanu delivers through Ion's death acquires religious connotations. At the bidding of the author, God punishes Ion. As for the priest's minor feelings of guilt, they are assuaged by a pompous funeral. The tone of the description is ironic; the priest's scheming, humorous; the overlapping of religion and economic interest, definitive.

At the end of the novel, a bishop visits Pripas for the consecration (*sfințire*) of the new church. The display of church pomp and wealth is excessive:

> The bishop arrived at ten, in a coupé drawn by four horses, escorted by a host of young men from Pripas, who, according to the priest's orders, had escorted him on horseback from the bridge over the Someș. The coupé was followed by six other carriages containing His Grace's suite, made up of a number of higher clergymen. (401–2)

*Episcopul sosi pe la zece, într-un cupeu închis, tras de patru cai, în-
conjurat de o ceată de flăcăi pripășeni, călări, care îl așteptaseră la podul
de peste Someș, după ordinele preotului. Cupeul era urmat de vreo zece
alte trăsuri în care se găsea suita episcopului, alcătuită din înalte fețe
bisericești.* (563)

The bishop arrives in style, like a king, identified by his protruding belly. The
description of the event satirically borrows from the language of fairy tales:
"Fifty-two priests, headed by the bishop, took part in the consecration service.
The gold-threaded vestments filled the church with their radiance [*Cincizeci și
doi de preoți, cu episcopul în frunte, slujiră sfințirea. Veșmintele bătute cu fir um-
pleau biserica de strălucire*]" (402, 564). The Romanian Transylvanian peasants
in Pripas feel oppressed by wealthier landowners and by the imperial state. And
yet this religious event offers a display of wealth like no other in the novel—
carriages, golden garments, a lavish feast. The spectacle is awe inspiring.[64]

The inter-imperial nationalist plot thus offers a triangular configuration: Ion
wants to acquire land, Titu wants to hear the Romanian language spoken everywhere in Transylvania, and Belciug wants a new church. A similar passion moves
the three projects:

> His dearest aim in life was now to see a holy shrine of stone, rise, proud
> and stately, instead of the old weather-worn church that was unworthy
> of him and the village. For the past ten years he had been collecting one
> penny after another, with ever growing enthusiasm, contributing him-
> self practically all the revenues of the church, making all possible econ-
> omies to see his dream come true. The campaign for the erection of
> the church had begun with a subscription list, which two of the most
> prominent peasant-farmers, Toma Bulbuc and Ștefan Hotnog, had car-
> ried round all the villages of Transylvania, armed with an authoriza-
> tion given by the Bishop. As a large amount of money was necessary,
> Belciug tried to inspire the peasants with the idea of making offerings
> for the new church building, on every occasion, and especially at wed-
> dings, christenings and funerals. . . . In his pious reveries, Belciug saw
> the new church soaring skywards triumphantly, proclaiming to all the
> world the worthy endeavors of a modest minister of God. (186)

> *Căci râvna lui cea mai scumpă în viață era să vadă înălțându-se un
> sfânt locaș de piatră, falnic și frumos, în locul celui vechi și dărăpănat
> care îi făcea necinste atât lui, cât și satului întreg. De vreo zece ani aduna
> ban peste ban, cu o patimă mereu crescând, contribuind el însuși cu
> aproape toate veniturile bisericii și impunându-și singur toate economiile*

în favoarea visului său. Realizarea începuse printr-o colectă, făcută de
doi săteni fruntași, Toma Bulbuc și Ștefan Hotnog, prin toate comunele
Ardealului, cu o scrisoare de învoire din partea episcopului. Trebuind
bani mulți, Belciug caută să insufle și țăranilor ambiția de a dărui pen-
tru biserica cea nouă la toate prilejurile, dar mai ales la nunți, la bote-
zuri, la morți. . . . În reveriile lui cucernice, Belciug vedea noua biserică
triumfătoare, trâmbițând lumii silințele vrednice ale unui preot modest.
(263)

Belciug imagines a stately church tower. The church will become the visual fo-
cal point of the region, its grandeur a testament to the ambition of a falsely modest village priest. The free, indirect style mixes the narrative voice with that of
the character, midsentence. The thought belongs to the character, the irony to
the modernist narrator.

Belciug's strategy enlists the spirituality of the peasants to achieve his ambition: "In Pripas, God now meant the new church [*Dumnezeu însemna acuma în*
Pripas biserica cea nouă]" (244, 342). Transylvania's relation to secularity is ironically condensed in this one sentence: "now" (in modern times), the sign "God"
is redefined to include in its semantic field "the new church" (i.e., donations for
the building of the new church). Simply put, God means cash. The thought of
God should trigger an impulse to donate to the church. Peasants' religiosity becomes monetized. The plot of capitalist integration explored in chapter 2 has
reached its limit—and its goal: the church is a capitalist institution. Belciug's
church turns out to be a seemingly retrograde economic force when it comes
to self-serving labor arrangements, but it is otherwise fully integrated into the
capitalist system.

We have come full circle. The land Ion Glanetașu and Vasile Baciu negotiated with inter-imperial passion, the land that, in many ways, served as the hero
of the novel, has become the property of the church. If, at the end of *Madame
Bovary*, the demagoguery of a Monsieur Homais triumphs, at the end of *Ion*, the
triumph belongs to the scheming of the priest Belciug. His medal of honor is the
new church, built under his dedicated supervision at the heart of Pripas and consecrated in the last chapter of the novel by an impressive collection of fifty-two
priests and a bishop (*un sobor de preoți*). At the end of the first modern Romanian novel, as a prefiguration of the future, Pripas gets a new church, a pulpit
for the new nationalism and a refusal of its creolized history.

Notes

INTRODUCTION

1. "Xenia, fata lui Ion, nu a citit romanul lui Rebreanu [Xenia, Ion's daughter, has not read Rebreanu's novel]," *Adevărul*, June 15, 2009.

2. Laura Doyle, *Inter-Imperiality: Vying Empires, Gendered Labor, and the Literary Arts of Alliance* (Durham, NC: Duke University Press, 2020).

3. The global entanglements of East Europe go back to emergence of the modern world-system, which rested on the rise to power of West European imperial entities through two concomitant processes: the conquest of the Americas and the gradual transformation of East European feudal economies. See Immanuel Wallerstein, *The Modern World-System I: Capitalist Agriculture and the Origins of the European World-Economy in the Sixteenth Century* (Berkeley: University of California Press, 2011), 94–95.

4. Pascale Casanova, *The World Republic of Letters*, trans. M. B. DeBevoise (Cambridge, MA: Harvard University Press, 2007).

5. Nina Glick Schiller, Ayşe Çağlar, and Thaddeus Guldbrandsen, "Beyond the Ethnic Lens: Locality, Globality, and Born-Again Incorporation," *American Ethnologist* 33, no. 4 (2006): 612–33.

6. On method and East Europe more broadly, see Anca Parvulescu, "Eastern Europe as Method," *SEEJ* 63, no. 4 (2019): 470–81.

7. Other scholars have written similar accounts of the world seen from a small place. See Donald R. Wright, *The World and a Very Small Place in Africa: A History of Globalization in Niumi, the Gambia* (Armonk, NY: M. E. Sharpe, 2010). Similarly, Jeremy Prestholdt, who has traced globalization from the vantage point of East African nineteenth-century consumerism, challenges us to "accept the possibility that seemingly marginal actors can, at times, significantly affect seemingly powerful ones." Jeremy Prestholdt, *Domesticating the World: African Consumerism and the Genealogies of Globalization* (Berkeley: University of California Press, 2008), 60.

8. Raymond Williams, *The Country and the City* (Oxford: Oxford University Press, 1975). For an account of ruralism and Romanian-language literature, see Ștefan Baghiu, Vlad Pojoga, and Maria Sass, eds., *Ruralism and Literature in Romania* (Berlin: Peter Lang, 2020).

9. Julie Skurski and Fernando Coronil, "Country and City in a Postcolonial Landscape: Double Discourse and the Geo-Politics of Truth in Latin America," in *Views beyond the Border Country: Raymond Williams and Cultural Politics*, ed. Dennis L. Dworkin and Leslie G. Roman (New York: Routledge, 1993), 244–46.

10. Encarnación Gutiérrez Rodríguez and Shirley Anne Tate, *Creolizing Europe: Legacies and Transformations* (Liverpool: Liverpool University Press, 2017); Manuela Boatcă, "Caribbean Europe: Out of Sight, out of Mind?" in *Constructing the Pluriverse*, ed. Bernd Reiter (Durham, NC: Duke University Press, 2018), 197–218.

11. On the Caribbean, see Kamau Brathwaite, *The Development of Creole Society in Jamaica, 1770–1820* (Oxford: Clarendon Press, 1971). On the expansion of the term *creolization*, see Robin Cohen and Paola Toninato, eds., *The Creolization Reader: Studies in Mixed Identities and Cultures* (London: Routledge, 2010).

12. According to Stuart Hall, "Creolization always entails inequality, hierarchization, issues of domination and subalternity, mastery and servitude, control and resistance. Questions of *power*, as well as questions of *entanglement*, are always at stake. It is important to keep these contradictory tendencies together, rather than singling out their celebratory aspects." Stuart Hall, "Créolité and the Process of Creolization," in Cohen and Toninato, *Creolization Reader*, 29.

13. One of the most forceful arguments for creolization outside the Caribbean comes from the Indian Ocean. See Françoise Vergès and Carpanin Marimoutou, "Moorings: Indian Ocean Creolizations," *Portal: Journal of Multidisciplinary International Studies* 9 (June 29, 2012). For recent work on transoceanic creolization, see Ananya Jahanara Kabir, "Elmina as Postcolonial Space: Transoceanic Creolization and the Fabric of Memory," *Interventions* 22, no. 8 (2020): 994–1012; Ananya Jahanara Kabir, "Rapsodia Ibero-Indiana: Transoceanic Creolization and the Mando of Goa," *Modern Asian Studies*, 2021, 1–56. For a critique of the extension of the term beyond the Caribbean, see Stephan Palmié, "Creolization and Its Discontents," *Annual Review of Anthropology* 35 (2006): 433–56.

14. On creolization and translated societies, see Hall, "Créolité and the Process of Creolization," 29. On creolization as a mode of relation, see Édouard Glissant, *Poetics of Relation*, trans. Betsy Wing (Ann Arbor: University of Michigan Press, 2010).

15. Aníbal Quijano and Immanuel Wallerstein, "Americanity as a Concept, or the Americas in the Modern World," *International Social Science Journal* 44, no. 4 (1992): 549–57; Sidney W. Mintz, "The Localization of Anthropological Practice: From Area Studies to Transnationalism," *Critique of Anthropology* 18, no. 2 (1998): 117–33.

16. Françoise Lionnet and Shu-mei Shih, eds., *The Creolization of Theory* (Durham, NC: Duke University Press, 2011).

17. Edward W. Said, "Yeats and Decolonization," in *Culture and Imperialism* (New York: Vintage, 1994).

18. Andre Gunder Frank, "Nothing New in the East: No New World Order," *Social Justice* 19, no. 1 (1992): 34–61; Rossen Vassilev, "The 'Third-Worldization' of a 'Second-World' Nation: De-Development in Post-Communist Bulgaria," *New Political Science* 25, no. 1 (2010): 99–112.

19. Maria Todorova, *Imagining the Balkans* (New York: Oxford University Press, 2009), 195.

20. Walter D. Mignolo, *The Darker Side of Western Modernity: Global Futures, Decolonial Options* (Durham, NC: Duke University Press, 2011); Fernando Coronil, "Latin American Postcolonial Studies and Global Decolonization," *The Worlds & Knowledges Otherwise Project* 3, no. 3 (2013); Ramón Grosfoguel, "From Postcolonial Studies to Decolonial Studies: Decolonizing Postcolonial Studies," *Review (Fernand Braudel Center)* 29, no. 2 (2006): 141–220; Mabel Moraña, Enrique D. Dussel, and Carlos A. Jáuregui, eds., *Coloniality at Large: Latin America and the Postcolonial Debate* (Durham, NC: Duke University Press, 2008).

21. Manuela Boatcă, "Uneasy Postcolonialisms," *The Worlds & Knowledges Otherwise Project* 3, no. 3 (2013).

22. Quijano and Wallerstein, "Americanity as a Concept"; Walter D. Mignolo, *Local Histories/Global Designs: Coloniality, Subaltern Knowledges, and Border Thinking* (Princeton, NJ: Princeton University Press, 2000); Ramón Grosfoguel, Nelson Maldonado-Torres, and José David Saldivar, eds., *Latin@s in the World-System: Decolonization Struggles in the 21st Century U.S. Empire* (New York: Routledge, 2016).

23. Wallerstein, *The Modern World-System I*; Daniel Chirot, *Social Change in a Peripheral Society: The Creation of a Balkan Colony* (New York: Academic Press, 1976); Iván T. Berend and György Ránki, *The European Periphery and Industrialization 1780–1914* (Cambridge: Cambridge University Press, 1982); Iván T. Berend, "Past Convergence

within Europe: Core–Periphery Diversity in Modern Economic Development," in *Economic Convergence and Divergence in Europe: Growth and Regional Development in an Enlarged European Union*, ed. Gertrude Tumpel-Gugerell and Peter Mooslechner (Cheltenham, UK: Elgar, 2003), 9–23; Nataša Kovačević, *Narrating Post/Communism: Colonial Discourse and Europe's Borderline Civilization* (New York: Routledge, 2008); Anca Parvulescu, *The Traffic in Women's Work: East European Migration and the Making of Europe* (Chicago: University of Chicago Press, 2014); Manuela Boatcă, "Multiple Europes and the Politics of Difference Within," in *The Worlds & Knowledges Otherwise Project* 3, no. 3 (Spring 2013); József Böröcz, *The European Union and Global Social Change: A Critical Geopolitical-Economic Analysis* (London: Routledge, 2010).

24. On the colonial-imperial distinction, see Walter D. Mignolo, "Colonialidad global, capitalism y hegemonía epistémica" [Global coloniality, capitalism and epistemic hegemony] in *Indisciplinar las ciencias sociales: Geopoliticas del conocimiento y colonialidad del poder* [Undisciplining the social sciences: Geopolitics of knowledge and coloniality of power], ed. Catherine Walsh, Freya Schiwy, and Santiago Castro-Gómez (Quito: Ediciones Abya-Yala, 2002).

25. Immanuel Wallerstein, *The Modern World-System III: The Second Era of Great Expansion of the Capitalist World-Economy, 1730s–1840s* (Berkeley: University of California Press, 2011), 75.

26. On the Orient, see Said, *Culture and Imperialism*; Todorova, *Imagining the Balkans*, 195.

27. Todorova, 60.

28. Miloš Jovanović and Giulia Carabelli, "Introduction," *History of the Present* 10, no. 1 (2020): 6.

29. For exceptions that confirm the rule, see Teresa Kulawik and Zhanna Kravchenko, eds., *Borderlands in European Gender Studies: Beyond the East–West Frontier* (London: Routledge, 2019); Redi Koobak, Madina Tlostanova, and Suruchi Thapar-Björkert, eds., *Postcolonial and Postsocialist Dialogues: Intersections, Opacities, Challenges in Feminist Theorizing and Practice* (London: Routledge, 2021); Danijela Majstorović, *Discourse and Affect in Postsocialist Bosnia and Herzegovina: Peripheral Selves* (London: Palgrave Macmillan, 2021).

30. See Walter Mignolo, "Imperial/Colonial Metamorphosis: A Decolonial Narrative, from the Ottoman Sultanate and Spanish Empire to the US and the EU," in *The Oxford Handbook of Postcolonial Studies*, ed. Graham Huggan (Oxford: Oxford University Press, 2013).

31. Laura Doyle, "Thinking Back through Empires," *Modernism/modernity* 2, no. 4 (2018).

32. Kristin Hoganson and Jay Sexton, "Introduction," in *Crossing Empires: Taking U.S. History into Transimperial Terrain* (Durham, NC: Duke University Press, 2020), 10. For a recent exploration of trans-imperial dynamics, see M'hamed Oualdi, *A Slave between Empires: A Transimperial History of North Africa* (New York: Columbia University Press, 2020).

33. Anna Amelina, Devrimsel D. Nergiz, Thomas Faist, and Nina Glick Schiller, eds., *Beyond Methodological Nationalism: Research Methodologies for Cross-Border Studies* (New York: Routledge, 2012); Anna Amelina, Manuela Boatcă, Gregor Bongaerts, and Anja Weiß, "Theorizing Societalization across Borders: Globality, Transnationality, Postcoloniality," *Current Sociology* 69, no. 3 (2021): 303–14.

34. Liviu Rebreanu, *Ion*, trans. A. Hillard (London: Peter Owen, 1965); Liviu Rebreanu, *Ion*, ed. Niculae Gheran, vol. 4, *Opere* (Bucharest: Editura Minerva, 1970). We modified some translations. Hereafter, parenthetical citations from the novel refer to these two editions in the above order.

35. On the extended case study as used in ethnography, see Michael Burawoy, *The Extended Case Method: Four Countries, Four Decades, Four Great Transformations, and One Theoretical Tradition* (Berkeley: University of California Press, 2009). On the history of the case study and its interdisciplinary uses, see Lauren Berlant, "On the Case," *Critical Inquiry* 33, no. 4 (2007): 663–72.

36. Doyle, *Inter-Imperiality*, 25.

37. On comparative audiences, see Rebecca L. Walkowitz, *Born Translated: The Contemporary Novel in the Age of World Literature* (New York: Columbia University Press, 2017).

38. See Franco Moretti, "Conjectures on World Literature," *New Left Review* 1 (2000): 54–68.

39. In 1935 George Călinescu referred to *Ion* as "the first true Romanian modern novel." *Adevărul literar și artistic*, December 8, 1935. Reviewing this literature in 1967, Lucian Raicu concluded: "Rebreanu is for us the true and only creator of this genre." Lucian Raicu, *Liviu Rebreanu* (Bucharest: Editura pentru literatură, 1967), 353.

40. Mohammed Hussein Haikal, *Zainab* (London: Darf Publishers, 2016); Futabatei Shimei, *Japan's First Modern Novel:* Ukigumo *of Futabatei Shimei*, trans. Marleigh Grayer Ryan (Ann Arbor, MI: Center for Japanese Studies, University of Michigan, 1990); Lu Xun, *The Real Story of Ah-Q and Other Tales of China: The Complete Fiction of Lu Xun*, trans. Julia Lovell (London: Penguin Classics, 2010).

41. On this intersection, see Pheng Cheah, *What Is a World? On Postcolonial Literature as World Literature* (Durham, NC: Duke University Press, 2016).

42. Mircea Martin, Christian Moraru, and Andrei Terian, eds., *Romanian Literature as World Literature* (New York: Bloomsbury Academic, 2017).

43. Gayatri Chakravorty Spivak speaks of the "sanctioned ignorance of the theoretical elite." Gayatri Chakravorty Spivak, *A Critique of Postcolonial Reason: Toward a History of the Vanishing Present* (Cambridge, MA: Harvard University Press, 1999), x. On asymmetrical ignorance, see Dipesh Chakrabarty, *Provincializing Europe: Postcolonial Thought and Historical Difference* (Princeton, NJ: Princeton University Press, 2000).

44. Boaventura de Sousa Santos, "Nuestra América," *Theory, Culture & Society* 18, no. 2–3 (2001): 185–217.

45. Raewyn Connell, *Southern Theory: The Global Dynamics of Knowledge in Social Science* (Cambridge: Polity Press, 2007); Wiebke Keim, Ercüment Çelik, Christian Ersche, and Veronika Wöhrer, eds., *Global Knowledge Production in the Social Sciences: Made in Circulation* (London: Routledge, 2016).

46. Gilles Deleuze and Félix Guattari, *Kafka: Toward a Minor Literature*, trans. Dana Polan (Minneapolis: University of Minnesota Press, 1986).

47. For a review of Romanian-language criticism, see Raicu, *Liviu Rebreanu*.

48. Rebreanu, *Ion*, 714.

49. Eugen Lovinescu, *Istoria civilizației române moderne* [History of Romanian modern civilization] (Bucharest: Editura Științifică, 1972), 71. Lovinescu added: "The social stratification of all peoples can hence be regarded as a blessing: at the base, a numerous peasantry, inert, passive, traditional, upholder of nationality, and above it the superior classes, once noble, today urban, intelligent, receptive, able to introduce all the elements of universal civilization and which, as a consequence, constitute the true factor of progress" (414).

50. Walkowitz, *Born Translated*, 26.

51. On the politics of translation, see Lawrence Venuti, *The Scandals of Translation: Towards an Ethics of Difference* (London: Taylor & Francis, 1998).

52. We focus on the young Rebreanu, the author who oversaw the writing and publication of *Ion*. Later in his career, Rebreanu engaged in problematic institutional politics and wrote admiringly about Mussolini.

53. Walkowitz, *Born Translated*, 25.

54. Carl E. Schorske, *Fin-de-Siècle Vienna: Politics and Culture* (New York: Vintage, 1981). Marjorie Perloff's study of Austro-modernism extends its purview to the multiethnic and multilingual edges of the Austro-Hungarian Empire (authors like Joseph Roth, Elias Canetti, Paul Celan), but Perloff's archive remains centered on Vienna and the German language. With this emphasis on the German language, the Jewish experience on the Austrian side of the empire and "high culture," comes an autumnal nostalgia for the golden age of Austro-Hungary, which the critic risks reproducing in the act of analysis. Within this framework, although the focus is on the edges of empire, non-German-speaking populations remain "Slavs of one kind or another." Marjorie Perloff, *Edge of Irony: Modernism in the Shadow of the Habsburg Empire* (Chicago: University of Chicago Press, 2016), 11, 51.

55. Laura Doyle and Laura Winkiel, eds., "Introduction," in *Geomodernisms: Race, Modernism, Modernity* (Bloomington: Indiana University Press, 2006), 1.

56. Doyle and Winkiel, 3.

57. Sanja Bahun, "The Balkans Uncovered: Towards Historie Croisée of Modernism," in *The Oxford Handbook of Global Modernism*, ed. Mark Wollaeger (New York: Oxford University Press, 2010), 25–47.

58. Since *Geomodernisms*, the literature on global modernism has expanded. See Jessica Berman, *Modernist Commitments: Ethics, Politics and Transnational Modernism* (New York: Columbia University Press, 2012); Susan Stanford Friedman, *Planetary Modernisms: Provocations on Modernity across Time* (New York: Columbia University Press, 2018); Eric Hayot and Rebecca Walkowitz, eds., *A New Vocabulary for Global Modernism* (New York: Columbia University Press, 2016).

59. C. P. Snow, *The Two Cultures*, ed. Stefan Collini (1959; reprint, Cambridge: Cambridge University Press, 2012).

60. The Gulbenkian Commission's 1996 report, "Open the Social Sciences," emphasized that "disciplinary boundaries are historical as well as political constructions, and that the emergence of the social sciences, as well as the intellectual division of labor between sociology, anthropology, political science, economics, and history, was concomitant as well as complicit with empire." Richard E. Lee and Immanuel Wallerstein, eds., *Overcoming the Two Cultures: Science vs. the Humanities in the Modern World-System* (New York: Routledge, 2015). On the relation between literary and sociological modernisms, see Claire Marie Class, "Beyond the Chicago School: Literature, Gender, and Modernist Sociology in America, 1892–1930" (PhD diss., Washington University in St Louis, 2017).

61. For an eloquent example, see David Palumbo-Liu, Bruce Robbins, and Nirvana Tanoukhi, eds., *Immanuel Wallerstein and the Problem of the World: System, Scale, Culture* (Durham, NC: Duke University Press, 2011).

62. For the broader debate, see Anca Parvulescu, "The World of World Literature and World-Systems Analysis," *symplokē* 28, no. 1–2 (2020): 375–83.

63. Manuela Boatcă, Sina Farzin, and Julian Go, "Postcolonialism and Sociology," *Soziologie-Forum der Deutschen Gesellschaft für Soziologie* 47, no. 4 (2018): 423–38.

64. Laszlo Peter, ed., *Historians and the History of Transylvania* (Boulder, CO: East European Monographs, 1993); László Kürti, *The Remote Borderland: Transylvania in the Hungarian Imagination* (Albany, NY: SUNY Press, 2001).

65. Gyula Kristó, *Hungarian History in the Ninth Century* (Szeged, Hungary: Szegedi Középkorász Műhely, 1996).

66. Katalin Szende, "*Iure Theutonico?* German Settlers and Legal Frameworks for Immigration to Hungary in an East-Central European Perspective," *Journal of Medieval History* 45, no. 3 (2019): 360–79.

67. Janet L. Abu-Lughod, *Before European Hegemony: The World System A.D. 1250–1350* (Oxford: Oxford University Press, 1989).

68. The first German settlements in Transylvania were primarily rural and tied to military service—Saxons defended Transylvania's border area. The settlements gradually became urbanized during the thirteenth and fourteenth centuries as the region's commercial importance increased and privileges given to German (and other) settlers were linked to the territory they inhabited rather than to single persons or groups. In 1224 King Andrew II conferred rights and duties on all the Saxons of Transylvania, irrespective of the settlements' urban or rural character. Katalin Szende, "Towns along the Way: Changing Patterns of Long-Distance Trade and the Urban Network of Medieval Hungary," *Towns and Communication* 2 (2011): 161–225.

69. Manuela Boatcă, "Second Slavery versus Second Serfdom: Local Labor Regimes of the Global Periphery," in *Social Theory and Regional Studies in the Global Age*, ed. Saïd Amir Arjomand (Albany, NY: SUNY Press, 2014), 361.

70. Marshall Lang, *The Armenians: A People in Exile* (London: Unwin Hyman, 1981), 103–4.

71. Gérard Chaliand and Jean-Pierre Rageau, *The Penguin Atlas of Diasporas* (New York: Penguin Books, 1995), 80.

72. Judit Pál, *Armenians in Transylvania: Their Contribution to the Urbanization and the Economic Development of the Province*, trans. Bogdan Aldea (Cluj-Napoca: Romanian Cultural Institute, 2005), 91.

73. On Prussia, see Stefan Berger, "Building the Nation among Visions of German Empire," in *Nationalizing Empires*, ed. Stefan Berger and Alexei Miller (Budapest: Central European University Press, 2015), 251.

74. For an intra-European account of the Habsburg Empire, see Pieter M. Judson, *The Habsburg Empire: A New History* (Cambridge, MA: Belknap Press, 2016). For the debate around Judson's history, see "An Imperial Dynamo? CEH Forum on Pieter Judson's *The Habsburg Empire: A New History*," *Central European History* 50, no. 2 (June 2017): 236–59, especially Tara Zahra's contribution. Working against nationalist narratives, Judson reevaluates the history of the Habsburg Empire as a modern European state, anchored in modernizing institutions and the rule of law (largely focusing on the Austrian side, with little attention paid to Transylvania). This is a "positive" recuperation of the history of empire in the region, risking the implication that critical evaluations (a focus on "the darker threads," in Zahra's terms) necessarily embrace a nationalist historiography. We hope that a revised account of this history, anchored in a world-historical perspective on comparative empires, yields an alternative challenge to nationalism.

75. Berger, "Building the Nation," 251.

76. Omer Bartov and Eric D. Weitz, eds., *Shatterzone of Empires: Coexistence and Violence in the German, Habsburg, Russian, and Ottoman Borderlands* (Bloomington: Indiana University Press, 2013); Kürti, *Remote Borderland*.

77. The distinction between ethnic groups with or without national (and nationalist) ambitions reflects different—and shifting—positions in the colonial and imperial racial matrix. In the eighteenth century Armenians in Transylvania (like Romanians) unsuccessfully requested recognition as a fourth Transylvanian "nation" (in the sense of a status group). Judit Pál, "Assimilation and Identity of the Transylvanian Armenians in the 19th Century," in *Building Identities in Transylvania: A Comparative Approach*, ed. Sorin Mitu (Cluj-Napoca, Romania: Argonaut, 2014). Likewise, Jewish organizations invoked the nation as a mode of activism. Ethan B. Katz, Lisa Moses Leff, and Maud S.

Mandel, eds., *Colonialism and the Jews* (Bloomington: Indiana University Press, 2017). When it comes to the Roma, an internal colonial Other whose humanity was denied, "no one suggested that they should be accorded the same political rights or status as Austria-Hungary's other nationalities (unless they successfully assimilated into another national community)." Tara Zahra, "Condemned to Rootlessness and Unable to Budge: Roma, Migration Panics, and Internment in the Habsburg Empire," *American Historical Review* 122, no. 3 (2017): 710. On the Carpatho-Rus minority, see Paul R. Magocsi, *The People from Nowhere: An Illustrated History of Carpatho-Rusyns* (Uzhgorod, Ukraine: Padjaka, 2006); Paul Robert Magocsi, *With Their Backs to the Mountains: A History of Carpathian Rus' and Carpatho-Rusyns* (Budapest: Central European University Press, 2015).

78. Andrea Komlosy, "Imperial Cohesion, Nation-Building, and Regional Integration in the Habsburg Monarchy," in Berger and Miller, *Nationalizing Empires*, 369–428.

79. Bálint Varga, "The Two Faces of the Hungarian Empire," *Austrian History Yearbook* 52 (2021): 118–30.

80. Tara Zahra reports that 3.5 million people left the Austro-Hungarian Empire between 1876 and 1910, or 7 to 8 percent of the population. Tara Zahra, *The Great Departure: Mass Migration from Eastern Europe and the Making of the Free World* (New York: W.W. Norton, 2016), 25, 30, 68.

81. Zahra, 72–73.

82. The most important reference point for this narrative is *Supplex Libellus Valachorum Transsilvaniae* (1791), which argued that the Romanian nation is the oldest in Transylvania. See Lucian Boia, *History and Myth in Romanian Consciousness* (Budapest: Central European University Press, 2001). For an analysis of Transylvania's mythical place in the Hungarian national imagination, see Kürti, *Remote Borderland*.

83. Walter D. Mignolo, "Huntington's Fears," in Grosfoguel et al., *Latin@s in the World-System*, 58. On the place of Romanian in Romance language philology, see Anca Parvulescu, "Istanbul, Capital of Comparative Literature," *MLN* 135, no. 5 (2020): 1232–57.

84. Immanuel Wallerstein, "Latin@s: What's in a Name?" in Grosfoguel et al., *Latin@s in the World-System*, 37–46.

85. On the enduring influence of classical empires, see Jane Burbank and Frederick Cooper, *Empires in World History: Power and the Politics of Difference* (Princeton, NJ: Princeton University Press, 2010).

86. Enrique D. Dussel, "Europe, Modernity, and Eurocentrism," trans. Javier Krauel and Virginia C. Tuma, *Nepantla: Views from South* 1, no. 3 (2000): 465–78.

87. On the tension between federalization and national self-determination, see Larry Wolff, *Woodrow Wilson and the Reimagining of Eastern Europe* (Stanford, CA: Stanford University Press, 2020).

88. Ezra Mendelsohn, *The Jews of East Central Europe between the World Wars* (Bloomington: Indiana University Press, 1987); Attila Gidó, "Identitatea evreilor ardeleni în perioada interbelică" [The identity of Transylvanian Jews in the interwar period]," *Revista de Istorie a Evreilor din România* 1 (2016): 52–64.

89. Hans-Christian Petersen and Jannis Panagiotidis, "Historischer Kontext: Deutsche in und aus Osteuropa," http://www.bpb.de. For a map of the imagined German cultural world, see *German Volks- und Kulturboden*, https://digital.library.cornell.edu/catalog/ss:3293930.

90. Stefan Berger and Alexei Miller, "Introduction: Building Nations in and with Empires: A Reassessment," in Berger and Miller, *Nationalizing Empires*, 26.

91. Stefano Bottoni, *Stalin's Legacy in Romania: The Hungarian Autonomous Region, 1952-1960* (Lanham, MA: Lexington Books, 2018).

92. Although not formally part of the nonalignment movement, Romania claimed a large degree of independence starting in the 1960s.

93. Ella Shohat, "Rethinking Jews and Muslims: Quincentennial Reflections," *Middle East Report* 22 (1992): 25.

1. THE FACE OF LAND

1. Parenthetical citations from the novel refer to the following editions: Liviu Rebreanu, *Ion*, trans. A. Hillard (London: Peter Owen, 1965); Liviu Rebreanu, *Ion*, ed. Niculae Gheran, vol. 4, *Opere* (Bucharest: Editura Minerva, 1970). We modified some translations.

2. On animals, especially dogs, in Rebreanu's novel, see Andrei Terian, "Zoopoetics in a Rural Environment," in *Ruralism and Literature in Romania*, ed. Ştefan Baghiu, Vlad Pojoga, and Maria Sass (Berlin: Peter Lang, 2020).

3. Edward W. Said, "Yeats and Decolonization," in *Culture and Imperialism* (New York: Vintage, 1994), 297.

4. Said, 299.

5. On space and modernism, see Eric Bulson, *Novels, Maps, Modernity: The Spatial Imagination, 1850–2000* (New York: Routledge, 2007).

6. Anne McClintock, *Imperial Leather: Race, Gender, and Sexuality in the Colonial Contest* (New York: Routledge, 1995), 27.

7. Local toponyms were collected in 1864–1865 though a questionnaire that asked villagers to record the names of villages, rivers, meadows, and forests. Simion Retegan, *Satele năsăudene la mijlocul secolului al XIX-lea: Mărturii documentare* [Villages in the Năsăud region in mid nineteenth century: documents] (Cluj-Napoca, Romania: Accent, 2002).

8. Jahan Ramazani, *The Hybrid Muse: Postcolonial Poetry in English* (Chicago: University of Chicago Press, 2001), 41.

9. Martina Tazzioli and Glenda Garelli, "Counter-Mapping, Refugees and Asylum Borders," in *Handbook on Critical Geographies of Migration* (Cheltenham, UK: Edward Elgar, 2019), 397.

10. Geographers Joel Wainwright and Joe Bryan point out that counter-mapping is primarily a critique of maps as self-evident representations—of national territory or indigenous property, for instance—and not an attempt to reverse perspectives by "replacing bad colonial maps with good anti-colonial ones." Joel Wainwright and Joe Bryan, "Cartography, Territory, Property: Postcolonial Reflections on Indigenous Counter-Mapping in Nicaragua and Belize," *Cultural Geographies* 16, no. 2 (2009): 154.

11. Liviu Rebreanu, *Amalgam*, ed. Niculae Gheran, vol. 15, *Opere* (Bucharest: Editura Minerva, 1991), 167.

12. Rebreanu, 169.

13. Romanian-language criticism of the novel has emphasized its comprehensive and definitive treatment of the land question. Lucian Raicu, *Liviu Rebreanu* (Bucharest: Editura pentru literatură, 1967), 103.

14. Fernando Coronil, "Beyond Occidentalism: Toward Nonimperial Geohistorical Categories," *Cultural Anthropology* 11, no. 1 (1996): 65.

15. Katherine Verdery, *Transylvanian Villagers: Three Centuries of Political, Economic, and Ethnic Change* (Berkeley: University of California Press, 1983), 151.

16. As Pieter M. Judson celebrates the Habsburg Empire's increasingly progressive policies toward peasants and their ensuing affective "attachment" to the empire, he acknowledges that members of the Hungarian nobility retained their privileges well into the nineteenth century and that emancipation from serfdom followed a different track in Hungary, in comparison to the Austrian side of the empire. Pieter M. Judson, *The Habsburg Empire: A New History* (Cambridge, MA: Belknap Press, 2016).

17. Immanuel Wallerstein, *The Modern World-System I. Capitalist Agriculture and the Origins of the European World-Economy in the Sixteenth Century* (Berkeley: University of California Press, 2011), 91.

18. Iosif Kovács, *Desființarea relațiilor feudale în Transilvania* [The abolition of feudal relations in Transylvania] (Cluj-Napoca, Romania: Editura Dacia, 1973).

19. Daniela Deteșan, ed., *Căsătorie și moștenire în Transilvania: Documente din a doua jumătate a secolului al XIX-lea* [Marriage and inheritance in Transylvania: documents from the second half of the nineteenth century] (Cluj-Napoca, Romania: Presa Universitară Clujană, 2013).

20. Sorina Paula Bolovan, *Familia în satul românesc din Transilvania* [The family in the Romanian village of Transylvania] (Cluj-Napoca, Romania: Fundația Culturală Română, 1999), 43.

21. George Barițiu, "Românii transilvăneni, ca proprietari de pământ [Transylvanian Romanians as land owners]," *Gazeta Transilvaniei* (1861), 94–95.

22. Jörg K. Hoensch, *A History of Modern Hungary 1867–1994* (London: Longman, 1996), 40.

23. Iván T. Berend and György Ránki, *East Central Europe in the 19th and 20th Centuries* (Budapest: Akadémiai Kiadó, 1977), 30.

24. See Viorel Roman and Hannes Hofbauer, *Transilvania: românii la încrucișarea intereselor imperiale* [Transylvania: Romanians at the crossroads of imperial interests] (Vienna: Editura Nova, 1998), 110. The authors note that working in Austrian- or Hungarian-owned mines in northern Transylvania became an alternative for some, but more than twelve-hour workdays and uncertain pay prompted both poor Romanian and Saxon peasants to migrate to the United States.

25. Zoltán Szász, "Political Life and Nationality Question," in *History of Transylvania*, vol. 3 (New York: Columbia University Press, 2002), 568, 590.

26. The literature on the border region is extensive. For an early history, see George Barițiu, *Istoria Regimentului II graniteriu transilvanu* [The history of the Transylvanian border regiment II] (Brașov, Romania, 1874). For more recent contributions, see Andrei Onofreiu, *Districtul Năsăud, 1861–1876* (Cluj-Napoca, Romania: Argonaut, 2010); Adrian Onofreiu and Ioan Bolovan, *Contribuții documentare privind istoria regimentului grăniceresc năsăudean* [Documentary contributions to the history of the Năsăud border regiment] (Bucharest: Editura Enciclopedică, 2006); Claudia Septimia Sabău, *"Și ne-au făcut din grăniceri, țărani . . ."* *Mentalități colective în satele năsăudene foste grănicerești în a doua jumătate a secolului al XIX-lea* ["And they transformed us from soldiers into peasants": collective mentalities in villages of the Năsăud region, formerly the border regiment, in the second half of the nineteenth century] (Cluj-Napoca, Romania: Editura Mega, 2015).

27. Sabău, *"Și ne-au făcut din grăniceri, țărani . . . ,"* 14, 39.

28. The irony of this situation is compounded by statistical data showing more economic growth on the Hungarian side of the empire than on the Austrian side by 1918. See Cornel Ban, "Romania and Transylvania on the Eve of the Great War: A Statistical View," *Acta Mvsei Porolissensis* vol. XLII (2020).

29. Roman and Hofbauer, *Transilvania*, 125.

30. Marilyn McArthur, "The Saxon Germans: Political Fate of an Ethnic Identity," *Dialectical Anthropology* 1, no. 1–4 (January 1975): 349–64.

31. See Roman and Hofbauer, *Transilvania*, 126. For a detailed account of the decade-long dispute involving the League of Nations, see Anders E. B. Blomqvist, "Economic Nationalizing in the Ethnic Borderlands of Hungary and Romania" (Stockholm University, 2014).

32. Roman and Hofbauer, *Transilvania*, 125.

33. The incorporation of external areas into the capitalist world-economy was complete by 1900—no place was "outside" the modern colonial world-system anymore. Andrea Komlosy, *Work: The Last 1,000 Years*, trans. Jacob K. Watson and Loren Balhorn (London: Verso, 2018), 123; Immanuel Wallerstein, *The Essential Wallerstein* (New York: New Press, 2000), 335.

34. Within literary studies, compare Kōjin Karatani, *Origins of Modern Japanese Literature*, trans. Brett de Bary (Durham, NC: Duke University Press, 1993).

35. Neelam Jabeen, "Women, Land, Embodiment: A Case of Postcolonial Ecofeminism," *Interventions* 22 no. 8 (2020): 1–15.

36. In one episode in Rebreanu's novel, Ana visits Ion's household and watches him eat: "she saw Ion sitting at the table, cutting a large, red onion with his pocket knife, and on the table she saw a barely started cornbread, a healthy cut of thick lard and some salt in a piece of cloth [*văzu pe Ion stând la masă, cu un briceag în mână și crestând o ceapă mare, roșie, iar pe masă văzu o pâine de mălai deabia începută, o bucată zdravănă de slănină groasă și niște sare pisată într-un nod de pânzătură*]" (167, 237).

37. Immanuel Wallerstein, *The Modern World-System IV: Centrist Liberalism Triumphant, 1789–1914* (Berkeley: University of California Press, 2011), 144.

38. Georges Clemenceau, *La Justice*, May 12, 1894.

39. Szász, "Political Life and Nationality Question," 647. On the Transylvanian electoral system, see Judit Pál, Vlad Popovici, Andrea Fehér, and Ovidiu Emil Iudean, eds., *Parliamentary Elections in Eastern Hungary and Transylvania (1865–1918)* (Berlin: Peter Lang, 2018).

40. "In Transylvania, one (a peasant) could qualify as a voter only if one paid a land tax according to a minimum net land income of 84 Gulden." Pál et al., *Parliamentary Elections in Eastern Hungary and Transylvania*, 26.

41. Máté Rigó, "The Long First World War and the Survival of Business Elites in East-Central Europe: Transylvania's Industrial Boom and the Enrichment of Economic Elites," *European Review of History: Revue européenne d'histoire* 24, no. 2 (2017): 254.

42. Tellingly, the terms *property* and *propriety* have a common etymology in English, derived from the Old French *propriété*, which linked notions of "suitability to a correct standard" and "ownership" at the same time the emerging capitalist world-economy started transforming notions of property and labor—in the long sixteenth century. https://www.etymonline.com/word/propriety.

43. Bolovan reports on the much-advertised slogan *Mia și călătoria* (a grand a trip). Bolovan, *Familia în satul românesc din Transilvania*, 49, 51. The journal of one such immigrant, a peasant named Vasile Triff, who immigrated from Transylvania to the United States in 1906, has recently been published as an online interactive documentary at https://strainul.kinokult.net/#Povestea_continua.

44. Roman and Hofbauer, *Transilvania*, 109.

45. Manuela Boatcă and Julia Roth, "Women on the Fast Track? Coloniality of Citizenship and Embodied Social Mobility," in *Gender and Development: The Economic Basis of Women's Power*, ed. Rae Lesser Blumberg and Samuel Cohn (Los Angeles: Sage, 2019).

46. Gayle Rubin, "The Traffic in Women: Notes on the 'Political Economy' of Sex," in *Toward an Anthropology of Women*, ed. Rayna R. Reiter (New York: Monthly Review Press, 1975), 157–210.

47. Raymond Williams, *The Country and the City* (Oxford: Oxford University Press, 1975), 61.

48. Sabău, "*Și ne-au făcut din grăniceri, țărani . . . ,*" 160.

49. Rebreanu, *Amalgam*, 164.

50. Sebastian Conrad writes about "a quasi-Romantic discourse among Hindu elites as they sought to affirm their organic connection to the land and to the agrarian workforce." Sebastian Conrad, *What Is Global History?* (Princeton, NJ: Princeton University Press, 2016), 85.

51. For an account of the commons in East Europe running on a "belated" parallel track to the commons in West Europe, see Miguel Laborda Pemán and Tine De Moor, "A Tale of Two Commons: Some Preliminary Hypotheses on the Long-Term Development of the Commons in Western and Eastern Europe, 11th–19th Centuries," *International Journal of the Commons* 7, no. 1 (2013): 7–33.

52. Adrian Onofreiu, *Districtul Năsăudului (1861–1876)* (Cluj-Napoca, Romania: Editura Argonaut, 2009), 43.

53. Wallerstein, "Land, Space, and People," 9.

54. Constantin C. Giurescu, *A History of the Romanian Forest* (Bucharest: Editura Academiei Republicii Socialiste România, 1980).

55. Williams, *Country and the City*, 280.

56. In an essay dedicated to Williams's work, Julie Skurski and Fernando Coronil write: "At the global level we may observe the same ideological concealment that operates domestically: a tendency to obscure the mutually constitutive relationship between center ('city') and periphery ('country') and to represent them as separate entities whose characteristics appear as the consequence of intrinsic attributes." Julie Skurski and Fernando Coronil, "Country and City in a Postcolonial Landscape: Double Discourse and the Geo-Politics of Truth in Latin America," in *Views beyond the Border Country: Raymond Williams and Cultural Politics*, ed. Dennis L. Dworkin and Leslie G. Roman (New York: Routledge, 1993), 244–46.

57. Onofreiu, *Districtul Năsăudului*, 62.

58. Nestor Șimon, *Vasile Nașcu: Viața și faptele lui* [Vasile Nașcu: his life and deeds] (Bistrița, Romania: Tipografia G. Matheiu, 1908).

59. Documents pertaining to the dispute are reproduced in Mircea Gelu Buta and Adrian Onofreiu, eds., *Petiții din granița năsăudeană în a doua jumătate a secolului al XIX-lea: Contribuții documentare* [Petitions from the Năsăud border in the second half of the nineteenth century: documentary contributions] (Cluj-Napoca, Romania: Eikon, 2012).

60. In discussing land rights in the world-system, Wallerstein as well as Farshad Araghi and Marina Karides see the land problem as arising with the shift from customary rights to property rights—native populations claim landownership based on oral knowledge and tradition, whereas an imperial administration attempts to formalize it through modern administrative documents. Immanuel Wallerstein, "Land, Space, and People: Constraints of the Capitalist World-Economy," *Journal of World-Systems Research* 18, no. 1 (2012): 6–14; Farshad Araghi and Marina Karides, "Land Dispossession and Global Crisis: Introduction to the Special Section on Land Rights in the World-System," *Journal of World-Systems Research* 18, no. 1 (2012): 1–5.

61. On the formalization of the commons in Transylvania, see Monica Vasile, "Formalizing Commons, Registering Rights: The Making of the Forest and Pasture Commons in the Romanian Carpathians from the 19th Century to Post-Socialism," *International Journal of the Commons* 12, no. 1 (2018): 170–201. Vasile examined property records, court documents, and commons bylaws and conducted interviews with commons council representatives.

62. On cases of enclosure, see Onofreiu, *Districtul Năsăudului*, 57.

63. Onofreiu, 77–79.

64. Wallerstein, "Land, Space, and People," 12.

65. Rețegan, *Satele năsăudene la mijlocul secolului al XIX-lea.*

66. Vasile, "Formalizing Commons, Registering Rights," 178.

67. Vasile, 179.

68. István Csucsuja, *Istoria pădurilor din Transilvania 1848–1914* [The history of forests in Transylvania 1848–1914] (Cluj-Napoca, Romania: Presa Universitară Clujeană, 1998).

69. R. J. W. Evans, *Austria, Hungary, and the Habsburgs: Essays on Central Europe c. 1683–1867* (Oxford: Oxford University Press, 2006), 213.

70. McArthur, "Saxon Germans."

71. See Valer Simion Cosma, "Inventing the Romanian Peasant in Transylvania during the Nineteenth Century," in *Ruralism and Literature in Romania*, ed. Ștefan Baghiu, Vlad Pojoga, and Maria Sass (Berlin: Peter Lang, 2020).

72. Compare Jennifer L. Fleissner, *Women, Compulsion, Modernity: The Moment of American Naturalism* (Chicago: University of Chicago Press, 2004), 9.

73. Aníbal Quijano, "Coloniality of Power, Eurocentrism, and Latin America," *Nepentla: Views from the South* 1, no. 3 (2000): 539.

74. Immanuel Wallerstein, *The Essential Wallerstein* (New York: The New Press, 2000), 91.

75. For a counterargument to this connection, see Pieter M. Judson, *The Habsburg Empire: A New History* (Cambridge, MA: Belknap Press, 2016).

76. Jason W. Moore, "Sugar and the Expansion of the Early Modern World-Economy: Commodity Frontiers, Ecological Transformation, and Industrialization," *Review (Fernand Braudel Center)* 23, no. 3 (2000): 411.

77. For a notable exception, see Enrico Dal Lago, "Second Slavery, Second Serfdom, and Beyond: The Atlantic Plantation System and the Eastern and Southern European Landed Estate System in Comparative Perspective, 1800–60," *Review (Fernand Braudel Center)* 32, no. 4 (2009): 391–420.

78. Immanuel Wallerstein, *The Modern World-System I: Capitalist Agriculture and the Origins of the European World-Economy in the Sixteenth Century* (Berkeley: University of California Press, 2011), 100.

79. Braudel is quoted in Wallerstein, 42; Komlosy, *Work*, 169.

80. Komlosy, *Work*, 169–71.

81. Komlosy, 171.

82. Araghi and Karides, 1.

83. Araghi and Karides, 1.

84. Wallerstein, "Land, Space, and People," 7.

85. Coronil, "Beyond Occidentalism."

86. Araghi and Karides, "Land Dispossession and Global Crisis," 1.

2. TRANSYLVANIA IN THE WORLD-SYSTEM

1. Zoltán Szász, "Political Life and Nationality Question," in *History of Transylvania*, vol. 3 (New York: Columbia University Press, 2002), 511.

2. Stefan Berger suggests that, as an imperial nation, Germany before 1914 had a complex structure, with Prussia as "the national core of the Empire" and four layers of peripheries stratified hierarchically: a first-line periphery made up of the other German states and statelets to be incorporated into the emerging nation-state; a second colonial periphery inside the nation-state, made up the ethnic minorities that did not regard themselves and were not regarded by the core as German, such as speakers of Polish in Prussia's eastern provinces, speakers of Danish in Schleswig, and Alsatians and Lorrainers in the Rhineland; a third periphery comprising about 24 million German speakers in Central and East Europe, who found themselves outside the borders of the German

Reich after 1871; and Germany's overseas colonies. Stefan Berger, "Building the Nation among Visions of German Empire," in *Nationalizing Empires*, ed. Stefan Berger and Alexei Miller (Budapest: Central European University Press, 2015), 247–308.

3. By contrast, Katherine Verdery writes in a note: "While this entity is commonly referred to as the Habsburg *Empire*, I consider its behavior to be perfectly consonant with treating it as an aspirant state in the European state system of its day." Katherine Verdery, *Transylvanian Villagers: Three Centuries of Political, Economic, and Ethnic Change* (Berkeley: University of California Press, 1983), 373.

4. Drawing on earlier work interrogating the relationship between the colonial state and the metropolitan state and the relationship between the making of nations and the making of empires, Laura Stoler proposes that we refer to Western states as *imperial formations*, which are "macropolities whose technologies of rule thrive on the production of exceptions and their uneven and changing proliferation. Territorial ambiguity, legal categories of belonging that produce quasi-membership (and ambiguous rules of access to that membership) and geographic and demographic zones of partially and indefinitely suspended rights are defining features." Laura Stoler, *Duress: Imperial Durabilities in Our Times* (Durham, NC: Duke University Press, 2016), 177.

5. Sylvia Walby, "The Myth of the Nation-State: Theorizing Society and Polities in a Global Era," *Sociology* 37, no. 3 (2003): 529–46; Frederick Cooper, *Colonialism in Question: Theory, Knowledge, History* (Berkeley: University of California Press, 2005); Andrea Komlosy, "Imperial Cohesion, Nation-Building, and Regional Integration in the Habsburg Monarchy," in Berger and Miller, *Nationalizing Empires*; Benjamin De Carvalho, Halvard Leira, and John M. Hobson, "The Big Bangs of IR: The Myths that Your Teachers Still Tell You about 1648 and 1919," *Millennium* 39, no. 3 (2011): 735–58.

6. Komlosy, "Imperial Cohesion, Nation-Building, and Regional Integration," 369.

7. Berger, "Building the Nation among Visions of German Empire," 305.

8. Max-Stephan Schulze and Nikolaus Wolf, "On the Origins of Border Effects: Insights from the Habsburg Empire," *Journal of Economic Geography* 9, no. 1 (2009): 117–36.

9. John Komlos, *The Habsburg Monarchy as a Customs Union: Economic Development in Austria-Hungary in the Nineteenth Century* (Princeton, NJ: Princeton University Press, 1983), 4.

10. Iván T. Berend and György Ránki report that "Budapest became the second largest milling center of the world after Minneapolis . . . grinding 24 million quintals annually and exporting about 8 million (the second largest flour export in the world)." Iván T. Berend and György Ránki, *East Central Europe in the 19th and 20th Centuries* (Budapest: Akadémiai Kiadó, 1977), 26.

11. Berger, "Building the Nation among Visions of German Empire," 257.

12. David Blackbourn, *Das Kaiserreich transnational: Eine Skizze* [The German Empire Transnationally: A Sketch], in Sebastian Conrad und Jürgen Osterhammel, eds., *Das Kaiserreich transnational: Deutschland in der Welt 1871–1914* [The German Empire Transnationally: Germany in the World 1871–1914] (Göttingen: Vandenhoeck und Ruprecht, 2004), 322.

13. Berend writes: "as intermediaries of Western banks, and as collectors of Austrian deposits, these banks became highly important financial institutions for the entire Austro-Hungarian empire, and for the Balkans as well. With some exaggeration, it can be said that no money went to Eastern Europe without passing through Viennese banks." Iván T. Berend, "Past Convergence within Europe: Core–Periphery Diversity in Modern Economic Development," in *Economic Convergence and Divergence in Europe: Growth and Regional Development in an Enlarged European Union*, ed. Gertrude Tumpel-Gugerell and Peter Mooslechner (Cheltenham, UK: Elgar, 2003), 22.

14. On the role of local banks, see Bujor Surdu, *Aspecte privind rolul băncilor în consolidarea burgheziei românești din Transilvania până la primul război mondial* [Aspects regarding the role of banks in the consolidation of the Romanian bourgeoisie in Transylvania before World War I] (Bucharest: Editura Academiei Republicii Populare Române, 1962); Lucian Dronca, *Băncile românești din Transilvania în perioada dualismului austro-ungar (1867–1918)* [Romanian banks in Transylvania during the period of Austro-Hungarian dualism (1867–1918)] (Cluj-Napoca, Romania: Presa Universitară Clujeană, 2003); Iosif Marin Balog, "Elitele financiar-bancare românești din Transilvania (1895–1918): Considerații teoretico-metodologice și evaluări statistice [Romanian financial/banking elites in Transylvania (1895–1918): theoretical methodological considerations and statistical evaluations]," *Anuarul Institutului de Istorie George Barițiu* 55, no. 55 (2016): 33–47; Iosif Marin Balog, "The Clergy's Involvement in the Romanian Credit System from Transylvania during the Late Nineteenth and the Early Twentieth Centuries. Case Study: The Greek-Catholic Clergy," in *Recruitment and Promotion among the Romanian Greek Catholic Ecclesiastical Elite in Transylvania (1853–1918)*, ed. Mirela Popa-Andrei (Cluj-Napoca, Romania: Editura Mega, 2014), 170–74.

15. Lucian Dronca, "Filiale, reuniuni de credit și asociații ale băncilor românești din Transilvania in epoca modernă (1867–1918) [Branches, co-ops, and associations of Romanian banks in Transylvania in the modern period (1867–1918)]," *Cumidava* 26 (2003): 112.

16. Schulze and Wolf argue that "the intensification of intra-empire economic nationalism led to asymmetric integration of regional markets within an overall integrating Habsburg economy . . . trade networks tend to evolve along social and ethnic contacts . . . *language* is estimated to be highly significant after controlling for distance or transport costs." Max-Stephan Schulze and Nikolaus Wolf, "Economic Nationalism and Economic Integration: The Austro-Hungarian Empire in the Late Nineteenth Century," *Economic History Review* 65, no. 2 (2012): 652–73.

17. Balog, "Clergy's Involvement in the Romanian Credit System."

18. On banks and economic nationalism, see Catherine Albrecht, "Rural Banks and Czech Nationalism in Bohemia, 1848–1914," *Agricultural History* 78, no. 3 (2004): 317–45.

19. According to Berend and Ránki, "The gentry despised commerce and industry; they shunned anyone with a business mentality, and did not want to become bourgeois. They flocked into government offices, which became a thick network of gentry kinships; one third to one half of the ministerial posts, three quarters of the county offices and a significant portion of the posts in the judiciary and officer corps were held by the gentry." Berend and Ránki, *East Central Europe in the 19th and 20th Centuries*, 32.

20. Komlos, *Habsburg Monarchy*, 389. On the British census, see Timothy Parsons, *The Rule of Empires: Those Who Built Them, Those Who Endured Them, and Why They Always Fall* (Oxford: Oxford University Press, 2010).

21. Stoler, *Duress*, 176.

22. Manuela Boatcă, "Thinking Europe Otherwise: Lessons from the Caribbean," *Current Sociology* 69, no. 3 (2021): 391.

23. Andrea Komlosy, *Work: The Last 1,000 Years*, trans. Jacob K. Watson and Loren Balhorn (London: Verso, 2018), 192.

24. Traude Horvath and Gerda Neyer, eds., *Auswanderungen aus Österreich: von der Mitte des 19. Jahrhunderts bis zur Gegenwart: mit einer umfassenden Bibliographie zur Österreichischen Migrationsgeschichte* [Emigration from Austria: From the mid-19th century until the present: with a comprehensive bibliography on Austria's migration history] (Vienna: Böhlau, 1996), 35.

25. Tara Zahra, *The Great Departure: Mass Migration from Eastern Europe and the Making of the Free World* (New York: W. W. Norton, 2016), 37; Benno Gammerl, *Sub-*

jects, Citizens, and Others: Administering Ethnic Heterogeneity in the British and Habsburg Empires, 1867–1918 (New York: Berghahn Books, 2018), 44.

26. Berger, "Building the Nation among Visions of German Empire," 298.

27. Iván T. Berend, *History Derailed: Central and Eastern Europe in the Long Nineteenth Century* (Berkeley: University of California Press, 2005), 172.

28. Iosif Marin Balog, "Transporturile și comunicațiile: evoluție și semnificație în procesul modernizării economice a Transilvaniei la mijlocul secolului al XIX-lea [Transportation and communication: their evolution and signification in the process of economic modernization of Transylvania in mid-nineteenth century]," *Revista Bistriței* 20 (2006): 235.

29. Dale Tomich, "World Slavery and Caribbean Capitalism: The Cuban Sugar Industry, 1760–1868," *Theory and Society* 20, no. 3 (1991): 302.

30. Tomich, 308; Oscar Zanetti and Alejandro García, *Sugar and Railroads: A Cuban History, 1837–1959* (Chapel Hill: University of North Carolina Press, 2017).

31. Tomich, "World Slavery and Caribbean Capitalism," 308.

32. Zanetti and García, *Sugar and Railroads*, 20.

33. Zoltán Ginelli, "Plotting the Semiperipheral Empire: Hungarian Balkanism and Global Colonialism in Geographical Knowledge, 1867–1948," in *De-Linking—Critical Thought and Radical Politics*, ed. Manuela Boatcă (Abingdon, VA: Routledge, forthcoming).

34. Teodor Păcățian, *Cartea de aur sau luptele naționale ale românilor de sub coroana ungară* [The golden book or, the Romanian national struggle under the Hungarian crown], vol. 8 (Sibiu, Romania: Tiparul Tipografiei Arhidiecezane, 1915), 488.

35. Balog, "Transporturile și comunicațiile," 245.

36. Fernando Coronil, "Beyond Occidentalism: Toward Nonimperial Geohistorical Categories," *Cultural Anthropology* 11, no. 1 (1996): 340.

37. Komlosy, *Work*, 193.

38. Kristin Hoganson and Jay Sexton, "Introduction," in *Crossing Empires: Taking U.S. History into Transimperial Terrain* (Durham, NC: Duke University Press, 2020).

39. Bernhard Siegert, *Relays: Literature as an Epoch of the Postal System* (Stanford, CA: Stanford University Press, 1999).

40. Warwick Research Collective, *Combined and Uneven Development: Towards a New Theory of World-Literature* (Liverpool: Liverpool University Press, 2015), 12.

41. On the concept of antisemitism, including the debate around the spelling of the word, see Deborah E. Lipstadt, *Antisemitism: Here and Now* (New York: Schocken, 2019).

42. David Nirenberg, *Anti-Judaism: The Western Tradition* (New York: W. W. Norton, 2013).

43. Szász, "Political Life and Nationality Question," 560.

44. Nirenberg, *Anti-Judaism*, 465–66.

45. Esther Benbassa and Aron Rodrigue, *The Jews of the Balkans: The Judeo-Spanish Community, 15th to 20th Centuries* (Oxford: Blackwell, 1995), 46–48. Judit Pál foregrounds the fact that the category "Greek" included traders belonging to a number of Balkan ethnic groups, including Romanians, Macedo-Romanians, Greeks, and Serbs. Judit Pál, *Armenians in Transylvania: Their Contribution to the Urbanization and the Economic Development of the Province*, trans. Bogdan Aldea (Cluj-Napoca: Romanian Cultural Institute, 2005), 116.

46. Andrei Oișteanu, *Imaginea evreului în cultura română* [The image of the Jew in Romanian culture] (Bucharest: Humanitas, 2001), 158–60.

47. On the Armenians' association with trade, as well as their gradual assimilation, see Judit Pál, "Armenian Society in 18th Century Transylvania," in *Studies in the History of Early Modern Transylvania*, ed. Gyöngy Kovács Kiss (New York: Columbia University

Press, 2011), 151–78. Rebreanu wrote a number of drafts staging stories about Transylvanian Armenians.

48. Moshe Carmilly-Weinberger, *Istoria evreilor din Transilvania (1623–1944)* [History of the Jews of Transylvania (1623–1944)] (Bucharest: Editura Enciclopedică, 1994), 35; Ladislau Gyémánt, *Evreii din Transilvania în epoca emancipării/The Jews of Transylvania in the Age of Emancipation (1790–1867)* (Bucharest: Editura Enciclopedică, 2000), 307–8, 323.

49. Pieter M. Judson, *The Habsburg Empire: A New History* (Cambridge, MA: Belknap Press, 2016), 68.

50. Judson, 68.

51. Steven Béla Várdy, *Baron Joseph Eötvös (1813–1871): A Literary Biography* (Boulder, CO: East European Monographs, 1987).

52. Ladislau Gyémánt, "The Transylvanian Jewish Identity's Avatars in the Epoch of Emancipation," in *Building Identities in Transylvania: A Comparative Approach*, ed. Sorin Mitu (Cluj-Napoca, Romania: Argonaut, 2014), 121–142, 134. Macaulay is known for his infamous "Minutes on Indian Education," which argued in favor of the English-language education of Indians. Gauri Viswanathan addresses Macauley's two essays— one on Jewish emancipation and the other on the education of colonized subjects in India—and argues that both served British commercial needs. Gauri Viswanathan, "Subjecting English and the Question of Representation," in *Disciplinarity at the Fin de Siècle*, ed. Amanda Anderson and Joseph Valente (Princeton, NJ: Princeton University Press 2002), 177–95.

53. On the debate on Jewish emancipation in Hungary, see Raphael Patai, *The Jews of Hungary: History, Culture, Psychology* (Detroit: Wayne State University Press, 1996). For a comparative account of Jewish emancipation, see David Sorkin, *Jewish Emancipation: A History across Five Centuries* (Princeton, NJ: Princeton University Press, 2019).

54. Salo W. Baron, "The Impact of the Revolution of 1848 on Jewish Emancipation," *Jewish Social Studies* 11, no. 3 (1949): 195–248.

55. Gyémánt, *Evreii din Transilvania în epoca emancipării*, 387, 400.

56. Berend, *History Derailed*, 202.

57. Immanuel Wallerstein, *The Modern World-System I: Capitalist Agriculture and the Origins of the European World-Economy in the Sixteenth Century* (Berkeley: University of California Press, 2011), 149.

58. Berend, *History Derailed*, 202.

59. Raul Cârstocea, "Between Europeanisation and Local Legacies: Holocaust Memory and Contemporary Anti-Semitism in Romania," *East European Politics and Societies* 35, no. 2 (2020): 313–35.

60. Micheal K. Silber, "The Making of Habsburg Jewry in the Long Eighteenth Century," in *The Cambridge History of Judaism*, vol. 7 (Cambridge: Cambridge University Press, 2017).

61. Gyémánt, *Evreii din Transilvania în epoca emancipării*, 402. Iveta Jusová writes about the Czech predicament: "Given the nineteenth-century nationalist struggle for independence, the Bohemian and Moravian Jews who identified with German culture and proclaimed their loyalty to the Habsburg dynasty—and in general, many other Jews—were regarded by Czechs with hostility. . . . The question remains to what extent the unwillingness among the Jewish population to adopt the Czech language and culture for their own was due to their perception of Czech bigotry and xenophobia." Iveta Jusová, "Figuring the Other in Nineteenth-Century Czech Literature: Gabriela Preissová and Bozena Viková-Kunetická," in *History of the Literary Cultures of East-Central Europe*, vol. IV, ed. Marcel Cornis-Pope and John Neubauer (Amsterdam: John Benjamins Publishing, 2010), 373.

62. Gyémánt, *Evreii din Transilvania în epoca emancipării*, 369, 403.

63. Writing about Kafka's relation to German as a Jewish language, Yasemin Yildiz joins a number of recent scholars who argue against a paradigm of Jewish linguistic assimilation. Once one rejects a proprietary mapping of language onto ethnos (Hungarians speak Hungarian, Romanians speak Romanian, etc.), all the languages of the region spoken by Jewish people can be conceived of as Jewish languages. Yasemin Yildiz, *Beyond the Mother Tongue: The Postmonolingual Condition* (New York: Fordham University Press, 2012).

64. Victor Neumann, *Istoria evreilor din Banat* [The history of Jews in Banat] (Bucharest: Atlas, 1999), 74–75.

65. Sorina Paula Bolovan, *Familia în satul românesc din Transilvania* [The family in the Romanian village of Transylvania] (Cluj-Napoca, Romania: Fundaţia Culturală Română, 1999), 54.

66. A complex analysis of Romanian antisemitism, from a cross-imperial perspective, is offered by Irina Marin, *Peasant Violence and Antisemitism in Early Twentieth-Century Eastern Europe* (Cham, Switzerland: Palgrave Macmillan, 2018).

67. Cârstocea, "Between Europeanisation and Local Legacies," 3.

68. For a list of such parallels, see Oişteanu, *Imaginea evreului în cultura română*, 306–11.

69. Attila Gidó, "Identitatea evreilor ardeleni în perioada interbelică" [The identity of Transylvanian Jews in the interwar period]," *Revista de Istorie a Evreilor din România* 1 (2016): 52–64.

70. Gyémánt, *Evreii din Transilvania în epoca emancipării*, 330–32; Ezra Mendelsohn, *The Jews of East Central Europe between the World Wars* (Bloomington: Indiana University Press, 1987), 171, 187.

71. Franz Liszt, *The Gipsy in Music*, trans. Edwin Evans (London: William Reeves, n.d.).

72. Parenthetical citations from the novel refer to the following editions: Liviu Rebreanu, *Ion*, trans. A. Hillard (London: Peter Owen, 1965); Liviu Rebreanu, *Ion*, ed. Niculae Gheran, vol. 4, *Opere* (Bucharest: Editura Minerva, 1970). We modified some translations.

73. On the stereotype attached to poisoning in a broader European context, see David Nirenberg, *Communities of Violence: Persecution of Minorities in the Middle Ages* (Princeton, NJ: Princeton University Press, 2015).

74. Gyémánt, *Evreii din Transilvania în epoca emancipării*, 391–92. Robert B. Pynsent writes about a similar development in Czech nationalism: "they threatened rural Czechness with distilleries and country pubs. Jews could be blamed for rural alcohol abuse as well as the unemployment and poverty that resulted from modernization." Robert B. Pynsent, "Mácha, the Czech National Poet," in *History of the Literary Cultures of East-Central Europe*, vol. IV, ed. Marcel Cornis-Pope and John Neubauer (Amsterdam: John Benjamins Publishing, 2010), 348.

75. The city of Năsăud/Nassod/Naszód had an ordinance that attempted to curtail the visits of young men from the region to the Jewish village of Tradam/Emtrádám/Unterdam. Two guards were stationed at the bridge separating the village from the city, with orders to record transgressors, who would be punished with labor time. Adrian Onofreiu, *Districtul Năsăudului (1861–1876)* (Cluj-Napoca, Romania: Editura Argonaut, 2009), 88.

76. Nirenberg, *Anti-Judaism*, 422. For a reversal of the term's connotations through a decolonial lens, see Santiago Slabodsky, *Decolonial Judaism: Triumphal Failures of Barbaric Thinking* (New York: Palgrave Macmillan, 2014). Slabodsky analyzes historical and conceptual overlaps between the history of anti-Judaism and experiences of colonization, reading Jewish resistance to imperial narratives of their "barbarism" as a decolonial project that he labels "decolonial Judaism."

77. "It is difficult," writes Nirenberg, "to think of a financial innovation, practice, or crisis that was not discussed in terms of Judaism in the nineteenth and twentieth centuries." Nirenberg, *Anti-Judaism*, 439.

78. Oişteanu, *Imaginea evreului în cultura română*, 131.

79. Mihai Eminescu, *Chestiunea evreiască* [The Jewish question] (Bucharest: Editura Vastala, 2000).

80. *Encyclopedia Judaica*, vol. 17.

81. Quoted in Liviu Rebreanu, *Ion*, ed. Niculae Gheran, vol. 4, *Opere* (Bucharest: Editura Minerva, 1970), 578.

82. On this rhetorical strategy, see Oişteanu, *Imaginea evreului în cultura română*, 237.

83. Jusová, "Figuring the Other in Nineteenth-Century Czech Literature," 374.

84. Because different constituencies voted in groups, hooting and even aggression were not uncommon. Judit Pál, Vlad Popovici, Andrea Fehér, and Ovidiu Emil Iudean, eds., *Parliamentary Elections in Eastern Hungary and Transylvania (1865–1918)* (Berlin: Peter Lang, 2018), 32–33.

85. Rebreanu wrote a short story titled "Iţic Ştrul, dezertor" (1919), a case study in Jewish "betrayal" that nonetheless ends with the main character refusing to desert to the enemy and hanging himself instead.

86. Marin, *Peasant Violence and Antisemitism*.

87. Rebreanu explained: "The committee tasked, after the Union, with checking and revising the names of all villages in Greater Romania, adopted the name Jidoviţa instead of Tradam, the name I gave it in the novel, which in a way expresses a reality, Jidoviţa being a pure Jewish village in our pure Romanian region, otherwise the only Jewish village in Transylvania, except of course Maramureş [*Comisia oficială, care după Unire, a revizuit şi verificat numele tuturor localităţilor din Romînia Mare, a adoptat în loc de Tradam numele Jidoviţa pe care i l-am dat eu în roman şi care exprimă într-un fel şi o realitate, Jidoviţa fiind un sat pur jidovesc în regiunea noastră pur românească, de altfel unicul sat jidovesc din Ardeal, afară, binenţeles, de Maramureş*]." Liviu Rebreanu, *Amalgam*, in *Opere* vol. 15 (Bucharest: Editura Minerva, 1991), 174.

88. Rebreanu elaborated in *Amalgam*: "Creating people does not mean imitating nature and real existing individuals. Such realism or naturalism is less valuable than a bad photograph. Literary creation can only be synthesis [*A crea oameni nu înseamnă a crea după natură indivizi existenţi. Asemenea realism sau naturalism e mai puţin valoros ca o fotografie proastă. Creaţia literară nu poate fi decât sinteză*]." Rebreanu, *Amalgam*, 162.

89. Gérard Genette defines metalepsis as an "intrusion by the extradiegetic narrator or narratee into the diegetic universe (or by the diegetic characters into a metadiegetic universe)." Gérard Genette, *Narrative Discourse: An Essay in Method*, trans. Jane E. Lewin (Ithaca, NY: Cornell University Press, 1980), 236.

3. THE *LONGUE DURÉE* OF ENSLAVEMENT

1. On the imbrication of enslavement and indentured labor, see Shu-mei Shih, "Comparison as Relation," in *Comparison: Theories, Approaches, Uses*, ed. Rita Felski and Susan Stanford Friedman (Baltimore, MD: Johns Hopkins University Press, 2013).

2. On linguistic conventions used to refer to Roma, see Yaron Matras, *The Romani Gypsies* (Cambridge, MA: Belknap Press, 2015).

3. Romani history is absent from both the school curriculum in contemporary Romania and the prevailing definition of Romanianness. It is seen as detrimental to the way Romania and its citizens are portrayed abroad, particularly in West Europe. In an effort to be included in the notion of proper Europeanness—associated with whiteness, Christianity, and Occidentality—contemporary Romanians, from intellectuals to politicians to

the wider population, often mobilize forms of anti-Roma racism, ranging from denouncing the association between Roma and Romanians as false etymology to engaging in violent invectives and behavior toward Roma and actively promoting school segregation. Alyosxa Tudor, "The Desire for Categories," *Feminist Review* blog, 2018, https://femrev.wordpress.com/2018/03/19/the-desire-for-categories/; Ioanida Costache, "Until We Are Able to Gas Them Like the Nazis, the Roma Will Infect the Nation: Roma and the Ethnicization of COVID-19 in Romania," *DOR*, April 2020, www.dor.ro/roma-and-the-ethnicization-of-covid-19-in-romania/; Margareta Matache and Jacqueline Bhabha, "Anti-Roma Racism Is Spiraling during COVID-19 Pandemic," *Health and Human Rights* 22, no. 1 (2020): 379–82.

4. On the concept of the racial field, see Claire Jean Kim, *Bitter Fruit: The Politics of Black-Korean Conflict in New York City* (New Haven, CT: Yale University Press, 2003); Shu-mei Shih, "Comparative Racialization: An Introduction," *PMLA* 123, no. 5 (2008): 1347–62.

5. Franz Liszt, *The Gipsy in Music*, trans. Edwin Evans (London: William Reeves, n.d.), 105, 116.

6. James Clifford, *Routes: Travel and Translation in the Late Twentieth Century* (Cambridge, MA: Harvard University Press, 1997).

7. Katie Trumpener, "Béla Bartók and the Rise of Comparative Ethnomusicology: Nationalism, Race Purity, and the Legacy of the Austro-Hungarian Empire," in *Music and the Racial Imagination*, ed. Ronald Radano and Philip V. Bohlman (Chicago: University of Chicago Press, 2000), 403–34.

8. Annegret Fauser reports that Romani musicians' success representing Hungary at the 1889 World's Fair was "tempered by the even more exotic and more 'authentic' gypsy music from Romania and Spain." These musicians were perceived as "primitives and thus true gypsies. They were so attuned to their art that they became 'almost instruments themselves.'" Annegret Fauser, *Musical Encounters at the 1889 Paris World's Fair* (Rochester, NY: University of Rochester Press, 2005), 257. For an account of Romani musicians representing Romania at the fair, see Georges Bibesco, *Exposition Universalle: La Roumanie* (Paris: Imprimerie Typographique J. Kugelmann, 1890).

9. On minorness, see Alex Woloch, *The One vs. the Many: Minor Characters and the Space of the Protagonist in the Novel* (Princeton, NJ: Princeton University Press, 2003). The scene dramatizes a musical construction of Transylvanian Romanian nationalism; see Michael Murphy and Harry White, eds., *Musical Constructions of Nationalism: Essays on the History and Ideology of European Musical Culture 1800–1945* (Cork, Ireland: Cork University Press, 2001).

10. Liviu Rebreanu, *Ion*, trans. A. Hillard (London: Peter Owen, 1965); Liviu Rebreanu, *Ion*, ed. Niculae Gheran, vol. IV, *Opere* (Bucharest: Editura Minerva, 1970). We modified some translations.

11. On this omission, see Ian Hancock, *The Pariah Syndrome: An Account of Gypsy Slavery and Persecution* (Ann Arbor, MI: Karoma Publishers, 1988); Mihaela Mudure, "Blackening Gypsy Slavery: The Romanian Case," in *Blackening Europe: The African American Presence*, ed. Heike Raphael-Hernandez (New York: Routledge, 2004); Margareta Matache and Cornel West, "Roma and African Americans Share a Common Struggle," *The Guardian*, 20 February, 2018.

12. Fatima El-Tayeb, *European Others: Queering Ethnicity in Postnational Europe* (Minneapolis: University of Minnesota Press, 2011), xxvii.

13. David Theo Goldberg has called for a relational account of "racial Europeanization" that would trace the link between European antisemitism and the production of race in European colonies. Such an account would have to include a study of the racialization

of Roma in East Europe in relation to antisemitism, Orientalism, and the history of enslavement. The history of camps and encampment as it pertains to the racialization of the Roma, detailed by Tara Zahra, should also be included in this account. David Theo Goldberg, "Racial Europeanization," *Ethnic and Racial Studies* 29 (2006): 331–64.

14. Felix B. Chang and Sunnie T. Rucker-Chang, *Roma Rights and Civil Rights: A Transatlantic Comparison* (Cambridge: Cambridge University Press, 2020); Manuela Boatcă, "Politics of Memory under Two Pandemics," *EuropeNow* 40 (2021), https://www.europenowjournal.org/2021/04/01/politics-of-memory-under-two-pandemics/; Marius Turda, "Anti-Roma Racism in Romania," *EuropeNow* 40 (2021), https://www.europenowjournal.org/2021/04/01/anti-roma-racism-in-romania/.

15. Viorel Achim, *The Roma in Romanian History* (Budapest: CEU Press, 1998), 28.

16. On the historical use of the juridical term *robie*, see Ion Radu Mircea, "Termenii rob, șerb și holop în documentele slave și române [The meanings of rob, șerb and holop in Slavonic and Romanian documents]," in *Robia țiganilor în Țările Române* [Gypsy slavery in the Romanian principalities], ed. Vasile Ionescu (Bucharest: Editura Centrului Rromilor pentru politici publice "Aven amentza," 2000), 61–74; Petre Petcuț, *Rromii: Sclavie și libertate* [Roms: slavery and freedom] (Bucharest: Editura Centrului National de Cultură a Romilor, 2016). On the distinction between the institutions of serfdom and enslavement, see Cristina Codarcea, *Société et pouvoir en Valachie (1601–1654): Entre la coutume et la loi* [Society and power in Wallachia (1601–1654): Between custom and law] (Bucharest: Editura Enciclopedică, 2002). Our translation of *robie* as *slavery* draws on comparative sources and methodologies: "Despite historical and cultural variations, slaves have generally been defined as chattels personal, incapable of legal marriage, property ownership, or judicial testimony; they have been subject to the authority of a private or institutional owner; their labor and services have been totally at the disposal of others." David Brion Davis, *The Problem of Slavery in Western Culture* (New York: Oxford University Press, 1988), 58.

17. The distinction appears in a 1646 legal code, *Sobornicescul Hrisov*: "the Gypsy belonging to the prince or the boyars or the monasteries or whoever [*țiganul domnesc ori boeresc ori mănăstiresc sau ori a cui*]." Andrei Rădulescu, ed., *Sobornicescul Hristov* (Bucharest: Editura Academiei Republicii Populare Române, 1958), 25.

18. Adrian-Nicolae Furtună and Victor-Claudiu Turcitu have collected a vast number of archival documents pertaining to the enslavement of Romani people—legal, economic and journalistic. See *Sclavia romilor și locurile memoriei—album de istorie socială* [Roma slavery and the places of memory—album of social history], ed. Adrian-Nicolae Furtună and Victor-Claudiu Turcitu (Bucharest: Dykhta! Publishing House, 2021).

19. Andrei Rădulescu, *Pagini din istoria dreptului românesc* [Pages from the history of Romanian law] (Bucharest: Editura Academiei Republicii Socialiste România, 1970). For a recent, comprehensive engagement with Romani enslavement as "law of the land," see the article series curated by Margareta Matache, "Obiceiul pământului" [Law of the Land], *DoR*, https://www.dor.ro/obiceiulpamantului/.

20. Michel-Rolph Trouillot, *Silencing the Past: Power and the Production of History* (Boston: Beacon Press, 1995); Susan Buck-Morss, *Hegel, Haiti, and Universal History* (Pittsburgh: University of Pittsburgh Press, 2009).

21. On the history of Romani resistance, see N. Grigoraș, "Robia în Moldova [Slavery in Moldova]," in Ionescu, *Robia țiganilor în Țările Române*.

22. Before *Legiuirea Caragea*, other legal documents regulated enslavement in Wallachia: *Îndreptarea Legii* (1652) and *Pravălniceasca Condică* (1780). *Caragea* was followed by *Regulamentul Organic* (1832).

23. Andrei Rădulescu, ed., *Legiuirea Caragea* (Bucharest: Editura Academiei Republicii Populare Române, 1955), 6.

24. Rădulescu, 10.
25. Rădulescu, 10.
26. Rădulescu, 10.
27. Rădulescu, 10–12.
28. Before *Codul Calimach*, other Moldovan codes regulated enslavement: *Carte românească de învățătură* (1646) and *Sobornicescul Hrisov* (1785). After *Calimach* came *Regulamentul Organic al Moldovei* (1831).
29. Andrei Rădulescu, ed., *Codul Calimach* (Bucharest: Editura Academiei Republicii Populare Române, 1958), 75.
30. An earlier law mentioned that the enslaved could be beaten, but not to death; if they were beaten too harshly or without cause, they could hit back and even kill the enslaver. Andrei Rădulescu, ed., *Carte românească de învățătură* (Bucharest: Editura Academiei Republicii Populare Române, 1961), 101.
31. The enslaved vacillated between the legal status of thing and person also because, as earlier codes specified, the law did not punish an affront to the honor of an enslaved person. Although dishonor (*sudalma*) was punishable, dishonoring the enslaved was punishable only if it reflected negatively on the enslaver. Rădulescu, 154. On honor, see Orlando Patterson, *Slavery and Social Death: A Comparative Study* (Cambridge. MA: Harvard University Press, 1982).
32. Rădulescu, *Legiuirea Caragea*, 26.
33. Mircea, "Termenii rob, șerb și holop în documentele slave și române," 64.
34. Rădulescu, *Codul Calimach*, 333. An earlier Moldovan law foregrounded the legal principle of *protimisis*: estates, which claim the enslaved who labor on them, cannot be estranged; when they are put up for sale, preference should be given to family members and other local boyars. Rădulescu, *Sobornicescul Hristov*, 19; *Pravilniceasca Condică* (Bucharest: Editura Academiei Republicii Populare Române, 1957), 148.
35. Rădulescu, *Legiuirea Caragea*, 80.
36. Dumitru Vitcu, ed., *Regulamentul Organic al Moldovei* (Iași, Romania: Editura Junimea, 2004), 245. Neagu Djuvara reports that, through regulations on landownership and endogamy, a few dozen families retained their privileges over a few centuries. Neagu Djuvara, *Între Orient și Occident: Țările române la începutul epocii moderne (1800–1848)* [Between Orient and Occident: the Romanian principalities at the dawn of the modern era (1800–1848)], trans. Maria Carpov (Bucharest: Humanitas, 1995), 124.
37. For a systematic analysis of the control of enslaved women's sexuality and reproduction on Caribbean plantations, see Rhoda Reddock, "Women and Slavery in the Caribbean: A Feminist Perspective," *Latin American Perspectives*, 12, no. 1 (Winter 1985), 63–80.
38. Rădulescu, *Codul Calimach*, 117.
39. Ioana Szeman writes: "racial differences between Romanians and Roma during slavery were created and maintained through marriage legislation, antiamalgamation (racial intermarriage) laws, and unwritten laws of sexual control and exploitation of female Roma slaves." Ioana Szeman, "'Black and White Are One': Anti-Amalgamation Laws, Roma Slaves, and the Romanian Nation on the Mid-Nineteenth-Century Moldavian Stage," in *Uncle Tom's Cabins: The Transnational History of America's Most Mutable Book*, ed. Tracy C. Davis and Stefka Mihaylova (Ann Arbor: University of Michigan Press, 2020), 167.
40. Rădulescu, *Codul Calimach*, 245.
41. Rădulescu, 121.
42. Rădulescu, 123.
43. An older legislative code in Moldova, *Carte românească de învățătură* (1646), regulated situations under the rubric of prostitution (*hotrie*), whereby an enslaver offered

enslaved women to other men for sex. In such cases, which defied religious mores, an enslaved woman should become free, and the enslaver should find her a husband. Rădulescu, *Carte românească de învățătură*, 125.

44. Rădulescu, *Codul Calimach*, 123.

45. Indentured laborers recruited from India to work on Caribbean sugar plantations after the abolition of slavery were subjected to the same gendering logic at the hands of the colonial state, the planter class, and male migrants. As Rhoda Reddock pointed out for Trinindad and Tobago, unmarried Indian women who came as indentured labourers at the end of the nineteenth century were under constant suspicion of being "prostitutes, social outcasts, or [. . .] prone to immoral conduct," while Indian men both participated in and benefitted from the construction of the women's independence as immorality. Rhoda Reddock, "Freedom Denied: Indian Women and Indentureship in Trinidad and Tobago, 1845–1917," *Economic and Political Weekly*, 20, no. 43 (1985): WS79–WS87.

46. Henri H. Stahl, "Théories des processus de 'modernisation' des Principautés Danubiennes et de l'ancien Royaume de Roumanie (1850–1920)" [Theories on the process of 'modernization' of the Danubian Principalities and the Old Kingdom of Romania (1850–1920)], *Review (Fernand Braudel Center)* 16, no. 1 (1993): 85–111.

47. Miloš Jovanović has found traces of wealth derived from the enslavement of Roma in several buildings in Belgrade, built by families that owned estates in Wallachia ("Cities of Dust and Mud: Urbanism and Bourgeois Fantasy in the Balkans," book manuscript).

48. On reparations, see the work of Margareta Matache, including the contribution to the recent comparative study, *Time for Reparations: A Global Perspective*, ed. Jacqueline Bhabha, Margareta Matache and Caroline Elkins (Philadelphia: University of Pennsylvania Press, 2021).

49. Harriet Beecher Stowe, *Coliba lui Moșu Toma* [Uncle Tom's cabin], trans. Teodor Codrescu (Iași, Romania: Tipografia Buciumul Român, 1853). On the reception of this translation against the background of the local emancipation movement, see Szeman, "'Black and White Are One.'"

50. Constantin Iordachi, *Liberalism, Constitutional Nationalism, and Minorities: The Making of Romanian Citizenship, c. 1750–1918* (Leiden, Netherlands: Brill, 2019), 159.

51. Achim, *Roma in Romanian History*, 20.

52. George Potra, *Contribuțiuni la istoricul țiganilor din România* [Contributions to the history of Gypsies in Romania] (Bucharest: Fundația Regelui Carol I, 1939), 47.

53. A. Gebora, "Situația juridică a țiganilor în Ardeal [The juridical situation of Gypsies in Transylvania]," in *Rromii în istoria României* [Roma in Romanian History] (Bucharest: Editura Centrului Rromilor, 2002).

54. Achim, *Roma in Romanian History*, 42.

55. *Uricariul* (Iași: Tipografia Buciumul Român).

56. Djuvara, *Între Orient și Occident*.

57. On this process of consolidation, see Pieter M. Judson, *The Habsburg Empire: A New History* (Cambridge, MA: Belknap Press, 2016). Although Judson traces the impact of centralizing efforts on the empire's Jewish population, the regulation of the Romani population does not factor into his account.

58. On the various provisions of *Regulatione*, see Matras, *Romani Gypsies*, 186. Achim writes: "the concentration of Gypsies in one place was forbidden, and, where necessary, orders were given for them to be moved elsewhere. However, it was proposed that Gypsies dispersed in this manner in the villages in small groups should be settled on the very edge of the villages. . . . The number of Gypsies living in each village was small, as a rule around two to three families." Achim, *Roma in Romanian History*, 133.

59. On the German-language circulation of Grellmann's text in Transylvania, see Marian Zăloagă, *Romii în cultura săsească din secolele al XVIII-lea și al XIX-lea* [Roma in

the Saxon culture of the 18th and 19th centuries] (Cluj-Napoca: Institutul pentru Studierea Problemelor Minorităților Naționale, 2015).

60. George Borrow, *The Zincali: An Account of the Gypsies of Spain* (London: John Murray, 1907), 76–80.

61. H. Grellmann, *Dissertation on the Gipseys* (London: Printed by William Ballintine, 1807), ix.

62. Grellmann, 100.

63. Grellmann, 100.

64. Tara Zahra, "Condemned to Rootlessness and Unable to Budge: Roma, Migration Panics, and Internment in the Habsburg Empire," *American Historical Review* 122, no. 3 (2017): 702–26.

65. On this discourse of orientalism, see Nicholas Saul, *Gypsies and Orientalism in German Literature and Anthropology of the Long Nineteenth Century* (London: Legenda, 2007).

66. E. Horvathová and S. Augustini, "Nachwort," in *Cigáni v Uhorsku/Zigeuner in Ungarn* [Gypsies in Hungary] (Bratislava: Štúdio DD, 1995).

67. Horvathová and Augustini, 190.

68. Grellmann, *Dissertation on the Gipseys*, viii.

69. Grellmann, 31.

70. Grellmann, 133, 200.

71. Sylvia Wynter, "Unsettling the Coloniality of Being/Power/Truth/Freedom: Towards the Human, after Man, Its Overrepresentation—An Argument," *CR: The New Centennial Review* 3, no. 3 (2003): 257–337.

72. Grellmann, *Dissertation on the Gipseys*, 38.

73. Grellmann, 43–44.

74. Liszt, *Gipsy in Music*, 69.

75. For a comparative account of how this figure functions in Spanish literature and art, see Lou Charnon-Deutsch, *The Spanish Gypsy: The History of a European Obsession* (University Park, PA: Pennsylvania State University Press, 2004).

76. Liszt, *Gipsy in Music*, 297.

77. Heinrich von Wlislocki, *Asupra vieții și obiceiurilor țiganilor transilvăneni* [On the lives and customs of Transylvanian Gypsies], trans. Sorin Georgescu (Bucharest: Editura Kriterion, 1998), 17.

78. E. Gerard, *The Land beyond the Forest: Facts, Figures, and Fancies from Transylvania* (New York: Harper & Brothers, 1888), 99–100.

79. Gerard, 99–100.

80. Achim, *Roma in Romanian History*, 135.

81. Viorel Cosma, *Figuri de lăutari* [Figures of musicians] (Bucharest: Editura Muzicală, 1960), 80.

82. Achim, *Roma in Romanian History*, 47.

83. On the Ottoman connection, see Anna G. Piotrowska, *Gypsy Music in European Culture: From the Late Eighteenth to the Early Twentieth Centuries*, trans. Guy R. Torr (Boston: Northeastern University Press, 2013), 23.

84. Cosma, *Figuri de lăutari*, 24.

85. The encounter between Liszt and Lăutaru was described in *La Vie Parisienne*, November 28, 1874, as well as in *Convorbiri Literare* (March 1, 1888) and *România Liberă* (March 12–13, 1888).

86. On the concept of musical tableau, see Tili Boon Cuillé, *Narrative Interludes: Musical Tableaux in Eighteenth-Century French Texts* (Toronto: Toronto University Press, 2006).

87. Liszt's book was known and debated in Transylvania. One of the editors of *ACLU*, the comparative literature journal discussed in the next chapter, wrote a rejoinder to it:

Sámuel Brassai, *Magyar-vagy czigány-zene?* [Hungarian or Gipsy music?] (Kolozsvár: Stein János Bizománya, 1860). On Liszt's popularity in the region, see Octavian Beu, *Franz Liszt în țara noastră* [Franz Liszt in our country] (Sibiu: Kraft & Dortleff, 1933).

88. In Romanian, *harap* is an archaic word for *Arab*. It is also an archaic word for *Rom*. Potra, *Contribuțiuni la istoricul țiganilor din România*, 16.

89. Methodologically and relationally, see Toni Morrison, *Playing in the Dark* (New York: Vintage, 1992).

90. On Indian modernism, see Priyamvada Gopal, *Literary Radicalism in India: Gender, Nation and the Transition to Independence* (London: Routledge, 2012).

91. Tara Zahra, *The Great Departure: Mass Migration from Eastern Europe and the Making of the Free World* (New York: W. W. Norton, 2016), 49.

92. Booker T. Washington and Robert E. Park, *The Man Farthest Down: A Record of Observation and Study in Europe* (New Brunswick, NJ: Transaction Books, 1984), 233.

93. Viorel Cosma records a number of historical events, from diplomatic occasions to military celebrations, accompanied by Romani music. Cosma, *Figuri de lăutari*, 131.

94. For a reading of this event in a nationalist mise-en-scène, see Ștefan Pascu, *A History of Transylvania*, trans. Robert Ladd (Detroit: Wayne State University Press, 1982). For a critique of this reading, which became possible only in the mid-nineteenth century, see Lucian Boia, *History and Myth in Romanian Consciousness* (Budapest: Central European University Press, 2001), 39–42.

95. Gruia Bădescu, "Rewritten in Stone: Imperial Heritage in the Sacred Place of the Nation," *Cultural Studies* 34, no. 5 (2020): 707–29.

96. C. Bobulescu, *Lăutarii noștri* [Our musicians] (Bucharest: Tipăritura Națională Jean Ionescu, 1922), 67.

97. Codarcea, *Société et pouvoir en Valachie*, 148.

98. Morrison, *Playing in the Dark*, 69.

99. Wynter writes: "one cannot 'unsettle' the 'coloniality of power' without a redescription of the human outside the terms of our present descriptive statement of the human, Man, and its over-representation." Wynter, "Unsettling the Coloniality of Being/Power/Truth/Freedom," 268. Rebreanu's novel relies on a sedimented, racialized trope of comparison throughout the narrative. The village teacher admonishes Ion: "The lowest gypsies wouldn't dare act and talk as you do! [*Nici țiganii cei mai nemernici n-ar îndrăzni să facă și să grăiască precum îndrăznești tu!*]" (182, 256). In turn, the priest scolds Ion, reminding him that, "after all Ion was not a vagabond gypsy [*că doar nici Ion nu-i țigan*]" (187, 264). As negotiations over Ana's dowry become heated, the priest rebukes the participants: "Now it's up to you to reach an agreement like honest-minded people. Feuds are only good among gypsies [*Acu să vă tocmiți și să vă învoiți ca oamenii, că vrajba-i bună numai între țigani*]" (188, 266). The debate continues, with women taking the lead: "The women did most of the talking, squabbling like gypsies [*Cuvântul însă îl aveau îndeosebi femeile care se certau țigănește*]" (190, 270). Eventually, Ana's father makes an offer of a dowry and reassures his future in-laws: "Then no one will be able to say that when Vasile Baciu's daughter married, she was no better off than a gipsy girl [*Să nu zică nimeni ca fata lui Vasile Baciu s-a măritat ca o țigancă*]" (277, 318). In turn, Gheran quotes Rebreanu's use of a racialized comparison in his description of the literary world: "Writers are, in a sense, like Gypsies; they argue even in the cemetery." Niculae Gheran, *Tânărul Rebreanu* [Young Rebreanu] (Bucharest: Editura Albatros, 1986), 23.

100. Morrison, *Playing in the Dark*, 67.

101. Cosma, *Figuri de lăutari*, 160–63.

102. Rebreanu's map of Pripas is similar to that drawn by sociologist Aurel Boia, who included a map of a village in the same region, Șanț/Újradna/Neurodna, in his 1938 study of the Roma's relative integration into a Transylvanian Romanian community. Boia's

study, steeped in racialized language, offers sociological details of racial spatial segregation. He also records interviews in which Roma report their desire to own land. Aurel Boia, "Integrarea țiganilor din Sanț (Năsăud) în comunitatea Românească a satului [The integration of Gypsies in Sanț (Năsăud) in the Romanian village community]," *Sociologie Românească* 7–9 (1938).

103. Boia, 352.

104. Goghi's obituary appeared in *Arhiva Someșană* 20 (1936).

105. On the cultural politics of minstrelsy in the United States, see Michael North, *The Dialect of Modernism: Race, Language, and Twentieth-Century Literature* (Oxford: Oxford University Press, 1994).

106. On the likely Romani etymology of the word *cioară*, see A. Juillard, "Le vocabulaire argotique roumain d'origine tsigane," *Cahiers Sextil Pușcariu* 1 (1952): 162.

107. For an account of Taiwanese indigenous literature as an example of another literary minority nestled within multiple inter-imperial literary traditions, see Andrea Bachner, "At the Margins of the Minor: Rethinking Scalarity, Relationality, and Translation," *Journal of World Literature* 2, no. 2 (2017): 139–57.

108. Jahan Ramazani, "Code-Switching, Code-Stitching: A Macaronic Poetics?" *Dibur Literary Journal*, 2015.

109. Piotrowska, *Gypsy Music in European Culture*, 4.

110. The comparative literature journal *ACLU* published Transylvanian Romani folk songs. Two collections edited by Hugo von Meltzl that included Romani folk songs were translated into English: *The Black Wodas: An Inedited Gipsy Ballad* (1879) and *Volk-Songs* (1885). For a collection of Romani literature, see Ian Hancock, Siobhan Dowd, and Rajko Djurić, eds., *The Roads of the Roma: A PEN Anthology of Gypsy Writers* (Hatfield, UK: University of Hertfordshire Press, 1998).

111. Janet Lyon traces "the figure of the Gypsy" in modernism. Janet Lyon, "Gadže Modernism," *Modernism/modernity* 11, no. 3 (2004): 517–38. Yasemin Yildiz cites Kafka's invocation of "a literature impossible in all respects, a gypsy literature," as illustrative of Kafka's relation to the German language. Yasemin Yildiz, *Beyond the Mother Tongue: The Postmonolingual Condition* (New York: Fordham University Press, 2012), 63. For an account of the subalternization of the Romani people and the question of access to the means of representation, see Gayatri Chakravorty Spivak, "Making Visible," in *On Productive Shame, Reconciliation, and Agency*, ed. Suzana Milevska (Vienna: Stenberg Press, 2019), 92–100.

4. COUNTING AND DISCOUNTING LANGUAGES

1. Borbála Zsuzsanna Török, *Exploring Transylvania: Geographies of Knowledge and Entangled Histories in a Multiethnic Province, 1790–1918* (Leiden, Netherlands: Brill, 2016), 56.

2. Mary Louise Pratt, "Language and the Afterlives of Empire," *PMLA* 130, no. 2 (2015): 355.

3. Haun Saussy, "Exquisite Cadavers Stitched from Fresh Nightmares," in *Comparative Literature in an Age of Globalization*, ed. Haun Saussy (Baltimore: The Johns Hopkins UP, 2006), 3–42; David Damrosch, "Rebirth of a Discipline: The Global Origins of Comparative Studies," *Comparative Critical Studies* 3, no. 1–2 (2006): 99–112; David Damrosch, "Global Regionalism," *European Review* 15, no. 1 (2007): 135–43. For two alternative genealogies of the discipline, see Shu-mei Shih, "Theory in a Relational World," *Comparative Literature Studies* 53, no. 4 (2016): 722–46; Shaden M. Tageldin, "One Comparative Literature? 'Birth' of a Discipline in French-Egyptian Translation, 1810–1834," *Comparative Literature Studies* 47, no. 4 (2010): 417–45.

4. On the frontispiece of the first issue of *ACLU*, Brassai and Meltzl listed their family name first, following the Hungarian convention that is often not observed today. In other contexts, Meltzl signed his name Hugo von Meltzl, Hugo Meltzl von Lomnitz, Hugo de Meltzl, or Hugo Meltzl.

5. For a thorough analysis of the link between the creolization of languages and the racial order of coloniality, as well as the implications of both, see Jane Anna Gordon, *Creolizing Political Theory: Reading Rousseau through Fanon* (New York: Fordham University Press, 2014).

6. Pratt, "Language and the Afterlives of Empire," 351–52.

7. On the use of Latin in the region, see Lav Šubarić, "National Identities and the Latin Language in Hungary and Croatia: Language Conflicts 1784–1848," in *Major versus Minor? Languages and Literatures in a Globalized World*, ed. Theo D'haen, Iannis Goerlandt, and Roger D. Sell (Amsterdam: John Benjamins Publishing, 2015), 53–66; Gábor Almási and Lav Šubarić, eds., "Introduction," in *Latin at the Crossroads of Identity: The Evolution of Linguistic Nationalism in the Kingdom of Hungary* (Leiden, Netherlands: Brill, 2015).

8. On the belatedness of German, see David Damrosch, *What Is World Literature?* (Princeton, NJ: Princeton University Press, 2018).

9. Ágnes Deák, "Antencedentele din Austria ale legii naționalităților din 1868 [Austrian precedents to the nationalities law of 1868]," in *140 de ani de legislație minoritară în Europa Centrală și de Est* [140 years of minority legislation in East-Central Europe] (Cluj-Napoca, Romania: Editura Institutului pentru Studierea Minorităților Naționale, 2010), 23–48.

10. Yiddish—and, in a different way, Romani—both belonged and did not belong on this list. The Jewish community of Transylvania was multilingual; there were multiple "Jewish languages." Jewish people spoke two or three of the languages of Transylvania— Hungarian, German, and Romanian. Sephardic Jews included Ladino in the mix, and Hebrew continued to be a language of religion. At the same time, the political project of obtaining rights necessitated the inclusion of the Jewish minority on the list of ethnic minorities and Yiddish on the list of minority languages. On Jewish languages, see Anita Norich and Joshua L. Miller, *Languages of Modern Jewish Cultures: Comparative Perspectives* (Ann Arbor: University of Michigan Press, 2016). As Yasemin Yildiz explains, the shift in the scholarship on Jewish languages emerged out of "an ethical injunction to transcend proprietary thinking vis-à-vis language(s)." Yasemin Yildiz, *Beyond the Mother Tongue: The Postmonolingual Condition* (New York: Fordham University Press, 2012), 42.

11. Max Weinreich, *History of the Yiddish Language* (New Haven, CT: Yale University Press, 2008), 349.

12. Judson argues that the Germanizing perception was retroactively projected onto this moment in the nineteenth century. Pieter M. Judson, *The Habsburg Empire: A New History* (Cambridge, MA: Belknap Press, 2016), 55.

13. István Margócsy, "When Language Became Ideology: Hungary in the Eighteenth Century," in Almási and Šubarić, *Latin at the Crossroads of Identity*, 32–33.

14. Almási and Šubarić, "Introduction," 20.

15. Robert J. C. Young, "That Which Is Casually Called a Language," *PMLA* 131, no. 5 (2016): 1207–21.

16. Eugen Brote, *Cestiunea română în Transilvania și Ungaria* [The Romanian question in Transylvania and Hungary] (Bucharest: Tipografia Voința Națională, 1895), 87.

17. On the German monolingual paradigm on the Austrian side of the Austro-Hungarian Empire, see Yildiz, *Beyond the Mother Tongue*.

18. On the co-implication of language and power on the Austrian side, see Rosita Rindler Schjerve, *Diglossia and Power: Language Policies and Practice in the 19th Century Habsburg Empire* (Berlin: Mouton de Gruyter, 2003). On German-language Jewish writ-

ing, see Marjorie Perloff, *Edge of Irony: Modernism in the Shadow of the Habsburg Empire* (Chicago: University of Chicago Press, 2016).

19. Eötvös's advocacy for the law of nationalities was anchored in a theoretical text he authored in 1865.

20. Susan Gal, "Polyglot Nationalism: Alternative Perspectives on Language in Nineteenth Century Hungary," *Langage et Société* 2, no. 136 (2011): 31–54.

21. Hoensch writes on the law's implementation: "the ruling elites observed neither the letter nor the spirit of the nationalities agreements. Over the years a nationalism which had been originally liberal in character began to identify itself wholly with the traditional Magyar sense of national mission, which viewed the Magyars' historic task in the second half of the nineteenth century as pioneering the new bourgeois economic, social and cultural progress in eastern Europe and the Balkans and transmitting the achievements of western European civilisation to its peoples." Jörg K. Hoensch, *A History of Modern Hungary 1867–1994* (London: Longman, 1996), 29.

22. Attila Demeter, "Concepţiile despre naţionalitate ale lui József Eötvös [József Eötvös's understanding of nationality]," in *140 de ani de legislaţie minoritară*, 59.

23. Teodor Botiş, *Monografia familiei Mocioni* [Monograph of the Mocioni family] (Bucharest: Editura Fundaţia pentru Literatură şi Artă "Regele Carol II," 1939), 132. Mocioni went on to have a long career in the service of Romanian nationalism in Banat and Transylvania, later supporting positions that were at odds with this early positing of six nations, six languages.

24. Quoted in Luminiţa Ignat-Coman, "Identitate reprimată: Legislaţie şi deznaţionalizare în Transilvania dualistă [Repressed identity: legislation and denationalizing in dualist Transylvania]," in *140 de ani de legislaţie minoritară*, 124.

25. Sorin Mitu, *Transilvania mea: Istorii, mentalităţi, identităţi* [My Transylvania: histories, mentalities, identities] (Iaşi, Romania: Polirom, 2006), 417.

26. Teodor Păcăţian, *Cartea de aur sau luptele naţionale ale românilor de sub coroana ungară* [The golden book or, the Romanian national struggle under the Hungarian crown], vol. 8 (Sibiu, Romania: Tiparul Tipografiei Arhidiecezane, 1915), 150. Kürti quotes Arthur J. Patterson, who referred to Transylvania as "a Hungarian Ireland." László Kürti, *The Remote Borderland: Transylvania in the Hungarian Imagination* (Albany, NY: SUNY Press, 2001), 230.

27. For a Saidian reading of nineteenth-century Transylvania, see Sorin Mitu, *Ungurii despre români: Naşterea unei imagini etnice* [Hungarians about Romanians: the birth of an ethnic image] (Iaşi, Romania: Polirom, 2014).

28. Gayatri Chakravorty Spivak, *Death of a Discipline* (New York: Columbia University Press, 2003), 10–11.

29. On Meltzl, see Horst Fassel, ed., *Hugo Meltzl und die die Anfänge der Komparatistik* [Hugo Meltzl and the Beginnings of Comparative Literature] (Stuttgart: Franz Steiner Ferlag, 2005). Brassai, who was a prominent theorist of foreign language acquisition, is often unjustly neglected in accounts of the journal, including accounts of polyglottism. On this neglect, see Levente T. Szabó, "À la recherche . . . de l'editeur perdu: Sámuel Brassai and the First International Journal of Comparative Literary Studies," in *Storia, Identità e Canoni Letterari*, ed. Ioana Both, Ayşe Saraçgil, and Angela Tarantino (Florence: Firenze University Press, 2013).

30. The three articles appeared in *ACLU* 9 (May 1877), 15 (October 1877), and 24 (February 1878). The first two articles were translated in 1973 for Hans-Joachim Schultz and Phillip H. Rhein, eds, *Comparative Literature: The Early Years* (Chapel Hill, NC: University of North Carolina Press, 1973); and were reproduced in David Damrosch, Mbongiseni Buthelezi, and Natalie Melas, eds., *The Princeton Sourcebook in Comparative Literature: From the European Enlightenment to the Global Present* (Princeton, NJ: Princeton

University Press, 2009). Original issues of *ACLU* are available at http://documente.bcucluj
.ro/web/bibdigit/periodice/osszehasonlitoirodalomtortenelmi/1877.html.

31. Hugo Meltzl, "Present Tasks of Comparative Literature," in Damrosch, Buthelezi, and Melas, *Princeton Sourcebook in Comparative Literature*, 44.

32. Meltzl, 44. On the endurance of this principle, see Haun Saussy, "Exquisite Cadavers Stitched from Fresh Nightmares," in *Comparative Literature in an Age of Globalization*, ed. Haun Saussy (Baltimore: Johns Hopkins University Press, 2006), 3–42.

33. Meltzl, "Present Tasks of Comparative Literature," 45. On the inherent polyglottism of literature, see Rebecca L. Walkowitz, *Born Translated: The Contemporary Novel in the Age of World Literature* (New York: Columbia University Press, 2017).

34. Meltzl, "Present Tasks of Comparative Literature," 46, 45. The question of endangered languages was taken up by Simon Gikandi, "The Fragility of Languages," *PMLA* 130, no. 1 (2015): 9–14. The plight of "literatureless peoples" was revisited by Caroline Levine, "The Great Unwritten: World Literature and the Effacement of Orality," *Modern Language Quarterly* 74, no. 2 (2013): 217–37.

35. On literature and the postal system, see Bernhard Siegert, *Relays: Literature as an Epoch of the Postal System* (Stanford, CA: Stanford University Press, 1999).

36. Dora d'Istria (Elena Ghica) was proficient in French, Romanian, Albanian, Italian, Russian, German, and Greek. She traveled extensively and was the author of *Les femmes en Orient* and *La poésie des Ottomans*. She also authored *La nationalité roumaine d'après les chants populaires*—and similar accounts of Albanian, Greek, and Serb folk traditions. She published regularly in *ACLU* and conducted an extensive correspondence with Meltzl in French.

37. Meltzl, "Present Tasks of Comparative Literature," 47. The gesture toward a normative ideal was revisited by Pheng Cheah, *What Is a World? On Postcolonial Literature as World Literature* (Durham, NC: Duke University Press, 2016).

38. Various texts in the journal appeared in other languages, including Albanian, Romani, Icelandic, Japanese, Latin, and Catalan.

39. On the renewed interest in minor literary traditions, see "Ultraminor Literatures," special issue, *Journal of World Literature* (2017).

40. Theo D'haen, *The Routledge Concise History of World Literature* (London: Routledge, 2012), 56.

41. Meltzl articulated this position in the third installment of "The Present Tasks of Comparative Literature," not included in the current English translation. He writes: "The literatures of the Danes, Norwegians, Latvians, Finns, Estonians, Basques, Irish, Bretons, Poles, Czechs, Slavs, Serbs, Russians, (Modern) Greeks, Albanians, Romanians, Turks, as well as of the other small people of Europe, are still either merely folk literature or, when they are literature, they are more recent and they are certainly natural or at best of a Romantic color. Hungarian is perhaps the only non-Germanic area literature among the small literatures that has thoroughly broken with Romanticism and turned to a true classicism. [*Die Litteraturen der Dänen, Norweger, Letten, Finnen, Esten, Basken, Iren, Bretonén, Polen, Czechen, Wenden, Serben, Russen, Neugriechen, Albanesen, Rumänen, Türken, sowie der übrigen, kleineren Volksstämme Europas, sind entweder nur noch Volksliederlitt., oder aber, wenn Kunstlitteraturen so meist jüngeren Datums' u. von durchwegs naturalistischer, besten Falls Romantischer Färbung. Das magyarische ist vielleicht das einzige nicht-germanische Litteraturgebiet unter den kleineren Litteraturen, das mit dem Romanticismus bereits gründlich gebrochen u. zu wahrhaftigem Classicismus sich hinaufgeschwungen hat*].*"

42. Walter D. Mignolo, *Local Histories/Global Designs: Coloniality, Subaltern Knowledges, and Border Thinking* (Princeton, NJ: Princeton University Press, 2000), 226.

43. In June 1877, the Eötvös motto was replaced with a fragment from Schiller, in French. In 1879, the motto from Schiller was translated into Latin.

44. Sándor Kerekes, *Lomnitzi Meltzl Hugó 1846–1908* (Budapest: Minerva-Könyvtár, 1937), 119.

45. On Eötvös's languages and the place of his literary writings in the Hungarian national imagination, see Kürti, *Remote Borderland*, 81, 86.

46. On Meltzl's collaboration with Silaşi, see Engel Károly, "*Contribuţii ale comparatiştilor maghiari din Transilvania până la al doilea război mondial* [Contributions of Hungarian comparatists from Transylvania before WWI]," *Istoria şi teoria comparatismului în România [History and theory of Romanian comparatism]* (Bucharest: Editura Academiei Republicii Socialiste România, 1972), 139–50.

47. Márta Nagy Zabán, "The Relationship between National Identity and Literature Education in Cluj in the Last Quarter of the 19th Century," in Both, Saraçgil and Tarantino, *Storia, Identità e Canoni Letterari*.

48. Minutes of faculty meetings are reproduced, in Hungarian, in Levente T. Szabó and Márta Zabán, *Dokumentumok a kolozsvári Bölcsészet-, Nyelv- és Történettudományi Kar Történetéhez (1872–1892)* (Cluj-Napoca, Romania: Presa Universitară Clujeană, 2012).

49. *ACLU* 1, no. 16–20 (1886). Szabó reads the inclusion of the article by Silaşi as a form of silent protest. Levente T. Szabó, "Cultural Brokers, Forms of Hybridity and the Emergence of the First International Comparative Literary Journal," *Philobiblon: Transylvanian Journal of Multidisciplinary Research in the Humanities* 22, no. 2 (2017): 67–80.

50. *ACLU* 11, no. 5–8 (1884).

51. *ACLU* included rubrics such as *Petőfi Polyglotte* and *Petőfiana*, as well as *Petőfi in Italy*, *Petőfi in German*, *Petőfi in Cluj*. See Mircea Popa, "Un comparatist sas din Transilvania: Hugo Meltzl (1846–1908) [A Saxon comparatist from Transylvania: Hugo Meltzl (1846–1908)]," *Convergenţe europene [European convergences]* (Oradea, Romania: Editura Cogito, 1995), 187–200, 193.

52. Eszter Szabó-Resnek, "Meltzl Hugó és a kolozsvári Petőfi-ellenkánon: Kísérlet a 'nemzeti költő' regionális újraértelmezésére [Hugó Meltzl and the Petőfi anti-canon from Kolozsvár: Attempts at a regional reinterpretation of the 'national poet']," *Irodalomtörténeti Közlemények* 120, no. 2 (2016): 215–24.

53. Interest in folklore included an appeal for colonial functionaries in South Africa to collect African folklore (*ACLU* 6, no. 7–10 [1881]) and for a collection of Indian folklore in the United States (*ACLU* 4, no. 4 [1880]). On *ACLU*'s London connection, see Annamária Codău, "The Acta Comparationis Litterarum Universarum (1877–1888) from the Perspective of Its British Collaborators," *Hungarian Cultural Studies* 10 (2017): 106–119.

54. In the context of his polemic over the nationalist interpretation of Petőfi, Meltzl was accused of being an "immigrant," that is, someone not of Hungarian ethnic origin, who should refrain from discussing the national poet. Szabó-Resnek, "Meltzl Hugó és a kolozsvári Petőfi-ellenkánon," 220–21. On the institutional framing of Meltzl's work within Hungarian literature and the expectation of vindication, see Levente T. Szabó, "Negotiating the Borders of Hungarian National Literature: The Beginnings of the Acta Comparationis Litterarum Universarum and the Rise of Hungarian Studies (Hungarologie)." *Transylvanian Review* XXII, no. 1 (2013): 48–61.

55. Walkowitz, *Born Translated*, 45.

56. Yildiz invokes the concept of "selective multilingualism."

57. Aamir R. Mufti, "Auerbach in Istanbul: Edward Said, Secular Criticism, and the Question of Minority Culture," *Critical Inquiry* 25, no. 1 (1998): 124–25.

58. For a revised account of Istanbul within comparative literature, see Anca Parvulescu, "Istanbul, Capital of Comparative Literature," *MLN* 135, no. 5 (2020): 1232–57.

59. On the de–Cold War project, see Khuan-Hsing Chen, *Asia as Method: On Deimperialization* (Durham, NC: Duke University Press, 2010). On the resonance of this project in East Europe, see Anca Parvulescu, "Eastern Europe as Method," *SEEJ* 63, no. 4 (2019): 470–81.

60. Niculae Gheran, *Tânărul Rebreanu* [Young Rebreanu] (Bucharest: Editura Albatros, 1986), 105.

61. Gheran, 115.

62. Gheran, 170.

63. Vasile Voia, "Liviu Rebreanu în Ungaria [Liviu Rebreanu in Hungary]," in *Aspecte ale comparatismului românesc*, 146–56.

64. Gheran, *Tânărul Rebreanu*, 214.

65. Gheran, 396.

66. Mignolo, *Local Histories/Global Designs*, 225.

67. Elias Canetti, *The Tongue Set Free*, trans. Joachim Neugroschel (New York: Farrar, Straus & Giroux, 1979), 27.

68. Viktor Shklovsky's 1917 "Art as Technique" invoked multilingualism as one strategy of defamiliarization. Viktor Shklovsky, "Art as Technique" in *Russian Formalist Criticism: Four Essays* (Lincoln: University of Nebraska Press, 1965). On modernism and multilingualism, see Joshua L. Miller, *Accented America: The Cultural Politics of Multilingual Modernism* (Oxford: Oxford University Press, 2011). It is important to note that one form of American literary multilingual modernism is a function of immigration from East-Central Europe.

69. On the educational pilgrimage, see Benedict Anderson, *Imagined Communities: Reflections on the Origin and Spread of Nationalism* (London: Verso, 2006).

70. Liviu Rebreanu, *Ion*, trans. A. Hillard (London: Peter Owen, 1965); Liviu Rebreanu, *Ion*, ed. Niculae Gheran, vol. 4, *Opere* (Bucharest: Editura Minerva, 1970). We modified some translations.

71. Hoensch reports: "Whereas approximately 10 per cent of all civil servants belonged to the population's non-Magyar groups in 1910, Hungarian was spoken as a first language by 96 per cent of civil servants and 91.2 per cent of all state employees." Hoensch, *History of Modern Hungary*, 31.

72. Păcățian, *Cartea de aur*, 8:551.

73. Păcățian, 391.

74. Stefan Berger and Alexei Miller, "Introduction: Building Nations in and with Empires: A Reassessment," in *Nationalizing Empires*, ed. Stefan Berger and Alexei Miller (Budapest: Central European University Press, 2015), 26.

75. Compare, for example, descriptions of modernized facial hair in Tagore's novels about Indian modernity, or in the first Japanese modern novel, *Ukigumo*. Rabindranath Tagore, *The Home and the World*, trans. Surendranath Tagore (London: Penguin Books, 2005); Futabatei Shimei, *Japan's First Modern Novel: Ukigumo of Futabatei Shimei*, trans. Marleigh Grayer Ryan (Ann Arbor, MI: Center for Japanese Studies, University of Michigan, 1990).

76. For a comparative account of this phenomenon, see Ben Conisbee Baer, *Indigenous Vanguards: Education, National Liberation, and the Limits of Modernism* (New York: Columbia University Press, 2019).

77. Păcățian, *Cartea de aur*, 8:556.

78. Păcățian, 520.

79. For a comparative account of the imbrication of coloniality, multilingualism, and religion, see Sumathi Ramaswamy, *Passions of the Tongue: Language Devotion in Tamil India, 1891–1970* (Berkeley: University of California Press, 1997).

80. On the revision of Roman Jakobson's metalingual function to account for interlingual situations, see Vladimir Zorić, "Radiating Nests: Metalingual Tropes in Poetry of Exile," *Comparative Literature* 62, no. 3 (2010): 201–27.

81. Interventions in the Hungarian parliament mentioned high translation fees. Păcățian, *Cartea de aur*, 8:379.

82. On translators functioning as "professional Romanians," see Roger Brubaker, *Nationalist Politics and Everyday Ethnicity in a Transylvanian Town* (Princeton, NJ: Princeton University Press, 2006).

83. Thirteen percent of Transylvania's population was urban; a quarter of the urban population was Romanian speaking. Brubaker, 66.

84. Titu's perception is one-sided; there were large Hungarian- and Saxon-speaking rural areas.

85. The word *renegade* applied especially to Romanian Transylvanian politicians who participated in the Hungarian parliamentary system. See Ovidiu Emil Iudean, *The Romanian Governmental Representatives in the Budapest Parliament* (Cluj-Napoca, Romania: Mega Publishing House, 2016).

86. Meltzl, "Present Tasks of Comparative Literature," 46.

87. Ngũgĩ wa Thiong'o, *Decolonizing the Mind* (London: J. Currey, 1986).

88. Păcățian, *Cartea de aur*, 8:150.

89. Gloria Anzaldúa, *Boderlands / La Frontera: The New Mestiza* (San Francisco, CA: Aunt Lute Books, 2012).

90. On the process of Romanianization, see Irina Livezeanu, *Cultural Politics in Greater Romania: Regionalism, Nation Building, and Ethnic Struggle, 1918–1930* (Ithaca, NY: Cornell University Press, 2000).

91. Brubaker, *Nationalist Politics and Everyday Ethnicity*, 76.

92. Intellectuals like Titu became major power brokers after 1918, participating in a cultural process sometimes described as a reversed "colonizing mission." Livezeanu, *Cultural Politics in Greater Romania*, 183–84.

93. For an account of how this narrative developed in Romanian-language historiography, see Lucian Boia, *History and Myth in Romanian Consciousness* (Budapest: Central European University Press, 2001).

94. For a comparative account of the imperial desires of post-1918 nation-states in the region, see Judson, *Habsburg Empire*, 448. Kate Brown argues that "nation itself worked in a colonial pattern as a formula to replace localized identities and cultural complexities, which made modern governance so difficult in places like the borderlands." Kate Brown, *A Biography of No Place: From Ethnic Borderland to Soviet Heartland* (Cambridge, MA: Harvard University Press, 2004), 11.

95. Gheran, *Tânărul Rebreanu*, 176, 240, 417.

96. Jahan Ramazani, *The Hybrid Muse: Postcolonial Poetry in English* (Chicago: University of Chicago Press, 2001), 13.

97. When he was invited to join the Romanian Academy in 1940, in the midst of accelerated interwar nationalism, Rebreanu gave a lecture glorifying a *monoglot* Romanian peasant. Liviu Rebreanu, *Lauda țăranului român* [In praise of the Romanian peasant] (Bucharest: Imprimeria Națională, 1940).

98. On a Francophone Romania, which included a period when French was declared the language of education, see Adela Beiu, "The Nation and the Absurd: A Romanian Story of Modernity," *Modernism/modernity* 21, no. 4 (2015): 961–75. On a Francophone Transylvania, see Coralia Telea, *George Barițiu: Un francophile transylvain* (Cluj-Napoca, Romania: Editura Mega, 2013).

99. Interwar Bucharest-based avant-garde figures such as Tristan Tzara—a status to which Rebreanu aspired—now represent Romanian modernism within global modernism, and they often do so through their polyglot credentials. For an inter-imperial reading of this modernism, see Sanja Bahun, "The Balkans Uncovered: Towards Historie Croisée of Modernism," in *The Oxford Handbook of Global Modernism*, ed. Mark Wollaeger (New York: Oxford University Press, 2010), 25–47.

100. Păcățian, *Cartea de aur*, 8:335.

101. On the novel's irony, see Béla Bíró, "Constructed Spaces in Liviu Rebreanu's *Ion*," *Acta Universitatis Sapientiae, Philologica* 4, no. 1 (2012): 117–48.

102. Perloff identifies irony as one of the signature features of Central European modernism. Perloff, *Edge of Irony*.

103. Mufti, "Auerbach in Istanbul," 157.

104. Keith Hitchins, *A Nation Affirmed: The Romanian National Movement in Transylvania, 1860–1914* (Bucharest: Encyclopaedic Publishing House, 1999), 220.

105. Armenians in Transylvania often spoke three or four languages (Hungarian, Romanian, German, and Armenian) but increasingly identified themselves as speakers of Hungarian. Judit Pál, *Armenians in Transylvania: Their Contribution to the Urbanization and the Economic Development of the Province*, trans. Bogdan Aldea (Cluj-Napoca, Romania: Romanian Cultural Institute, 2005), 154.

106. Yildiz invokes the "radical difference between multilingualism before and after the monolingual paradigm." Yildiz, *Beyond the Mother Tongue*, 4.

5. THE INTER-IMPERIAL DOWRY PLOT

1. On feminist movements and women's writing in the Austro-Hungarian Empire, see Agatha Schwartz, *Shifting Voices: Feminist Thought and Women's Writing in Fin-de-Siècle Austria and Hungary* (Montreal: McGill-Queen's University Press, 2008); Harriet Anderson, *Utopian Feminism: Women's Movements in Fin-de-Siècle Vienna* (New Haven, CT: Yale University Press, 1992).

2. See especially Marnia Lazreg, *The Eloquence of Silence: Algerian Women in Question* (New York: Routledge, 1994); Gayatri Chakrabarty Spivak, "Can the Subaltern Speak?" in *Can the Subaltern Speak? Reflections on the History of an Idea*, ed. Rosalind C. Morris (New York: Columbia University Press, 2010).

3. Robin Blackburn, *The Overthrow of Colonial Slavery, 1776–1848* (London: Verso, 1988).

4. Blackburn, *Overthrow of Colonial Slavery*.

5. Martha Mamozai, *Herrenmenschen: Frauen im deutschen Kolonialismus* [Master People: Women during German Colonial Rule] (Hamburg: Rowohlt, 1982).

6. Fatima El-Tayeb, "'Blood Is a Very Special Juice': Racialized Bodies and Citizenship in Twentieth-Century Germany," *International Review of Social History* 44, no. S7 (1999): 149–69.

7. Tara Zahra, "Condemned to Rootlessness and Unable to Budge: Roma, Migration Panics, and Internment in the Habsburg Empire," *American Historical Review* 122, no. 3 (2017): 719.

8. Ayelet Shachar, *The Birthright Lottery: Citizenship and Global Inequality* (Cambridge, MA: Harvard University Press, 2009).

9. Shachar, 38.

10. Roberto Patricio Korzeniewicz and Timothy Patrick Moran, *Unveiling Inequality: A World-Historical Perspective* (New York: Russell Sage Foundation, 2009).

11. Manuela Boatcă and Julia Roth, "Unequal and Gendered: Notes on the Coloniality of Citizenship," *Current Sociology* 64, no. 2 (2016): 191–212.

12. Gerald Horne, *Confronting Black Jacobins: The United States, the Haitian Revolution, and the Origins of the Dominican Republic* (New York: NYU Press, 2015), 102.

13. Virginia Woolf, "Professions for Women," in *Selected Essays* (Oxford: Oxford University Press, 2008), 141.

14. On masculinity, see R. W. Connell and James W. Messerschmidt, "Hegemonic Masculinity: Rethinking the Concept," *Gender and Society* 19, no. 6 (2005): 829–59.

15. Warwick Research Collective, *Combined and Uneven Development: Towards a New Theory of World-Literature* (Liverpool: Liverpool University Press, 2015), 66.

16. Warwick Research Collective, 67. For an account of Rebreanu's realism, which excludes the possibility of its convergence with modernism, see Ion Simuț, *Liviu Rebreanu și contradicțiile realismului* [Liviu Rebreanu and the contradictions of realism] (Cluj-Napoca, Romania: Editura Dacia, 2010).

17. Jennifer L. Fleissner, *Women, Compulsion, Modernity: The Moment of American Naturalism* (Chicago: University of Chicago Press, 2004).

18. On the global reverberations of naturalism, see Christopher L. Hill, "Travels of Naturalism and the Challenges of a World Literary History," *Literature Compass* 6, no. 6 (2009): 1198–210.

19. For a review of debates on modernism in Romanian-language literary criticism, see Andrei Terian, "Faces of Modernity in Romanian Literature: A Conceptual Analysis," *Alea* 16, no. 1 (2014): 15–34.

20. Warwick Research Collective, *Combined and Uneven Development*, 68.

21. On naturalism and prostitution, see Christopher L. Hill, "Nana in the World: Novel, Gender, and Transnational Form," *Modern Language Quarterly* 72, no. 1 (2011): 75–105. On debates on prostitution in the Austro-Hungarian Empire, see Nancy M. Wingfield, *The World of Prostitution in Late Imperial Austria* (Oxford: Oxford University Press, 2017). Zahra reports on a debate concerning women from the Austro-Hungarian Empire participating in sex work in the Ottoman Empire. Tara Zahra, *The Great Departure: Mass Migration from Eastern Europe and the Making of the Free World* (New York: W. W. Norton, 2016), 50.

22. Schwartz, *Shifting Voices*, 57, 59. For the global resonances of this argument, see Alix Kates Shulman, ed., *Red Emma Speaks: An Emma Goldman Reader* (New York: Open Road Media, 2012).

23. Liviu Rebreanu, *Ion*, trans. A. Hillard (London: Peter Owen, 1965); Liviu Rebreanu, *Ion*, ed. Niculae Gheran, vol. IV, *Opere* (Bucharest: Editura Minerva, 1970). We modified some translations.

24. On this mutation, see Sorina Paula Bolovan, *Familia în satul românesc din Transilvania* [The family in the Romanian village of Transylvania] (Cluj-Napoca, Romania: Fundația Culturală Română, 1999), 163.

25. Gayle Rubin, "The Traffic in Women: Notes on the 'Political Economy' of Sex," in *Toward an Anthropology of Women*, ed. Rayna R. Reiter (New York: Monthly Review Press, 1975), 157–210.

26. Raymond Williams, *The Country and the City* (Oxford: Oxford University Press, 1975), 53.

27. Claudia Septimia Sabău, *"Și ne-au făcut din grăniceri, țărani . . ." Mentalități colective în satele năsăudene foste grănicerești în a doua jumătate a secolului al XIX-lea ["And they transformed us from soldiers into peasants": collective mentalities in villages of the Năsăud region, formerly the border regiment, in the second half of the nineteenth century]* (Cluj-Napoca, Romania: Editura Mega, 2015), 241.

28. On the power dynamic between deflowerer and virgin, see Sigmund Freud, "The Taboo of Virginity," in *The Standard Edition of the Complete Psychological Works of Sigmund Freud*, vol. 11, trans. James Strachey (London: Hogarth Press, 1966), 193–208.

29. Rebreanu also wrote a short story titled *Ofilirea* (Wilting), about a young peasant girl abandoned by her lover.

30. Wolfgang Iser, "Interaction between Text and Reader," in *The Reader in the Text: Essays on Audience and Interpretation*, ed. Inge Crosman and Susan Rubin Suleiman (Princeton, NJ: Princeton University Press, 1980), 111.

31. Nicolae Iorga invoked the rape in *Ion* in 1934; quoted in Lucian Raicu, *Liviu Rebreanu* (Bucharest: Editura pentru literatură, 1967), 74.

32. On the guilt associated with the loss of virginity in the broader Romanian-language culture, see Constanța Vintilă-Ghițulescu, *Focul amorului: Despre dragoste și*

sexualitate în societatea românească (1750–1830) [The heat of passion: on love and sexuality in Romanian society (1750–1830)] (Bucharest: Humanitas, 2006).

33. Andrei Oişteanu, *Sexualitate şi societate: Istorie, religie şi literatură* [Sexuality and society: history, religion and literature] (Iaşi, Romania: Polirom, 2016), 91.

34. On the rural virtues, see Williams, *Country and the City*, 12. In a series of articles in 1890, Ştefan Buzilă reported on an ethnographic study of wedding rituals in the region. He repeatedly underscored that weddings among the rural Transylvanian Romanian population followed Roman custom. Ştefan Buzilă, "Nunta la ţăranul român din jurul Năsăudului [Romanian peasants' wedding rituals in the Năsăud region]," ed. Claudia Septimia Peteanu, *Studii şi cercetări etnoculturale* 15 (2010): 145–56.

35. Sabău, *"Şi ne-au făcut din grăniceri, ţărani. . . ."*

36. Michel Foucault, *The History of Sexuality: An Introduction*, trans. Robert Hurley (New York: Vintage, 1990).

37. Bolovan documents the high rate of intermarriage in late-nineteenth-century Transylvania and anxieties associated with it. Ioan Bolovan, "The Quantitative Dimension of Mixed Marriages in Transylvania at the End of the Long Nineteenth Century," in *Intermarriage in Transylvania, 1895–2010*, ed. Ioan Bolovan and Luminiţa Dumănescu (Frankfurt: Peter Lang, 2017). In 1890 Buzilă emphasized that "the daughter of a Romanian peasant will never marry a Jew, a Hungarian or a Gypsy, etc." Buzilă, "Nunta la ţăranul român din jurul Năsăudului," 130.

38. On virginity, see Lloyd Davis, "The Virgin Body as Victorian Text: An Introduction," in *Virginal Sexuality and Textuality in Victorian Literature*, ed. Lloyd Davis (Albany: State University of New York Press, 1993), 3–24.

39. In the early modern period, a law in a neighboring Romanian-language community in Moldova required that rapists marry their victims. Oişteanu, *Sexualitate şi societate*, 382.

40. Daniela Deteşan, ed., *Căsătorie şi moştenire în Transilvania: Documente din a doua jumătate a secolului al XIX-lea* [Marriage and inheritance in Transylvania: documents from the second half of the nineteenth century] (Cluj-Napoca, Romania: Presa Universitară Clujană, 2013), 41.

41. The portrayal of Ion's father as unmanly is crucial to how Rebreanu describes the household in which Ion grew up. The novel reports that Ion's mother, Zenobia, is "a woman as efficient as any man [*o femeie ca un bărbat*]" (39, 56). Indeed, given her husband's inefficiency, "she became man and master of the place [*s-a făcut ea bărbat şi a dus casa*]" (40, 57). Zenobia thus challenges the local gender system, temporarily becoming the head of the household. There is a sense, however, that the household still lacks a head, which explains its downward mobility. As Ion matures, he takes over the household, and things slowly return to "normal." A sign of this normalcy is Ion's willingness to strike his mother to indicate her new place in the household.

42. In 1894 the imperial state secularized marriage, limiting the authority of the church in matrimonial law. Bolovan, *Familia în satul românesc din Transilvania*, 67. Churches continued to function as major actors, especially with regard to civil and moral issues.

43. Ioan Corjescu, trans., *Codul Austriac* [The Austrian legal code] (Bucharest: Imprimeria Statului, 1921), 195.

44. The dowry itemized by Deteşan on the basis of Transylvanian church and notary records is almost identical to Rebreanu's fictional list. Deteşan, *Căsătorie şi moştenire în Transilvania*, 37.

45. A rhetoric of animalization is deployed to describe the character of Savista, who is disabled: "Savista, the village cripple, crept through the gate, worming her way through the people's legs. . . . Her legs were maimed from birth and her long wiry arms served as

hooks to drag her crippled body along. The whitish lips of her enormous mouth covered froth-flecked gums and sparse pointed stubs of yellow teeth [*Tocmai atunci se târăşte pe poartă, printre picioarele oamenilor, Savista, oloaga satului. . . . Are picioarele încârcite din naştere, iar braţele lungi şi osoase ca nişte căngi anume spre a-şi târî schilozenia, şi o gură enormă cu buzele alburii de sub care se întind gingiile îmbălate, cu colţi de dinţi galbeni, rari şi lungi]"* (14, 18–19).

46. Maria Mies, *Patriarchy and Accumulation on a World Scale: Women in the International Division of Labour* (London: Zed Books, 1986).

47. Williams, *Country and the City*, 30.

48. Reddock, *Women and Slavery*, 78.

49. Quoted in Zahra, *Great Departure*, 94.

50. On the global dimensions of this argument, see Alice Kessler-Harris, "Gender and Work: Possibilities for a Global, Historical Overview," in *Women's History in Global Perspective*, ed. Bonnie G. Smith (Urbana: University of Illinois Press, 2004), 154.

51. A survey from the 1930s reported that peasant women in the region had, at most, only a few days of rest before and after childbirth. Thus, they were likely to give birth while they worked in the household or in the fields. See Petru Râmneanţu, "Studiu asupra depopulării Banatului. Cauzele depopulării. Rezultatele anchetei demografice din comuna Banloc, judeţul Timiş/Torontal." *Buletin Eugenic şi Biopolitic* 6, nos. 10-11-12, (1935): 311.

52. Quoted in Niculae Gheran, *Tânărul Rebreanu* [Young Rebreanu] (Bucharest: Editura Albatros, 1986), 103.

53. On corporal punishment in Transylvanian schools, see Sabău, "*Şi ne-au făcut din grăniceri, ţărani . . . ,*" 146.

54. Oişteanu, *Sexualitate şi societate*, 153.

55. Oişteanu writes matter-of-factly about this phenomenon in the broader Romanian-language culture: "The custom of the husband beating his wife was considered one of his inalienable 'rights.' This was a usual perception even among women. It is a problem of traditional mentality, profoundly instilled . . . the well-intentioned intervention of a stranger was perceived like an intrusion, being considered more brutal than the violence administered by one's own husband." Oişteanu, 152–53.

56. Michel Foucault, *Discipline and Punish: The Birth of the Prison*, trans. Alan Sheridan (New York: Vintage, 1995).

57. Partha Chatterjee, "The Nationalist Resolution of the Woman's Question," in *Recasting Women: Essays in Indian Colonial History*, ed. Kumkum Sangari and Sudesh Vaid (New Brunswick, NJ: Rutgers University Press, 1990), 233–53.

58. Reddock, *Women and Slavery*, 77.

59. Williams, *Country and the City*.

60. Ida Blom, ed., *Gendered Nations: Nationalisms and Gender Order in the Long Nineteenth Century* (Oxford: Berg, 2000).

61. Romanian-language literary critic Nicolae Manolescu argues that the greatness of the naturalist novel depends on characters like Ana: "The naturalist novel owes its greatness to the cultivation of these people without a chance, to these destinies without hope." Nicolae Manolescu, *Arca lui Noe* (Bucharest: Editura Minerva, 1980), 175–76.

62. Fleissner describes a naturalist pattern: "an ongoing, nonlinear, repetitive motion—back and forth, around and around, on and on—that has the distinctive effect of seeming also like a stuckness in place." Fleissner, *Women, Compulsion, Modernity*, 9.

63. Nancy M. Wingfield documents the racialized discourse on the trafficking of girls and women from the empire's eastern borderlands into sex work both within Austria-Hungary and in the Ottoman Empire, Argentina, and India. This discourse racialized

traffickers as Jewish, and it Orientalized the destinations for sex work. Wingfield writes: "the vision of upstanding, unwilling girls from the Monarchy being delivered to exotic, faraway, 'less civilized,' non-European countries—Argentina or the 'Orient'—excited the Austrian public's imagination." Wingfield, *World of Prostitution*, 182.

64. Zahra, *Great Departure*, 90.

65. Anita Kurimay, *Queer Budapest (1873–1961)* (Chicago: The University of Chicago Press, 2020).

66. Franz Fanon, *Black Skin, White Masks*, trans. Constance Farrington (New York: Grove Press, 1994).

6. FEMINIST WHIMS

1. Virginia Woolf, *A Room of One's Own* (San Diego: Harcourt, 1981), 89.

2. Woolf, 90.

3. Woolf, 39.

4. Liviu Rebreanu, *Ion*, trans. A. Hillard (London: Peter Owen, 1965); Liviu Rebreanu, *Ion*, ed. Niculae Gheran, vol. IV, *Opere* (Bucharest: Editura Minerva, 1970). We modified some translations.

5. See, especially, Kumari Jayawardena, *Feminism and Nationalism in the Third World* (New York: Verso, 2016); Chandra Talpade Mohanty, Ann Russo, and Lourdes Torres, eds., *Third World Women and the Politics of Feminism* (Bloomington: Indiana University Press, 1991).

6. Mohanty, Russo, and Torres, *Third World Women and the Politics of Feminism*.

7. George Bariț, "Despre educațiunea femeiloru la națiunea românească [On the education of women of the Romanian nation]," *Transilvania*, September 1, 1869, 34. On the broader discourse on women's education in Transylvania, see Ileana Vlassa, "Condiția intelectuală a femeii oglindită în discursul pedagogic românesc al secolului al XIX-lea [The intellectual condition of women as mirrored by the Romanian pedagogical discourse of the nineteenth century]," *Sargetia. Acta Musei Devensis*, no. 3 (2012): 287–95.

8. Teodor Păcățian, *Cartea de aur sau luptele naționale ale românilor de sub coroana ungară* [The golden book or, the Romanian national struggle under the Hungarian crown], vol. 8 (Sibiu, Romania: Tiparul Tipografiei Arhidiecezane, 1915).

9. The text considered Japan's "first modern novel," *Ukigumo*, dramatized the issue of women's education, including risks for the nation. Futabatei Shimei, *Japan's First Modern Novel: Ukigumo of Futabatei Shimei*, trans. Marleigh Grayer Ryan (Ann Arbor: University of Michigan, 1990).

10. On modernist spinsters, see Emma Liggins, *Odd Women? Spinsters, Lesbians and Widows in British Women's Fiction, 1850s–1930s* (Manchester, UK: Manchester University Press, 2016).

11. On gendering as a systemwide process that entailed the economic disadvantaging of women and their exclusion from public space, as well as their construction as threats to public order, see Sheila Margaret Pelizzon, "But Can She Spin? The Decline in the Social Standing of Women in the Transition from Feudalism to Capitalism" (PhD diss., State University of New York at Binghamton, 1999). The same logic was at work in the transition from feudalism to capitalism, as described by Maria Mies, *Patriarchy and Accumulation on a World Scale: Women in the International Division of Labour* (London: Zed Books, 1986); Silvia Federici, *Caliban and the Witch: Women, the Body, and Primitive Accumulation* (New York: Autonomedia, 2004).

12. On the globalization of the image of the modern girl, especially through cosmetics, see Alys Eve Weinbaum, Lynn M. Thomas, Priti Ramamurthy, Uta G. Poiger, Madeleine Yue Dong, and Tani E. Barlow, eds., *The Modern Girl around the World: Consumption, Modernity, and Globalization* (Durham, NC: Duke University Press, 2008).

13. Rebecca Houze, *Textiles, Fashion, and Design Reform in Austria-Hungary before the First World War: Principles of Dress* (Burlington, VT: Ashgate Publishing, 2015), 54.

14. Werner Sombart, *Luxury and Capitalism*, trans. W. R. Dittmar (Ann Arbor: University of Michigan Press, 1967).

15. In two of Odette's most sexualized appearances in *Swann's Way*, she wears a silk dress; her boudoir is likewise filled with silk. Marcel Proust, *Swann's Way*, trans. Lydia Davis (New York: Penguin Books, 2002), 228–29.

16. Houze, *Textiles, Fashion, and Design Reform*, 250.

17. On the construction of authenticity in art history, see Prita Meier, "Authenticity and Its Modernist Discontents: The Colonial Encounter and African and Middle Eastern Art History," *Arab Studies Journal* 18, no. 1 (2010): 12–45.

18. Weinbaum and colleagues write: "both policing of actual Modern Girls and of representations of Modern Girls characterized modern nationalisms worldwide in the 1920s and 1930s. In order to ensure their continuous production and consolidation, hegemonic nationalisms seem to have required control over Modern Girls as historical agents and as images—thus the vigilant containment of the Modern Girl's sexuality, consumption, and not least her representation in the variety of cultural texts." Weinbaum et al., *Modern Girl around the World*, 16.

19. Ioan Bolovan, "The Quantitative Dimension of Mixed Marriages in Transylvania at the End of the Long Nineteenth Century," in *Intermarriage in Transylvania, 1895–2010*, ed. Ioan Bolovan and Luminiţa Dumănescu (Frankfurt: Peter Lang, 2017), 68. On the stakes of intermarriage, see Matthijs Kalmijn, "Intermarriage and Homogamy: Causes, Patterns, Trends," *Annual Review of Sociology* 24, no. 1 (1998): 395–421.

20. Partha Chatterjee, "The Nationalist Resolution of the Woman's Question," in *Recasting Women: Essays in Indian Colonial History*, ed. Kumkum Sangari and Sudesh Vaid (New Brunswick, NJ: Rutgers University Press, 1990), 233–53.

21. Mrinalini Sinha, "Gender and Nation," in *Women's History in Global Perspective*, ed. Bonnie G. Smith, vol. 1 (Urbana: Illinois University Press, 2004), 254.

22. Jayawardena analyzes women's movements in the colonial and semicolonial world "against the background of nationalist struggles aimed at achieving political independence, asserting a national identity, and modernizing society." In these contexts, "the new woman could not be a total negation of traditional culture" because women "still had to act as guardians of national culture, indigenous religion and family traditions—in other words, to be both 'modern' and 'traditional.'" Jayawardena, *Feminism and Nationalism in the Third World*, 3, 14.

23. Chatterjee, "Nationalist Resolution of the Woman's Question," 237.

24. Maria Baiulescu, "Opening Speech at the Congress of the Federation of Romanian Women (1914)," in *Shaking the Empire, Shaking the Patriarchy: The Growth of a Feminist Consciousness across the Austro-Hungarian Monarchy* (Riverside, CA: Ariadne Press, 2014), 229.

25. Constanţa Hodoş, *Transilvania*, May 1920 (our translations).

26. Judith Szapor, *Hungarian Women's Activism in the Wake of the First World War: From Rights to Revanche* (New York: Bloomsbury Publishing, 2017), 8.

27. Emma de Ritoók and Charlotte de Geőcze, *Le problème de la Hongrie: les femmes hongroises aux femmes du monde civilisé* [The problem of Hungary: Hungarian women address the women of the civilized world] (Budapest: Ferdinand Pfeifer Libraires-Editeurs, 1920), 33.

28. Marius Turda has analyzed the eugenic rhetoric used in Hungary to react to the Treaty of Trianon. Marius Turda. "In Pursuit of Greater Hungary: Eugenic Ideas of Social and Biological Improvement, 1940–1941." *The Journal of Modern History* 85, no.3 (2013): 558–591.

29. Ritoók and Geőcze, *Le problème de la Hongrie*, 6. Szapor describes the imperial dimension of this feminist project: "they [Ritoók and Geőcze] made clever use of the vocabulary of British and French imperialism to drive home their points about the benign and civilizing influence of prewar Hungarian rule, the professionalism of its public service, the quality education and public-health services it provided, fighting corruption, ignorance, and a general lack of culture amongst non-Hungarian subjects." Szapor, *Hungarian Women's Activism*, 101.

30. Gudrun-Liane Ittu, "Aspecte ale emancipării femeii în mediul protestant (lutheran) german (săsesc) din Transilvania, în a doua jumătate a sec. al XIX-lea şi începutul sec. XX-lea [Aspects of women's emancipation in the Protestant (Lutheran) German (Saxon) milieu in the second half of the nineteenth century and the beginning of the twentieth century]," in *Anuarul Institutului de Cercetări Socio-Umane* (Sibiu, Romania: Editura Academiei Române, 2005).

31. Susan Groag Bell and Karen M. Offen, *Women, the Family, and Freedom: 1750–1880* (Stanford, CA: Stanford University Press, 1983).

32. On Berde's Transylvanianism, see John Neubauer and Marcel Cornis-Pope, "Transylvania's Literary Cultures," in *History of the Literary Cultures of East-Central Europe*, ed. Marcel Cornis-Pope and John Neubauer, vol. 2 (Amsterdam: John Benjamins Publishing, 2004).

33. Charlotte Perkins Gilman, *The New Mothers of a New World* (New York: Charlton, 1913).

34. Szapor, *Hungarian Women's Activism*, 15.

35. Under the Austrian Code, the optimal ages for marriage were eighteen for men and sixteen for women; later, the age for men was raised to twenty-two, on military grounds. Most marriages at the turn of the century were contracted at ages twenty-four to twenty-five for men and nineteen to twenty for women. Minors could ask for dispensations, but men could not be younger than fourteen and women could not be younger than twelve. Sorina Paula Bolovan, *Familia în satul românesc din Transilvania* [The family in the Romanian village of Transylvania] (Cluj-Napoca, Romania: Fundaţia Culturală Română, 1999), 81, 97, 202.

36. One of the Occidentalist distinctions between the West and the rest, codified in the 1960s as the "Hajnal line," refers to women's age at the time of their first marriage.

37. On husband hunting in women's literature, see Agatha Schwartz, *Shifting Voices: Feminist Thought and Women's Writing in Fin-de-Siècle Austria and Hungary* (Montreal: McGill-Queen's University Press, 2008), 172.

38. Juliette Leeb-du Toit, *isishweshwe: A History of the Indigenisation of Blueprint in South Africa* (Pietermaritzburg, South Africa: University of KwaZulu-Natal Press, 2017).

39. On the association of *Blaudruck/kékfestö* with the Romanian minority in Hungary, see Leeb-du Toit, 98.

40. Simone de Beauvoir, *The Second Sex*, trans. Constance Borde (New York: Vintage Books, 2011).

41. Virginia Woolf, *To the Lighthouse* (New York: Harvest Books, 1989), 49.

42. Nancy M. Wingfield, *The World of Prostitution in Late Imperial Austria* (Oxford: Oxford University Press, 2017), 12. Rebreanu's novel also includes a scene in which Transylvanian Romanian men sexually harass the young wife of a Jewish tavern owner.

43. On secular criticism, see Aamir R. Mufti, "Auerbach in Istanbul: Edward Said, Secular Criticism, and the Question of Minority Culture," *Critical Inquiry* 25, no. 1 (1998): 95–125.

44. Quoted in Schwartz, *Shifting Voices*, 57.

45. Compare Sinha's reading of Chatterjee: Mrinalini Sinha, "Refashioning Mother India: Feminism and Nationalism in Late-Colonial India," *Feminist Studies* 26, no. 3 (2000): 625.

46. For one such use, see Baiulescu, "Opening Speech at the Congress of the Federation of Romanian Women," 234. Wollstonecraft, an antislavery activist, used analogies to both transatlantic slavery and Muslim women to bolster the case for Western women's emancipation through education. See Mary Wollstonecraft, *A Vindication of the Rights of Woman* (New York: Dover, 1996); Ruth Bernard Yeazell, *Harems of the Mind: Passages of Western Art and Literature* (New Haven, CT: Yale University Press, 2000).

47. Mies, *Patriarchy and Accumulation on a World Scale*; Claudia von Werlhof, Maria Mies, and Veronika Bennholdt-Thomsen, eds., *Frauen, die letzte Kolonie* [Women: The last colony] (Hamburg: Rowohlt, 1983).

48. The education of female teachers in the Civil Greek Catholic School for Girls in Beiuş/Belényes/Binsch, for example, which opened in 1896 and had a boarding school, included a mix of the following institutions, which taught in one or more of the three languages of education: Astra's Civil School in Sibiu/Hermannstadt/Nagyszeben, Ursuline Nuns' School in Oradea/Nagyvárad/Großwardein, Notre Dame Civil School in Timişoara/Temesvár/Temeswar, and Sancta Maria Institute for Teachers in Budapest. Iudita Căluşer, "Cadrele didactice de la şcoala civilă unită de fete din Beiuş, elita intelectualităţii feminine locale [The faculty of the Uniate Civil School for girls in Beiuş, the elite of the local female intellectual class]," in *240 de ani de la moartea marelui arhiereu şi luptător naţional Ioan Inochentie Micu-Klein 1768–2008* [240 years since the death of the great archbishop and national fighter Ioan Inochentie Micu-Klein 1768–2008] (Oradea, Romania: Editura Episcop Vasile Aftenie, 2009).

49. Reuniunea Femeilor Române din Braşov, *Regulament pentru internatul-orfelinat* [Regulation of boarding school / orphanage] (Braşov, Romania: Tipografia A. Mureşianu, 1910).

50. Jayawardena, *Feminism and Nationalism in the Third World*, 16–17.

51. Schwartz, *Shifting Voices*, 116. In the interwar period, Ritoók's work took an antisemitic turn.

52. Historian Jörg K. Hoensch writes: "the social cohesion of Rumanian and Ruthenian peasant communities, which still lived a very traditional life, formed an effective protection against magyarisation measures. The higher a citizen climbed on the social ladder, the more likely he was to change his national identity." Jörg K. Hoensch, *A History of Modern Hungary 1867–1994* (London: Longman, 1996), 31.

53. See Katie Trumpener's account of Béla Bartók's racially inflected advocacy of Hungarian women's antifeminist and anticosmopolitan monolingualism, which was meant to safeguard the Hungarian soul. Katie Trumpener, "Béla Bartók and the Rise of Comparative Ethnomusicology: Nationalism, Race Purity, and the Legacy of the Austro-Hungarian Empire," in *Music and the Racial Imagination*, ed. Ronald Radano and Philip V. Bohlman (Chicago: University of Chicago Press, 2000), 403–34.

54. Romanian nationalist politician Alexandru Mocioni drew up a contract for his family members in 1901, obligating them to commit to the family's national and religious character or risk being excluded from the family and losing their inheritance. Teodor Botiş, *Monografia familiei Mocioni* [Monograph of the Mocioni family] (Bucharest: Editura Fundaţia pentru Literatură şi Artă "Regele Carol II," 1939).

55. Laura is modeled after one of Rebreanu's sisters, Livia, who published a volume of poetry in 1920, the same year *Ion* was published.

56. Woolf, *To the Lighthouse*, 86.

57. Constanţa Hodoş, *Martirii* [The martyrs] (Bucharest: Minerva, 1908), 60.

58. When George Călinescu wrote the history of Romanian literature in 1941, he credited Rebreanu with creating the Romanian novel and offered a misogynistic interpretation of Papadat-Bengescu's work. Călinescu avers that women writers cannot abstract; they can only write about their immediate world and their own sensations. George Călinescu, *Istoria literaturii române* [History of Romanian literature] (Bucharest: Fundaţia regală pentru

cultură și artă, 1941), 737–38. Importantly, Rebreanu was a supporter of Papadat-Bengescu's literary career.

59. Hortensia Papadat-Bengescu, *Ape adânci* [Deep waters] (Bucharest: Editura Librăriei Alcalay, 1919), 32.

60. Papadat-Bengescu, 141.

61. On the politics of modernist cosmopolitanism, see Rebecca L. Walkowitz, *Cosmopolitan Style: Modernism beyond the Nation* (New York: Columbia University Press, 2006). On Papadat-Bengescu's transnational reach, see Eugenia Tudor-Anton, *Hortensia Papadat-Bengescu, marea europeană* (Bucharest: Editura National, 2001).

7. GOD IS THE NEW CHURCH

1. Sabbatarians or Szambatos based their faith and rituals on the Old Testament, modeled on the Sephardic rite. Twenty thousand Szeklers converted to Sabbatarianism in the late sixteenth and early seventeenth centuries. Raphael Patai, *The Jews of Hungary: History, Culture, Psychology* (Detroit: Wayne State University Press, 1996), 158.

2. Ferenc Pozsony, "The Ethnicization of Religious Identity: The Case of Szekler Sabbatarians," in *Integrating Minorities: Traditional Communities and Modernization*, ed. Agnieszka Barszczewska and Lehel Peti (Cluj-Napoca, Romania: Romanian Institute for Research on National Minorities, 2011), 119–38.

3. Patai, *Jews of Hungary*, 378.

4. A paradigmatic model for understanding the translation between religious options was the 1956 conversion of Indian Dalits to Buddhism. See Gauri Viswanathan, "Religious Conversion and the Politics of Dissent," in *Conversion to Modernities: The Globalization of Christianity*, ed. Peter van der Veer (New York: Routledge, 1996), 89–114.

5. The schism, as Robert Bideleux and Ian Jeffries argue, amplified divisions that were "more important and significant than the later cleavage within Western Christianity, between the Roman Catholic and Protestant Churches. They solidified and gave sharper doctrinal edge to an enduring East-West divide within European civilization." Robert Bideleux and Ian Jeffries, *A History of Eastern Europe: Crisis and Change* (London: Routledge, 1998), 48. The schism of 451 had divided Christianity into Chalcedonian and non-Chalcedonian, a division that survived within Eastern Christianity after the 1054 schism.

6. Stephen Fischer-Galati writes: "As an Eastern power expanding westward, the Ottoman Turks came into conflict with a Western power expanding westward. The unavoidable clash occurred over Hungary . . . Lutheran campaign for legal recognition in Germany exploited the insoluble Habsburg-Ottoman conflict over Hungary." Stephen Fischer-Galati, "The Protestant Reformation and Islam," in *The Mutual Effects of the Islamic and Judeo-Christian Worlds: The East European Pattern*, ed. Abraham Ascher, Tibor Halasi-Kun, and Béla K. Király (New York: Brooklyn College Press, 1979), 58–59.

7. Karen Barkey, "Empire and Toleration: A Comparative Sociology of Toleration within Empire," in *Boundaries of Toleration*, ed. Alfred Stepan and Charles Taylor (New York: Columbia University Press, 2014), 218.

8. Susan Ritchie, "The Pasha of Buda and the Edict of Torda," *Journal of Unitarian Universalist History*, 2005, 36–54.

9. The toleration enacted by Joseph's edict was economically motivated, intended to guarantee free trade in regions with competing religious groups. Barkey, "Empire and Toleration," 208, 225.

10. Ira Katznelson describes toleration as "a willful decision to permit disliked groups, beliefs, or practices to persist despite the ability to do otherwise," which is needed in cases of "antipathy often closer to outrage and revulsion." For Katznelson, toleration consti-

tutes "a willful act of omission, a deliberate silence or restraint, a suspension of commitment, and a willingness to share geographic and political space with others who deviate from true belief, correct values, and proper behavior." Ira Katznelson, "A Form of Liberty and Indulgence: Toleration as a Layered Institution," in Stepan and Taylor, *Boundaries of Toleration*, 40–41.

11. The authors write: "'Tolerance' is premised on a prior normativity, an assumption of major and minor elements in a society. Even the tolerance within the Abrahamic 'religions of the book' marginalizes those who adhere to other nonmonotheistic religions or to nonscriptural religions or to those who prefer no religion at all. Tolerance also encodes class superiority by forgetting that the powerless can also practice 'tolerance' without learning it from their 'betters.'" Robert Stam and Ella Shohat, *Race in Translation: Culture Wars around the Postcolonial Atlantic* (New York: NYU Press, 2012), 119.

12. Converts experienced increased persecution and discrimination for allegedly conspiring against Christianity or secretly practicing a non-Christian faith. Walter D. Mignolo, *Local Histories/Global Designs: Coloniality, Subaltern Knowledges, and Border Thinking* (Princeton, NJ: Princeton University Press, 2000); Max-Sebastián Hering Torres, *Rassismus in der Vormoderne: Die "Reinheit Des Blutes" im Spanien der frühen Neuzeit* [Racism during Premodernity: The 'Purity of Blood' in Early Modern Spain] (Frankfurt: Campus Verlag, 2006); Stam and Shohat, *Race in Translation*.

13. Jane S. Gerber, *The Jews of Spain: A History of the Sephardic Experience* (New York: Free Press, 1994), 127.

14. Stam and Shohat, in *Race in Translation*, argue for the need to simultaneously conceptualize the "two 1492s," which resulted in Iberian antisemitism and Islamophobia being projected outward onto Native American and African populations in the New World.

15. See H. Micheal Tarver and Emily Slape, *The Spanish Empire: A Historical Encyclopedia* (Santa Barbara, CA: ABC-CLIO, 2016), 161. Henry Kamen notes that Charles V's union of European and American territories encompassed "a greater number of realms than had ever before been accumulated by any European ruler; the entire Burgundian inheritance, centred on the Netherlands; the immense hereditary Habsburg lands, including Austria within the Empire and Hungary outside it; the whole of peninsular Spain as well as the Italian territories of Spain and Sicily; and the continent of America." Henry Kamen, *Spain's Road to Empire: The Making of a World Power, 1492–1763* (London: Penguin, 2003), 50.

16. Nicolae Iorga, *Istoria bisericii românești și a vieții religioase a românilor* [History of the Romanian church and of the religious life of Romanians], vol. 1 (Vălenii-de-munte, Romania: Tipăritura Neamul Românesc, 1908), 277.

17. Saba Mahmood, *Religious Difference in a Secular Age: A Minority Report* (Princeton, NJ: Princeton University Press, 2016), 44–45.

18. Talal Asad, *Formations of the Secular: Christianity, Islam, Modernity* (Stanford, CA: Stanford University Press, 2003).

19. Tomoko Masuzawa, *The Invention of World Religions: Or, How European Universalism Was Preserved in the Language of Pluralism* (Chicago: University of Chicago Press, 2005), 264.

20. Shalini Randeria, Martin Fuchs, and Antje Linkenbach, "Konfigurationen der Moderne: Zur Einleitung," *Konfigurationen der Moderne: Diskurse zu Indien* [Configurations of Modernity: An Introduction, *Configurations of Modernity: Discourses on India*], *Soziale Welt* 15 (2004): 1–34.

21. Compare the case of Goa, colonized by the Portuguese in the sixteenth century. Ananya Kabir analyzes the *dekhni*, one of the oldest dance forms in the region, through the prism of Christianity as a creolizing matrix. The *dekhni* evokes the Hindu temple

culture that had been banished, symbolically and materially, to "the other side of the river" during the conversion of Goan elites to Catholicism. In this perspective, conversion becomes "the watershed that separated the new from the pre-existent." Ananya Jahanara Kabir, "Rapsodia Ibero-Indiana: Transoceanic Creolization and the Mando of Goa," *Modern Asian Studies*, 2021, 1–56, 40.

22. Peter van der Veer, *Conversion to Modernities: The Globalization of Christianity* (New York: Routledge, 1996), 4, 7.

23. Paul J. Shore, *Narratives of Adversity: Jesuits in the Eastern Peripheries of the Habsburg Realms (1640–1773)* (Budapest: Central European University Press, 2012), 288. Shore writes: "It is probably going too far to say that the Roma, Romanians and Ruthenians were denied consideration as a 'fully human type' in the way the *Indios* of Peru were viewed by sixteenth and seventeenth century Jesuits. Yet an unmistakable antipathy flavors documentation of the Society's interactions with these populations. This antipathy is both a result and a cause of the Jesuits' less than uniformly successful experience with each of these groups." Shore, 292.

24. Quoted in Keith Hitchins, *Orthodoxy and Nationality: Andreiu Şaguna and the Rumanians of Transylvania, 1846–1873* (Cambridge, MA: Harvard University Press, 1977), 197.

25. Charles Taylor, "Afterword and Corrections," in *A Secular Age beyond the West: Religion, Law and the State in Asia, the Middle East and North Africa*, ed. Mirjam Künkler, John Madeley, and Shylashri Shankar (Cambridge: Cambridge University Press, 2018), 386.

26. For Shalini Randeria, this dialectic is part of the shared and connected histories that colonialism engendered and that juxtaposed secularization in Europe to the evangelization of the colonies. Randeria writes: "drawing attention, for example, to the fervent missionary activities of modern Europeans in the colonies unsettles the modernist narrative of a progressive secularization of Europe, which makes it possible to overlook, or at least underplay, the role of the churches, missionary societies and of religious associations in modern western civil societies, and regard these as characteristic of backward or imperfect non-European ones." Shalini Randeria, "Entangled Histories of Uneven Modernities: Civil Society, Caste Solidarities and Legal Pluralism in Post-Colonial India," in *Unraveling Ties: From Social Cohesion to New Practices of Connectedness*, ed. Yehuda Elkana, Ivan Krastev, Elísio Macamo, and Shalini Randeria (Frankfurt: Campus Verlag, 2002), 284–311.

27. Saba Mahmood, *Religious Difference in a Secular Age: A Minority Report* (Princeton, NJ: Princeton University Press, 2015), 2.

28. On comparative secularisms, see Linell E. Cady and Tracy Fessenden, eds., *Religion, the Secular, and the Politics of Sexual Difference* (New York: Columbia University Press, 2013).

29. Mahmood writes: "Eastern Orthodox Christianity and Oriental Orthodox Christianity are just as alien in such theorizations of the secular [Taylor's] as Islam." Mahmood, *Religious Difference in a Secular Age* (2015), 206. Tellingly, in *A Secular Age*, Taylor borrows from the language of European Union integration to describe different speeds at which secularism is achieved: Latin Christendom experienced increasing unbelief at one speed, whereas the Eastern churches did so at a slower speed.

30. Enrique D. Dussel, *The Underside of Modernity: Apel, Ricoeur, Rorty, Taylor, and the Philosophy of Liberation*, trans. Eduardo Mendieta (Atlantic Highlands, NJ: Humanities Press, 1996), 134.

31. Charles Taylor, *A Secular Age* (Cambridge, MA: Harvard University Press, 2007), 374.

32. Steven Béla Várdy, *Baron Joseph Eötvös (1813–1871): A Literary Biography* (Boulder, CO: East European Monographs, 1987), 29.

33. Emancipation also made conversion to Judaism possible. The inhabitants of the formerly Transylvanian Sabbatarian village of Bözödujfalu/Bezidul Nou reconverted to Judaism and became, according to Patai, "the only proselyte Jewish congregation in modern European history." Patai, *Jews of Hungary*, 160.

34. Mahmood, *Religious Difference in a Secular Age*, 3.

35. Teodor Botiş, *Monografia familiei Mocioni* [Monograph of the Mocioni family] (Bucharest: Editura Fundaţia pentru Literatură şi Artă "Regele Carol II," 1939), 120–21.

36. Taylor, *Secular Age*, 2.

37. Hitchins, *Orthodoxy and Nationality*, 5. Hitchins summarizes the influence of the Orthodox church in Transylvania in the 1830s: "The church's dominance of Romanian society in the 1830s extended well beyond the realm of politics to include education, literature, and philosophy, not to mention the spiritual and moral upbringing of the vast majority of the population. The only Romanian institutions of higher learning in Transylvania were the gymnasium at Blaj and the Orthodox seminary at Sibiu; the village elementary schools throughout the country were in the hands of the two churches as was the training of their teachers, and, consequently, the curricula and textbooks emphasized traditional religious teachings; the only Romanian publishing house in Transylvania was operated by the Uniate Church at Blaj; the district protopopes and the parish priests were the spiritual and, usually, the political leaders of their people; and the majority of Romanian intellectuals were either priests or the sons of priests." Hitchins, 201.

38. Piro Rexhepi, "Imperial Inventories, 'Illegal Mosques' and Institutionalized Islam: Coloniality and the Islamic Community of Bosnia and Herzegovina," *History and Anthropology* 30, no. 4 (2019): 481.

39. Taylor, *Secular Age*, 299.

40. Botiş, *Monografia familiei Mocioni*, 337, 343.

41. See Clifford Geertz, "Religion as a Cultural System," in *The Interpretation of Cultures: Selected Essays* (New York: Basic Books, 1973).

42. Steve Bruce, *God Is Dead: Secularization in the West* (Oxford: Blackwell, 2002), 31.

43. Aamir R. Mufti, "Auerbach in Istanbul: Edward Said, Secular Criticism, and the Question of Minority Culture," *Critical Inquiry* 25, no. 1 (1998): 113.

44. Mufti, 116.

45. Liviu Rebreanu, *Ion*, trans. A. Hillard (London: Peter Owen, 1965); Liviu Rebreanu, *Ion*, ed. Niculae Gheran, vol. IV, *Opere* (Bucharest: Editura Minerva, 1970). We modified some translations.

46. Hitchins, *Orthodoxy and Nationality*, 170, 174.

47. Prislop/Priszlop had 458 Greek Catholic believers and four Jewish inhabitants, while the dependent villages of Cepan, Nagy-Demeter, and Tradam had a mix of Greek Catholic, Protestant, and Jewish inhabitants. Ioan V. Boţan, *Prislop-Liviu Rebreanu, Judeţul Bistriţa-Năsăud (1392–2007): Studiu monografic* (Cluj-Napoca, Romania: Editura Mega, 2008), 143.

48. Boţan, 137.

49. Ion Simuţ argues that Ion is caught between the priest and the teacher; he is an individual "partially manipulated." Ion Simuţ, *Liviu Rebreanu şi contradicţiile realismului* [Liviu Rebreanu and the contradictions of realism] (Cluj-Napoca, Romania: Editura Dacia, 2010), 127. For Simuţ, this means that Ion is caught between the priest's religious mission and the teacher's secular-social mission. Simuţ, 132. In contrast, Liviu Maliţa agrees that Ion is positioned between the priest and the teacher but challenges the assumption of manipulation, arguing that Ion uses his position to achieve his own ends. Liviu Maliţa, *Alt Rebreanu* [A different Rebreanu] (Cluj-Napoca, Romania: Cartimpex, 2000), 85, 98.

50. Philip Gorski writes: "There was also an underlying and often unspoken disagreement as to whether secularization should be mourned or cheered, reflecting the split

between religious and irreligious sociologists of religion. The former were more apt to see secularization in tragic terms, as Weber did, as a loss of 'meaning' or cultural coherence. . . . The latter were more apt to see it in comic terms, as Comte did, as a process of liberation and enlightenment." Philip Gorski, "Secularity 1: Varieties and Dilemmas," in Künkler, Madeley, and Shankar, *Secular Age beyond the West*, 36.

51. Deborah Brandt, "Sponsors of Literacy," *College Composition and Communication* 49, no. 2 (1998): 165–85.

52. Hitchins, *Orthodoxy and Nationality*, 202.

53. Edward Said, *Orientalism* (London, Vintage, 1978).

54. On the history of the term, see Julien Benda, *The Treason of the Intellectuals* (London: Routledge, 2017).

55. Edward W. Said, *Representations of the Intellectual* (London: Vintage, 2012).

56. On the debate regarding the moral corruption of Uniate priests, see Sorin Mitu, *Transilvania mea: Istorii, mentalități, identități* [My Transylvania: histories, mentalities, identities] (Iași, Romania: Polirom, 2006), 190–94. On the figure of the priest as lover (*ibovnicul satelor*) in the Romanian-language culture, see Constanța Vintilă-Ghițulescu, *Focul amorului: Despre dragoste și sexualitate în societatea românească (1750–1830)* [The heat of passion: on love and sexuality in Romanian society (1750–1830)] (Bucharest: Humanitas, 2006).

57. Max Weber, "Science as a Vocation," trans. Hans H. Gerth and C. Wright Mills, in *Max Weber: Sociological Writings*, ed. Wolf Heydebrand (New York: Continuum, 1994), 302–303.

58. Valer Simion Cosma, "Preoțimea între tradiție și modernitate: Intrarea în modernitate [Priesthood between tradition and modernity: entering modernity]," *Caiete de Antropologie Istorică*, no. 15 (2009): 55–68.

59. Purushottama Bilimoria, "Disenchantments of Secularism: The West and India," in *Secularisations and Their Debates: Perspectives on the Return of Religion in the Contemporary West*, ed. Matthew Sharpe and Dylan Nickelson (Dordrecht, Netherlands: Springer, 2014), 36.

60. One historical document mentions that villagers asked not to be treated like serfs in their labor obligations to the church ["*poporenii să nu fie de tot asupriți și însărcinați cu obligăminte iobăgești, cari ad actum nu mai esistă*"]. Priests received eighty to one hundred Austrian francs as salary. Simion Retegan, *Satele năsăudene la mijlocul secolului al XIX-lea: Mărturii documentare* [Villages in the Năsăud region in mid nineteenth century: documents] (Cluj-Napoca, Romania: Accent, 2002), 262.

61. On the tension between patriotism as attachment to the empire and patriotism as devotion to the nation, see Pieter M. Judson, *The Habsburg Empire: A New History* (Cambridge, MA: Belknap Press, 2016).

62. Hitchins, *Orthodoxy and Nationality*, 184–85.

63. Daniela Deteșan argues that this was a fairly widespread practice. Daniela Deteșan, ed., *Căsătorie și moștenire în Transilvania: Documente din a doua jumătate a secolului al XIX-lea* [Marriage and inheritance in Transylvania: documents from the second half of the nineteenth century] (Cluj-Napoca, Romania: Presa Universitară Clujană, 2013), 231.

64. Hitchins writes about the history of such visits: "Lay leaders pointed out to the bishops that their arrival in a village was one of the most important events in the lives of its inhabitants: their visit had not only spiritual but also cultural significance because almost the entire cultural life of the peasants took place within the framework of the church and under the influence of religion." Hitchins, *Orthodoxy and Nationality*, 180.

Bibliography

Abu-Lughod, Janet L. *Before European Hegemony: The World System A.D. 1250–1350.* Oxford: Oxford University Press, 1989.

Achim, Viorel. *The Roma in Romanian History.* Budapest: CEU Press, 1998.

Albrecht, Catherine. "Rural Banks and Czech Nationalism in Bohemia, 1848–1914." *Agricultural History* 78, no. 3 (2004): 317–45.

Almási, Gábor, and Lav Šubarić. "Introduction." In *Latin at the Crossroads of Identity: The Evolution of Linguistic Nationalism in the Kingdom of Hungary*, edited by Gábor Almási and Lav Šubarić. Leiden, Netherlands: Brill, 2015.

Amelina, Anna, Manuela Boatcă, Gregor Bongaerts, and Anja Weiß. "Theorizing Societalization across Borders: Globality, Transnationality, Postcoloniality." *Current Sociology* 69, no. 3 (2021): 303–14.

Amelina, Anna, Devrimsel D. Nergiz, Thomas Faist, and Nina Glick Schiller, eds. *Beyond Methodological Nationalism: Research Methodologies for Cross-Border Studies.* New York: Routledge, 2012.

Anderson, Benedict. *Imagined Communities: Reflections on the Origin and Spread of Nationalism.* London: Verso, 2006.

Anderson, Harriet. *Utopian Feminism: Women's Movements in Fin-de-Siècle Vienna.* New Haven, CT: Yale University Press, 1992.

Anzaldúa, Gloria. *Boderlands / La Frontera: The New Mestiza* (San Francisco, CA: Aunt Lute Books, 2012).

Araghi, Farshad, and Marina Karides. "Land Dispossession and Global Crisis: Introduction to the Special Section on Land Rights in the World-System." *Journal of World-Systems Research* 18, no. 1 (2012): 1–5.

Asad, Talal. *Formations of the Secular: Christianity, Islam, Modernity.* Stanford, CA: Stanford University Press, 2003.

Bachner, Andrea. "At the Margins of the Minor: Rethinking Scalarity, Relationality, and Translation." *Journal of World Literature* 2, no. 2 (2017): 139–57.

Bădescu, Gruia. "Rewritten in Stone: Imperial Heritage in the Sacred Place of the Nation." *Cultural Studies* 34, no. 5 (2020): 707–29.

Baer, Ben Conisbee. *Indigenous Vanguards: Education, National Liberation, and the Limits of Modernism.* New York: Columbia University Press, 2019.

Baghiu, Ștefan, Vlad Pojoga, and Maria Sass, eds. *Ruralism and Literature in Romania.* Berlin: Peter Lang, 2020.

Bahun, Sanja. "The Balkans Uncovered: Towards Historie Croisée of Modernism." In *The Oxford Handbook of Global Modernism*, edited by Mark Wollaeger, 25–47. New York: Oxford University Press, 2010.

Baiulescu, Maria. "Opening Speech at the Congress of the Federation of Romanian Women (1914)." In *Shaking the Empire, Shaking the Patriarchy: The Growth of a Feminist Consciousness across the Austro-Hungarian Monarchy*, 228–35. Riverside, CA: Ariadne Press, 2014.

Baker, Catherine. *Race and the Yugoslav Region: Postsocialist, Post-Conflict, Postcolonial?* Manchester: Manchester University Press, 2018.

Balog, Iosif Marin. "Elitele financiar-bancare românești din Transilvania (1895–1918): Considerații teoretico-metodologice și evaluări statistice [Romanian financial/

banking elites in Transylvania (1895–1918): Theoretical methodological considerations and statistical evaluations]." *Anuarul Institutului de Istorie George Barițiu* 55, no. LV/Sup (2016): 33–47.

——. "The Clergy's Involvement in the Romanian Credit System from Transylvania during the Late Nineteenth and the Early Twentieth Centuries. Case Study: The Greek-Catholic Clergy." In *Recruitment and Promotion among the Romanian Greek Catholic Ecclesiastical Elite in Transylvania (1853–1918)*, edited by Mirela Popa-Andrei, 170–74. Cluj-Napoca, Romania: Editura Mega, 2014.

——. "Transporturile și comunicațiile: evoluție și semnificație în procesul modernizării economice a Transilvaniei la mijlocul secolului al XIX-lea [Transportation and communication: their evolution and signification in the process of economic modernization of Transylvania in mid-nineteenth century]." *Revista Bistriței* 20 (2006): 235–47.

Barkey, Karen. "Empire and Toleration: A Comparative Sociology of Toleration within Empire." In *Boundaries of Toleration*, edited by Alfred Stepan and Charles Taylor, 203–32. New York: Columbia University Press, 2014.

Baron, Salo W. "The Impact of the Revolution of 1848 on Jewish Emancipation." *Jewish Social Studies* 11, no. 3 (1949): 195–248.

Bartov, Omer, and Eric D. Weitz, eds. *Shatterzone of Empires: Coexistence and Violence in the German, Habsburg, Russian, and Ottoman Borderlands.* Bloomington: Indiana University Press, 2013.

Beauvoir, Simone de. *The Second Sex.* Translated by Constance Borde. New York: Vintage Books, 2011.

Beiu, Adela. "The Nation and the Absurd: A Romanian Story of Modernity." *Modernism/modernity* 21, no. 4 (2015): 961–75.

Bell, Susan Groag, and Karen M. Offen. *Women, the Family, and Freedom: 1750–1880.* Stanford, CA: Stanford University Press, 1983.

Benbassa, Esther, and Aron Rodrigue. *The Jews of the Balkans: The Judeo-Spanish Community, 15th to 20th Centuries.* Oxford: Blackwell, 1995.

Benda, Julien. *The Treason of the Intellectuals.* Translated by Richard Aldington. London: Routledge, 2017.

Berend, Iván T. *History Derailed: Central and Eastern Europe in the Long Nineteenth Century.* Berkeley: University of California Press, 2005.

——. "Past Convergence within Europe: Core–Periphery Diversity in Modern Economic Development." In *Economic Convergence and Divergence in Europe: Growth and Regional Development in an Enlarged European Union*, edited by Gertrude Tumpel-Gugerell and Peter Mooslechner, 9–23. Cheltenham, UK: Elgar, 2003.

Berend, Iván T., and György Ránki. *East Central Europe in the 19th and 20th Centuries.* Budapest: Akadémiai Kiadó, 1977.

——. *The European Periphery and Industrialization 1780–1914.* Cambridge: Cambridge University Press, 1982.

Berger, Stefan. "Building the Nation among Visions of German Empire." In *Nationalizing Empires*, edited by Stefan Berger and Alexei Miller, 247–308. Budapest: Central European University Press, 2015.

Berger, Stefan, and Alexei Miller. "Introduction: Building Nations in and with Empires: A Reassessment." In *Nationalizing Empires*, edited by Stefan Berger and Alexei Miller, 1–30. Budapest: Central European University Press, 2015.

Berlant, Lauren. "On the Case." *Critical Inquiry* 33, no. 4 (2007): 663–72.

Berman, Jessica. *Modernist Commitments: Ethics, Politics and Transnational Modernism.* New York: Columbia University Press, 2012.

Beu, Octavian. *Franz Liszt în țara noastră* [Franz Liszt in our country]. Sibiu, Romania: Kraft & Dortleff, 1933.

Bibesco, Georges. *Exposition Universalle: La Roumanie*. Paris: Imprimerie Typographique J. Kugelmann, 1890.

Bideleux, Robert, and Ian Jeffries. *A History of Eastern Europe: Crisis and Change*. London: Routledge, 1998.

Bilimoria, Purushottama. "Disenchantments of Secularism: The West and India." In *Secularisations and Their Debates: Perspectives on the Return of Religion in the Contemporary West*, edited by Matthew Sharpe and Dylan Nickelson, 21–37. Dordrecht, Netherlands: Springer, 2014.

Bíró, Béla. "Constructed Spaces in Liviu Rebreanu's *Ion*." *Acta Universitatis Sapientiae, Philologica* 4, no. 1 (2012): 117–48.

Blackbourn, David. *Das Kaiserreich transnational: Eine Skizze* [The German Empire Transnationally: A Sketch], in *Das Kaiserreich transnational: Deutschland in der Welt 1871–1914* [The German Empire Transnationally: Germany in the World 1871–1914], edited by Sebastian Conrad und Jürgen Osterhammel. Göttingen: Vandenhoeck und Ruprecht, 2004.

Blackburn, Robin. *The Overthrow of Colonial Slavery, 1776–1848*. London: Verso, 1988.

Blom, Ida, ed. *Gendered Nations: Nationalisms and Gender Order in the Long Nineteenth Century*. Oxford: Berg, 2000.

Blomqvist, Anders E. B. "Economic Nationalizing in the Ethnic Borderlands of Hungary and Romania." Södertorn University, 2014.

Boatcă, Manuela. "Caribbean Europe: Out of Sight, out of Mind?" In *Constructing the Pluriverse*, edited by Bernd Reiter, 197–218. Durham, NC: Duke University Press, 2018.

——. "Multiple Europes and the Politics of Difference within." In *Worlds & Knowledges Otherwise*. Spring 2013. 3, no. 3, https://globalstudies.trinity.duke.edu/projects/wko-uneasy-postcolonialisms.

——. "Politics of Memory under Two Pandemics." *EuropeNow* 40 (2021). https://www.europenowjournal.org/2021/04/01/politics-of-memory-under-two-pandemics/.

——. "Second Slavery versus Second Serfdom: Local Labor Regimes of the Global Periphery." In *Social Theory and Regional Studies in the Global Age*, edited by Saïd Amir Arjomand, 361–88. Albany, NY: SUNY Press, 2014.

——. "Thinking Europe Otherwise: Lessons from the Caribbean." *Current Sociology* 69, no. 3 (2021): 389–414.

——. "Uneasy Postcolonialisms." *Worlds & Knowledges Otherwise* 3, no. 3 (2013). https://globalstudies.trinity.duke.edu/projects/wko-uneasy-postcolonialisms.

Boatcă, Manuela, Sina Farzin, and Julian Go. "Postcolonialism and Sociology." *Soziologie-Forum der Deutschen Gesellschaft für Soziologie* 47, no. 4 (2018): 423–38.

Boatcă, Manuela, and Julia Roth. "Unequal and Gendered: Notes on the Coloniality of Citizenship." *Current Sociology* 64, no. 2 (2016): 191–212.

——. "Women on the Fast Track? Coloniality of Citizenship and Embodied Social Mobility." In *Gender and Development: The Economic Basis of Women's Power*, edited by Rae Lesser Blumberg and Samuel Cohn. Los Angeles: Sage, 2019.

Bobulescu, C. *Lăutarii noștri* [Our musicians]. Bucharest: Tipăritura Națională Jean Ionescu, 1922.

Boia, Aurel. "Integrarea țiganilor din Sanț (Năsăud) în comunitatea Românească a satului [The integration of Gypsies in Sanț (Năsăud) in the Romanian village community]." *Sociologie Românească* 7–9 (1938).

Boia, Lucian. *History and Myth in Romanian Consciousness*. Budapest: Central European University Press, 2001.

Bolovan, Ioan. "The Quantitative Dimension of Mixed Marriages in Transylvania at the End of the Long Nineteenth Century." In *Intermarriage in Transylvania, 1895–2010*, edited by Ioan Bolovan and Luminiţa Dumănescu. Frankfurt: Peter Lang, 2017.

Bolovan, Sorina Paula. *Familia în satul românesc din Transilvania* [The family in the Romanian village of Transylvania]. Cluj-Napoca, Romania: Fundaţia Culturală Română, 1999.

Böröcz, József. *The European Union and Global Social Change: A Critical Geopolitical-Economic Analysis*. London: Routledge, 2010.

Borrow, George. *The Zincali: An Account of the Gypsies of Spain*. London: John Murray, 1907.

Boţan, Ioan V. *Prislop-Liviu Rebreanu, Judeţul Bistriţa-Năsăud (1392–2007): Studiu Monografic*. Cluj-Napoca, Romania: Editura Mega, 2008.

Botiş, Teodor. *Monografia familiei Mocioni* [Monograph of the Mocioni family]. Bucharest: Editura Fundaţia pentru Literatură şi Artă "Regele Carol II," 1939.

Bottoni, Stefano. *Stalin's Legacy in Romania: The Hungarian Autonomous Region, 1952–1960*. Lanham, MA: Lexington Books, 2018.

Brandt, Deborah. "Sponsors of Literacy." *College Composition and Communication* 49, no. 2 (1998): 165–85.

Brassai, Sámuel. *Magyar-vagy czigány-zene?* [Hungarian or Gipsy music?] Kolozsvár: Stein János Bizománya, 1860.

Brathwaite, Kamau. *The Development of Creole Society in Jamaica, 1770–1820*. Oxford: Clarendon Press, 1971.

Brote, Eugen. *Cestiunea română în Transilvania şi Ungaria* [The Romanian question in Transylvania and Hungary]. Bucharest: Tipografia Voinţa Naţională, 1895.

Brown, Kate. *A Biography of No Place: From Ethnic Borderland to Soviet Heartland*. Cambridge, MA: Harvard University Press, 2004.

Brubaker, Roger. *Nationalist Politics and Everyday Ethnicity in a Transylvanian Town*. Princeton, NJ: Princeton University Press, 2006.

Bruce, Steve. *God Is Dead: Secularization in the West*. Oxford: Blackwell, 2002.

Buck-Morss, Susan. *Hegel, Haiti, and Universal History*. Pittsburgh: University of Pittsburgh Press, 2009.

Bulson, Eric. *Novels, Maps, Modernity: The Spatial Imagination, 1850–2000*. New York: Routledge, 2007.

Burawoy, Michael. *The Extended Case Method: Four Countries, Four Decades, Four Great Transformations, and One Theoretical Tradition*. Berkeley: University of California Press, 2009.

Burbank, Jane, and Frederick Cooper. *Empires in World History: Power and the Politics of Difference*. Princeton, NJ: Princeton University Press, 2010.

Buta, Mircea Gelu, and Adrian Onofreiu, eds. *Petiţii din graniţa năsăudeană în a doua jumătate a secolului al XIX-lea: Contribuţii documentare* [Petitions from the Năsăud border in the second half of the nineteenth century: documentary contributions]. Cluj-Napoca, Romania: Eikon, 2012.

Buzilă, Ştefan. "Nunta la ţăranul român din jurul Năsăudului [Romanian peasants' wedding rituals in the Năsăud region]." In *Studii şi cercetări etnoculturale*, edited by Claudia Septimia Peteanu, XV:145–56, 2010.

Cady, Linell E., and Tracy Fessenden, eds. *Religion, the Secular, and the Politics of Sexual Difference*. New York: Columbia University Press, 2013.

Căluşer, Iudita. "Cadrele didactice de la şcoala civilă unită de fete din Beiuş, elita intelectualităţii feminine locale [The faculty of the Uniate Civil School for Girls in Beiuş, the elite of the local female intellectual class]." In *240 de ani de la mo-*

artea marelui arhiereu și luptător național Ioan Inochentie Micu-Klein 1768–2008 [240 years since the death of the great archbishop and national fighter Ioan Inochentie Micu-Klein 1768–2008]. Oradea, Romania: Editura Episcop Vasile Aftenie, 2009.

Canetti, Elias. *The Tongue Set Free.* Translated by Joachim Neugroschel. New York: Farrar, Straus & Giroux, 1979.

Carmilly-Weinberger, Moshe. *Istoria evreilor din Transilvania (1623–1944)* [History of the Jews of Transylvania (1623–1944)]. Bucharest: Editura Enciclopedică, 1994.

Cârstocea, Raul. "Between Europeanisation and Local Legacies: Holocaust Memory and Contemporary Anti-Semitism in Romania." *East European Politics and Societies* 35, no. 2 (2020): 313–35.

Casanova, Pascale. *The World Republic of Letters.* Translated by M. B. DeBevoise. Cambridge, MA: Harvard University Press, 2007.

Chakrabarty, Dipesh. *Provincializing Europe: Postcolonial Thought and Historical Difference.* Princeton, NJ: Princeton University Press, 2000.

Chaliand, Gérard, and Jean-Pierre Rageau. *The Penguin Atlas of Diasporas.* New York: Penguin Books, 1995.

Chang, Felix B., and Sunnie T. Rucker-Chang. *Roma Rights and Civil Rights: A Transatlantic Comparison.* Cambridge: Cambridge University Press, 2020.

Charnon-Deutsch, Lou. *The Spanish Gypsy: The History of a European Obsession.* University Park: Pennsylvania State University Press, 2004.

Chatterjee, Partha. "The Nationalist Resolution of the Woman's Question." In *Recasting Women: Essays in Indian Colonial History,* edited by Kumkum Sangari and Sudesh Vaid, 233–53. New Brunswick, NJ: Rutgers University Press, 1990.

Cheah, Pheng. *What Is a World? On Postcolonial Literature as World Literature.* Durham, NC: Duke University Press, 2016.

Chen, Khuan-Hsing. *Asia as Method: On Deimperialization.* Durham, NC: Duke University Press, 2010.

Chirot, Daniel. *Social Change in a Peripheral Society: The Creation of a Balkan Colony.* New York: Academic Press, 1976.

Class, Claire Marie. "Beyond the Chicago School: Literature, Gender, and Modernist Sociology in America, 1892–1930." Washington University in St. Louis, 2017.

Clifford, James. *Routes: Travel and Translation in the Late Twentieth Century.* Cambridge, MA: Harvard University Press, 1997.

Codarcea, Cristina. *Société et pouvoir en Valachie (1601–1654): Entre la coutume et la loi* [Society and power in Wallachia (1601–1654): between custom and law]. Bucharest: Editura Enciclopedică, 2002.

Codău, Annamária. "The Acta Comparationis Litterarum Universarum (1877–1888) from the Perspective of Its British Collaborators." *Hungarian Cultural Studies* 10 (2017).

Cohen, Robin, and Paola Toninato, eds. *The Creolization Reader: Studies in Mixed Identities and Cultures.* London: Routledge, 2010.

Connell, Raewyn. *Southern Theory: The Global Dynamics of Knowledge in Social Science.* Cambridge: Polity Press, 2007.

Connell, R. W., and James W. Messerschmidt. "Hegemonic Masculinity: Rethinking the Concept." *Gender and Society* 19, no. 6 (2005): 829–59.

Conrad, Sebastian. *What Is Global History?* Princeton, NJ: Princeton University Press, 2016.

Cooper, Frederick. *Colonialism in Question: Theory, Knowledge, History.* Berkeley: University of California Press, 2005.

Corjescu, Ioan, trans. *Codul Austriac* [The Austrian legal code]. Bucharest: Imprimeria Statului, 1921.

Coronil, Fernando. "Beyond Occidentalism: Toward Nonimperial Geohistorical Categories." *Cultural Anthropology* 11, no. 1 (1996): 51–87.

———. "Latin American Postcolonial Studies and Global Decolonization." *Worlds & Knowledge Otherwise* 3, no. 3 (2013).

Cosma, Viorel. *Figuri de lăutari* [Figures of musicians]. Bucharest: Editura Muzicală, 1960.

Cosma, Valer Simion. "Inventing the Romanian Peasant in Transylvania during the Nineteenth Century." In *Ruralism and Literature in Romania*, edited by Ştefan Baghiu, Vlad Pojoga, and Maria Sass. Berlin: Peter Lang, 2020.

———. "Preoţimea între tradiţie şi modernitate: Intrarea în modernitate [Priesthood between tradition and modernity: entering modernity]." *Caiete de Antropologie Istorică*, no. 15 (2009): 55–68.

Costache, Ioanida. "Until We Are Able to Gas Them Like the Nazis, the Roma Will Infect the Nation: Roma and the Ethnicization of COVID-19 in Romania." *DOR*, April 2020. www.dor.ro/roma-and-the-ethnicization-of-covid-19-in-romania/.

Csucsuja, István. *Istoria pădurilor din Transilvania 1848–1914* [The history of forests in Transylvania 1848–1914]. Cluj-Napoca, Romania: Presa Universitară Clujeană, 1998.

Cuillé, Tili Boon. *Narrative Interludes: Musical Tableaux in Eighteenth-Century French Texts*. Toronto: Toronto University, 2006.

Damrosch, David. "Global Regionalism." *European Review* 15, no. 1 (2007): 135–43.

———. "Rebirth of a Discipline: The Global Origins of Comparative Studies." *Comparative Critical Studies* 3, no. 1–2 (2006): 99–112.

———. *What Is World Literature?* Princeton, NJ: Princeton University Press, 2018.

Davis, David Brion. *The Problem of Slavery in Western Culture*. New York: Oxford University Press, 1988.

Davis, Lloyd. "The Virgin Body as Victorian Text: An Introduction." In *Virginal Sexuality and Textuality in Victorian Literature*, edited by Lloyd Davis, 3–24. Albany: State University of New York Press, 1993.

De Carvalho, Benjamin, Halvard Leira, and John M. Hobson. "The Big Bangs of IR: The Myths that Your Teachers Still Tell You about 1648 and 1919." *Millennium* 39, no. 3 (2011): 735–58.

Deák, Ágnes. "Antencedentele din Austria ale Legii naţionalităţilor din 1868 [Austrian precedents to the nationalities law of 1868]." In *140 de ani de legislaţie minoritară în Europa Centrală şi de Est* [140 years of minority legislation in East-Central Europe], 23–48. Cluj-Napoca, Romania: Editura Institutului pentru Studierea Minorităţilor Naţionale, 2010.

Deleuze, Gilles, and Félix Guattari. *Kafka: Toward a Minor Literature*. Translated by Dana Polan. Minneapolis: University of Minnesota Press, 1986.

Demeter, Attila. "Concepţiile despre naţionalitate ale lui József Eötvös [József Eötvös's understanding of nationality]." In *140 de ani de legislaţie minoritară în Europa Centrală şi de Est* [140 years of minority legislation in East-Central Europe]. Cluj-Napoca, Romania: Editura Institutului pentru Studierea Minorităţilor Naţionale, 2010.

Deteşan, Daniela, ed. *Căsătorie şi moştenire în Transilvania: Documente din a doua jumătate a secolului al XIX-lea* [Marriage and inheritance in Transylvania: documents from the second half of the nineteenth century]. Cluj-Napoca, Romania: Presa Universitară Clujeană, 2013.

D'haen, Theo. *The Routledge Concise History of World Literature*. London: Routledge, 2012.

Djuvara, Neagu. *Între Orient şi Occident: Ţările române la începutul epocii moderne (1800–1848)* [Between Orient and Occident: the Romanian principalities at the dawn of the modern era (1800–1848)]. Translated by Maria Carpov. Bucharest: Humanitas, 1995.

Doyle, Laura. *Inter-Imperiality: Vying Empires, Gendered Labor, and the Literary Arts of Alliance*. Durham, NC: Duke University Press, 2020.

——. "Thinking Back through Empires." *Modernism/modernity* 2, no. 4 (2018).

Doyle, Laura, and Laura Winkiel. "Introduction." In *Geomodernisms: Race, Modernism, Modernity*, edited by Laura Doyle and Laura Winkiel. Bloomington: Indiana University Press, 2006.

Dronca, Lucian. *Băncile româneşti din Transilvania în perioada dualismului austro-ungar (1867–1918)* [Romanian banks in Transylvania during the period of Austro-Hungarian dualism (1867–1918)]. Cluj-Napoca, Romania: Presa Universitară Clujeană, 2003.

——. "Filiale, reuniuni de credit şi asociaţii ale băncilor româneşti din Transilvania in epoca modernă (1867–1918) [Branches, co-ops, and associations of Romanian banks in Transylvania in the modern period (1867–1918)]." *Cumidava* 26 (2003): 106–18.

Dussel, Enrique D. *The Underside of Modernity: Apel, Ricoeur, Rorty, Taylor, and the Philosophy of Liberation*. Translated by Eduardo Mendieta. Atlantic Highlands, NJ: Humanities Press, 1996.

Dussel, Enrique D. "Europe, Modernity, and Eurocentrism." Translated by Javier Krauen and Virginia C. Tuma. *Nepantla: Views from South* 1, no. 3 (2000): 465–78.

El-Tayeb, Fatima. "'Blood Is a Very Special Juice': Racialized Bodies and Citizenship in Twentieth-Century Germany." *International Review of Social History* 44, no. S7 (December 1999): 149–69.

——. *European Others: Queering Ethnicity in Postnational Europe*. Minneapolis: University of Minnesota Press, 2011.

Eminescu, Mihai. *Chestiunea evreiască* [The Jewish question]. Bucharest: Editura Vastala, 2000.

Evans, R. J. W. *Austria, Hungary, and the Habsburgs: Essays on Central Europe c. 1683–1867*. Oxford: Oxford University Press, 2006.

Fanon, Franz. *Black Skin, White Masks*. Translated by Constance Farrington. New York: Grove Press, 1994.

Fassel, Horst, ed. *Hugo Meltzl und die Anfänge der Komparatistik* [Hugo Meltzl and the Beginnings of Comparative Literature]. Stuttgart: Franz Steiner Ferlag, 2005.

Fauser, A. *Musical Encounters at the 1889 Paris World's Fair*. Rochester, NY: University of Rochester Press, 2005.

Federici, Silvia. *Caliban and the Witch: Women, the Body, and Primitive Accumulation*. New York: Autonomedia, 2004.

Fischer-Galati, Stephen. "The Protestant Reformation and Islam." In *The Mutual Effects of the Islamic and Judeo-Christian Worlds: The East European Pattern*, edited by Abraham Ascher, Tibor Halasi-Kun, and Béla K. Király, 53–64. New York: Brooklyn College Press, 1979.

Fleissner, Jennifer L. *Women, Compulsion, Modernity: The Moment of American Naturalism*. Chicago: University of Chicago Press, 2004.

Foucault, Michel. *Discipline and Punish: The Birth of the Prison*. Translated by Alan Sheridan. New York: Vintage, 1995.

——. *The History of Sexuality: An Introduction*. Translated by Robert Hurley. New York: Vintage, 1990.

Frank, Andre Gunder. "Nothing New in the East: No New World Order." *Social Justice* 19, no. 1 (1992).

Freud, Sigmund. "The Taboo of Virginity." In *The Standard Edition of the Complete Psychological Works of Sigmund Freud*. Vol. 11. Translated by James Strachey, 193–208. London: Hogarth Press, 1966.

Friedman, Susan Stanford. *Planetary Modernisms: Provocations on Modernity across Time*. New York: Columbia University Press, 2018.

Furtună, Adrian-Nicolae, and Victor-Claudiu Turcitu, eds. *Sclavia romilor și locurile memoriei—album de istorie socială* [Roma slavery and the places of memory—album of social history] (Bucharest: Dykhta! Publishing House, 2021).

Futabatei, Shimei. *Japan's First Modern Novel: Ukigumo of Futabatei Shimei*. Translated by Marleigh Grayer Ryan. Ann Arbor: Center for Japanese Studies, University of Michigan, 1990.

Gal, Susan. "Polyglot Nationalism: Alternative Perspectives on Language in Nineteenth Century Hungary." *Langage et Société* 2, no. 136 (2011): 31–54.

Gammerl, Benno. *Subjects, Citizens, and Others: Administering Ethnic Heterogeneity in the British and Habsburg Empires, 1867–1918*. New York: Berghahn Books, 2018.

Gebora, A. "Situația juridică a țiganilor în Ardeal [The juridical situation of Gypsies in Transylvania]." In *Rromii în istoria României*. Bucharest: Editura Centrului Rromilor, 2002.

Geertz, Clifford. *The Interpretation of Cultures: Selected Essays* (New York: Basic Books: 1973).

Genette, Gérard. *Narrative Discourse: An Essay in Method*. Translated by Jane E. Lewin. Ithaca, NY: Cornell University Press, 1980.

Gerard, Emily. *The Land beyond the Forest: Facts, Figures, and Fancies from Transylvania*. New York: Harper & Brothers, 1888.

Gerber, Jane S. *The Jews of Spain: A History of the Sephardic Experience*. New York: Free Press, 1994.

Gheran, Niculae. *Tânărul Rebreanu* [Young Rebreanu]. Bucharest: Editura Albatros, 1986.

Gidó, Attila. "Identitatea evreilor ardeleni în perioada interbelică" [The identity of Transylvanian Jews in the interwar period]." *Revista de Istorie a Evreilor din România* 1 (2016): 52–64.

Gikandi, Simon. "The Fragility of Languages." *PMLA* 130, no. 1 (2015): 9–14.

Gilman, Charlotte Perkins. *The New Mothers of a New World*. New York: Charlton, 1913.

Ginelli, Zoltán. "Plotting the Semiperipheral Empire: Hungarian Balkanism and Global Colonialism in Geographical Knowledge, 1867–1948." In *De-Linking—Critical Thought and Radical Politics*, edited by Manuela Boatcă. Abingdon, VA: Routledge, forthcoming.

Giurescu, Constantin C. *A History of the Romanian Forest*. Bucharest: Editura Academiei Republicii Socialiste România, 1980.

Glick-Schiller, Nina, Ayşe Çağlar, and Thaddeus Guldbrandsen. "Beyond the Ethnic Lens: Locality, Globality, and Born-Again Incorporation." *American Ethnologist* 33, no. 4 (2006): 612–33.

Glissant, Édouard. *Poetics of Relation*. Translated by Betsy Wing. Ann Arbor: University of Michigan Press, 2010.

Goldberg, David Theo. "Racial Europeanization." *Ethnic and Racial Studies* 29 (2006): 331–64.

Gopal, Priyamvada. *Literary Radicalism in India: Gender, Nation and the Transition to Independence*. London: Routledge, 2012.

Gorski, Philip. "Secularity 1: Varieties and Dilemmas." In *A Secular Age beyond the West: Religion, Law and the State in Asia, the Middle East and North Africa*, edited by

Mirjam Künkler, John Madeley, and Shylashri Shankar. Cambridge: Cambridge University Press, 2018.

Grellmann, H. *Dissertation on the Gipseys.* London: Printed by William Ballintine, 1807.

Grigoraş, N. "Robia în Moldova [Slavery in Moldova]." In *Robia ţiganilor în Ţările Române,* edited by Vasile Ionescu. Bucharest: Editura Centrului Rromilor, 2000.

Grosfoguel, Ramón. "From Postcolonial Studies to Decolonial Studies: Decolonizing Postcolonial Studies." *Review (Fernand Braudel Center)* 29, no. 2 (2006): 141–220.

Grosfoguel, Ramón, Nelson Maldonado-Torres, and José David Saldivar, eds. *Latin@s in the World-System: Decolonization Struggles in the 21st Century U.S. Empire.* New York: Routledge, 2016.

Gutiérrez Rodríguez, Encarnación, and Shirley Anne Tate. *Creolizing Europe: Legacies and Transformations.* Liverpool: Liverpool University Press, 2017.

Gyémánt, Ladislau. *Evreii din Transilvania în epoca emancipării/The Jews of Transylvania in the Age of Emancipation (1790–1867).* Bucharest: Editura Enciclopedică, 2000.

——. "The Transylvanian Jewish Identity's Avatars in the Epoch of Emancipation." In *Building Identities in Transylvania: A Comparative Approach,* edited by Sorin Mitu. Cluj-Napoca, Romania: Argonaut, 2014.

Hall, Stuart. "Créolité and the Process of Creolization." In *The Creolization Reader: Studies in Mixed Identities and Cultures,* edited by Robin Cohen and Paola Toninato, 26–38. London: Routledge, 2010.

Hancock, Ian. *The Pariah Syndrome: An Account of Gypsy Slavery and Persecution.* Ann Arbor, MI: Karoma Publishers, 1988.

Hancock, Ian, Siobhan Dowd, and Rajko Djurić, eds. *The Roads of the Roma: A PEN Anthology of Gypsy Writers.* Hatfield, UK: University of Hertfordshire Press, 1998.

Hayot, Eric, and Rebecca Walkowitz, eds. *A New Vocabulary for Global Modernism.* New York: Columbia University Press, 2016.

Hering Torres, Max-Sebastián. *Rassismus in der Vormoderne: Die "Reinheit des Blutes" im Spanien der Frühen Neuzeit* [Racism during Premodernity: The 'Purity of Blood' in Early Modern Spain]. Frankfurt: Campus Verlag, 2006.

Hill, Christopher L. "Nana in the World: Novel, Gender, and Transnational Form." *Modern Language Quarterly* 72, no. 1 (2011): 75–105.

——. "Travels of Naturalism and the Challenges of a World Literary History." *Literature Compass* 6, no. 6 (2009): 1198–1210.

Hitchins, Keith. *A Nation Affirmed: The Romanian National Movement in Transylvania, 1860–1914.* Bucharest: Encyclopaedic Publishing House, 1999.

——. *Orthodoxy and Nationality: Andreiu Şaguna and the Rumanians of Transylvania, 1846–1873.* Cambridge, MA: Harvard University Press, 1977.

Hodoş, Constanţa. *Martirii* [The martyrs]. Bucharest: Minerva, 1908.

Hoensch, Jörg K. *A History of Modern Hungary 1867–1994.* London: Longman, 1996.

Hoganson, Kristin L., and Jay Sexton. "Introduction." In *Crossing Empires: Taking U.S. History into Transimperial Terrain.* Durham, NC: Duke University Press, 2020.

Horne, Gerald. *Confronting Black Jacobins: The United States, the Haitian Revolution, and the Origins of the Dominican Republic.* New York: NYU Press, 2015.

Horvath, Traude, and Gerda Neyer, eds. *Auswanderungen aus Österreich: von der Mitte des 19. Jahrhunderts bis zur Gegenwart: mit einer umfassenden Bibliographie zur Österreichischen Migrationsgeschichte* [Emigration from Austria: From the mid-19th century until the present: with a comprehensive bibliography on Austria's migration history]. Vienna: Böhlau, 1996.

Horvathová, E., and S. Augustini. "Nachwort." In *Cigáni v Uhorsku/Zigeuner in Ungarn* [Gypsies in Hungary]. Bratislava, Slovakia: Štúdio DD, 1995.

Houze, Rebecca. *Textiles, Fashion, and Design Reform in Austria-Hungary before the First World War: Principles of Dress*. Burlington, VT: Ashgate Publishing, 2015.

Ignat-Coman, Luminița. "Identitate reprimată: Legislație și deznaționalizare în Transilvania dualistă [Repressed identity: legislation and denationalizing in dualist Transylvania]." In *140 de ani de legislație minoritară în Europa Centrală și de Est* [140 years of minority legislation in East-Central Europe]. Cluj-Napoca, Romania: Editura Institutului pentru Studierea Minorităților Naționale, 2010.

"An Imperial Dynamo? CEH Forum on Pieter Judson's *The Habsburg Empire: A New History*." *Central European History* 50, no. 2 (June 2017): 236–59.

Iordachi, Constantin. *Liberalism, Constitutional Nationalism, and Minorities: The Making of Romanian Citizenship, c. 1750–1918*. Leiden: Brill, 2019.

Iorga, Nicolae. *Istoria bisericii românești și a vietii religioase a românilor* [History of the Romanian church and of the religious life of Romanians]. Vol. 1. Vălenii-de-munte: Tipografia Neamul Românesc, 1908.

Iser, Wolfgang. "Interaction between Text and Reader." In *The Reader in the Text: Essays on Audience and Interpretation*, edited by Inge Crosman and Susan Rubin Suleiman. Princeton, NJ: Princeton University Press, 1980.

Ittu, Gudrun-Liane. "Aspecte ale emancipării femeii în mediul protestant (lutheran) german (săsesc) din Transilvania, în a doua jumătate a sec. al XIX-lea și începutul sec. XX-lea [Aspects of women's emancipation in the Protestant (Lutheran) German (Saxon) milieu in the second half of the nineteenth century and the beginning of the twentieth century]." In *Anuarul Institutului de Cercetări Socio-Umane*. Sibiu, Romania: Editura Academiei Române, 2005.

Iudean, Ovidiu Emil. *The Romanian Governmental Representatives in the Budapest Parliament*. Cluj-Napoca, Romania: Mega Publishing House, 2016.

Jabeen, Neelam. "Women, Land, Embodiment: A Case of Postcolonial Ecofeminism." *Interventions* 22, no 8 (2020): 1–15.

Jayawardena, Kumari. *Feminism and Nationalism in the Third World*. New York: Verso, 2016.

Jovanović, Miloš, and Giulia Carabelli. "Introduction." *History of the Present* 10, no. 1 (2020).

Judson, Pieter M. *The Habsburg Empire: A New History*. Cambridge, MA: Belknap Press, 2016.

Juillard, A. "Le vocabulaire argotique roumain d'origine tsigane." *Cahiers Sextil Pușcariu* 1 (1952): 151–81.

Jusová, Iveta. "Figuring the Other in Nineteenth-Century Czech Literature: Gabriela Preissová and Bozena Viková-Kunetická." In *History of the Literary Cultures of East-Central Europe*, edited by Marcel Cornis-Pope and John Neubauer, 367–77. Amsterdam: John Benjamins Publishing, 2010.

Kabir, Ananya Jahanara. "Elmina as Postcolonial Space: Transoceanic Creolization and the Fabric of Memory." *Interventions* 22, no. 8 (2020): 994–1012.

——. "Rapsodia Ibero-Indiana: Transoceanic Creolization and the Mando of Goa." *Modern Asian Studies*, 2021, 1–56.

Kalmijn, Matthijs. "Intermarriage and Homogamy: Causes, Patterns, Trends." *Annual Review of Sociology* 24, no. 1 (1998): 395–421.

Kamen, Henry. *Spain's Road to Empire: The Making of a World Power, 1492–1763*. London: Penguin, 2003.

Karatani, Kōjin. *Origins of Modern Japanese Literature*. Translated by Brett de Bary. Durham, NC: Duke University Press, 1993.

Katz, Ethan B., Lisa Moses Leff, and Maud S. Mandel, eds. *Colonialism and the Jews*. Bloomington: Indiana University Press, 2017.

Katznelson, Ira. "A Form of Liberty and Indulgence: Toleration as a Layered Institution." In *Boundaries of Toleration*, edited by Alfred Stepan and Charles Taylor, 37–58. New York: Columbia University Press, 2014.

Keim, Wiebke, Ercüment Çelik, Christian Ersche, and Veronika Wöhrer, eds. *Global Knowledge Production in the Social Sciences: Made in Circulation*. London: Routledge, 2016.

Kerekes, Sándor. *Lomnitzi Meltzl Hugó 1846–1908*. Budapest: Minerva-Könyvtár, 1937.

Kessler-Harris, Alice. "Gender and Work: Possibilities for a Global, Historical Overview." In *Women's History in Global Perspective*, edited by Bonnie G. Smith, 145–94. Urbana: University of Illinois Press, 2004.

Kim, Claire Jean. *Bitter Fruit: The Politics of Black-Korean Conflict in New York City*. New Haven, CT: Yale University Press, 2003.

Komlos, John. *The Habsburg Monarchy as a Customs Union: Economic Development in Austria-Hungary in the Nineteenth Century*. Princeton, NJ: Princeton University Press, 1983.

Komlosy, Andrea. "Imperial Cohesion, Nation-Building, and Regional Integration in the Habsburg Monarchy." In *Nationalizing Empires*, edited by Stefan Berger and Alexei Miller. Budapest: Central European University Press, 2015.

——. *Work: The Last 1,000 Years*. Translated by Jacob K. Watson and Loren Balhorn. London: Verso, 2018.

Koobak, Redi, Madina Tlostanova, and Suruchi Thapar-Björkert, eds. *Postcolonial and Postsocialist Dialogues: Intersections, Opacities, Challenges in Feminist Theorizing and Practice*. London: Routledge, 2021.

Korzeniewicz, Roberto Patricio, and Timothy Patrick Moran. *Unveiling Inequality: A World-Historical Perspective*. New York: Russell Sage Foundation, 2009.

Kovačević, Nataša. *Narrating Post/Communism: Colonial Discourse and Europe's Borderline Civilization*. New York: Routledge, 2008.

Kovács, Iosif. *Desființarea relațiilor feudale în Transilvania* [The abolition of feudal relations in Transylvania]. Cluj-Napoca, Romania: Editura Dacia, 1973.

Kristó, Gyula. *Hungarian History in the Ninth Century*. Szeged, Hungary: Szegedi Középkorász Műhely, 1996.

Kulawik, Teresa, and Zhanna Kravchenko, eds. *Borderlands in European Gender Studies: Beyond the East–West Frontier*. London: Routledge, 2019.

Kürti, László. *The Remote Borderland: Transylvania in the Hungarian Imagination*. Albany, NY: SUNY Press, 2001.

Lago, Enrico Dal. "Second Slavery, Second Serfdom, and Beyond: The Atlantic Plantation System and the Eastern and Southern European Landed Estate System in Comparative Perspective, 1800–60." *Review (Fernand Braudel Center)* 32, no. 4 (2009): 391–420.

Lang, Marshall. *The Armenians: A People in Exile*. London: Unwin Hyman, 1981.

Lazreg, Marnia. *The Eloquence of Silence: Algerian Women in Question*. New York: Routledge, 1994.

Lee, Richard E., and Immanuel Wallerstein, eds. *Overcoming the Two Cultures: Science vs. the Humanities in the Modern World-System*. New York: Routledge, 2015.

Leeb-du Toit, Juliette. *isishweshwe: A History of the Indigenisation of Blueprint in South Africa*. Pietermaritzburg, South Africa: University of KwaZulu-Natal Press, 2017.

Levine, Caroline. "The Great Unwritten: World Literature and the Effacement of Orality." *Modern Language Quarterly* 74, no. 2 (2013): 217–37.

Liggins, Emma. *Odd Women? Spinsters, Lesbians and Widows in British Women's Fiction, 1850s–1930s*. Manchester, UK: Manchester University Press, 2016.

Lionnet, Françoise, and Shu-mei Shih, eds. *The Creolization of Theory*. Durham, NC: Duke University Press, 2011.

Lipstadt, Deborah E. *Antisemitism: Here and Now*. New York: Schocken, 2019.

Liszt, Franz. *The Gipsy in Music*. Translated by Edwin Evans. London: William Reeves, n.d.

Livezeanu, Irina. *Cultural Politics in Greater Romania: Regionalism, Nation Building, and Ethnic Struggle, 1918–1930*. Ithaca, NY: Cornell University Press, 2000.

Lovinescu, Eugen. *Istoria civilizației române moderne* [History of Romanian modern civilization]. Bucharest: Editura Științifică, 1972.

Lyon, Janet. "Gadže Modernism." *Modernism/modernity* 11, no. 3 (2004): 517–38.

Magocsi, Paul R. *The People from Nowhere: An Illustrated History of Carpatho-Rusyns*. Uzhgorod, Ukraine: Padjaka, 2006.

——. *With Their Backs to the Mountains: A History of Carpathian Rus' and Carpatho-Rusyns*. Budapest: Central European University Press, 2015.

Mahmood, Saba. *Religious Difference in a Secular Age: A Minority Report*. Princeton, NJ: Princeton University Press, 2015.

Majstorović, Danijela. *Discourse and Affect in Postsocialist Bosnia and Herzegovina: Peripheral Selves*. London: Palgrave Macmillan, 2021.

Malița, Liviu. *Alt Rebreanu* [A different Rebreanu]. Cluj-Napoca, Romania: Cartimpex, 2000.

Mamozai, Martha. *Herrenmenschen: Frauen im deutschen Kolonialismus* [Master People: Women during German Colonial Rule]. Hamburg: Rowohlt, 1982.

Manolescu, Nicolae. *Arca lui Noe*. Bucharest: Editura Minerva, 1980.

Margócsy, István. "When Language Became Ideology: Hungary in the Eighteenth Century." In *Latin at the Crossroads of Identity*, edited by Gábor Almási and Lav Šubarić, 32–33. Leiden, Netherlands: Brill, 2015.

Marin, Irina. *Peasant Violence and Antisemitism in Early Twentieth-Century Eastern Europe*. Cham, Switzerland: Springer, 2018.

Martin, Mircea, Christian Moraru, and Andrei Terian, eds. *Romanian Literature as World Literature*. New York: Bloomsbury Academic, 2017.

Masuzawa, Tomoko. *The Invention of World Religions: Or, How European Universalism Was Preserved in the Language of Pluralism*. Chicago: University of Chicago Press, 2005.

Matache, Margareta, and Cornel West. "Roma and African Americans Share a Common Struggle." *The Guardian*, February 20, 2018.

Matache, Margareta, and Jacqueline Bhabha. "Anti-Roma Racism Is Spiraling during COVID-19 Pandemic." *Health and Human Rights* 22, no. 1 (2020): 379–82.

Matras, Yaron. *The Romani Gypsies*. Cambridge, MA: Belknap Press, 2015.

McArthur, Marilyn. "The Saxon Germans: Political Fate of an Ethnic Identity." *Dialectical Anthropology* 1, no. 1–4 (January 1975): 349–64.

McClintock, Anne. *Imperial Leather: Race, Gender, and Sexuality in the Colonial Contest*. New York: Routledge, 1995.

Meier, Prita. "Authenticity and Its Modernist Discontents: The Colonial Encounter and African and Middle Eastern Art History." *Arab Studies Journal* 18, no. 1 (2010): 12–45.

Meltzl, Hugo. "Present Tasks of Comparative Literature." In *The Princeton Sourcebook in Comparative Literature: From the European Enlightenment to the Global Present*, edited by David Damrosch, Mbongiseni Buthelezi, and Natalie Melas, 41–49. Princeton, NJ: Princeton University Press, 2009.

Mendelsohn, Ezra. *The Jews of East Central Europe between the World Wars*. Bloomington: Indiana University Press, 1987.

Mies, Maria. *Patriarchy and Accumulation on a World Scale: Women in the International Division of Labour*. London: Zed Books, 1986.

Mignolo, Walter. "Imperial/Colonial Metamorphosis: A Decolonial Narrative, from the Ottoman Sultanate and Spanish Empire to the US and the EU." In *The Oxford Handbook of Postcolonial Studies*, edited by Graham Huggan. Oxford: Oxford University Press, 2013.

Mignolo, Walter D. "Colonialidad global, capitalism y hegemonía epistémica [Global coloniality, capitalism and epistemic hegemony]." In *Indisciplinar las ciencias sociales: Geopoliticas del conocimiento y colonialidad del poder* [Undisciplining the social sciences: Geopolitics of knowledge and coloniality of power], edited by Catherine Walsh, Freya Schiwy, and Santiago Castro-Gómez. Quito, Ecuador: Ediciones Abya-Yala, 2002.

——. *The Darker Side of Western Modernity: Global Futures, Decolonial Options*. Durham, NC: Duke University Press, 2011.

——. "Huntington's Fears." In *Latin@s in the World-System: Decolonization Struggles in the 21st Century US Empire*, edited by Ramón Grosfoguel, Nelson Maldonado-Torres, and José David Saldivar. New York: Routledge, 2016.

——. *Local Histories/Global Designs: Coloniality, Subaltern Knowledges, and Border Thinking*. Princeton, NJ: Princeton University Press, 2000.

Miller, Joshua L. *Accented America: The Cultural Politics of Multilingual Modernism*. Oxford: Oxford University Press, 2011.

Mintz, Sidney W. "The Localization of Anthropological Practice: From Area Studies to Transnationalism." *Critique of Anthropology* 18, no. 2 (1998): 117–33.

Mircea, I. R. "Termenii rob, șerb și holop în documentele slave și române [The meanings of rob, șerb and holop in Slavonic and Romanian documents]." In *Robia țiganilor în Țările Române* [Gypsy slavery in the Romanian principalities], edited by Vasile Ionescu, 61–74. Bucharest: Editura Centrului Rromilor pentru politici publice "Aven amentza," 2000.

Mitu, Sorin. *Transilvania mea: Istorii, mentalități, identități* [My Transylvania: histories, mentalities, identities]. Iași, Romania: Polirom, 2006.

——. *Ungurii despre români: Nașterea unei imagini etnice* [Hungarians about Romanians: the birth of an ethnic image]. Iași, Romania: Polirom, 2014.

Mohanty, Chandra Talpade, Ann Russo, and Lourdes Torres, eds. *Third World Women and the Politics of Feminism*. Bloomington: Indiana University Press, 1991.

Moore, Jason W. "Sugar and the Expansion of the Early Modern World-Economy: Commodity Frontiers, Ecological Transformation, and Industrialization." *Review (Fernand Braudel Center)* 23, no. 3 (2000): 409–33.

Moraña, Mabel, Enrique D. Dussel, and Carlos A. Jáuregui, eds. *Coloniality at Large: Latin America and the Postcolonial Debate*. Durham, NC: Duke University Press, 2008.

Moretti, Franco. "Conjectures on World Literature." *New Left Review* 1 (2000): 54–68.

Morrison, Toni. *Playing in the Dark*. New York: Vintage, 1992.

Mudure, Mihaela. "Blackening Gypsy Slavery: The Romanian Case." In *Blackening Europe: The African American Presence*, edited by Heike Raphael-Hernandez. New York: Routledge, 2004.

Mufti, Aamir R. "Auerbach in Istanbul: Edward Said, Secular Criticism, and the Question of Minority Culture." *Critical Inquiry* 25, no. 1 (1998): 95–125.

Murphy, Michael, and Harry White, eds. *Musical Constructions of Nationalism: Essays on the History and Ideology of European Musical Culture 1800–1945*. Cork, Ireland: Cork University Press, 2001.

Neubauer, John, and Marcel Cornis-Pope. "Transylvania's Literary Cultures." In *History of the Literary Cultures of East-Central Europe*, edited by Marcel Cornis-Pope and John Neubauer. Vol. 2. Amsterdam: John Benjamins Publishing, 2004.

Neumann, Victor. *Istoria evreilor din Banat* [The history of Jews in Banat]. Bucharest: Atlas, 1999.

Nirenberg, David. *Anti-Judaism: The Western Tradition*. New York: W. W. Norton, 2013.

——. *Communities of Violence: Persecution of Minorities in the Middle Ages*. Princeton, NJ: Princeton University Press, 2015.

Norich, Anita, and Joshua L. Miller. *Languages of Modern Jewish Cultures: Comparative Perspectives*. Ann Arbor: University of Michigan Press, 2016.

North, Michael. *The Dialect of Modernism: Race, Language, and Twentieth-Century Literature*. Oxford: Oxford University Press, 1994.

Oişteanu, Andrei. *Imaginea evreului în cultura română* [The image of the Jew in Romanian culture]. Bucharest: Humanitas, 2001.

——. *Sexualitate şi societate: Istorie, religie şi literatură* [Sexuality and society: history, religion and literature]. Iaşi, Romania: Polirom, 2016.

Onofreiu, Adrian. *Districtul Năsăudului (1861–1876)*. Cluj-Napoca, Romania: Editura Argonaut, 2009.

Onofreiu, Adrian, and Ioan Bolovan. *Contribuţii documentare privind istoria regimentului grăniceresc năsăudean* [Documentary contributions to the history of the Năsăud border regiment]. Bucharest: Editura Enciclopedică, 2006.

Oualdi, M'hamed. *A Slave between Empires: A Transimperial History of North Africa*. New York: Columbia University Press, 2020.

Păcăţian, Teodor. *Cartea de aur sau luptele naţionale ale românilor de sub coroana ungară* [The golden book or, the Romanian national struggle under the Hungarian crown]. Vol. 8. Sibiu, Romania: Tiparul Tipografiei Arhidiecezane, 1915.

Pál, Judit. "Armenian Society in 18th Century Transylvania." In *Studies in the History of Early Modern Transylvania*, edited by Gyöngy Kovács Kiss, 151–78. New York: Columbia University Press, 2011.

——. *Armenians in Transylvania: Their Contribution to the Urbanization and the Economic Development of the Province*. Translated by Bogdan Aldea. Cluj-Napoca: Romanian Cultural Institute, 2005.

——. "Assimilation and Identity of the Transylvanian Armenians in the 19th Century." In *Building Identities in Transylvania: A Comparative Approach*, edited by Sorin Mitu. Cluj-Napoca, Romania: Argonaut, 2014.

Pál, Judit, Vlad Popovici, Andrea Fehér, and Ovidiu Emil Iudean, eds. *Parliamentary Elections in Eastern Hungary and Transylvania (1865–1918)*. Berlin: Peter Lang, 2018.

Palmié, Stephan. "Creolization and Its Discontents." *Annual Review of Anthropology* 35 (2006): 433–56.

Palumbo-Liu, David, Bruce Robbins, and Nirvana Tanoukhi, eds. *Immanuel Wallerstein and the Problem of the World: System, Scale, Culture*. Durham, NC: Duke University Press, 2011.

Papadat-Bengescu, Hortensia. *Ape adânci* [Deep waters]. Bucharest: Editura Librăriei Alcalay, 1919.

Parsons, Timothy. *The Rule of Empires: Those Who Built Them, Those Who Endured Them, and Why They Always Fall*. Oxford: Oxford University Press, 2010.

Parvulescu, Anca. "Eastern Europe as Method." *SEEJ* 63, no. 4 (2019): 470–81.

——. "Istanbul, Capital of Comparative Literature." *MLN* 135, no. 5 (2020): 1232–57.

——. *The Traffic in Women's Work: East European Migration and the Making of Europe*. Chicago: University of Chicago Press, 2014.

——. "The World of World Literature and World-Systems Analysis." *symplokē* 28, no. 1–2 (2020): 375–83.

Pascu, Ștefan. *A History of Transylvania*. Translated by Robert Ladd. Detroit: Wayne State University Press, 1982.

Patai, Raphael. *The Jews of Hungary: History, Culture, Psychology*. Detroit: Wayne State University Press, 1996.

Patterson, Orlando. *Slavery and Social Death: A Comparative Study*. Cambridge, MA: Harvard University Press, 1982.

Pelizzon, Sheila Margaret. "But Can She Spin? The Decline in the Social Standing of Women in the Transition from Feudalism to Capitalism." State University of New York at Binghamton, 1999.

Pemán, Miguel Laborda, and Tine De Moor. "A Tale of Two Commons. Some Preliminary Hypotheses on the Long-Term Development of the Commons in Western and Eastern Europe, 11th–19th Centuries." *International Journal of the Commons* 7, no. 1 (2013).

Perloff, Marjorie. *Edge of Irony: Modernism in the Shadow of the Habsburg Empire*. Chicago: University of Chicago Press, 2016.

Petcuț, Petre. *Rromii: Sclavie și libertate* [Roma: slavery and freedom]. Bucharest: Editura Centrului Național de Cultură a Romilor, 2016.

Péter, László, ed. *Historians and the History of Transylvania*. Boulder, CO: East European Monographs, 1993.

Petersen, Hans-Christian, and Jannis Panagiotidis. "Historischer Kontext: Deutsche in und aus Osteuropa | bpb." https://www.bpb.de/izpb/298553/historischer-kontext -deutsche-in-und-aus-osteuropa.

Piotrowska, Anna G. *Gypsy Music in European Culture: From the Late Eighteenth to the Early Twentieth Centuries*. Translated by Guy R. Torr. Boston: Northeastern University Press, 2013.

Popa, Mircea. "Un comparatist sas din Transilvania: Hugo Meltzl (1846–1908) [A Saxon comparatist from Transylvania: Hugo Meltzl (1846–1908)]," *Convergențe europene* [European convergences] (Oradea, Romania: Editura Cogito, 1995), 187–200.

Potra, George. *Contribuțiuni la istoricul țiganilor din România* [Contributions to the history of Gypsies in Romania]. Bucharest: Fundația Regelui Carol I, 1939.

Pozsony, Ferenc. "The Ethnicization of Religious Identity: The Case of Szekler Sabbatarians." In *Integrating Minorities: Traditional Communities and Modernization*, edited by Agnieszka Barszczewska and Lehel Peti, 119–38. Cluj-Napoca: Romanian Institute for Research on National Minorities, 2011.

Pratt, Mary Louise. "Language and the Afterlives of Empire." *PMLA* 130, no. 2 (2015): 348–57.

Prestholdt, Jeremy. *Domesticating the World: African Consumerism and the Genealogies of Globalization*. Berkeley: University of California Press, 2008.

Proust, Marcel. *Swann's Way*. Translated by Lydia Davis. New York: Penguin Books, 2002.

Quijano, Aníbal. "Coloniality of Power, Eurocentrism, and Latin America." *Nepantla: Views from South* 1, no. 3 (2000): 533–80.

Quijano, Aníbal, and Immanuel Wallerstein. "Americanity as a Concept, or the Americas in the Modern World." *International Social Science Journal* 44, no. 4 (1992): 549–57.

Rădulescu, Andrei, ed. *Carte românească de învățătură*. Bucharest: Editura Academiei Republicii Populare Române, 1961.

——, ed. *Codul Calimach*. Bucharest: Editura Academiei Republicii Populare Române, 1958.

——, ed. *Legiuirea Caragea*. Bucharest: Editura Academiei Republicii Populare Române, 1955.

——. *Pagini din istoria dreptului românesc* [Pages from the history of Romanian law]. Bucharest: Editura Academiei Republicii Socialiste România, 1970.

——, ed. *Pravilniceasca Condică*. Bucharest: Editura Academiei Republicii Populare Române, 1957.

——, ed. *Sobornicescul Hristov*. Bucharest: Editura Academiei Republicii Populare Române, 1958.

Raicu, Lucian. *Liviu Rebreanu*. Bucharest: Editura pentru literatură, 1967.

Ramaswamy, Sumathi. *Passions of the Tongue: Language Devotion in Tamil India, 1891–1970*. Berkeley: University of California Press, 1997.

Ramazani, Jahan. "Code-Switching, Code-Stitching: A Macaronic Poetics?" *Dibur Literary Journal*, 2015.

——. *The Hybrid Muse: Postcolonial Poetry in English*. Chicago: University of Chicago Press, 2001.

Râmneanțu, Petru. "Studiu asupra depopulării Banatului. Cauzele depopularii. Rezultatele anchetei demografice din comuna Banloc, județul Timiș/Torontal." *Buletin Eugenic si Biopolitic* 6, no.10-11-12 (1935): 310–311.

Randeria, Shalini. "Entangled Histories of Uneven Modernities: Civil Society, Caste Solidarities and Legal Pluralism in Post-Colonial India." In *Unraveling Ties: From Social Cohesion to New Practices of Connectedness*, edited by Yehuda Elkana, Ivan Krastev, Elísio Macamo, and Shalini Randeria, 284–311. Frankfurt: Campus Verlag, 2002.

Randeria, Shalini, Martin Fuchs, and Antje Linkenbach. "Konfigurationen der Moderne: Zur Einleitung [Configurations of Modernity: An Introduction]." In *Konfiguration der Moderne: Diskurse Zu Indien* [Configurations of Modernity: Discourses on India], *Soziale Welt Sonderband* 15 (2004): 1–34.

Rebreanu, Liviu. *Amalgam*, ed. Niculae Gheran, vol. 15, *Opere*. Bucharest: Editura Minerva, 1991.

——. *Ion*. Translated by A. Hillard. London: Peter Owen, 1965.

——. *Ion*. Edited by Niculae Gheran. Vol. 4. *Opere*. Bucharest: Editura Minerva, 1970.

——. *Lauda țăranului român* [In praise of the Romanian peasant]. Bucharest: Imprimeria Națională, 1940.

Reddock, Rhoda. "Women and Slavery in the Caribbean: A Feminist Perspective." *Latin American Perspectives* 44, no. 12/1 (1985), 63–80.

Retegan, Simion. *Satele năsăudene la mijlocul secolului al XIX-lea: Mărturii documentare* [Villages in the Năsăud region in mid nineteenth century: documents]. Cluj-Napoca, Romania: Accent, 2002.

Rexhepi, Piro. "Imperial Inventories, 'Illegal Mosques' and Institutionalized Islam: Coloniality and the Islamic Community of Bosnia and Herzegovina." *History and Anthropology* 30, no. 4 (2019): 477–89.

Rigó, Máté. "The Long First World War and the Survival of Business Elites in East-Central Europe: Transylvania's Industrial Boom and the Enrichment of Economic Elites." *European Review of History: Revue européenne d'histoire* 24, no. 2 (2017): 250–72.

Rindler Schjerve, Rosita. *Diglossia and Power: Language Policies and Practice in the 19th Century Habsburg Empire*. Berlin: Mouton de Gruyter, 2003.

Ritchie, Susan. "The Pasha of Buda and the Edict of Torda." *Journal of Unitarian Universalist History* 30 (2005): 36–54.

Ritoók, Emma de, and Charlotte de Geőcze. *Le problème de la Hongrie: les femmes hongroises aux femmes du monde civilisé* [The problem of Hungary: Hungarian women address the women of the civilized world]. Budapest: Ferdinand Pfeifer Libraires-Editeurs, 1920.

Roman, Viorel, and Hannes Hofbauer. *Transilvania: românii la încrucişarea intereselor imperiale* [Transylvania: Romanians at the crossroads of imperial interests]. Vienna: Editura Nova, 1998.

Rubin, Gayle. "The Traffic in Women: Notes on the 'Political Economy' of Sex." In *Toward an Anthropology of Women*, edited by Rayna R. Reiter, 157–210. New York: Monthly Review Press, 1975.

Sabău, Claudia Septimia. *"Şi ne-au făcut din grăniceri, ţărani . . ." Mentalităţi colective în satele năsăudene foste grănicereşti în a doua jumătate a secolului al XIX-lea* ["And they transformed us from soldiers into peasants": collective mentalities in villages of the Năsăud region, formerly the border regiment, in the second half of the nineteenth century]. Cluj-Napoca, Romania: Editura Mega, 2015.

Said, Edward W. *Culture and Imperialism*. New York: Vintage, 1994.

——. *Representations of the Intellectual*. New York: Vintage, 2012.

——. "Yeats and Decolonization." In *Culture and Imperialism*. New York: Vintage, 1994.

Santos, Boaventura de Sousa. "Nuestra América." *Theory, Culture & Society* 18, no. 2–3 (2001): 185–217.

Saul, Nicholas. *Gypsies and Orientalism in German Literature and Anthropology of the Long Nineteenth Century*. London: Legenda, 2007.

Saussy, Haun. "Exquisite Cadavers Stitched from Fresh Nightmares." In *Comparative Literature in an Age of Globalization*, edited by Haun Saussy. Baltimore: Johns Hopkins University Press, 2006.

Schorske, Carl E. *Fin-de-Siècle Vienna: Politics and Culture*. New York: Vintage, 1981.

Schultz, Hans-Joachim, and Phillip H. Rhein, eds. *Comparative Literature: The Early Years* (Chapel Hill: University of North Carolina Press, 1973).

Schulze, Max-Stephan, and Nikolaus Wolf. "Economic Nationalism and Economic Integration: The Austro-Hungarian Empire in the Late Nineteenth Century." *Economic History Review* 65, no. 2 (2012): 652–73.

——. "On the Origins of Border Effects: Insights from the Habsburg Empire." *Journal of Economic Geography* 9, no. 1 (2009): 117–36.

Schwartz, Agatha. *Shifting Voices: Feminist Thought and Women's Writing in Fin-de-Siècle Austria and Hungary*. Montreal: McGill-Queen's University Press, 2008.

Shachar, Ayelet. *The Birthright Lottery: Citizenship and Global Inequality*. Cambridge, MA: Harvard University Press, 2009.

Shih, Shu-mei. "Comparative Racialization: An Introduction." *PMLA* 123, no. 5 (2008): 1347–62.

——. "Comparison as Relation." In *Comparison: Theories, Approaches, Uses*, edited by Rita Felski and Susan Stanford Friedman. Baltimore: Johns Hopkins University Press, 2013.

——. "Theory in a Relational World," *Comparative Literature Studies* 53, no. 4 (2016): 722–46.

Shklovsky, Viktor. "Art as Technique" in *Russian Formalist Criticism: Four Essays*. Lincoln: University of Nebraska Press, 1965.

Shohat, Ella. "Rethinking Jews and Muslims: Quincentennial Reflections." *Middle East Report* 22 (1992): 25.

Shore, Paul J. *Narratives of Adversity: Jesuits in the Eastern Peripheries of the Habsburg Realms (1640–1773)*. Budapest: Central European University Press, 2012.

Shulman, Alix Kates. *Red Emma Speaks: An Emma Goldman Reader*. New York: Open Road Media, 2012.

Siegert, Bernhard. *Relays: Literature as an Epoch of the Postal System*. Stanford, CA: Stanford University Press, 1999.

Silber, Micheal K. "The Making of Habsburg Jewry in the Long Eighteenth Century." In *The Cambridge History of Judaism*. Vol. 7. Cambridge: Cambridge University Press, 2017.

Şimon, Nestor. *Vasile Naşcu: Viaţa şi faptele lui* [Vasile Naşcu: his life and deeds]. Bistriţa, Romania: Tipografia G. Matheiu, 1908.

Simuţ, Ion. *Liviu Rebreanu şi contradicţiile realismului* [Liviu Rebreanu and the contradictions of realism]. Cluj-Napoca, Romania: Editura Dacia, 2010.

Sinha, Mrinalini. "Gender and Nation." In *Women's History in Global Perspective*, edited by Bonnie G. Smith. Vol. 1. Urbana: Illinois University Press, 2004.

——. "Refashioning Mother India: Feminism and Nationalism in Late-Colonial India." *Feminist Studies* 26, no. 3 (2000): 623–44.

Skurski, Julie, and Fernando Coronil. "Country and City in a Postcolonial Landscape: Double Discourse and the Geo-Politics of Truth in Latin America." In *Views beyond the Border Country: Raymond Williams and Cultural Politics*, edited by Dennis L. Dworkin and Leslie G. Roman, 244–46. New York: Routledge, 1993.

Slabodsky, Santiago. *Decolonial Judaism: Triumphal Failures of Barbaric Thinking*. New York: Palgrave Macmillan, 2014.

Snow, C. P. *The Two Cultures*. Edited by Stefan Collini. Cambridge: Cambridge University Press, 2012.

Sombart, Werner. *Luxury and Capitalism*. Translated by W. R. Dittmar. Ann Arbor: University of Michigan Press, 1967.

Sorkin, David. *Jewish Emancipation: A History across Five Centuries*. Princeton, NJ: Princeton University Press, 2019.

Spivak, Gayatri Chakrabarty. "Can the Subaltern Speak?" In *Can the Subaltern Speak? Reflections on the History of an Idea*, edited by Rosalind C. Morris. New York: Columbia University Press, 2010.

——. *A Critique of Postcolonial Reason: Toward a History of the Vanishing Present*. Cambridge, MA: Harvard University Press, 1999.

——. *Death of a Discipline*. New York: Columbia University Press, 2003.

——. "Making Visible." In *On Productive Shame, Reconciliation, and Agency*, edited by Suzana Milevska, 92–100. Vienna: Stenberg Press, 2019.

Stahl, Henri H. "Théories des processus de 'modernisation' des principautés danubiennes et de l'ancien Royaume de Roumanie (1850–1920) [Theories on the process of 'modernization' of the Danubian Principalities and the Old Kingdom of Romania (1850–1920)]." *Review (Fernand Braudel Center)* 16, no. 1 (1993): 85–111.

Stam, Robert, and Ella Shohat. *Race in Translation: Culture Wars around the Postcolonial Atlantic*. New York: NYU Press, 2012.

Stoler, Laura. *Duress: Imperial Durabilities in Our Times*. Durham, NC: Duke University Press, 2016.

Stowe, Harriet Beecher. *Coliba lui Moşu Toma* [Uncle Tom's cabin]. Translated by Teodor Codrescu. Iaşi, Romania: Tipografia Buciumul Român, 1853.

Šubarić, Lav. "National Identities and the Latin Language in Hungary and Croatia: Language Conflicts 1784–1848." In *Major versus Minor? Languages and Literatures in a Globalized World*, edited by Theo D'haen, Iannis Goerlandt, and Roger D. Sell, 53–66. Amsterdam: John Benjamins Publishing, 2015.

Surdu, Bujor. *Aspecte privind rolul băncilor în consolidarea burgheziei româneşti din Transilvania până la primul război mondial* [Aspects regarding the role of banks in the consolidation of the Romanian bourgeoisie in Transylvania before World War I]. Bucharest: Editura Academiei Republicii Populare Române, 1962.

Szabó, Levente T. "Cultural Brokers, Forms of Hybridity and the Emergence of the First International Comparative Literary Journal." *Philobiblon: Transylvanian Journal of Multidisciplinary Research in the Humanities* 22, no. 2 (2017): 67–80.

———. "À la recherche … de l'editeur perdu: Sámuel Brassai and the First International Journal of Comparative Literary Studies." In *Storia, Identità e Canoni Letterari*, edited by Ioana Both, Ayşe Saraçgil, and Angela Tarantino. Florence: Firenze University Press, 2013.

Szabó, Levente T., and Márta Zabán. *Dokumentumok a kolozsvári Bölcsészet-, Nyelv- és Történettudományi Kar Történetéhez (1872–1892)*. Cluj-Napoca, Romania: Presa Universitară Clujeană, 2012.

Szabó-Resnek, Eszter. "Meltzl Hugó és a kolozsvári Petőfi-ellenkánon: Kísérlet a 'nemzeti költő' regionális újraértelmezésére [Hugó Meltzl and the Petőfi anti-canon from Kolozsvár: Attempts at a regional reinterpretation of the 'national poet']." *Irodalomtörténeti Közlemények* 120, no. 2 (2016): 215–24.

Szapor, Judith. *Hungarian Women's Activism in the Wake of the First World War: From Rights to Revanche*. New York: Bloomsbury Publishing, 2017.

Szász, Zoltán. "Political Life and Nationality Question." In *History of Transylvania*. Vol. 3. New York: Columbia University Press, 2002.

Szeman, Ioana. "'Black and White Are One': Anti-Amalgamation Laws, Roma Slaves, and the Romanian Nation on the Mid-Nineteenth-Century Moldavian Stage." In *Uncle Tom's Cabins: The Transnational History of America's Most Mutable Book*, edited by Tracy C. Davis and Stefka Mihaylova. Ann Arbor: University of Michigan Press, 2020.

Szende, Katalin. "*Iure Theutonico*? German Settlers and Legal Frameworks for Immigration to Hungary in an East-Central European Perspective." *Journal of Medieval History* 45, no. 3 (2019): 360–79.

———. "Towns along the Way: Changing Patterns of Long-Distance Trade and the Urban Network of Medieval Hungary." *Towns and Communication* 2 (2011): 161–225.

Tageldin, Shaden M. "One Comparative Literature? 'Birth' of a Discipline in French-Egyptian Translation, 1810–1834," *Comparative Literature Studies* 47, no. 4 (2010): 417–45.

Tagore, Rabindranath. *The Home and the World*, trans. Surendranath Tagore (London: Penguin Books, 2005).

Tarver, H. Micheal, and Emily Slape. *The Spanish Empire: A Historical Encyclopedia*. Santa Barbara, CA: ABC-CLIO, 2016.

Taylor, Charles. "Afterword and Corrections." In *A Secular Age beyond the West: Religion, Law and the State in Asia, the Middle East and North Africa*, edited by Mirjam Künkler, John Madeley, and Shylashri Shankar, 385–96. Cambridge: Cambridge University Press, 2018.

———. *A Secular Age*. Cambridge, MA: Harvard University Press, 2007.

Tazzioli, Martina, and Glenda Garelli. "Counter-Mapping, Refugees and Asylum Borders." In *Handbook on Critical Geographies of Migration*. Cheltenham, UK: Edward Elgar, 2019.

Telea, Coralia. *George Barițiu: Un francophile transylvain*. Cluj-Napoca, Romania: Editura Mega, 2013.

Terian, Andrei. "Faces of Modernity in Romanian Literature: A Conceptual Analysis." *Alea* 16, no. 1 (2014): 15–34.

———. "Zoopoetics in a Rural Environment." In *Ruralism and Literature in Romania*, edited by Ștefan Baghiu, Vlad Pojoga, and Maria Sass. Berlin: Peter Lang, 2020.

Thiong'o, Ngũgĩ wa. *Decolonizing the Mind*. London: J. Currey, 1986.

Todorova, Maria. *Imagining the Balkans*. New York: Oxford University Press, 2009.

Tomich, Dale. "World Slavery and Caribbean Capitalism: The Cuban Sugar Industry, 1760–1868." *Theory and Society* 20, no. 3 (1991): 297–319.

Török, Borbála Zsuzsanna. *Exploring Transylvania: Geographies of Knowledge and Entangled Histories in a Multiethnic Province, 1790–1918*. Leiden, Netherlands: Brill, 2016.

Trouillot, Michel-Rolph. *Silencing the Past: Power and the Production of History*. Boston: Beacon Press, 1995.

Trumpener, Katie. "Béla Bartók and the Rise of Comparative Ethnomusicology: Nationalism, Race Purity, and the Legacy of the Austro-Hungarian Empire." In *Music and the Racial Imagination*, edited by Ronald Radano and Philip V. Bohlman, 403–34. Chicago: University of Chicago Press, 2000.

Tudor, Alyosxa. "The Desire for Categories." *Feminist Review* blog, 2018. https://femrev.wordpress.com/2018/03/19/the-desire-for-categories/.

Tudor-Anton, Eugenia. *Hortensia Papadat-Bengescu, marea europeană* [Hortensia Papadat-Bengescu, the great European]. Bucharest: Editura National, 2001.

Turda, Marius. "Anti-Roma Racism in Romania", *EuropeNow* 40 (2021), https://www.europenowjournal.org/2021/04/01/anti-roma-racism-in-romania/.

——. "In Pursuit of Greater Hungary: Eugenic Ideas of Social and Biological Improvement, 1940–1941." *The Journal of Modern History* 85, no.3 (2013): 558–91.

Várdy, Steven Béla. *Baron Joseph Eötvös (1813–1871): A Literary Biography*. Boulder, CO: East European Monographs, 1987.

Varga, Bálint. "The Two Faces of the Hungarian Empire." *Austrian History Yearbook* 52 (2021): 118–30.

Vasile, Monica. "Formalizing Commons, Registering Rights: The Making of the Forest and Pasture Commons in the Romanian Carpathians from the 19th Century to Post-Socialism." *International Journal of the Commons* 12, no. 1 (2018): 170–201.

Vassilev, Rossen. "The 'Third-Worldization' of a 'Second-World' Nation: De-Development in Post-Communist Bulgaria." *New Political Science* 25, no. 1 (2010): 99–112.

Veer, Peter van der, ed. *Conversion to Modernities: The Globalization of Christianity*. New York: Routledge, 1996.

Venuti, Lawrence. *The Scandals of Translation: Towards an Ethics of Difference*. London: Taylor & Francis, 1998.

Verdery, Katherine. *Transylvanian Villagers: Three Centuries of Political, Economic, and Ethnic Change*. Berkeley: University of California Press, 1983.

Vergès, Françoise, and Carpanin Marimoutou. "Moorings: Indian Ocean Creolizations." *Portal: Journal of Multidisciplinary International Studies* 9, no. 1 (2012).

Vintilă-Ghițulescu, Constanța. *Focul amorului: Despre dragoste și sexualitate în societatea românească (1750–1830)* [The heat of passion: on love and sexuality in Romanian society (1750–1830)]. Bucharest: Humanitas, 2006.

Viswanathan, Gauri. "Religious Conversion and the Politics of Dissent." In *Conversion to Modernities: The Globalization of Christianity*, edited by Peter van der Veer, 89–114. New York: Routledge, 1996.

——. "Subjecting English and the Question of Representation." In *Disciplinarity at the Fin de Siècle*, edited by Amanda Anderson and Joseph Valente, 177–95. Princeton, NJ: Princeton University Press, 2002.

Vitcu, Dumitru, ed. *Regulamentul Organic al Moldovei*. Iași, Romania: Editura Junimea, 2004.

Vlassa, Ileana. "Condiția intelectuală a femeii oglindită în discursul pedagogic românesc al secolului al XIX-lea [The intellectual condition of women as mirrored by the Romanian pedagogical discourse of the nineteenth century]." *Sargetia. Acta Musei Devensis*, no. 3 (2012): 287–95.

Voia, Vasile. "Liviu Rebreanu în Ungaria [Liviu Rebreanu in Hungary]." In *Aspecte ale comparatismului românesc* [Aspects of Romanian comparatism], 146–56. Cluj-Napoca, Romania: Editura Dacia, 2002.

Wainwright, Joel, and Joe Bryan. "Cartography, Territory, Property: Postcolonial Reflections on Indigenous Counter-Mapping in Nicaragua and Belize." *Cultural Geographies* 16, no. 2 (2009): 153–78.

Walby, Sylvia. "The Myth of the Nation-State: Theorizing Society and Polities in a Global Era." *Sociology* 37, no. 3 (2003): 529–46.

Walkowitz, Rebecca L. *Born Translated: The Contemporary Novel in the Age of World Literature.* New York: Columbia University Press, 2017.

——. *Cosmopolitan Style: Modernism beyond the Nation.* New York: Columbia University Press, 2006.

Wallerstein, Immanuel. *The Essential Wallerstein.* New York: New Press, 2000.

——. "Land, Space, and People: Constraints of the Capitalist World-Economy." *Journal of World-Systems Research* 18, no. 1 (2012): 6–14.

——. "Latin@s: What's in a Name?" In *Latin@s in the World-System: Decolonization Struggles in the 21st Century US Empire,* edited by Ramón Grosfoguel, Nelson Maldonado-Torres, and José David Saldivar, 37–46. New York: Routledge, 2016.

——. *The Modern World-System I: Capitalist Agriculture and the Origins of the European World-Economy in the Sixteenth Century.* Berkeley: University of California Press, 2011.

——. *The Modern World-System III: The Second Era of Great Expansion of the Capitalist World-Economy, 1730s–1840s.* Berkeley: University of California Press, 2011.

——. *The Modern World-System IV: Centrist Liberalism Triumphant, 1789–1914.* Berkeley: University of California Press, 2011.

Warwick Research Collective. *Combined and Uneven Development: Towards a New Theory of World-Literature.* Liverpool: Liverpool University Press, 2015.

Washington, Booker T., and Robert E. Park. *The Man Farthest Down: A Record of Observation and Study in Europe.* New Brunswick, NJ: Transaction Books, 1984.

Weinbaum, Alys Eve, Lynn M. Thomas, Priti Ramamurthy, Uta G. Poiger, Madeleine Yue Dong, and Tani E. Barlow, eds. *The Modern Girl around the World: Consumption, Modernity, and Globalization.* Durham, NC: Duke University Press, 2008.

Weinreich, Max. *History of the Yiddish Language.* New Haven, CT: Yale University Press, 2008.

Werlhof, Claudia von, Maria Mies, and Veronika Bennholdt-Thomsen, eds. *Frauen, die letzte Kolonie* [Women: The last colony]. Hamburg: Rowohlt, 1983.

Williams, Raymond. *The Country and the City.* Oxford: Oxford University Press, 1975.

Wingfield, Nancy M. *The World of Prostitution in Late Imperial Austria.* Oxford: Oxford University Press, 2017.

Wlislocki, Heinrich von. *Asupra vieții și obiceiurilor țiganilor transilvăneni* [On the lives and customs of Transylvanian Gypsies]. Translated by Sorin Georgescu. Bucharest: Editura Kriterion, 1998.

Wolff, Larry. *Woodrow Wilson and the Reimagining of Eastern Europe.* Stanford, CA: Stanford University Press, 2020.

Woloch, Alex. *The One vs. the Many: Minor Characters and the Space of the Protagonist in the Novel.* Princeton, NJ: Princeton University Press, 2003.

Wollstonecraft, Mary. *A Vindication of the Rights of Woman.* London: Dover, 1996.

Woolf, Virginia. "Professions for Women." In *Selected Essays,* 140–45. Oxford: Oxford University Press, 2008.

——. *A Room of One's Own.* San Diego: Harcourt, 1981.

———. *To the Lighthouse*. San Diego: Harvest Books, 1989.

Wright, Donald R. *The World and a Very Small Place in Africa: A History of Globalization in Niumi, the Gambia*. Armonk, NY: M. E. Sharpe, 2010.

Wynter, Sylvia. "Unsettling the Coloniality of Being/Power/Truth/Freedom: Towards the Human, after Man, Its Overrepresentation—An Argument." *CR: The New Centennial Review* 3, no. 3 (2003): 257–337.

"Xenia, fata lui Ion, nu a citit romanul lui Rebreanu." *Adevărul*, June 15, 2009.

Yeazell, Ruth Bernard. *Harems of the Mind: Passages of Western Art and Literature*. New Haven, CT: Yale University Press, 2000.

Yildiz, Yasemin. *Beyond the Mother Tongue: The Postmonolingual Condition*. New York: Fordham University Press, 2012.

Young, Robert J. C. "That Which Is Casually Called a Language." *PMLA* 131, no. 5 (2016): 1207–21.

Zabán, Márta Nagy. "The Relationship between National Identity and Literature Education in Cluj in the Last Quarter of the 19th Century." In *Storia, Identità e Canoni Letterari*, edited by Ioana Both, Ayşe Saraçgil, and Angela Tarantino. Florence: Firenze University Press, 2013.

Zahra, Tara. "Condemned to Rootlessness and Unable to Budge: Roma, Migration Panics, and Internment in the Habsburg Empire." *American Historical Review* 122, no. 3 (2017): 702–26.

———. *The Great Departure: Mass Migration from Eastern Europe and the Making of the Free World*. New York: W. W. Norton, 2016.

Zăloagă, Marian. *Romii în cultura săsească din secolele al XVIII-lea şi al XIX-lea* [Roma in the Saxon culture of the 18th and 19th centuries]. Cluj-Napoca, Romania: Institutul pentru Studierea Problemelor Minorităţilor Naţionale, 2015.

Zanetti, Oscar, and Alejandro García. *Sugar and Railroads: A Cuban History, 1837–1959*. Chapel Hill: University of North Carolina Press, 2017.

Zorić, Vladimir. "Radiating Nests: Metalingual Tropes in Poetry of Exile." *Comparative Literature* 62, no. 3 (2010): 201–27.

Index

Note: Page numbers in italics indicate a figure.

247

CPSIA information can be obtained
at www.ICGtesting.com
Printed in the USA
LVHW040202161022
730794LV00001B/89